D0296450

HARVARD STUDIES IN ENGLISH

VOLUME XVII

BEN JONSON ON THE ENGLISH STAGE
1660–1776

BY

ROBERT GALE NOYES

BEN JONSON

BEN JONSON ON THE
ENGLISH STAGE
1660–1776

BY

ROBERT GALE NOYES

BENJAMIN BLOM
New York

Printed in U.S.A. by
NOBLE OFFSET PRINTERS, INC.
NEW YORK 3, N. Y.

TO THE MEMORY OF

MY FATHER AND MOTHER

PREFACE

FOR many years there has been need for a comprehensive stage-history of Ben Jonson's plays. Scholarship in the nineteenth and twentieth centuries has been occupied with criticizing "rare Ben," annotating his works, tracing his sources, and writing his biography. No study of the fortunes of his plays on the stage, based on records which have become increasingly available, has been made since the remarkable but very incomplete account of John Genest appeared more than a hundred years ago. The influence of Ben Jonson on the later comedy of humors has not yet been adequately traced; before an investigation so tenuous and so important is made, perhaps the most desirable preparation is a detailed chronicle of the facts in his own posthumous fate, when his comedies and tragedies were still living forces in the theatres.

My interest in Jonson was stimulated by Professor J. Tucker Murray, to whom I wish to express appreciation for encouragement. Since, in Jonson's words, "they are not, Sir, worst owers that do pay debts when they can," it is a pleasure to thank many other friends for aid. Professor George Lyman Kittredge is so prodigal a creditor to those whom he advises that one must pass his days in the most delightful debtors' prison in the world. To my former teacher, Miss Anna Elizabeth Gilbert, I am grateful for transcribing data from the Kemble-Devonshire playbills in the Henry E. Huntington Library and Art Gallery. Among other friends and associates who have contributed details, I wish particularly to thank Mrs. Lillian Arvilla Hall, custodian of the Harvard Theatre Collection, whose resourcefulness has been always at my disposal; Professor and Mrs. Richmond P. Bond, Professors

Leslie Hotson, Arthur Colby Sprague, J. B. Martin, and Mr. Harold Freeze Folland. The late Robert Gould Shaw purchased for my use several rare pamphlets; every student of the stage honors the memory of so keen a lover of the theatre. Without the courtesies and privileges of the Harvard College Library, the Yale University Library, the British Museum, the Bodleian Library, the Guildhall Library, the Public Record Office, and the Boston Public Library, this project would have been impossible. Professor Hyder Edward Rollins, who has patiently instructed me in the art of making books, has committed me to a debt embarrassingly great.

R. G. N.

Dunster House
Cambridge, Massachusetts
August 21, 1935

CONTENTS

ILLUSTRATIONS

BEN JONSON ON THE ENGLISH STAGE
1660–1776

CHAPTER I

Main Currents in the Criticism of Ben Jonson, 1660–1776

WHILE the critical reputation of Shakspere in the Restoration and the eighteenth century has furnished a rich mine for students, who have investigated his posthumous fame from almost every conceivable angle, the reputation of his greatest contemporary, Ben Jonson, has been singularly neglected. The reasons are, no doubt, clear enough. The name of Jonson stirs excitement in few modern readers, who are content rather to protest that he and his plays are dull, obsolete, and heavy. Fearing Jonson for his excessive learning, the timorous literary researcher is afraid to examine his works, because of the "double sorwe" involved in the mastery not only of the poet's own times, but also of those classic stores from which he so generously borrowed; and many desirable essays are wanting on one of England's staunchest men of letters. Among them may be mentioned a study of Jonson's influence on subsequent authors of comedies of humors, an elusive but necessary investigation; and, second, an outline of the main tendencies in the course of his own fate, demonstrating by what processes the plays of the one-time dramatic idol came to be considered sorry reading. The latter problem forms, of course, a vital complement to the actual history of Jonson's plays on the London stage, since the history of the plays themselves as acting dramas largely determined what was written about their author. Although the emphasis of the present study lies on the actual stage records of the plays, — the number of performances, the actors

and actresses, and the reception granted them by the public, — some indication of the fortunes of Ben Jonson at the
hands of the critics will serve as an introduction and, possibly, as an interesting illustration of the shifting of the
winds of doctrine over a period of years.

At the very beginning, a word of limitation. In no sense
is this critical essay an allusion-book. For the forty years
following the Restoration, most of the important references
to Ben Jonson have been assembled in *The Jonson
Allusion-Book*,[1] and some notice has been taken of the im-
pact of his mind on the greatest poetic and critical talent
of the Restoration, John Dryden.[2] By consulting these
materials, one may conveniently witness the place of
honor which Jonson occupied before the eighteenth century. For the most part, he and his works were regarded
with uncompromising adulation, as we shall see later in
the chapters on the plays, to which criticism of specific
comedies and tragedies may be confined. As for Jonson
the man, admired by Dryden and worshiped by Shadwell,
Restoration writers described him as "our unimitable
Johnson," a poet with "fewer Failings, than all the *English
Poets*,"[3] "incomparably the best Dramatick Poet that
ever was,"[4] and "the most learned, judicious and correct
. . . of our *English* Comedians,"[5] — opinions which were
focussed in the greatest single tribute to Jonson in the
Restoration, John Oldham's *Upon the Works of Ben Johnson. Written in 1678.*[6]

The main streams in Jonsonian criticism, exclusive of
that based on individual plays, may be classified. There

1. Ed. J. F. Bradley and J. Q. Adams, New Haven, 1922.
2. "Dryden and Jonson," Sir Walter Scott and George Saintsbury, *The
Works of John Dryden*, Edinburgh, XVIII (1893), 285–289. For refutation of
some of Dryden's strictures see Gerard Langbaine, *An Account of the English
Dramatick Poets*, Oxford, 1691, pp. 136–138, 145–150, and Jeremy Collier, *A
Short View of the Immorality and Profaneness of the English Stage*, 1698, *passim*.
3. *The Jonson Allusion-Book*, pp. 360, 363.
4. Page 385.   5. Page 378.
6. *Poems and Translations. By the Author of The Satyrs upon the Jesuits*,
1683, pp. 69–86.

was an intense admiration for his robust personality; a definite appreciation of his dramatic virtues, illustrative of the standards of the century from Dryden to Dr. Johnson, which singled out for special commendation his correctness and judgment, his adherence to nature, his satirical power, his technical excellence in plots and drawing of characters of humors. The critics admitted freely his faults, which consisted primarily of a too servile imitation of classic models, a lack of interest in love, and an inadequate representation of women, all of which rendered his comedies cold and cynical. Then, by an inevitable process, the critics set up a possibly natural, but certainly unphilosophical, comparison of Jonson with his friend Shakspere, which underwent a significant alteration of emphasis in the course of a century. As the plays grew older and manners and modes of life changed, the important question of the obsolescence of the comedies arose. There was dispute, in the first place, about the value of reviving old plays in general and Jonson's plays in particular, for although they required no alteration for acting, the comedies were becoming museum pieces; a new school of actors found them very difficult to act; the public preferred new poets to old; and changing theatrical taste, which was being debauched by the newly discovered pantomimes, bade fair to banish Jonson and the older playwrights completely from the stage. But in spite of all difficulty, the public found pleasure and the managers profit in Jonson's three famous comedies, *The Fox*, *The Alchemist*, and *The Silent Woman* (and also, for twenty-five years, in *Every Man in his Humour*), which were to hold the stage under the stimulus of Garrick's antiquarian interest and the genius of the Drury Lane and Covent Garden comedians until the farewell of "Roscius" to the theatre in 1776.

So far as personality was concerned, the neo-classic age was inclined to recall the eccentricities of "rugged," "surly" Ben. As Jonson was accustomed to write about people who represented abnormalities and idiosyncracies of character, so his own nature left an impression on a later age, which was fond of recalling his occupation as bricklayer, his ready, quip-like wit and sharp tongue, his love of potations, the fashion in which he demolished his enemies and censors, and his habits of roaring down opposition to his theory and practise in comedy. The forms which this reminiscence of "old Ben" took were almost always amusing, and from them one might draw many anecdotes which seem a trifle musty to modern taste in wit. Ben Jonson's ghost was occasionally employed to speak a prologue at the revival of one of his own plays, often in condemnation of the reigning taste.[1] In 1705, when the stage was in decline as the result of foreign *divertissements*, Ned Ward promised the public dire results unless conditions improved:

> *Shakespere* and *Ben. Johnson's* Ghosts, will in a little time pay a Visit to both Playhouses; and if their Fury be not appeased by a fair Promise of a new Regulation of their Stages, with Scorpion Rods, borrowed from the Furies, they will whip the *Barnet* Mimick and the *French* Tumblers out of both Houses, and convince the Spectators, a good old Play is a better Entertainment for a sensible Audience, than a modern Farce with *Bartholomew-fair* Sauce to it.[2]

The attitude which regarded Shakspere and Jonson as fathers and defenders of the English stage was common. Instead of using Jonson's ghost, the critic often arranged a little scene in the underworld, with Jonson sitting in Rhadamanthine judgment on visitors, who were either manglers of his comedies on the stage or creditable performers deserving praise from his own lips. An amusing example appeared in 1704 in the anonymous *Visits From the Shades; or, Dialogues Serious, Comical, and Political*:[3]

1. See the three prologues to Edward Howard's *The Womens Conquest*, 1671, sigs. C2–C4; and Sackville's epilogue to *Every Man in his Humour*, in *A Collection of Poems Written upon several Occasions*, 1673, pp. 29–32. For a print of Jonson's ghost see William Hogarth's *A Just View of the British Stage*, 1725.

2. *A Comical View of London and Westminster*, 1705, part ii, p. 162.

3. Dialogue VI, p. 38.

Jon[*son*]. I have heard how presumptuously you upstart Authors wou'd lessen the Glory of the last Age, to cry up your Tinsel, Flash and Whipt-cream Wit. But I have kept a Correspondence with your Theater for these forty Years, and cou'd never yet find any of you come to the perfection of *Shakespear*; and, to speak without vaunting, any thing comparable to my *Volpone*, or *Silent Woman*.

A later example, including an interesting character-sketch of the poet, occurred in an article entitled "The Apotheosis of Milton. A Vision," in *The Gentleman's Magazine* for May, 1738. The writer fell asleep in Westminster Abbey and had a vision of the poets, including Chaucer, Drayton, and Spenser:

The next who appeared was a fresh-coloured Old Man, whom at first I took for an *English* Country Gentleman, but upon considering his Dress, I found it such as is described in Pictures about 160 Years ago: it seemed to be of coarse Cloth, but was extreamly well fitted for his Body, and gave him, notwithstanding his Homeliness, a very agreeable Look, which grew more so, the longer I ey'd him. I observed, that as he went up to his Seat, he was attacked by every one he passed with some Jest, but he always answered them in a manner that got him the Laugh on his side. When he sat down, the President gave him a Nod, which let me understand that the greatest Familiarity subsisted betwixt 'em. After he was seated, I viewed his Face more narrowly, and found, that tho' his Features were very strong, yet they appeared regular, and his Look not so churlish as I at first took it to be. I own, had it not been for my Companion, I should never have known him to be *Ben Johnson*. Upon perceiving his Pockets stuffed with Books, I asked my Conductor what the Meaning of that was. *These Books*, answered he, *are the Works of* Cicero, Horace, *and* Salust; *his Genius being too mechanical to catch the fine Sentiments of these Authors, to render them natural to himself by a long Familiarity with them, he always carries their Works about him; and has the Art, upon every Occasion, to quote them so justly, and so much* a propos, *that they receive new Beauties by his Applications.*

All the rest of the company "were constantly employ'd in studying the Motions of the Muscles of *Ben's* Face, and by them they framed their own, till they had caught all the Sourness and Rusticity of his Air, without any of its Sincerity and Frankness.¹"

Another form of homage to Ben Jonson was the use of his name by subsequent authors as a pseudonym. In 1672 a miscellaneous collection of poems appeared by "Ben Johnson Junior." ² In 1708 the author of *Sport upon Sport*; *or, The London Frolick* wrote under the *nom de plume* "Ben Johnson," a device adopted by the author of the periodical *The Censor* (1715), who claimed lineal descent from the poet, under a

Resolution to let the World know, that there is still a poor Branch of that *Immortal* Family remaining, sworn and avow'd Foes to Nonsense, Bad Poets, illiterate Fops, affected Coxcombs, and all the Spawn of Follies and Impertinence, that make up and incumber the present Generation. . . . Folly shall no more be bawl'd in our Streets, nor Sense and Nonsense sold currently at the same Price, if the Spirit of *Ben Johnson* can work any Reformation.³

Ten days later, he promised readers his family tree and regaled them with some anecdotes on Jonson's comedies which he said had come down as part of his heritage.

Anecdotes about Jonson himself were very common in the eighteenth-century jest-books. The same stories, dealing usually with his famous power of repartee or his love of canary, were reprinted, apparently without end.⁴ A divert-

1. VIII, 234.
2. See Edward Arber, *The Term Catalogues*, I (1903), 87; Edmond Malone, *The Plays and Poems of William Shakspeare*, 1790, I, part ii, 171; *Notes and Queries*, 5th series, II (1874), 208, 6th series, VI (1882), 475; W. C. Hazlitt, *Bibliographical Collections and Notes*, 3d series, 1887, p. 218.
3. No. 1, April 11, 1715.
4. See T. S. Graves, "Jonson in the Jest Books," *The Manly Anniversary Studies*, Chicago, 1923, pp. 127–139; *Fragmenta Aulica; or, Court and State Jests in Noble Drollery*, 1662; *Polly Peachum's Jests*, 1733; *Joe Miller's Jests*, 1739; *Ben Johnson's last Legacy to the Sons of wit, mirth, and jollyty*, 1756; *Ben Johnson's Jests*, 6th ed., 1760.

ing episode in the history of Jonson's tomb, more amusing
than the recent discussion of "O rare" *vs.* "*Orare,*" occurred in 1723, when a writer in *The British Journal* noted
that the sculptor had carved the buttons on the left side of
Jonson's coat.[1] The discovery inspired a poem, *Ben Johnson's Bust, lately set up in Westminster Abby with the Buttons
on the wrong Side*:

> O rare *Ben Johnson*! what, a Turn-coat grown?
> Thou ne'er wert such, till thou wert clad in Stone:
> When Time thy Coat, thy only Coat impairs,
> Thou'lt find a Patron in a hundred Years:
> Then let not this Mistake disturb thy Sprite,
> Another Age shall set thy Buttons right.[2]

A somewhat more profane poem appeared in 1756:

> On seeing *Ben Jonson* turn'd out of Place in a Turn'd-Coat.
>
> If *Ben's* pale Ghost, at Noon of Night,
>   (Like *Cæsar's* Shadow on the Stage)
> Should rise and contemplate the Sight,
>   How would his growling Spirit rage?
>
> Why, what a Jack-an-apes is here!
>   This meant for me! away, be gone!
> (Why this would make a Parson swear!)
>   A Turn'd-coat too! Zounds! turn'd to Stone!
>
> Give me my other Coat again,
>   And place me where I was before;
> This cannot be the famous *Ben*,
>   This is some upstart Son of a Whore![3]

As late as 1753 an audience might be mildly amused by

---

1. No. XXXII, April 27, 1723. See my letter in *The Saturday Review of
Literature*, December 31, 1927, p. 494.
2. *Miscellaneous Poems by Several Hands Published by D. Lewis*, 1726, p. 148;
Joseph Yarrow, *A Choice Collection of Poetry, by the Most Ingenious Men of the
Age*, York, 1738, p. 65; W. R. Chetwood, *Memoirs of the Life and Writings of
Ben. Jonson, Esq.*, Dublin, 1756, p. 52. Chetwood declared that the poem was
by "the late reverend Mr. *Wesley.*"
3. Chetwood, p. 53. He exploited Jonson's personality so generously that
the editors of *The Jonson Allusion-Book* (p. vi) refused to include any of his
jingles.

allusions to Jonson's original occupation as bricklayer,[1] and it was primarily interest in his personality which evoked a series of articles called "Miscellaneous Observations *on the Genius and Writings of* Ben Johnson" in *The Town and Country Magazine* from April to October, 1775.[2] For well over a century legends arose round the personality of Jonson. Critics might find all manner of fault with his works, but even they were fascinated by the nimbus of stern yet whimsical and merry charm which enveloped the poet's honest brow.

About Jonson's correctness in dramatic composition, the critics were agreed. Their evaluations of it, however, varied. His admirers considered correctness a virtue in itself; but his detractors argued that it prevented Jonson from those wild flights of poesy which enraptured them in Shakspere, and caused Jonson's coldness and want of passion. The contrast between the two dramatists was the oft-repeated one between art and nature, or between judgment and genius. Jonson went to the schools, while Shakspere, "Fancy's child," warbled "his native woodnotes wild." Jonson was the trimmed and ordered formal garden; Shakspere, the wild prospect of primordial nature. The correctness of Jonson was regarded as the outcome of excessive learning.

Shakespear excelled in a natural Vein . . . and *Johnson* in Gravity and ponderousness of Style; whose onely fault was, he was too elaborate; and had he mixt less erudition with his Playes, they had been more pleasant and delightful then they are. Comparing him with *Shakespear*, you shall see the difference betwixt Nature and Art.[3]

The opinion that Jonson was rather defective in genius than a product of the classics was expressed by James

1. Epilogue to *The Earl of Essex*, spoken by Mrs. Cibber, *The Universal Magazine*, XII (1753), 123–124.
2. VII, 199, 291, 407, 532.
3. Richard Flecknoe, *A Short Discourse of the English Stage*, affixed to *Love's Kingdom*, 1664, sig. G6.

Beattie in his *Remarks on the Utility of Classical Learning* (1769):

Ben Johnson's misfortune was, not that he knew too much, but that he could not make a proper use of his knowledge; a misfortune, which arose rather from a defect of genius or taste, than from a superabundance of erudition. With the same genius, and less learning, he would probably have made a worse figure.[1]

This opinion was echoed by an anonymous writer in *The Town and Country Magazine* for June, 1775, who observed that Jonson's good sense seemed "to have forsaken him whenever he forsook the guides of antiquity, and trusted to his own natural strength." He found that Jonson failed to touch the heart, and in true romantic fashion considered that a writer "must go to his domestic and inward monitor, and there search for the secret springs and motives of action. In a word, he must have the proper feeling before he can attain to the proper expression: in this science his contemporary Shakespeare has greatly the preference."[2]

The authors just quoted considered Jonson's correctness and learning rather a fault than a virtue. But critics more typical of the neo-classic love of chaste outline and the rules praised him as law-giver and model. Their attitude found expression in Robert Gould's *The Play-House. A Satyr* (1689):

> Thee, mighty *Ben*! we ever shall affect,
> Thee ever mention with profound Respect;
> Thou most Judicious *Poet*! most correct!
> I know not on what single Play to fall;
> Thou did'st arrive t'an Excellence in all.
> Yet we must give thee but thy just desert;
> Thou'd'st less of *nature*, though much more of *Art*:
> The Springs that move our Souls thou did'st not touch:
> But then thy *Judgment, care* and *pains* were such,

---

1. *Essays on Poetry and Music*, Edinburgh, 1778, p. 527.
2. VII, 292.

> We ne'r yet, nor e'r shall an *Author* see,
> That wrote so many *perfect Plays* as thee:
> Not one vain humour thy strict view escapes,
> All Follies thou hadst drest in all their proper shapes.[1]

In 1694 Sir Thomas Pope Blount recalled that Winstanley had judged

Ben. Johnson . . . paramount in the *Dramatick* part of *Poetry*, and taught the Stage an exact conformity to the Laws of *Comedians*, being accounted the most Learned, Judicious, and Correct of all the *English Poets*; and the more to be admir'd for being so, for that neither the height of Natural Parts, for he was no *Shakespear*; nor the Cost of extraordinary Education, but his own proper Industry, and Application to Books, advanc'd him to this perfection.[2]

Jonson could still please for his correctness in 1713, for "Mr. Webster," in his poem *The Stage*, praised Jonson:

> 'T was he first methodiz'd the Muse's Rage,
> To him we owe Correctness on the Stage.[3]

And in 1715 Mr. Hepburn, writing *A Discourse concerning the Character of a Man of Genius*, remarked that there are men

of a *great*, but more *correct Genius*, who have confin'd their Wit and Invention to proper Bounds. Improv'd by Education, they have restrain'd the Exuberancy of Fancy, by the just Force of their Judgment. There is an Air of Politeness, and a *fine Taste*, that shines in all their Writings. . . . Of this Sort . . . our *Island* has produc'd a *Ben: Johnson*.[4]

Hepburn's definition of the meaning of correctness is excellent.

In 1720 Jonson was declared "the most consummate Comick Poet that ever was, and as just and severe a

---

1. *Poems Chiefly consisting of Satyrs and Satyrical Epistles*, p. 178.
2. *De Re Poetica*, "Characters and Censures," p. 106.
3. Page 9. Mr. F. W. Bateson proved that "Mr. Webster" was really Francis Reynardson; see *Modern Language Notes*, XLV (1930), 27-29.
4. Page 3.

Critick, and vehement Contender for the Laws of *Helicon*,"[1] and when Charles Churchill wrote the section on Jonson in *The Rosciad* (1761), he could merely expand on the opinions of Jonson's correctness expressed by his predecessors:

> NEXT JOHNSON sat, — in antient learning train'd,
> His rigid judgment Fancy's flight restrain'd,
> Correctly prun'd each wild luxuriant thought,
> Mark'd out her course, nor spar'd a glorious fault.
> The Book of Man he read with nicest art,
> And ransack'd all the secrets of the heart;
>
> .   .   .   .
>
> His comic humour kept the world in awe,
> And Laughter fright'ned Folly more than Law.[2]

For over a century after the Restoration, whether for praise or blame, the correctness of Jonson's composition was universally admitted.

One of the primary tests of realism is the requirement that it closely adhere to the facts of nature. For the purpose of correcting human nature, the realist may portray excess and abnormality, but the roots of his art are firmly grounded in the normal and the representative. Since Jonson was one of the greatest English realists, the critics applied their test and did not find him wanting. In 1702 Charles Gildon, in *A Comparison Between the Two Stages*, stated the *desiderata* of an excellent comedy:

Sull [*en*]. I wou'd have a Play founded either on Truth, or some Story very near it; *aut Veram aut Verisimilem*; I wou'd have every Scene made probable, and of force to make an impression on the Fancy: Nor must you say this is not to be done, what d'ee yee think of . . . several of *Shakespear's*, . . . all *Ben's*; there Nature is followed so close, we take the Picture to be the Life; nor are they less diverting, for being confin'd within Reason.[3]

---

1. *The Battle of the Authors Lately Fought in Covent-Garden*, p. 30. For a similar opinion by Gildon see *The Laws of Poetry* . . . *Explain'd and Illustrated*, 1721, p. 33.
2. Pages 7–8.
3. Page 146. Gildon's authorship of this work is questioned.

Gildon's view was propagated by the author of an essay, "Of Plays," in *The London Magazine* for December, 1733:

[True comedy] is not the smart *Jest*, the odd *Drollery*, or the lively *Repartee*, but the *natural View of Life;* the *Manners*, the *Singularity* and *Humours* of *Mankind*, pleasantly represented, which are alone worthy to be call'd the Entertainments of *Comedy*. Among all the Comic Writers of our Nation, none has drawn Nature stronger, or put the Follies or Vices of Mankind in a clearer Light than the judicious *Ben Johnson*, who in all his Plays has not only exhibited *Nature*, but *Nature* of the most beautiful Kind, as he not only excites Men to be *good*, but wou'd make *good* Men *better*.[1]

A Dissertation on Comedy. . . . By a Student of Oxford (1750) praised Jonson above all else for his observance of nature:

Ben Johnson . . . had a thorough Knowledge of human Nature, from its highest to its lowest Gradations, was perfectly well acquainted with the various Combinations of Passions, and the innumerable Blendings of Vice and Virtue, which distinguish one Character from another: But what more eminently exalted him above all comic Writers whatever, was the Art . . . of happily marking the different Shades of the same Colour, of distinguishing the Covetous from the Covetous, the Voluptuous from the Voluptuous, *&c.*[2]

Closely connected with the drawing of characters which followed natural models was the element of satire, the corrective quality, which could not escape the notice of the critics. It does not appear, however, to have been mentioned frequently. Dryden noted that "to make men appear pleasantly ridiculous on the stage, was . . . [Jonson's] talent,"[3] and the anonymous author of *The Satirist: In*

1. II, 618. For a rendering of this opinion in verse see *An Essay on the Theatres; or, The Art of Acting*, 1745, p. 15.
2. Pages 38–39. The essay is attributed to John Hippisley, son of the comedian.
3. *Works*, III (1883), 243.

Imitation of the Fourth Satire of the First Book of Horace (1733) wrote:

> When awful *Johnson* on th' improving Stage
> With comic Humour lash'd the vitious Age;
> When the strong Scene of *Wycherley* was fear'd,
> And *Congreve's* pointed Wit by Fools rever'd;
> No Vice or Folly did their Satire spare,
> But drew the Knave and Blockhead as they were;
> Aw'd by no Fear, expecting no Reward,
> Lash'd the rich Villain, or the courtly Lord.[1]

The technical accomplishments of Jonson's plays were admired fully as much as their content, and critics were almost unanimous in praising his plots and such of his comic characters as did not descend to the groveling wit of Cob. Dryden, in considering English plots fuller of variety than the French, declared that English plots were "weaved in English looms," deriving "the copiousness and well-knitting of the intrigues . . . from Jonson." [2] And in 1747 the dramatist Samuel Foote said that Ben Jonson was "most successful in his Plots." [3] These opinions, coming from two successful playwrights in different eras, are significant.

One of the best analyses of Jonson's method of character-drawing was written by Thomas Wilkes in his *General View of the Stage* (1759). It shows excellent understanding of the problem involved in the creation of a character of humors:

The antient Comic Writers drew their scenes from living manners; they grouped a variety of humours that were general, otherwise a Comic Character is not truly valuable; because, unless it strikes every spectator, it cannot afford proper instruction. A man of but mean talents may turn a particular character into ridicule, and expose a person infinitely more valuable to society than himself; but from the affectations and absurdities of many,

1. Page 3.
2. *Works*, XV (1892), 341.
3. *The Roman and English Comedy Consider'd and Compar'd*, p. 26.

to compile one Comic Character that may be useful while it diverts, and, at the same time, meet the approbation of correct judgment and refined taste, is a task which none but a great genius can fulfil. Ben Jonson has been accused of shewing himself in this poor confined light by the Morose of his Silent Woman, which he is supposed to have drawn from a person of his own acquaintance, who had this extravagant turn. Congreve, in a letter to Dennis, has defended him admirably, and proved, that the immortal Ben

> *Expos'd no single fop, but laid the load*
> *More equally; and spread the folly broad.*[1]

The usual fault to be found with Jonson's characters was not that they were unrepresentative but that they were studied and wanting in passion. The grounds of this criticism lay undoubtedly in the unphilosophical habit of comparing his comedies with the entirely different type of play written by Shakspere or Beaumont and Fletcher and in judging Jonson's realistic and satirical characters in the light of the more romantic creatures of his contemporaries. Not until Coleridge noted the absurdity of comparing such dissimilar attempts in art did critics begin to judge Jonson's comedies for what they were rather than for what they were not. But Dryden, I suspect, had an inkling of the true state of Jonsonian criticism when he wrote that Ben Jonson "can be taxed with fewer failings than any English poet," [2] and with his eye on Jonson himself, proceeded to explain the want of emotional quality in his plays on a natural rather than an artificial basis.

You seldom find him making love in any of his scenes, or endeavouring to move the passions; his genius was too sullen and saturnine to do it gracefully, especially when he knew he came after those who had performed both to such an height. Humour was his proper sphere; and in that he delighted most to represent mechanic people.[3]

1. Pages 47–48.   2. *Works*, III, 243.
3. XV, 347.

John Dennis in 1702 went so far as to praise Jonson, "one of the best Comick Poets that ever was in the World," for omitting emphasis on love and for concentrating on humor, because "Humour is harder to write than Love," and because the *Ridiculum* (without which comedy cannot exist) "is a great deal more to be found in Humour, than it is in Love."[1] Two years later, Tom Brown, in his first dialogue, resumed the discussion of Jonson's treatment of love. Bayes (Dryden) has just been discoursing on the operas he has written, which have banished Shakspere and Jonson from the stage.

Crites. But pray, *Bays*, what did you say to *Shakespear*, *Johnson*, and the rest of them? . . .

Bays. To prevent, Sir, all Storms that might have issued from that Quarter, I . . . so castrated these grave Old-fashioned Gentlemen, so disguised their true Features, by putting them in Modern Apparel, that upon the Stage, few, very few I-gad, could distinguish their Works, from my own proper Legitimate Productions. Then I fulminated *Johnson's* Affected Style, his dull way of making Love, his Thefts, and mean Characters . . . so often, do you observe me, Mr. *Crites*, that scarce one in a hundred had the Assurance to offer one Good Word in their Behalf.[2]

Throughout the entire period of performances of Jonson there was a convention among critics never to mention him without remarking on his imitation of the classics. To attempt to recount variations on the theme of Jonson's indebtedness to ancient models would be fruitless. One need only summarize various points of view. Some critics regarded his borrowing as an improvement of the source, considering that Jonson had given the classics "new Beauties by his Application," and in the Restoration no stigma of plagiarism was attached even to the translations from Cicero and Sallust in *Sejanus* and *Catiline*. As Dryden wrote in 1668:

1. *A Large Account of the Taste in Poetry*, ed. W. H. Durham, *Critical Essays of the XVIII Century*, New Haven, 1915, pp. 122–124.
2. *A Collection Of all the Dialogues Written by Mr. Thomas Brown*, 1704, p. 39.

He was deeply conversant in the ancients, both Greek and Latin, and borrowed boldly from them: there is scarce a poet or historian among the Roman authors of those times, whom he has not translated in "Sejanus" and "Catiline." But he has done his robberies so openly, that one may see he fears not to be taxed by any law. He invades authors like a monarch; and what would be theft in other poets, is only victory in him.[1]

This attitude was bound to suffer, however, with the growth of romanticism, when originality, spontaneous overflow, and genius were more to be desired than the fine gold of the ancients. Bishop Hurd, Edward Young, and Edward Capell, all ardent sponsors of originality, gave Jonson many hard knocks, some of which will appear in the chapters on the plays. Capell's attitude in 1766 was particularly severe:

Johnson's writings are one continued series of Imitations and allusions: where he not only literally translates the antients, many passages from whom are transfused into his performances, and chime in as regular and as if they were the product of his own invention; but he gleans as freely, and without reserve, from the moderns when they make for his purpose. . . . In a word, such a one was *Johnson*, that he seems to have made it his study to cull out others sentiments, and to place them in his works as from his own mint. This surely is an odd species of improvement from reading, and savours very little of Invention or Genius: It borders nearly upon, if it is not really plagiarism. . . . Thus much for *Johnson*, considered as a Maker, and who as such has very poor pretensions to the high place he holds among the English Bards, as there is no original manner to distinguish him, *and the tedious sameness visible in his plots* indicates a defect of Genius.[2]

Blows such as this were destined sooner or later to affect the fate of the plays as acting dramas, and grumbles of dis-

1. *Works*, XV, 347.
2. *Reflections on Originality in Authors: . . . with a Word or Two on the Characters of Ben. Johnson and Pope*, pp. 63–64.

content, latent for many years, began to appear even in the newspaper reviews. If ever the public grew set against imitation, Jonson's comedies must be the first to crash.[1]

Since Shakspere and Jonson were, by common consent, the greatest dramatists of their era, it was natural that later critics should attempt to judge which was the greater. There were two dangers, however, implicit in a comparative test. The first was that the critics might indulge in sheer impressionism, preferring that dramatist who best suited their temperaments and fancies. The second was more serious: the critics might judge Shakspere's plays in the light of Jonson's, and *vice versa*, a method essentially unsound because the schools of art which the poets represented and their entire mental attitudes were so thoroughly incompatible. Theoretically, of course, it ought to be impossible to say that Shakspere was greater than Jonson, or Jonson greater than Shakspere, since Shakspere wrote no comedies of humors, and Jonson wrote no romantic dramas, yet each was master of his chosen type. Actually, though, the entire world has been willing to admit the superior genius of Shakspere. The test *quod semper, quod ubique, quod ab omnibus* has not failed. Efforts to compare the two poets were legion, and almost all of them exhibited one fallacy or the other. The critical method which achieved a reconciliation of opposites was unknown until Coleridge, and surely nothing short of a highly esemplastic imagination could make a judicious balance between Jonson and Shakspere. We cannot expect, then, in the Restoration and eighteenth century any criticism which will satisfy modern notions of critical method, but we should remember that comparative criticism had been honored since the time of Plutarch.

Dryden's hedging comparison of the two poets is famous:

1. James Upton had pointed out many of Jonson's borrowings in *Remarks on Three Plays of Benjamin Johnson* (1749), a work used by Peter Whalley in his edition of *The Works of Ben. Jonson* (1756).

If I would compare him [Jonson] with Shakespeare, I must acknowledge him the more correct poet, but Shakespeare the greater wit. Shakespeare was the Homer, . . . Jonson was the Virgil. . . . I admire him, but I love Shakespeare.[1]

Several years later, Dryden expressed a more positive opinion in his *Prologue to Julius Cæsar*:

> The faultless *Iohnson* equally writ well,
> *Shakespear* made faults; but then did more excel.
> One close at Guard like some old Fencer lay,
> Tother more open, but he shew'd more play.
> In Imitation *Iohnsons* wit was shown,
> Heaven made his men but *Shakespear* made his own.
> Wise *Iohnson's* talent in observing lay,
> But others follies still made up his play.
> He drew the like in each elaborate line,
> But *Shakespear* like a Master did design.
> *Iohnson* with skill dissected humane kind,
> And show'd their faults that they their faults might find.
> But then as all Anatomists must do,
> He to the meanest of mankind did go.
> And took from Gibbets such as he would show.
> Both are so great that he must boldly dare,
> Who both of 'em does judge and both compare.
> If amongst Poets one more bold there be,
> The man that dare attempt in either way, is he.[2]

The last four lines are an admirable indication that Dryden, with his usual keenness, recognized the difficulty in comparing the two authors at all.

Definite preference for Shakspere's plays manifested itself early, appearing as soon as the critics began to admire him in spite of his own faults and in spite of the virtues of his rivals. A fair example of this early attitude appeared during the Collier controversy, when James Drake wrote *The Antient and Modern Stages survey'd* (1699):

1. *Works*, XV, 347-348.
2. *Covent Garden Drolery*, 1672, p. 10.

Shakespear . . . I must still think the *Proto-Dramatist* of *England*, tho he fell short of the Art of *Johnson*, and the Conversation of *Beaumont* and *Fletcher*. Upon that account he wants many of their Graces, yet his Beauties make large amends for his Defects, and Nature has richly provided him with the materials, tho his unkind Fortune denied him the Art of managing them to the best Advantage.[1]

As years passed, what had formerly seemed defects in Shakspere began to be treated as virtues, either through changing taste or admiration for "the glory of the imperfect." For example, no later than 1710 Shakspere's conversation, judged faulty by Drake, was praised by Gildon:

There is likewise ever a Sprightliness in his Dialogue, and often a Genteelness . . . which is very surprizing for that Age, and what the Learned BEN cou'd not attain by all his Industry; and I confess, if we make some small Allowance for a few Words and Expressions, I question whether any one has since excell'd him in it.[2]

As the century progressed, comparisons of the two dramatists were common, but variations in opinion were few. Critics merely paraphrased their predecessors, declaring for instance that "*Shakespear* excelled in the marvellous Boldness of his Invention, and the admirable Energy of his Expression; *Johnson*, in his prodigious art of weaving his Plots, and a nice distinction of Characters,"[3] or advising young poets to

> aim to soar in SHAKESPEAR's lofty strain;
> Or nature draw in JOHNSON's merry vein.[4]

Shakspere's debt to nature and Jonson's debt to art were emphasized almost *ad nauseam*, and only occasionally did

1. Pages 201–202.
2. *An Essay on the Art, Rise and Progress of the Stage*, Nicholas Rowe, *The Works of Mr. William Shakespear*, 1710, VII, v. Gildon did not prefer Shakspere, however. See his *Life of Mr. Thomas Betterton*, 1710, p. 173.
3. "Of Taste in Plays," *The Gentleman's Magazine*, I (1731), 153.
4. Page 493.

the point receive as much distinction as, in his edition of *The Works of Shakespeare* (1733), Lewis Theobald gave it:

An additional Word or two naturally falls in here upon the Genius of our Author, as compared with that of *Jonson*. . . . They are confessedly the greatest Writers our Nation could ever boast of in the *Drama*. The first, we say, owed all to his prodigious natural Genius; and the other a great deal to his Art and Learning. This, if attended to, will explain a very remarkable Appearance in their Writings. Besides those wonderful Masterpieces of Art and Genius, which each has given Us; They are the Authors of other Works very unworthy of them: But with this Difference; that in *Jonson's* bad Pieces we don't discover one single Trace of the Author of the *Fox* and *Alchemist*: but in the wild extravagant Notes of *Shakespeare*, you every now and then encounter Strains that recognize the divine Composer. This Difference may be thus accounted for. *Jonson*, as we said before, owing all his Excellence to his Art, by which he sometimes strain'd himself to an uncommon Pitch, when at other times he unbent and play'd with his Subject, having nothing then to support him, it is no wonder he wrote so far beneath himself. But *Shakespeare*, indebted more largely to Nature, than the Other to acquired Talents, in his most negligent Hours could never so totally divest himself of his Genius, but that it would frequently break out with astonishing Force and Splendor.[1]

There was an element of uncomfortable dichotomy in the minds of all the critics who attempted to compare Jonson and Shakspere in the early romantic period. They were near enough to the neo-classics to have some respect for the laws of taste and the canons of the older criticism, so that they were bound to make respectful mention of Jonson, the father of the passing school. But they were also laying the cornerstone of the newer school of sensibility, the return to nature, and freedom, all of which they found in Shakspere. They gave Jonson a chance, it is true, because they knew when they began that they were going to prefer Shakspere, but they soon omitted the preambles

---

1. I, xxxiii–xxxiv.

of somewhat hypocritical flattery and devoted all their pleasant adjectives to the overwhelming beauties of Shakspere. The most famous statement of the triumph of Shakspere over Jonson appeared in Edward Young's *Conjectures on Original Composition* (1759), where his thesis was that

Shakespeare mingled no water with his wine, lower'd his genius by no vapid imitation. *Shakespeare* gave us a *Shakespeare*, nor could the first in ancient fame have given us more. *Shakespeare* is not their son, but brother; their equal; and that, in spite of all his faults. Think you this too bold? . . . *Johnson*, in the serious drama, is as much an imitator, as *Shakespeare* is an original.[1]

The identical opinion expressed by Young was versified in 1763:

Ars naturâ sit perfectior?

Great Shakespear, with genius disdaining all rules,
Above the cold phlegm or the fripp'ry of schools,
Appeal'd to the heart for success of his plays,
And trusted to Nature alone for the bays.

Despairing of glory but what rose from Art;
Old Johnson apply'd to the head, not the heart;
On the niceness of rules he founded his cause,
And ravish'd from regular method applause.

May we judge from the honours each author has shar'd,
Insipid is Art when with Nature compar'd.[2]

One must not infer that there was no critic acute enough to perceive that the palace of art was spacious enough to shelter both Jonson and Shakspere. Even at a time when the majority of writers considered Shakspere paramount, there was evidence of the fair-minded attitude in the anonymous author of *The Rational Rosciad* (1767):[3]

1. Pages 78–80. The section quoted was reprinted in *The Gentleman's Magazine*, XXIX (1759), 231. For an admirable critical comparison of Jonson and Shakspere see Corbyn Morris, *An Essay Towards Fixing the True Standards of Wit, Humour, Raillery, Satire, and Ridicule*, 1744, pp. 29–34.

2. *The St. James Magazine*, March, 1763, p. 63; *The Universal Magazine*, XXXVII (1765), 209.   3. Pages 5–6.

> JOHNSON to future times his fame may trust,
> Who is tho' seldom striking, always just.
> Tho' cool, correct, tho' modest, yet severe,
> Strong without passion, without dulness clear;
> Humorous with elegance, jocose with ease,
> Sublime to charm, satirical to please;
> SHAKESPEAR'S strong genius ever unconfin'd,
> Darts on the soul, and captivates the mind;
> While JOHNSON, by more regular essays,
> Attacks the dangerous avenues of praise.

The next two selections are extremely destructive of Jonson, but they indicate the prevailing attitude in those very years of the 1770's when his plays were appearing with greatest frequency. *The Dramatic Censor* (1770), by Francis Gentleman, who was subsequently to alter two of Jonson's comedies, contained critiques of fourteen of Shakspere's plays and none of Jonson's. The ungrateful Gentleman wrote of Jonson:

BEN JOHNSON, though ranked so high in literary fame, does not appear to us deserving of so honourable a station; his tragedies are the most stiff, uncouth, laborious, unaffecting, productions we know, spun out to an intolerable length, by tedious, unessential, declamatory passages, translated from the classics; three of his comedies have justly received the stamp of general approbation; VOLPONE, SILENT WOMAN, and EVERY MAN IN HIS HUMOUR; yet even in these nature seems rather carricatur'd [*sic*], and there are many blamable intrusions upon delicacy of idea and expression; the remainder of his works might have dubbed any man, less lucky, with the title of a bad writer, and we are perfectly of opinion that naming him with his great cotemporary, is pairing authors as poulterers do rabbits, a fat and a lean one.[1]

The Gentleman's Magazine for November, 1772, printed the following communication from "Horatio":

It would be an invidious task to run a long parallel between Johnson and Shakespeare; to do it effectually, would only shew the poor stock of one writer, and the vast treasures of the other.

1. II, 461.

Ben was rather a good satyrist than a complete poet. He pleased himself with personifying vices and passions; while his great cotemporary drew characters, such as Nature presented to him. . . . One *exalted*, the other *debased*, the human species. You despise Bobadil, though he makes you laugh. You wish to spend a jolly evening with Falstaff, tho' you cannot esteem him. In short, Ben contents himself with the humble praise of being the gentleman-usher of Fashion, while Shakespeare is not only Nature's companion, but sometimes her guide.

Two or three great actors, with much ado, keep alive three or four plays of Johnson; but many of Shakespeare's dramas, after they have lain dormant above half a century, are revived with fresh lustre, and are seen with perpetual pleasure, and repeated applause. . . . [Jonson's] Every man in his Humour, the Alchemist, Volpone, and the Silent Woman, are excellent pieces; but written with such labour and art, that Nature sometimes seems to lie buried under them. . . . his plays are incumbered with useless ornaments, and are totally divested of that ease and graceful air of negligence which distinguish the writings of Shakespeare.[1]

At length hypocrisy had been thrown to the winds and a critic had spoken his mind. From this time, Jonson's defenders were few.

If the critics were fond of emphasizing Jonson's imitation and his inferiority to Shakspere, they were equally fond of remarking that his plays were out-of-date and that revivals merely discouraged writers of new plays. Part of the neo-classic creed consisted of ardent allegiance to the age in which they lived. The quarrel of ancients and moderns exhausted no small degree of literary energy for seventy-five years after the Restoration, and one of the minor skirmishes took the form of antipathy to the serving-up of old plays.[2] By 1694 the revolt against old plays was directed specifically at Jonson in James Wright's *Country Conversations*, in which Lisander, Mitis, and Julio discussed comedies on their way to town. Lisander con-

1. XLII, 522–523.
2. See *Covent Garden Drolery*, p. 83; George Powell, *The Treacherous Brothers*, 1696, sig. A4.

sidered that the modern plays had "neither the Wit, Conduct, Honour, nor Design of those Writ by *Johnson*,
Shakspear, and *Fletcher*," but Mitis objected to those
ancient wits, believing rather that the object of comedy
was a "True and Lively Representation of the Manners
and Behaviour of Mankind in the times we Live in."

Our Poets, continued he, represent the Modern little Actions
of Debauchees, as *Ben Johnson* presented the Humours of his
Tankard Bearer, his Pauls Walkers, and his Collegiate Ladies,
&c. things then known and familiar to every Bodies Notice. . . .
These, Answered *Julio*, were *Ben Johnsons* Weaknesses. . . .
Such Representations are like a Painters taking a Picture after
the Life in the Apparel then Worn, which becomes Ungraceful or
Ridiculous in the next Age, when the Fashion is out.[1]

With the collapse of the union of the two companies in 1695
and the establishment of two rival theatres, the natural
outcome was competition productive of new dramas. Congreve, for example, rapidly gained an ascendancy over
Jonson, which he steadily kept during the eighteenth
century.[2]

The most trenchant attack on old plays was made by
Goldsmith, at first anonymously, in *An Enquiry into the
Present State of Polite Learning* (1759):[3]

Old pieces are revived, and scarce any new ones admitted.
The actor is ever in our eye, and the poet seldom permitted to
appear; the public are again obliged to ruminate [over] those
hashes of absurdity, which were disgusting to our ancestors even
in an age of ignorance. . . . What strange vamp'd comedies,
farcical tragedies . . . have we not of late seen! . . . The piece
pleases our critics, because it talks old English; and it pleases the
galleries, because it has ribaldry. . . . But great art must be
sometimes used before they can thus impose upon the public.

1. Pages 3–10.
2. *Memoirs of the Society of Grub-Street*, 1737, II, 324.
3. J. W. M. Gibbs, *The Works of Oliver Goldsmith*, III (1885), 518–520. See
the prologue at the revival of *Every Man in his Humour*, November 29, 1751.

To this purpose, a prologue written with some spirit generally precedes the piece, to inform us that it was composed by Shakespear, or old Ben, or somebody else who took them for his model.

Perhaps one need not add that Goldsmith's essay seriously displeased Garrick. But any suffering which he may have endured from slighting remarks on the attention he had paid the ancient poets was allayed by George Colman's *Critical Reflections on the Old English Dramatick Writers* (1761), in which Colman attributed the increasing reputation of Shakspere to Garrick's revivals, and bade the manager direct his energies to the merits of Jonson, Beaumont and Fletcher, and Massinger, for

the *Fox*, the *Alchymist*, the *Silent Woman*, *Every Man in his Humour* of *Jonson*, the *New Way to pay old Debts*, the *City Madam* of *Massinger*, &c. &c. all urge their Claim for a Rank in the ordinary Course of our Winter-Evening Entertainments.[1]

Answering the charge of obsolescence, Colman argued that it was both pleasant and instructive to see the manners of a former age pass in review, that the eye was gratified with the antique costumes, and that only proper curtailments were necessary to render many old plays as popular as Garrick's version of *Every Man in his Humour*.

In an amusing passage in *The Vicar of Wakefield* (1766), Goldsmith returned to the discussion of revivals. The vicar met a strolling player and asked him who were the Drydens and Otways of the day:

"I fancy, Sir," cried the player, "few of our modern dramatists would think themselves much honoured by being compared to the writers you mention. Dryden and Rowe's manner, Sir, are quite out of fashion; our taste has gone back a whole century, Fletcher, Ben Johnson, and all the plays of Shakespear, are the only things that go down." — "How," cried I, "is it possible the present age can be pleased with that antiquated

1. Page 17. The reviews in *The Monthly Review*, XXIV (1761), 200, and *The Critical Review*, XI (1761), 164, are interesting.

dialect, that obsolete humour, those over-charged characters, which abound in the works you mention?" — "Sir," returned my companion, "the publick think nothing about dialect, or humour, or character; for that is none of their business, they only go to be amused, and find themselves happy when they can enjoy a pantomime, under the sanction of Johnson's or Shakespeare's name." [1]

The number of performances of Jonson and Shakspere and the box-office receipts prove that the strolling player was a keen student of the contemporary theatre.

Closely related to the obsolescence of the plays was the problem of alteration. In the Restoration, so far as our evidence shows (inasmuch as there were no acting versions before the unaltered quartos of *The Fox*, *The Alchemist*, and *The Silent Woman* appeared in 1709), Jonson's comedies were unquestionably acted in unaltered form, and Dryden stated specifically that "in his works you find little to retrench or alter." [2] Not till *Every Man in his Humour* was produced unsuccessfully at Lincoln's Inn Fields in 1725 did the managers tamper with Jonson's text, a remarkable record in comparison with mutilations which the plays of Shakspere, and Beaumont and Fletcher, suffered beneath the ruthless pens of the improvers. [3] With the passage of time, however, the texts of *Bartholomew Fair*, *Every Man in his Humour*, *The Alchemist*, *Volpone*, and *The Silent Woman* were adapted to later theatrical taste, but most of the alterations consisted merely of reductions in speeches rather than of important structural changes. The intention was obviously to shorten the comedies to allow for the performance of an afterpiece and to reduce speeches and terms no longer comprehensible. The attitude of the anonymous author of *Memoirs of the Life of Robert Wilks*,

1. Chapter XVIII.
2. *Works*, XV, 346. For similar opinion see Eliza Haywood, *The Female Spectator*, 2d ed., 1748, II, 76.
3. See Hazelton Spencer, *Shakespeare Improved*, Cambridge, Mass., 1927, pp. 137–354; A. C. Sprague, *Beaumont and Fletcher on the Restoration Stage*, Cambridge, Mass., 1926, pp. 129–267.

Esq. (1732) was no doubt common. The public, lacking a degree of historical perspective, was mystified by some of the incidents in Jonson's plays:

Johnson, the Father of the *English* Comedy, is accused by some of having intended to represent particular Persons in his Plays: Every-body who knows any Thing of Dramatic Writing must have heard, That the Character of *Volpone* was intended for an old scraping Citizen, who by his great Cunning acquir'd a vast Fortune, and by leaving it to charitable Uses has acquired as large a Stock of Reputation in future Times: 'Tis highly probable that this Method of *Ben*'s might be of great Service, as to the immediate Fortune of his Plays, tho' at this Day it doubtless leaves us in the Dark, as to many Particulars which, if we had an exact Character of him against whom the Satyr is pointed, would become Beauties instead of being thought Defects; . . . such is the Variety of Characters presented in the Space of a few Years on the publick Theatre of Life, that in a short time the most striking grow antiquated, and the Publick by gazing continually on what passes in their own Times, lose all Ideas of what passed before. Hence it follows that not only *Johnson*'s Plays, but all the Tribe of Writers who followed him, fail of moving a Modern Audience upon the Stage, or of entertaining them in their Closets.[1]

By 1773 the plays of Jonson were considered thoroughly obsolete, even in altered form. Poetasters descended on them and began cutting them up into farces. The reviewer of *Memoirs of Samuel Foote, Esq.* dismissed Jonson in two sentences:

The dramatic characters of Shakespeare are the characters of people we meet with every day, while those of Ben Johnson are obsolete. The Alchymist, and Every Man in his Humour, are sufficient proofs of this observation.[2]

1. Pages vii–viii. For the original of Volpone see Andrew Clark, *Aubrey's 'Brief Lives,'* Oxford, 1898, II, 246. James Upton urged Jonson's need for explanation in 1749 (*Remarks on Three Plays*, sig. A4), which Peter Whalley attempted to furnish in his edition of *The Works*. See the review of Whalley's edition in *The Critical Review*, I (1756), 462–472.
2. Haymarket Scrap-book, Harvard Theatre Collection.

The plays were doomed as soon as the brilliant school of actors which Garrick had laboriously trained departed from the stage.

Thomas Davies remarked that the old actors always found Jonsonian rôles most difficult to play,[1] and as early as 1699 James Wright had noted that the actors of his day held a similar opinion:

> *Lovewit.* When the question has been asked, "Why these players do not revive the *Silent Woman* and some other of JOHNSON's plays, once of highest esteem?" They have answered truly, "Because there are none now living, who can rightly humour those parts: for all who [were] related to the 'Black-friars' (where they were acted in perfection) are now dead, and almost forgotten."[2]

The comedies were revived at Drury Lane immediately after Wright's observation, and the casts for Jonson's plays included the best actors in the company, but as time passed the common opinion was that the choice of actors for the old plays of Ben Jonson, Congreve, Steele, and Vanbrugh was very defective.[3] We know that Theophilus Cibber zanied Abel Drugger, and in 1746 there was common lamentation at the lack of honest acting. Critics deplored the degeneracy of the modern school of actors:

> Now turn we where discarded *Nature* turn'd adrift,
> They Comedy to low Buffoon'ry shift,
> Could *Laureat Ben* but from the Grave arise,
> And see his Manly Scenes in their *Disguise*,
> He'd curse the Time he spent with so much Toil
> To raise a Fabric but for them to spoil.[4]

With Garrick's assumption of the management of Drury Lane in 1747, the casts improved, and renewed attention

1. *Dramatic Miscellanies*, 1784, II, 94–95.
2. *Historia Histrionica*, ed. Edward Arber, *An English Garner*, II (1879), 273; R. W. Lowe, *An Apology for the Life of Mr. Colley Cibber*, 1889, I, xxiv.
3. *An Impartial Examen of the Present Contests Between the Town and the Manager of the Theatre. By Mr. Neither-Side*, 1744, p. 19.
4. *A Clear Stage and no Favour; or, Tragedy and Comedy at War* [ca. 1746], p. 8.

was paid to Jonson; surely no revival was ever more care-fully planned than that of *Every Man in his Humour* in 1751. But still the characters were considered difficult to perform, particularly the parts for women, and *The Theat-rical Examiner* (1757) published the following advice to young actresses:

> The great ladies of Ben. Johnson, are north country chamber-maids in point of breeding, Beaumont and Fletcher the same: I don't say this to rob either the former or latter of their merits: such were the modes of the times. I would recommend it to the actresses, who play prudish comedy, not to tone and tragedize; it is again out of nature.[1]

As Garrick's company and the excellent performers at Covent Garden included Jonson in their repertory each season, the public perceived that his plays were virtually preserved to the stage by the sheer genius of the acting of such men as Garrick, Woodward, Weston, and Shuter. It was no exaggeration of the critics that when these men had been associated for so many seasons with Abel Drugger, Bobadill, or Master Stephen, the public went to see the actors rather than the plays, a habit not entirely unknown today. In 1762 William Whitehead, the poet-laureate, wrote acutely of the audience:

> Or would ye sift more near these sons of fire,
> 'Tis Garrick, and not Shakespear they admire.
> Without his breath, inspiring every thought,
> They ne'er perhaps had known what Shakespear wrote;
> Without his eager, his becoming zeal,
> To teach them, tho' they scarce know why, to feel,
> A crude unmeaning mass had Johnson been,
> And a dead letter Shakespear's noblest scene.[2]

When Garrick retired and the personnel of the company changed, Jonson's plays died a natural death.

Another danger which threatened plays of the older dramatists and hastened their obsolescence was the rise of the pantomimes. These diversions, such as *Harlequin Dr.*

1. Page 78.   2. *A Charge to the Poets*, p. 15.

Faustus, Harlequin a Sorcerer, and *Harlequin Grand-Volgi,*
began to make place for themselves during the third
decade of the eighteenth century.   Lincoln's Inn Fields
theatre and later Covent Garden were the early haunts of
this form of entertainment, for which a special type of
actor had to be trained.   Lovers of the classical English
comedies feared promptly and ever increasingly that the
legitimate drama would be shoved to the wall.   Ned Ward is
the first writer I have discovered alluding to the danger
facing Jonson:

> Near to these Fields, as I before
> Have said, and now I say, *encore,*
> There stands a Fabrick of Renown,
> Erected to amuse the Town,
>
> .   .   .   .   .   .
>
> This House was, also, once design'd
> T'instruct, as well as please Mankind,
> That all degrees of humane Creatures
> Might learn their Duty to their Betters,
>
> .   .   .   .   .   .
>
> This also should have been the Seat
> Of Language, of Humour and of Wit,
> Of Musick, Poetry, and all
> The pleasing Arts Theatrical.
> Here *Shakespeare* to *Elizion* fled,
> And, *O rare Ben,* should live, tho' dead,
> That their inimitable Plays,   ⎫
> In others, might a Genius raise,   ⎬
> And teach 'em to deserve the Bays. ⎭
>
> .   .   .   .   .   .
>
> But now, the Stage revolts from these
> Dramatick Rules, that us'd to please,
> And does, in scorn of Wit, impose
> Upon the Town, *Dumb Raree Shows,*
> Compos'd of Vizards and Grimaces,
> Fine Scenes, Machine, and Antick Dresses;
> As if old Plays were, by the Proud,
> Thought too instructive for the Croud.[1]

---

1. *The Dancing Devils; or, The Roaring Dragon* [*ca.* 1722], pp. 5–9. Pictorial
satires appeared at once. See the *Catalogue of Prints and Drawings in the British
Museum, Division I, Satires,* III, part i (1877), Nos. 2354, 2466.

In 1732 the author of *Memoirs of the Life of Robert Wilks, Esq.* deplored the degeneracy of public taste, which had once boasted of the finest theatre in Europe, and warned readers that "it would be an irreparable Damage to the Reputation of the present Age, if we should now forfeit it for the sake of low Wit and Buffoonery, Pantomimes and Ballad Opera's." He prophesied that unless the stage were reformed, "JOHNSON in twenty Years [would] be an Author as antiquated as PLAUTUS." [1]

At the time of the differences between the actors and the managers in 1744, *The Disputes Between the Managers of the Theatres, and their Actors Adjusted* [2] blamed the managers for pantomimes and the rotation of worn-out plays, charging that because actors were paid badly, good players could scarcely afford to remain in the profession. Whether the managers were actually to blame or not is difficult to say. At any rate, they attempted to shift the blame to the public, as shown by the occasional prologue spoken at the opening of Drury Lane in September, 1750, [3] in which Garrick insisted that he was supplying the audience with what it wanted. This prologue was matched by one at Covent Garden, which considered Garrick's position specious and referred to him as a tyrant:

> If *Shakespear*'s passion, or if *Johnson*'s art,
> Can fire the fancy, or can warm the heart,
> That task be our's. — But if you damn their scenes,
> And heroes must give way to harlequins,
> We, too, can have recourse to mime and dance;
> Nay, there, I think, we have the better chance:
> And, should the town grow weary of the mute,
> Why — we'll produce — a child upon the flute. [4]

Two years later a writer in Bonnell Thornton's *Have at you all; or, The Drury-Lane Journal* wondered at the ridiculous admiration for harlequin performances, where "mere

1. Sig. A3. See Aaron Hill in *The Prompter*, January 30, 1736, and *The Usefulness of the Stage to Religion, and to Government*, 1738, pp. 12, 27, 40.
2. Pages 19–20.
3. *The Universal Magazine*, VII (1750), 135–136.　　4. Page 184.

apes of humanity" risked "their precious limbs in jostling
one another, to have an opportunity of staring at the
pretty feats of a dumb Harlequin, while the empty benches
reproach their deficiency of understanding, when SHAKE-
SPEARE or JONSON in vain exert the affecting powers of
reason and judgment." [1]   Animadversions flowed freely,
but the pantomimes continued.   Verse and prose were exhausted in an attempt to stem extravaganzas, afterpieces,
and mummeries.   One poet wrote:

> In this soft Age, when even Sense is found
> To lose her Charms, without the Charms of Sound:
> When Op'ra, waving high her Magic Wand,
> (And SHAKESPEAR quite forgot,) subdues the Land:
> When JOHNSON, OTWAY, all our Nation's Pride,
> For Noise, and Nonsense, are thrown quite aside:
> Is not some Tribute to those Mem'ries due,
> Who brought all Nature forth, and at a View
> Saw through the Whole? [2]

One wonders just what tribute the poet demanded. Was it
not enough that no less than seventeen plays of Shakspere
were performed at the two theatres in the season 1757–
1758, while two of Jonson's comedies were presented six
nights? The critics were somewhat more atrabiliar than
necessity demanded. None of them was more so than
Thomas Wilkes, who looked back to those glorious times
when the public had relished the polite arts and digested
"the manly sense of Shakespeare" and "the correct drawing of Jonson." He attributed the pantomimes to youths
who had taken the grand tour and had returned with a
vitiated taste which preferred performances by "an effemi-
nate treble-voiced fellow, whose tones are unnatural, and
those acquired by committing a violence upon nature" to
the noble classics of the English drama. [3]
    Theatrical affairs were in such parlous state that one
poet tried to imagine what the older actors would think if

1. Page 227.
2. *Candour: An Enquiry into the Real Merits of the Salisbury Comedians,*
1758, p. 24.   3. *A General View of the Stage,* p. 67.

they could return and see how debased the stage had
become. Quin's ghost comes in the dead of night to Garrick, and says that when he landed in Elysium, Ryan had
inquired for Garrick:

> He wished to know how matters went,
> In the *theatric* government:
> If acting now was just the same,
> And men of sense rever'd his name?
> I told him (and I told him true)
> The stage would dwindle but for you:
> That Rowe and Shakespear's tragic strain,
> Were ONLY heard at Drury-Lane.
> *Buffoonery* was gaining ground,
> And sense oblig'd to yield to sound.
> That merit was left unregarded,
> And impudence the best rewarded.
> The honest Vet'ran shook his head,
> Said he, it glads me that I'm dead;
> To live, and see what you impart,
> Would certainly have broke my heart.[1]

Charles Jenner imagined a rustic vicar visiting London
for pleasure and attending the theatre, where he found
nothing but pageants and stale jests.

> "Are these," he cries "the men of taste and learning,
> "So polish'd, so refin'd, and so discerning?
> "Are these the works, which envied praises crown
> "From that most dread tribunal, call'd *the town*?
> "Why did I ever quit my calm fireside,
> "Where common-sense with reason was my guide?
> "Where, all the critics useless rules laid by,
> "My heart inform'd me when to laugh or cry.
> "Let me return to *Shakespear* and old *Ben*;
> "I cannot brook these all-discerning men." [2]

In spite of the critics' fears, Jonson was holding the stage
with at least two plays, *The Alchemist* and *Every Man in his*

1. *The Interview; or, Jack Falstaff's Ghost. A Poem inscrib'd to David Garrick, Esq.*, 1766, pp. 12–13. Quin died in 1766.
2. *Town Eclogues*, 1772, pp. 3–4. For an account of entertainments made
from Jonson's masques see my forthcoming article, "Ben Jonson's Masques on
the Eighteenth-Century Stage," in *Studies in Philology*.

Humour. *Volpone* and *The Silent Woman* were soon to be revived, but critical analyses of the times were essentially correct. For Jonson's doom was near: after 1776 it was positively hazardous to revive any of his comedies.

Despite the vicissitudes of old age and the competition of the pantomimes, despite the fact that Jonson was ultimately to be judged of lesser genius than Shakspere, the merits of *The Fox*, *The Alchemist*, and *The Silent Woman* were recognized from the time that Dryden judged English humors superior to French and undertook "to find more variety of them in some one play of Ben Jonson's than in all theirs together: as he who has seen the 'Alchemist,' 'The Silent Woman,' or 'Bartholomew Fair,' cannot but acknowledge with me." [1] This opinion lasted to the days of the newspaper reviewers and the dramatic pamphleteers.

In 1675 Edward Phillips in his *Theatrum Poetarum* remarked that "In three of his Comedies, namely the *Fox*, *Alchymist* and *Silent Woman*; he may be compared, in the Judgment of Learned Men, for Decorum, Language, and well Humouring of the Parts, as well with the chief of the Ancient Greec [*sic*] and Latin Comedians as the prime of Modern *Italians*, who have been judg'd the best of *Europe* for a happy Vein in Comedies, nor is his *Bartholmew* [*sic*] *-Fair* much short of them." [2]

Eighteenth-century loyalty to the laws of poetry was manifested by John Dennis in 1720, in an attack on "Sir John Edgar" (Richard Steele), whom he warned not to meddle with criticism or the improvement of dramatic art. Sir John had attacked the rules, particularly those for the three unities, and Dennis defended them by the example of Jonson:

I am afraid we shall find, upon a strict scrutiny, that the very best of our Plays are the most regular. . . . "The Fox," "The Alchemist," "The Silent Woman" of BEN JONSON are incom-

1. *Works*, XV, 331.
2. "The Modern Poets," pp. 19–20. Copied in Blount's *De Re Poetica*, "Characters and Censures," p. 106.

parably the best of our Comedies; and they are certainly the most regular of them all. . . . it was the opinion of the greatest of our Comic Poets, that the Rules were absolutely necessary to perfection.[1]

Corbyn Morris described the three comedies as "most exquisite *Satires*," [2] and a poetical appreciation appeared in 1749 in a Latin poem, *An Accurate tho' Compendious Encomium on the Most Illustrious Persons, Whose Monuments are Erected in Westminster-Abbey*: [3]

> *Cernitur hìc, nullâ Famæ dignata Tabellâ,*
> JOHNSONI *Effigies; omni memorabilis Ævo!*
> *Qui mores Hominum tenui depinxit Avenâ,*
> *Stultitiam Vulgi, Curas, et inania Vota.*
> *Comicus ipsi labor ridenti* Dramate *nomen*
> *Efferat, et laudes* Mulier *taciturnu loquatur.*
> *Exuberat docili vafer* Alchymista *lepore,*
> *Et* Vulpes *fallax, Sale non pereunte, placebit.*

> BEHOLD! undignify'd, rare JOHNSON's Bust!
> No *Panegyric* celebrates his Dust:
> Whose hum'rous Vein display'd, on th' *English* Stage,
> The Wish, vain Cares, and Follies of the Age.
> Let then the Comic *Drama* speak his Praise,
> And due Applause the *Silent Woman* raise:
> His *Alchymist* unrivall'd Taste can boast,
> And crafty *Volpone* please, 'till Humour's lost.

The London Magazine for July, 1753, noted truly that "his Alchymist, his Volpone or the Fox, and his Silent Woman, have been performed to many crouded audiences, with universal applause," [4] and in 1770 Paul Hiffernan recommended a study of the triad to those who would know the best that had been written in English drama.[5]

When Thomas Davies wrote *Dramatic Miscellanies*, he expressed a unique opinion concerning the reasons for

1. John Nichols, *The Theatre, By Sir Richard Steele*, 1791, II, 378–379. See [Giles Jacob], *An Historical Account of the Lives and Writings of Our most Considerable English Poets*, 1720, p. 272.
2. *An Essay Towards Fixing the True Standards of Wit*, p. 33.
3. Pages 18–19.   4. XXII, 304.
5. *Dramatic Genius. In Five Books*, p. 95.

Jonson's success on the stage, attributing it not to any merit in the plays, but to the fear inspired in the public by the very name of Jonson, whom they dared not dislike!

The critics who lived in the same age with the author, and all who have succeeded till within these twenty or thirty years, have bestowed the most superlative commendations upon Volpone, the Silent Woman, and the Alchemist; and yet we find, by a contemporary, who seems to have no mean opinion of these comedies, that they were exhibited to empty benches, at a time when the name of Shakspeare was a charm sufficient to draw multitudes to see his dramatic works. . . . [Jonson] was never supported by the public voice, though kept alive by the critics and the excellent performance of the actors. He had bullied the authors of his own times into an extraordinary opinion of his vast merit; and, when he died, he left such a frown behind him, that he frightened all succeeding dramatic poets and critics, who were afraid to censure, what, in their hearts, they neither admired nor approved.[1]

Davies was wrong in several respects. It was true that Jonson's personality had exerted an influence somewhat of the quality he suggested, but if he had followed the course of criticism in his own century, he would have known that in no sense were writers so awed that they refrained from violently unfavorable comment, and he should have known also that no play is ever "kept alive by the critics" unless in some measure it satisfies public taste. Jonson's comedies held the stage only by virtue of their own excellence, enhanced by the skill of well-trained and imaginative actors. Even in obsolescence, they commanded tributes in prose and verse, the sincerity of which need never be questioned. That they grew out-of-date after a century and a half was not so much the fault of the plays and their author, as of the school of realism which Jonson represented to perfection, and without which English dramatic literature would have been infinitely less impressive.

1. II, 92–94.

CHAPTER II

Volpone; or, The Fox

I

1660–1700

TO MODERN poets and dramatists, *Volpone* has seemed the consummate achievement of Jonson's genius. Free from the prevailing humors of his other comedies and from the local customs and manners of Elizabethan and Jacobean times, this bitter play has a central theme of permanent moral value, the warping of human character wrought by avarice and the search for gold. There are five magnificent acting rôles: Volpone himself, the lively parasite Mosca, and the three legacy-hunters, Corbaccio, Corvino, and Voltore. Coleridge was "inclined to consider The Fox as the greatest of Ben Jonson's works," [1] and Symonds, Swinburne, and William Archer have written warmly about it. The fact that *Volpone* has been "discovered" by the German dramatist Stefan Zweig,[2] and that it has been produced fre-

---

1. W. G. T. Shedd, *The Complete Works of Samuel Taylor Coleridge*, New York, 1854, VI, 287.

2. *Ben Jonsons "Volpone" Eine lieblose Komödie in drei Akten*, Potsdam, 1926. For a comparison of this version with the original, by the present writer, see *The New York Times*, April 22, 1928. A French version was made by Jules Romains, *Volpone en collaboration avec Stefan Zweig*, Paris, 1929; there was an earlier adaptation by Emile Zola, *Les Héritiers Rabourdin*, produced at the Théâtre de Cluny, Paris, in 1874, for seventeen performances; this version was translated by A. Teixeira de Mattos, *The Heirs of Rabourdin*, 1894, and produced by J. T. Grein for the Independent Theatre, London, February 23, 1894, at the Opéra Comique. The reasons for its failure were analyzed by William Archer in *The Theatrical 'World' of 1894*, 1895, pp. 65–68. See also J. T. Grein, *Dramatic Criticism*, 1904, IV, 297. An independent prose translation in Italian was made by Alessandro De Stefani, *Volpone da Ben Jonson, Nuova Antologia*, CCLXXI

quently since 1926 in the foremost state-theatres of Germany,[1] whence it has made its way to New York in the successful production by the Theatre Guild,[2] speaks sufficiently for its excellence as an acting play.

Volpone was probably revived promptly after the Restoration. It had been popular until the closing of the theatres in 1642, as is witnessed by testimonial verses throughout the Jacobean and Caroline periods, and there are records of a performance on October 26, 1638, when Sir Humphrey Mildmay recorded in his diary that he saw "The Foxe playe with Fra. Wortley," and paid the very considerable sum of 4 *s*. 6 *d*.[3] There was another performance before the king and queen at "the Cocpit" at Whitehall, on November 8, 1638.[4] The comedy was remembered even during the Commonwealth period, for in 1658 Richard Flecknoe described the character "Of one that imitates the good companion another way" as "on[e] who now the stage is down Acts the *Parasites* part at Table; and since *Tailors* death, none can play Mosco's [*sic*] part so well as he."[5]

The Silent Woman, *The Alchemist*, and *Bartholomew Fair* had been acted in 1660 and 1661, but there is no record of production for *Volpone* after the Restoration until 1662, when Dr. Edward Browne, son of the illustrious Sir Thomas, noted in his memorandum book that he had paid 2 *s*. 6 *d*.

(1930), 429–451, CCLXXII (1930), 53–71, 157–177, 315–328. See also the German translation of *Volpone* in Margarete Mauthner, *Ben Jonson*, Berlin, 1912, pp. 117–223.

1. For reviews of the premières in Germany see *Berliner Tageblatt*, December 23, 1926; *Frankfurter Zeitung*, February 28, 1927; *Allgemeine Zeitung am Abend* (München), April 1, 1927; "*The Stage*" *Year Book*, 1927, p. 93. For stage settings, see *Das Theater*, 1927, pp. 22, 131, 232, 241, 527.

2. The New York première was at the Guild Theatre, April 9, 1928. All the reviews of the play itself and of the translation of Zweig's text by Ruth Langner were highly enthusiastic. See Helene Richter, "Ben Jonsons Volpone und sein Erneuerer Stefan Zweig," *Shakespeare-Jahrbuch*, LXIII (1927), 183–190.

3. J. Payne Collier, *The History of English Dramatic Poetry . . . and Annals of the Stage to the Restoration*, 1831, II, 86.

4. J. Q. Adams, *The Dramatic Records of Sir Henry Herbert*, New Haven, 1917, p. 77.

5. *Enigmaticall Characters*, p. 10.

to see *The Fox* "at the new new Theatre in Lincolnes Inne fields." [1] In the same year he saw *The Alchemist* and *Bartholomew Fair* at this theatre. His designation might lead one to confuse the theatre he meant with that of Sir William Davenant, who had opened the house in Lincoln's Inn Fields, under the patent granted to the Duke of York on June 28, 1661.[2] But Browne clearly meant the King's Company, acting in Vere Street, as may be determined from the actual list of the plays which he saw in this year and the fact that both Evelyn and Pepys spoke of the Vere Street house as being "near Lincolne's-Inn Fields." [3] If *Volpone* and *Bartholomew Fair* were produced at Lincoln's Inn Fields at this time by Davenant's company, there was a violation of that "private Rule or Argument" between the two capital houses, described by Cibber, whereby "both Houses were happily ty'd down" so that "no Play acted at one House, should ever be attempted at the other." [4] Futile rivalry was avoided, for all the leading plays of Shakspere, Fletcher, and Jonson were divided between them by the approval of the court and their own choice, so that the stage was furnished with a greater variety than could possibly have been presented, had both companies been employed simultaneously upon the same plays. However, Cibber's statement has been questioned,[5] and it is certain that at this early date the rule was not hard and fast, for the King's Company poached on the pre-

1. British Museum MS. Sloane 1900.

2. For detailed analysis of the difficult early years of the Restoration companies see Hazelton Spencer, *Shakespeare Improved*, pp. 3–110; A. C. Sprague, *Beaumont and Fletcher on the Restoration Stage*, pp. 1–24; Leslie Hotson, *The Commonwealth and Restoration Stage*, Cambridge, Mass., 1928, *passim*.

3. For further comment on Browne's use of the term "Lincoln's Inn Fields" with reference to the King's Company, see Sprague, pp. 17, 22, and Spencer, p. 58, n. 13. The King's Company did act at other theatres than their own in the summer of 1662 (Allardyce Nicoll, *A History of Restoration Drama*, Cambridge, 1923, p. 273), and Browne notes seeing them act at the "Cock Pit in Drewry Lane," probably, as Mr. Spencer surmised, because of repairs at Vere Street.

4. *Apology*, 2d ed., 1740, p. 77 (ed. R. W. Lowe, I, 91, which reads "Agreement" for "Argument").

5. [John Genest], *Some Account of the English Stage*, Bath, 1832, I, 404.

serves of the Duke's Company and produced some of the
plays of Beaumont and Fletcher, which were supposed to
be the property of Davenant's men;[1] but Davenant's
actors, according to the records, are not known to have
poached on the King's Company's rights to Jonson. It is
possible that this agreement did not go fully into effect
until the opening of the King's Company at the Theatre
Royal in Bridges Street on May 7, 1663. At any rate,
after Killigrew was established at the new house, nine
Jonson plays were included in the repertory as given by
the prompter John Downes, the famous triad of *The Fox*,
The Alchemist, and *The Silent Woman* being among "their
principal old stock plays," and the other six, *Catiline*,
Bartholomew Fair, *Every Man in his Humour*, *Every Man
out of his Humour*, *Sejanus*, and *The Devil is an Ass*, being
played "but now and then." [2]

Performances of all of Jonson's plays after 1662 share,
with negligible exceptions, the history and vicissitudes of
the King's Company, and, until well into the eighteenth
century, were given at Drury Lane. There was a division,
or rather a pooling, of the plays by the companies during
the union, which lasted from 1682 to 1695. Betterton revived *The Alchemist* at Lincoln's Inn Fields on October 9,
1702; the Jonson plays in the repertory accompanied the
players to the Haymarket when in 1705 Betterton opened
there, and continued to be acted until the new union of
Drury Lane and the Haymarket in 1708; they followed the
actors who deserted Rich under Swiney's management in
1709, and returned with them to Drury Lane in 1710,
where they were performed exclusively until the abortive
revival of *Every Man in his Humour* at Lincoln's Inn
Fields in 1725, and the successful revival of *Volpone* at that
theatre in 1727. This revival of *Volpone* lasted until the
opening of Covent Garden theatre under Rich on Decem-

1. Sprague, pp. 14-15.
2. *Roscius Anglicanus*, 1708, pp. 3-9.

ber 7, 1732, where it was acted until 1754. Until 1727 the fortunes of Jonson's comedies coincided with the fortunes of Drury Lane companies. After the opening of Covent Garden, however, there were only twelve seasons before 1776 in which Drury Lane presented the comedies without opposition from some other theatre, so that at least four times during that period one might find Jonson's plays presented on the same night at two houses.

The first performance of *Volpone* for which there is a definite date was that at court, unquestionably by Killigrew's actors, "before their Maties" on October 16, 1662, a performance seen by John Evelyn, at this time an infrequent spectator of the plays at public theatres, because "they were abused to an atheistical liberty, fowle and undecent women now (and never till now) permitted to appeare and act, who inflaming severall young noblemen and gallants, became their misses, and to some their wives."[1]

With these performances of the play in 1662 is associated the first influence of *Volpone* on foreign literature after the Restoration, and the earliest foreign influence, indeed, of any of Jonson's comedies; for in this year, Monsieur de Saint-Évremond, friend of the Duke of Buckingham and a frequent visitor at the English court, wrote his *Sir Politick Would-Be, Comedie à la Manière des Anglois*.[2] The editor observes that the piece was not exclusively the work of Saint-Évremond, but that "Le Duc de Buckingham, & M. d'Aubigny ont eu beaucoup de part à la composition."[3] Almost the only semblance it has to the original is the presence in the cast of the two characters, "Sir Politick Would-Be, Chevalier Anglois, Politique ridicule," and "La Femme de Sir Politick, grave & sottement capable." None of the others bears the slightest relation to the characters

1. William Bray and H. B. Wheatley, *Diary of John Evelyn*, 1879, II, 153, 211.
2. *Œuvres de Monsieur de Saint Evremond*, n.p., 1740, II, 175-318.
3. II, 177 n.; I, 64.

in *Volpone*. The comedy, the scene of which is laid at Venice, has no plot and is no more than a collection of conversations on international politics. To the modern reader it is insufferably dull, and Voltaire, while admitting the excellence of Saint-Évremond's taste and wit, called it a miserable performance.[1]

On Thursday, January 1, 1663, *Volpone* was presented at Oxford, as noted by Anthony Wood: "given to see Volponey acted at the town hall by prentices and tradesmen, 6*d*.," and on January 6, "given to see Volponey acted againe, 6*d*." [2]

After the opening on May 7, 1663, of the King's Company at the Theatre Royal in Bridges Street (the house was also called "Drury Lane," "Covent Garden," and "The King's") the play, together with *The Alchemist* and *The Silent Woman* became, as has been said, the official property of Killigrew's company. The cast as given by Downes [3] follows: Volpone, Major Mohun; Mosca, Mr. Hart; Voltore, Mr. Shatterel; Corbaccio, Mr. Cartwright; Corvino, Mr. Burt; Politick Would-be, Mr. Lacy; Peregrine, Mr. Kynaston; Lady Would-be, Mrs. Corey; Celia, Mrs. Marshall. No doubt these actors performed when Pepys saw "Vulpone" at the new theatre on January 14, 1665, and considered it "a most excellent play; the best I think I ever saw, and well acted." [4]

John Downes remains the chief authority for the physical characteristics and the various rôles of the Restoration actors, the descriptions of whom he spices with racy anecdotes. Although successive historians of the stage have borrowed his material along with his blunders, it must be repeated here in order that one may study the fitness of each actor in relation to Jonson's comedies and may not

1. See Karl Lachmann and Franz Muncker, *Gotthold Ephraim Lessings sämtliche Schriften*, Stuttgart, X (1894), 124.
2. Andrew Clark, *The Life and Times of Anthony Wood*, *antiquary*, Oxford, I (1891), 467.   3. Page 4.
4. H. B. Wheatley, *The Diary of Samuel Pepys*, 1926, IV, 309.

treat these plays in isolation from the other dramas appearing at the same time.

Since Michael Mohun, a great favorite with King Charles, was trained as an actor of female parts before the wars, he brought to the Restoration stage earlier traditions of acting. He was short but muscular, and his forte lay in grave, austere parts, though upon occasion he appeared in gay and buoyant rôles like Valentine in *Wit without Money*, and Face in *The Alchemist*. His parts included such varied characters as Truewit in *The Silent Woman*, Cethegus in *Catiline*, Melantius in *The Maid's Tragedy*, Ventidius in *All for Love*, and Pinchwife in *The Country Wife*. "In all his Parts," says Downes, "he was most Accurate and Correct." In 1678 when, as a Popish recusant, he was in danger of exile, he wrote to the king that if he were forced to leave London, the theatre would have to close. The king issued him a license to stay, but Mohun was suffering so severely from gout that he could not call for it.[1] An epilogue written by the Earl of Rochester in 1675 to decry the bad acting of the day referred to Mohun's decrepitude, and denounced those "half Players" who, "like half Wits, can't be endur'd."

> *Yet these are they, who durst expose the Age*
> *Of the great* Wonder *of our English Stage.*
> *Whom Nature seem'd to form for your delight,*
> *And bid him speak, as she bid* Shakespeare *write.*
> *Those Blades indeed are Cripples in their Art*
> *Mimmick his Foot, but not his speaking part.*
> *Let them the* Traytor *or* Volpone *try;*
> *Could they . . .*
> *Rage like* Cethegus, *or like* Cassius *die,*
> *They ne'er had sent to* Paris *for such Fancies,*
> *As* Monster's *heads, and Merry* Andrew's *Dances.*[2]

---

1. *Calendar of State Papers, Domestic Series, March 1, 1678, to December 31, 1678,* 1913, p. 571.
2. Sir Francis Fane, *Love in the Dark,* pp. 95–96; *The Works of John, Earl of Rochester,* 1714, pp. 102–103.

Charles Hart was so eminent an actor that Downes, after praising the exactness and perfection of all his tragic and comic parts, confesses that "not any of his Successors have Equall'd him." He succeeded his colleague Lacy in the favor of Nell Gwyn, shared in the management of the theatre, and acted as distinguished a series of characters as may be found in the history of the stage during the Restoration: Catiline; Arbaces in Beaumont and Fletcher's *A King and No King*; Amintor in *The Maid's Tragedy*; Othello, Brutus, Antony, Hotspur; Almanzor in *The Conquest of Granada*; Aureng-Zebe, Bussy D'Ambois, Philaster; Manly in *The Plain Dealer*; Horner in *The Country Wife*; and Don John in *The Chances*.

The other members of the cast had played various parts. Robert Shatterel acted Sir John Daw in *The Silent Woman*, Calianax in *The Maid's Tragedy*, and Poins in *Henry IV*. William Cartwright, the first Falstaff of the Restoration, acted in Jonson's plays as Morose and Sir Epicure Mammon; he was famous for Brabantio in *The Moor of Venice* (*Othello*), Major Oldfox in *The Plain Dealer*, and Hermogenes in *Marriage à la Mode*. Nicholas Burt played Ned Clerimont in *The Silent Woman* and Surly in *The Alchemist*. A few of his other rôles were the Elder Loveless in *The Scornful Lady*, the Moor in *The Moor of Venice*, and Prince Hal in *Henry IV*.

John Lacy, author of four plays, excelled in characters of humors. Of all the king's actors he was Pepys's favorite; the diarist thought Lacy's rôle as the dancing-master in *The French Dancing-Master* "the best in the world," and in *Love in a Maze* the life of the play was Lacy's part, the clown.[1] Langbaine described him as "of a rare Shape of Body, and good Complexion,"[2] and his qualifications for playing the garrulous English knight, Sir Politick Would-be, may be seen from other parts he held: Otter in

1. II, 225–226.
2. [Charles Gildon], *The Lives and Characters of the English Dramatick Poets. ... First begun by Mr. Langbain* [*ca.* 1699], p. 84.

The Silent Woman, Ananias in *The Alchemist*, Falstaff, Scruple in *The Cheats*, Teague in *The Committee*, and the original Bayes in *The Rehearsal*.

Edward Kynaston "made a Compleat Female Stage Beauty," says Downes: he acted Evadne in *The Maid's Tragedy*; Ismenia in *The Maid in the Mill*, and the princess in *The Mad Lover*. But actresses were introduced, it is supposed, on December 8, 1660, at a production of *Othello*,[1] and Kynaston probably relinquished most of his female rôles, although the supply of actresses was so scarce at first that "there was still a Necessity, for some time, to put the handsomest young Men into Petticoats,"[2] and there is no doubt that he was acting Epicoene on January 7, 1661.[3] By 1663, however, in the cast given by Downes, the part had been assumed by Pepys's admired friend Mrs. Knepp. Kynaston played Antony in *Julius Caesar*, Henry IV, Freeman in *The Plain Dealer*, Harcourt in *The Country Wife*, and Morat in *Aureng-Zebe*.

Of the women in *Volpone*, Mrs. Corey was famous for Mrs. Otter in *The Silent Woman*, Dol Common in *The Alchemist*, Abigail in *The Scornful Lady*, Widow Blackacre in *The Plain Dealer*, and Octavia in *All for Love*. There were two Mrs. Marshalls connected with the King's Company, Ann and Rebecca. Since Ann Marshall was acting in 1663 [4] and Rebecca came into the company "a few years after," it was probably Ann who played Celia.

On August 28, 1667, the Theatre Royal company played *Volpone* at court, receiving £20 for the performance.[5] In 1668 Dryden wrote the first Restoration critique of *Volpone* in *An Essay of Dramatic Poesy*. Lisideius, who represented the French neo-classic attitude, advocated a strong central character as the best basis for comedy, but Dryden him-

---

1. Nicoll, p. 71. See Montague Summers, *The Playhouse of Pepys*, 1935, pp. 83–86.
2. Colley Cibber, *Apology*, 2d ed., 1740, p. 100.
3. Pepys, I, 297. 4. *Roscius Anglicanus*, p. 3.
5. Nicoll, p. 306.

self, in true English fashion, wanted more than one memorable character. For

it is evident, that the more the persons are, the greater will be the variety of the plot. If then the parts are managed so regularly, that the beauty of the whole be kept entire, and that the variety become not a perplexed and confused mass of accidents, you will find it infinitely pleasing to be led in a labyrinth of design, where you see some of your way before you, yet discern not the end till you arrive at it. And that all this is practicable, I can produce for examples many of our English plays: as "The Maid's Tragedy," "The Alchymist," "The Silent Woman;" I was going to have named "The Fox," but that the unity of design seems not exactly observed in it; for there appear two actions in the play, the first naturally ending with the fourth act, the second forced from it in the fifth: which yet is the less to be condemned in him, because the disguise of Volpone, though it suited not with his character as a crafty or covetous person, agreed well enough with that of a voluptuary; and by it the poet gained the end at which he aimed, the punishment of vice, and the reward of virtue, both which that disguise produced. So that to judge equally of it, it was an excellent fifth act, but not so naturally proceeding from the former.[1]

About January 12, 1669, fourteen of Jonson's plays were allotted to Killigrew. There is nothing to prove, since they are not given in Downes's lists, that five of them were acted at all after the Civil Wars: *The New Inn*, *A Tale of A Tub*, *The Magnetick Lady*, *The Staple of News*, and *Cynthia's Revels*. *Every Man out of his Humour* was apparently produced only once, in 1675, and the production of two plays, *Sejanus* and *The Devil is an Ass*, is doubtful,[2] so that the

1. *Works*, XV, 335–336. On the double plot see Peter Whalley, *The Works of Ben. Jonson*, 1756, II, 405.

2. Nicoll (pp. 82, 169) writes that "fully seven" of Jonson's comedies and two of his tragedies were performed at Vere Street and elsewhere between 1660 and May, 1663. We have actual records for only four comedies between these dates. Downes's list is for the plays performed by Killigrew's company *after* April 8, 1663, his date of the opening of the New Theatre in Drury Lane. *Catiline* was certainly not produced until 1668, and there is only the evidence of Downes for the production of *Sejanus* and *The Devil is an Ass*.

history of Ben Jonson on the stage is the history of the remaining six: *The Fox, The Alchemist, The Silent Woman, Bartholomew Fair, Catiline,* and *Every Man in his Humour.*

The last actual record of *Volpone* in the seventeenth century dates its performance January 17, 1676, at the Theatre Royal. Royalty was present, and the remuneration to the actors was £10.[1] There is some reason, however, for thinking that the play continued during the dark years of the eighties. Sir William Soame's translation of Boileau's *Art of Poetry* (1680) was first published in 1683, after revision by Dryden, who substituted the names of English writers for the French. The section on tragedy included the following lines:

> Observe the Town, and study well the Court;
> For thither various Characters resort:
> Thus 'twas great *Johnson* purchas'd his renown,
> And in his Art had born away the Crown;
> If less desirous of the Peoples praise,
> He had not with low Farce debas'd his Playes;
> Mixing dull Buffoonry with Wit refin'd,
> And *Harlequin* with noble *Terence* joyn'd.
> When in the Fox I see the Tortois hist,
> I lose the Author of the Alchymist.[2]

In April, 1682, bad management caused the Theatre Royal to close its doors and to seek a union with the other patent company. The articles were signed by Killigrew, Betterton, Davenant, and William Smith on May 4, and the united companies of Drury Lane and Dorset Garden probably acted for the first time on November 15. If one were to credit Gildon's account of the state of the stage between 1675 and 1695, one would be tempted to say that there were no performances of Jonson during those twenty years. When theatrical rivalry was raging between Lincoln's Inn Fields and Drury Lane in 1695, both stages were

1. Nicoll, p. 308.
2. *The Art of Poetry, Written in French by the Sieur de Boileau,* 1683, pp. 51–52; *The Works of John Dryden,* XV, 246–247. The offensive scene of Would-be's tortoise shell was omitted in the later acting version.

hard put to it; many new authors were appearing, but their plays met a cold reception. Hence Betterton arranged a revival of Shakspere which "put *Drury-Lane* to a nonplus." As a foil, Rich went to his garret, taking Ben Jonson's picture with him, and prayed:

Most mighty Ben! *Father of the Stage, and Parent of the whole* Dramatick *Generation*! *May it please thy venerable Shade to cast an Eye on the unhappy Circumstances of thy Children: May it please thee to bedew the Sands of our scorcht* Lybia, *and bless the stubborn Earth till it raises up some nourishment for us who hunger.* . . . The Picture seem'd to Nod, which was a token of consent, up he rose, and very devoutly return'd the charitable Image to its place in his own *Theatre*. Then they fell to task on the *Fox*, the *Alchymist*, and *Silent Woman*, who had lain twenty Years in Peace, they drew up these in Battalia against *Harry* the 4th and *Harry* the 8th, and then the Fight began.[1]

But Jonson had not fallen into such complete desuetude as this. Downes says that *Bartholomew Fair* was acted by the united companies after 1682, and on January 15, 1685, the same actors received £5 for playing "The Silent Weoman" before the king and queen. In 1691 Langbaine noted that *The Fox* and *Catiline* were presented at the theatre, and of *The Fox* he wrote, "It is still in vogue at the Theatre in *Dorset-Garden*." [2] In the same year an allusion to Sir Politick Would-be implies a rather frequent appearance of *Volpone* on the stage.[3] The name was used as a synonym for a silly courtier, just as Volpone at this time was the title for a crafty politician, particularly applied, with surprising results, to the Earl of Godolphin.[4]

1. *A Comparison Between the Two Stages*, pp. 43–44. For confirmation of Gildon's observation see John Bancroft, *King Edward the Third, with the Fall of Mortimer*, 1691, prologue, sig. A3.

2. *An Account of the English Dramatick Poets*, p. 298.

3. *Mr. Pope's Literary Correspondence*, 1735, III, 168.

4. See my article, "Volpone; or, The Fox — The Evolution of a Nickname," *Harvard Studies and Notes in Philology and Literature*, XVI (1934), 161–175; C. H. Firth, *Memoirs of the Life of Colonel Hutchinson*, 1885, II, 17; *The Memoirs of Edmund Ludlow*, Oxford, 1894, II, 407; *Catalogue of Prints and Drawings in the British Museum, Division I, Satires*, II (1873), 821.

The union of the companies ended in 1695. On April 29 the best actors — Elizabeth Barry, Anne Bracegirdle, John Verbruggen, John Bowman, Cave Underhill, and Elizabeth Leigh — opened at a new theatre in Lincoln's Inn Fields under the leadership of Betterton, where they acted until April 9, 1705. Drury Lane remained under the management of Christopher Rich and Sir Thomas Skipwith, both of whom had been directing the fate of the theatre since March 24, 1690, when Alexander Davenant had sold his share in the patent to Rich. The rivalry of the two companies began in 1695. The company at Drury Lane enlisted young and able actors, and the quality of their acting improved steadily. That Rich did actually revive Jonson's plays is practically certain. But records fail; the decade from 1690 to 1700 forms the blankest period in the history of the stage. There is no Pepys to make comments, the Public Record Office has as yet yielded few documents of the first importance, and adequate records do not become available until the founding of *The Daily Courant* in 1702.

Possibly it was Rich's revival of Jonson that called forth the examen of *Volpone* in 1695 by John Dennis, in a letter to Congreve, which, with the succeeding letter, caused Congreve to write his famous *Letter Concerning Humour in Comedy* on July 10, 1695. Dennis criticized Mosca's introduction of Bonario into Volpone's house as unreasonable; he objected to making comedy at the expense of a personal defect such as Corbaccio's deafness; he regarded the Would-be underplot as an excrescence and the character of Volpone as inconsistent:

The Inconsistence of the Character appears in this, that *Volpone* in the fifth Act behaves himself like a Giddy Coxcombe, in the Conduct of that very Affair which he manag'd so Craftily in the first four. . . . For so strange an Alteration, in so little a time, is not in Nature, unless it happens by the Accident of some violent passion; which is not the case here. *Volpone* on the sudden behaves himself without common Discretion, in the

Conduct of that very Affair which he had manag'd with so much Dexterity, for the space of three Years together. For why does he disguise himself? or why does he repose the last Confidence in *Mosca*? Why does he cause it to be given out that he's Dead? Why, only to Plague his Bubbles. To Plague them, for what? Why only for having been his Bubbles. So that here is the greatest alteration in the World, in the space of twenty-four hours, without any apparent cause. The design of *Volpone* is to Cheat, he has carried on a Cheat for three years together, with Cunning and with Success. And yet he on a sudden in cold blood does a thing, which he cannot but know must Endanger the ruining all.[1]

Dennis's criticism is sound. He makes the same point about the inconsistency in Volpone's character that Dryden had previously discussed, but unlike Dryden, he does not hedge and declare the last act "excellent." Subsequent critics were to support Dennis to such a degree that in 1785 when the play was presented at Drury Lane for three performances, the underplot of the Would-be's was completely omitted.

Jeremy Collier in 1698 found most of Jonson's comedies irreproachable in point of morality. The preface to *Volpone*, in which Ben announced his platonic theory of poetry, namely, that the good poet must be a good man, naturally coincided with Collier's own notions, and he appeared to delight in defending Jonson's comedies against charges of immorality, while attacking Dryden's worst offenses. He objected in particular to the manner in which Dryden appeared to hide behind the skirts of Jonson's practise,[2] defending *The Mock Astrologer* by *The Silent Woman* and *The Fox*. "*Ben Johnson's Fox* is clearly against Mr. *Dryden*," says Collier. "And here I have his own Confession for proof. He declares the *Poet's end in*

---

1. *Letters Upon several Occasions: Written by and between Mr. Dryden, Mr. Wycherley, Mr. ———, Mr. Congreve, and Mr. Dennis*, 1696, pp. 73–75. See also pp. 76–79.
2. *A Short View of the Immorality and Profaneness of the English Stage*, pp. 151 ff.

this Play was the Punishment of Vice, and the Reward of Virtue. Ben was forced to strain for this Piece of Justice, and break through the *Unity of Design.* This Mr. *Dryden* remarks upon him: However he is pleased to commend the Performance, and calls it an excellent *Fifth Act.*" [1] Collier saw clearly that inconsistency in Dryden's critical writing which makes any discussion of his convictions so difficult. Of the two views, that of Dennis is the more valid. The end of the century leads us out of the darkness of the really "naughty nineties" into the new century, when theory and conjecture are no longer necessary in relating the chronicle of our plays.

II

1700–1727

Until recently the definite dating of performances of Jonson's plays began in 1702 with the materials derived from *The Daily Courant*, which was the first newspaper to print daily notices of the theatres. Through the happy discovery by Mr. Hotson [2] of the accounts rendered to Lady Morley for plays seen at Drury Lane, where she appears to have been a box-holder during the years 1700, 1701, and earlier, one is able to date many performances formerly unknown. In the first year of the century *The Fox* was played twice and *The Silent Woman* once. By exploring all available sources, one can account for thirty-eight productions of Jonson, unnoted by Genest, in the first decade of the century. In 1709 there were twelve performances; in 1707 ten, and in only one year were there as few as two. From 1700 to 1710 there were fifty-eight in all, surely an astonishing number for a dramatist who was perpetually accused of obsolescence. These figures furnish, perhaps, the strongest arguments for the continuous acting of the plays during the uncharted years of the Restoration. They certainly prejudice one in favor of the statement of

1. Page 153.   2. Pages 378–379.

Gildon that the comedies were revived at Drury Lane in 1695. There is a curious anomaly in the history of Jonson's plays: the more obsolete they became, the more frequently they were played, until in 1734 there were sixteen performances, in 1762 eighteen for only two comedies, *The Alchemist*, and *Every Man in his Humour*, and in 1772, if one may count an afterpiece derived in part from one of Jonson's masques, twenty-two performances. The anomaly is merely heightened when it is observed that upon Garrick's retirement in 1776, Jonson's plays fell immediately into a decline from which they have never recovered.

Volpone was performed on May 2 and December 27, 1700, and on March 18, 1701. At all of these performances Lady Morley was present, twice alone, and once with three friends, paying for box seats at the rate of four shillings apiece. We may draw some conclusions about these performances, owing to the fortunate fact that some Puritan, more hidebound than the relentless Collier, scented impurity and sought to have the play suppressed. The actors were presented before the grand jury for Middlesex in Easter term, 1701, and an indictment was found,[1] charging John Powell, John Mills, Robert Wilks, Elizabeth Verbruggen, Maria Oldfield, Benjamin Johnson, William Pinkethman, William Bullock, Philip Griffin, Colley Cibber, and Jane Rogers with having acted obscene, profane, and pernicious comedies at Drury Lane between June 24, 1700, and February 24, 1701. The offensive passages were selected from *Volpone*, *The Humours of the Age*, and *Sir Courtly Nice*. The passage from *Volpone* was the shortest:

Pray, Sir, make use of me, pray while you stay make use of me and the oft'ner you use me I shall take it for granted you have forgotten the Injury I have done you. Be damn'd.[2]

1. Public Record Office, King's Bench 10–11, London and Middlesex Indictments, Easter 13 William III. See J. W. Krutch, *Comedy and Conscience after the Restoration*, New York, 1924, pp. 175–176.
2. These words of Lady Would-be to Peregrine are misquoted to create a

The jury found all but Pinkethman not guilty, and the case was postponed *sine die*.[1]

The charge of immorality may have frightened the players. At any rate, *Volpone* was not produced for over two years, when on May 20 and 21, 1703, *The Daily Courant* announced that "At the Desire of several Persons of Quality" there would "be reviv'd that celebrated Comedy call'd *Volpone, or the Fox*. Written by the Famous *Ben. Johnson*." The parts were to "be perform'd to the best advantage" and the part of Corbaccio was to be "acted by *Ben. Johnson, For his own Benefit*." To the poor soul experienced in London's climate, it seems ludicrous to read that "By reason of the extream hot Weather, this Play being deferr'd to be acted on Wednesday last, the same will now be positively perform'd." As a result of the "revival," the play was presented five times before the end of the year. Since in no other year of the first decade was it acted more than three times, the record-breaking productions of 1703 look suspiciously like reaction or even defiance.

In 1702 there appeared *A Comparison Between the Two Stages*, in which Gildon caused his characters Critick and Ramble to discuss the faults of Jonson's use of song:

Cri. But this error of Musick is not Yesterdays invention; old *Ben* with all his exactness stumbles here sometimes: It does not well become me to arraign so establish'd an Author, but I'm sure he has Faults of all kinds, and to the purpose in Hand I take the Song sung to *Celia* in the *Fox*, to be one; 'tis in the *Seventh Scene of the Third Act*: He brings her in by a Stratagem to *Volpone*, who is supposed to be Paralytick and quite disabled for Woman's Sport; but finding himself alone with *Celia*, he shakes of [*sic*] his Hypocrisie and his Furs, and runs in an extasie to her Arms: She is ready to dye with the surprize, fain wou'd fly away, but

---

double entendre; there is no profanity in Jonson's text. Compare *Volpone*, IV. i. The actors may have improvised.

1. Public Record Office, King's Bench 29 (Controlment Roll, 360).

he forces her to stay, and she, without saying one Word, is suppos'd to listen to an entertainment of Musick, tho' in all the
Agony that the Poet cou'd give her. One wou'd think she shou'd
rend, and tear, and cry out for help, as she did afterwards with
fury enough; but that wou'd ha' spoil'd the Song: I beg *Ben's*
pardon for this presumption, but this being to the purpose it
came into my Mind.

Ramb. Your Example of *Ben* is enough to justifie this practice in some Men's Opinion.[1]

The song continued to be sung, however, if one may judge
from the acting versions of the play, down to the productions at Covent Garden from 1771 to 1773, when the version "regulated from the Prompt-Book" indicates its
omission.[2]

In 1704 there were three performances; for the second,
the parts of Volpone and Mosca were acted by Powell and
Wilks, and the play was furnished "with a new Prologue to
the Town" which does not appear to be extant. The performances usually began at half-past five (or in the winter
at five), and must have been exceedingly long, for there
were numerous *divertissements*, such as Italian sonatas by
Signor Gasperini and Mr. Paisable, "the new Boy," "the
Famous Signiora Francisca Margaretta de l'Epine," who
performed "several Entertainments of Singing in Italian
and English, compos'd by Signior Bononcini Scarletti and
the late Mr. Henry Purcell," dancing by "the famous Du
Ruell" and his wife, who were making "but a short stay in
England," "the Devonshire Girl," and "comical Entertainments between *Scaramouch, Harlaquin,* and *Pun-
chanello.*"

The play was acted at Drury Lane on June 5, 1705, but
what with the rivalry of the late Lincoln's Inn Fields com-

1. Pages 52–53. The original music for the song "Come, my Celia, let us
prove," was composed by Alfonso Ferrabosco (*Ayres,* 1609, No. VI). I have
found no later setting. The words were reprinted in *Wit's Interpreter: The
English Parnassus,* 1655, p. 141 (2d ed., 1662, p. 246); *The Hive, ca.* 1733, III,
198; *A Collection of Songs,* Edinburgh, 1762, p. 28.
2. *Bell's British Theatre,* XIX (1778), 55–56.

pany, which had removed on April 9 to the Haymarket, and the necessity for furnishing songs and dances, sonatas and harlequinades, the actors had a difficult time. One of Her Majesty's players at Drury Lane wrote to a strolling actor:

"Volpone," or "Tamerlane," will hardly fetch us a tolerable audience, unless we stuff the bills with long entertainments of dances, songs, scaramouched entries, and what not.[1]

In view of this critical state of affairs, the lord chamberlain began to put pressure on Rich, who was still the manager of Drury Lane, and suggested that he unite his forces with the Haymarket. Rich, who in the long run was managing a flourishing theatre, did not desire a union advocated by Vanbrugh, who was interested in the failing Haymarket. The sequel is told at first hand in a letter from Congreve to Joseph Keally, written on September 10, 1706:

The playhouses have undergone another revolution; and Swinny, with Wilks, Mrs. Olfield, Pinkethman, Bullock, and Dicky, are come over to the Hay-Market. Vanbrugh resigns his authority to Swinny, which occasioned the revolt. Mr. Rich complains and rails like Volpone when counterplotted by Mosca. My Lord Chamberlain approves and ratifies the desertion; and the design is, to have plays only at the Hay-Market, and operas only at Covent Garden. I think the design right to restore acting; but the houses are misapplied, which time may change.[2]

While at the Haymarket, the united company appeared in twelve performances of Jonson's plays: *The Fox* once; *Bartholomew Fair* four times; and *The Silent Woman* seven times. For the single performance of *Volpone* we have the first full cast since that given by Downes: Volpone, John

1. Percy Fitzgerald, *A New History of the English Stage*, 1882, I, 240. Compare a contemporary epilogue for the Theatre Royal, *The Diverting Post*, June 16, 1705.
2. G. M. Berkeley, *Literary Relics*, 1789, p. 348; Montague Summers, *The Complete Works of William Congreve*, 1923, I, 80.

Mills; Mosca, Robert Wilks; Voltore, Theophilus Keen; Corbaccio, Benjamin Johnson; Corvino, Colley Cibber; Politick Would-be, Henry Norris; Bonario, Barton Booth; Lady Would-be, Mrs. Leigh; Celia, Mrs. Oldfield. Except for the two women characters, these actors formed an almost standard cast for many years. Mills, though sharing the part with George Powell until 1712, played Volpone last on January 2, 1734; Wilks kept Mosca until just before his death, acting it for the last time on October 5, 1731; Keen was succeeded by Bickerstaff, January 31, 1717; Johnson played Corbaccio exclusively until the revival at Lincoln's Inn Fields on November 15, 1727 (when John Hippisley was substituted), and continued playing it at Drury Lane until his last appearance in the rôle on February 11, 1742. He acted the part for forty years. The part of Corvino fluctuated between Colley Cibber and John Mills; Cibber played it last on October 5, 1731, and Mills on October 21, 1736, with his son William Mills playing Mosca. Norris acted Would-be until September 24, 1730. The sole information about Booth's Bonario is that on January 31, 1717, the part was played by Lacy Ryan; the rôle is not cast in the bills during the second decade of the century. The rôles for the women changed very rapidly; during the century, thirteen actresses performed Lady Would-be and sixteen actresses played Celia.

The united company remained at the Haymarket until December 7, 1707, when performances at that house were limited to opera only, and on January 15, 1708, there was a new union of the actors from Drury Lane and the Haymarket, with all playing at Drury Lane, known as "Her Majesty's Only Company of Comedians," under Rich and Brett. On March 3 Henry Brett assigned Davenant's patent to Wilks, Estcourt, and Cibber. The union lasted until June 4, 1709.

On April 27, 1708, *Volpone* was performed "For the Benefit of Mr. Johnson," and was chosen four times for a similar purpose before 1716. Celia was played by Mrs.

Rogers, who probably, as we have seen, played it in 1701,
and Lady Would-be by Mrs. Kent, who acted no other
Jonsonian parts. On February 26, 1709, the play was
acted again, with a cast which differed little from the one
given in the quarto edition of 1709, the earliest acting version of the play. *The Daily Courant* gives Bickerstaff for
Peregrine on February 26; the quarto gives Fairbank, and
adds the names of the four *avocatori*: Corey, Carnaby,
Smith, and Cross. We have no other record of Fairbank as
Peregrine. Carnaby and Cross played respectively Lan-
thorn Leatherhead and Ursula in *Bartholomew Fair*.

For the next performance on May 27, 1709, we have the
first review of *Volpone*, written by Steele in *The Tatler*:

This night was acted the comedy, called, "The Fox"; but I
wonder the modern writers do not use their interest in the house
to suppress such representations. A man that has been at this,
will hardly like any other play during the season: therefore I
humbly move, that the writings, as well as dresses, of the last
age, should give way to the present fashion. We are come into a
good method enough (if we are not interrupted in our mirth by
such an apparition as a play of Jonson's) to be entertained at
more ease, both to the spectator and the writer, than in the days
of old. It is no difficulty to get hats, and swords, and wigs, and
shoes, and everything else, from the shops in town, and make a
man show himself by his habit, without more ado, to be a coun-
sellor, a fop, a courtier, or a citizen, and not be obliged to make
these characters talk in different dialects to be distinguished
from each other. This is certainly the surest and best way of
writing: but such a play as this makes a man for a month after
overrun with criticism, and inquire, what every man on the
stage said? What had such a one to do to meddle with such a
thing? How came the other, who was bred after such a manner,
to speak so like a man conversant among a different people?
These questions rob us of all our pleasure; for at this rate, no one
sentence in a play should be spoken by any one character, which
could possibly enter into the head of any other man represented
in it; but every sentiment should be peculiar to him only who
utters it. Laborious Ben's works will bear this sort of inquisi-

tion; but if the present writers were thus examined, and the offences against this rule cut out, few plays would be long enough for the whole evening's entertainment. But I don't know how they did in those old times: this same Ben Jonson has made every one's passion in this play be towards money, and yet not one of them expresses that desire, or endeavours to obtain it in any way but what is peculiar to him only: one sacrifices his wife, another his profession, another his posterity from the same motive; but their characters are kept so skilfully apart, that it seems prodigious their discourses should rise from the invention of the same author. But the poets are a nest of hornets, and I'll drive these thoughts no farther.[1]

Steele indicates clearly his opinion that the comedy of humors, as a type, had run its course, and that no author among the many imitators of Jonson after the Restoration, such as Shadwell, Lacy, and Sir Robert Howard, could compete with the originator and master of the form.

On June 4, 1709, Drury Lane was silenced by an order of the lord chamberlain, which brought the union of the companies to an end. On September 15, under the management of Owen Swiney, Betterton with Wilks and Mrs. Oldfield opened at the Haymarket in a new company, known as "Her Majesty's Company of Comedians in the Haymarket." The revolt was caused by the oppressive management of Rich. The company remained at the Haymarket until November 20, 1710, when they returned once more to Drury Lane, ending the stormy and complicated reversals of fortune in the early history of the eighteenth-century theatres until the last revolt against the managers in 1733.

While at the Haymarket, the comedians acted four of Jonson's comedies in seven performances: *The Silent Woman* three times, *The Alchemist* twice, and *Bartholomew Fair* and *Volpone* once each. No cast was given for *Volpone* in the bills, which indicated only that "all the parts [would] be perform'd to the best Advantage." However,

1. Ed. G. A. Aitken, I (1898), 177–178, No. 21; see also No. 42.

all the important Drury Lane actors were then at the Haymarket, — Mills, Johnson, Cibber, Wilks, — and the play was undoubtedly cast as usual.

The play was next presented "For the Benefit of Mr. Johnson" on April 29, 1712, and Steele, now writing for *The Spectator* concerning the moral influence of the stage on human conduct, noted:

When we come to Characters directly Comical, it is not to be imagin'd what Effect a well-regulated Stage would have upon Men's Manners. The Craft of an Usurer, the Absurdity of a rich Fool, the awkward Roughness of a Fellow of half Courage, the ungraceful Mirth of a Creature of half Wit, might be for ever put out of Countenance by proper Parts for *Dogget*. *Johnson* by acting *Corbacchio* the other Night, must have given all who saw him a thorough detestation of aged Avarice.[1]

The popularity of *Volpone* was manifested by the following criticism. The author speaks of Ben Jonson's

most applauded Play, called, *The Fox*, which does not yield to any Comedy of any other Nation whatsoever, for the Justness of Thought, Propriety of Expression, and the True Painting of the Characters, and may be said to be the most excellent as to the Variety of Incidents, the several Catastrophe's, and the compleat working up of the whole Design.[2]

From November 17, 1712, to January 26, 1716, no casts for *Volpone* were given in the newspaper bills. Some notes on the actors, indicating other rôles which they held, will help to throw light on their abilities in Jonson's comedies. George Powell acted the title-rôle of *Volpone* at least until the late spring of 1712. After Betterton's revolt at the close of the union in 1695, he inherited the great actor's rôles and played Hotspur, Edgar, and Jaffeir. Like many other men of the day, he was very intemperate, and it is said that his reputation decreased as his drinking in-

1. No. 370. Steele praises Wilks's Mosca in this paper.
2. [William King], *Useful Miscellanies*, 1712, p. 6.

creased. He wrote seven plays or adaptations that were produced in the nineties. When *Cato* appeared in 1713, Powell acted Portius. His rôles in Jonson's comedies were assumed as follows, so far as one is able to date first appearances: Volpone, 1704 or earlier; Quarlous in *Bartholomew Fair*, 1708; and Face in *The Alchemist*, 1709. He died on December 14, 1714. Gildon described him as "an idle Fellow, that neither minds his Business, nor lives quietly in any Community." [1]

Robert Wilks, "the finisht Copy of his Famous Predecessor, Mr. *Charles Hart*," [2] was, according to Benjamin Victor, "the unrivalled *fine Gentleman* of the Stage for more than twenty Years." [3] His most famous parts were Hamlet, Edgar, Macduff, Jaffeir, Castalio, and Sir Harry Wildair. An able man of business, he was associated with Swiney, Dogget, Cibber, and later with Collier, Steele, and Booth as licensee of Drury Lane theatre until his death on September 27, 1732. He played Mosca probably as early as 1701; Truewit in *The Silent Woman*, 1707; and Face, twice only, during the revolt at the Haymarket in 1710. The rôle of Mosca was considered particularly difficult. Thomas Davies, writing on the old actors, remarked on the difficulties involved in presenting Jonson:

It was a constant complaint of the old actors, who lived in Queen Anne's time, that if Jonson's plays were intermitted for a few years, they could not know how to personate his characters, they were so difficult, and their manners so distant, from those of all other authors. To preserve them required a kind of stage learning, which was traditionally hoarded up. Mosca, in Volpone, when he endeavours to work upon the avarice of Corvino, and to induce him to offer his wife to the pretendedly sick voluptuary, pronounces the word *think*, seven or eight times: there is a difficulty arises here in various pause and difference of

1. *A Comparison Between the Two Stages*, p. 199.
2. *Roscius Anglicanus*, p. 51.
3. *The History of the Theatres of London and Dublin, From the Year 1730 to the present Time*, 1761, II, 53.

sound. Many niceties of this kind were observed by the old comedians, which are now absolutely lost to the stage.[1]

Theophilus Keen was best known for Kent in *Lear*, the king in *Hamlet*, and Oroonoko. His figure and voice were neither elegant nor soft, but good, and his action was majestic. He acted Voltore for at least four years, as well as Justice Overdo at the Haymarket in 1707 and at Drury Lane in 1708.

Of Benjamin Johnson there is more criticism than of any other actor in *Volpone*. When he died in 1742, he had been on the stage forty-seven years, and from 1703 on there were only seven years in which he failed to act Corbaccio. He was the original Coupler in *The Relapse* and Alderman Smuggler in *The Constant Couple*; he was extremely successful in that fool-proof part of the first grave-digger in *Hamlet*; he played Bluff in *The Old Bachelor*, Justice Shallow, Morose in *The Silent Woman*, Waspe in *Bartholomew Fair*, and Ananias in *The Alchemist*. His playing impressed two generations of critics. In 1708 Downes expended a few exquisite Latin barbarisms on him:

Mr. *Johnson*, He's Skilful in the Art of Painting, which is a great Adjument, very Promovent to the Art of true Elocution, which is always requirable in him, that bears the Name of an Actor; he has the Happiness to gain Applause from Court and City: Witness, *Morose, Corbaccio*, Mr. *Hothead* and several others; He is a true Copy of Mr. *Underhill*, whom Sir *William Davenant*, judg'd 40 Year ago in *Lincolns-Inn-Fields*, the truest Comedian in his Company.[2]

Benjamin Victor considered that Johnson possessed the true *vis comica* and "could give Life to many Comedies that existed only by their extraordinary Performances. The *Morose*, in the *Silent Woman*, was one that died with this great Actor. His steady Countenance never betrayed the least Symptom of the Joke he was going to give

1. *Dramatic Miscellanies*, II, 94–95.
2. Page 52.

Utterance to," [1] a criticism paraphrased from the poetical epistle *The Actor*, written in the previous year by Robert Lloyd.[2] Concerning his acting in Jonson's comedies Chetwood remarked in 1749:

> He arrived to as great a Perfection in Acting, as his great Namesake did in Poetry. He seemed to be proud to wear that eminent Poet's double Name, being more particularly great in all that Author's Plays that were usually performed, *viz. Wasp* in the Play of *Bartholomew-Fair*, *Corbaccio* in the *Fox*, *Morose* in the *Silent Woman*, and *Ananias* in the *Alchymist*.[3]

Of Colley Cibber one need barely indicate the variety of parts which he played, for no other English actor has told us so much about himself as Cibber, the comedian, dramatist, successful manager, accomplished critic, and anything but prince of dullards. He acted Bayes in *The Rehearsal*, Lord Touchwood in *The Double Dealer*, Fondlewife in *The Old Bachelor*, Sir Novelty Fashion and Lord Foppington in his own comedies *Love's Last Shift* and *The Careless Husband*, Sir John Brute in *The Relapse*, and Corvino, Sir John Daw, Rabbi Busy, and Subtle in Jonson's plays.

The elder Mills was called by Victor "the most *useful Actor* that ever served a Theatre," [4] an enthusiasm not wholly shared by Cibber, who remarked that he had "as few Faults, as Excellencies," [5] Mills played an extraordinarily large number of characters over a period of forty years, including parts as widely varied as the Ghost in *Hamlet*, King Lear, Pierre in *Venice Preserved*, Falstaff, the original Manly in *The Provoked Husband*, Sir John Bevil in *The Conscious Lovers*, and Volpone, Corvino, Surly, Face, Clerimont, and Quarlous.

Barton Booth's term as Bonario is, we have noted, indeterminate. He acted Dauphine in *The Silent Woman* as

1. II, 63–64.   2. 3d ed., 1760, pp. 9–10.
3. *A General History of the Stage*, p. 174.
4. II, 59.   5. *Apology*, 2d ed., p. 213.

late as November 8, 1725, and Edgworth in *Bartholomew Fair* for only two seasons, 1707 and 1708. Downes, at the time Booth was playing Edgworth, thought him "A Gentleman of Liberal Education, of form Venust; of Mellifluent Pronuntiation, having proper Gesticulations, which are Graceful Attendants of true Elocution; of his time a most Compleat Tragedian." [1] Othello was his best part, but before his death in 1773, he played a prodigious list of characters in both tragedy and comedy.[2]

Henry Norris, called "Jubilee Dicky" because of his admirable performance of Dicky in *The Constant Couple*, derived considerable renown from an odd "little formal Figure, and his singular, squeaking Tone of Voice." [3] He acted Sir Politick Would-be continuously with no opposition at Drury Lane until September 24, 1730. At the next Drury Lane performance on October 5, 1731, Benjamin Griffin inherited the part. Norris also acted Dapper from 1709 to October 10, 1723, when he was succeeded by Theophilus Cibber; Cutbeard in *The Silent Woman*, from 1707 to January 29, 1729; and Littlewit in *Bartholomew Fair*, from 1707 to June 10, 1720; so that his appearances in Jonson's comedies were uninterrupted for a quarter-century.

John Bickerstaff played five rôles in Jonson, but none of them long. In *Volpone* he acted Voltore from 1717 to 1721; in *Bartholomew Fair*, Winwife and Rabbi Busy in 1708; and in *The Alchemist*, Lovewit, from the revival in 1709 indeterminately, since the part is not cast in the newspaper bills and the play was not acted from December 22, 1713, to October 25, 1721, when Shepard played the part.

As for the actresses, before the production of *Volpone* at Lincoln's Inn Fields in 1727, there were at least six Lady Would-bes and four Celias; the honors for retention

1. Page 52.
2. Genest, III, 214–217.
3. Benjamin Victor, II, 64.

of the part of Celia fall to Mrs. Hester Santlow, later Mrs. Booth, who required a substitute for only one night at Drury Lane from January 26, 1716, to October 5, 1731. Colley Cibber, speaking of her while she was still Mrs. Santlow, remarked on the "gentle Softness of her Voice, the composed Innocence of her Aspect, the Modesty of her Dress, the reserv'd Decency of her Gesture, and the Simplicity of the Sentiments, that naturally fell from her," [1] all of which would qualify her excellently for the part of the abused wife of Corvino. Mrs. Oldfield acted the part once, on December 3, 1706, when the Drury Lane company was in revolt at the Haymarket. Her only other Jonsonian character, Epicoene, brought her some fame, since she acted it until 1722.

From 1713 to 1716 there was but one performance of *Volpone* a year, and critical material is scarce.[2] In 1715 *The Censor*, a periodical written under the pseudonym of Ben Johnson, carried on the traditions of the real Ben's robust personality, especially of his reputation for heavy drinking, by publishing a series of memoranda supposed to have come down in the Jonson family. Concerning *Volpone* the note reads:

> I laid the Plot of my *Volpone*, and wrote most of it, after a Present of Ten Dozen of *Palm Sack*, from my very good Lord T——r; That Play I am positive will last to Posterity, and be acted when I and Envy are Friends, with Applause.[3]

The Censor noted that *The Alchemist, Catiline,* and *The Silent Woman* were written with similar inspiration.

From 1716 to 1727 there is little to record beyond the fact that *Volpone* was played at least once a year, except in

---

1. *Apology*, 2d ed., p. 348.
2. See an allusion to Volpone's struggle to seduce Celia in *A New Rehearsal; or, Bays the Younger*, 1714, p. 33. See also [Thomas Burnet], *A Second Tale of a Tub; or, The History of Robert Powel the Puppet-Show-Man*, 1715, pp. 73–76: "It's not to be imagin'd, Sir, how much the *Fox* of BEN JOHNSON's has taken of late."
3. 2d ed., 1717, No. 14.

Volpone or the fox.   Lud. Du Guernier inv. et Sculp.

1719; that James Quin acted for the first time in the comedy on May 15, 1717, as Voltore; and that the play was given twice before royalty, once at Hampton Court in 1718, and once at Drury Lane in 1722, when "their Royal Highnesses . . . saw VOLPONE, or The Fox, written by Ben Johnson, and were very much pleas'd with the Inimitable performance of Mr. Wilks." [1]   In 1724 Volpone's address to his gold was included in the *Thesaurus Dramaticus* as one of the poetical beauties of the ancient drama.[2]

On January 12, 1727, *Volpone* was presented at Drury Lane for the last time without rivalry. On November 15 the company at Lincoln's Inn Fields, under John Rich, produced it, and *Volpone* ceased to be important henceforth in the Drury Lane repertory. Indeed, until *Volpone* was dropped in 1773, it was presented at Lincoln's Inn Fields and Covent Garden three times as often as at its old home, — fifty-six nights at Covent Garden to nineteen at Drury Lane. Before exploring its fate with a new company, one should examine briefly its waning fortune with the old cast, who had played it every year except four since the beginning of the century.

III

DRURY LANE, 1727–1742

For two years after its revival at Lincoln's Inn Fields there was no production of *Volpone* at Drury Lane. But it was by now indelibly stamped upon the minds of the public as a play exposing avarice with great force; the term "Volpone" had already been disastrously effective in political satire, and was naturally enough used as a symbol in one of those moral essays of which the eighteenth century

1. *The Weekly Journal; or, British Gazetteer*, October 13, 1722.
2. II, 70–71. The collection contained no other passages from the major plays, but chose seven from *Catiline*. See *The Beauties of the English Stage*, 1737, I, 20, 176, 215, 225.

was fond. In 1728 James Ralph wrote *The Touch-Stone*, comprising "Historical, Critical, Political, Philosophical, and Theological Essays on the reigning Diversions of the Town," in which he contended that on the stage everything ought to be represented

larger than the Life, the readier to distaste the Beholders; and that the smallest Error being made plain on the Surface, no part of wrong Behaviour should escape . . . unregarded. Yet, on the Stage of Life, we every Day meet with those that are as ridiculously affected as *Lord Foppington*, as stupidly vicious as *Lord Brute*; as fawning as *Lord Plausible*; as impertinent as *Novel*; as impotently fond as *Limberham*; as treacherous as *Maskwell*; as superstitious as *Foresight*; as subtil as *Volpone*; as humoursome as *Morose*; as silly as *Sir Martin*; as hypocritical as *Tartuff*, and as jealous as *Fondle-wife*.[1]

Of the single performance in 1731 and the several from 1733 to 1735, Davies gives some account in the *Dramatic Miscellanies*:[2]

In the year 1731, the elder Mills acted Volpone; Wilks, Mosca; Colley Cibber, Corvino; Ben Jonson, Corbaccio; Mrs. Horton, Lady Would-be; and Celia by Mrs. Butler. About three years after, it was acted to still more advantage, for Quin excelled Mills in Volpone. In the Mountebank he assumed all the art, trick, and voluble impudence, of a charlatan; though W. Mills, who succeeded Wilks in Mosca, fell below his predecessor, yet his father, who submitted to play Corvino, was superior to C. Cibber in that part. Cibber seemed, I thought, to jest with the character. Mills was in earnest, and had a stronger voice to express passionate and jealous rage than the other. Jonson kept his old part, but Milward's Voltore was a fine copy of law oratory. Mrs. Clive, I need not say, gave infinite entertainment in Lady Wou'd-be. Though Celia is but a short part, to Mrs. Butler's great commendation, she rendered it extremely interesting.

To omit mentioning the part of the first avocatori [*sic*], or superior judge, would be an act of injustice; for it was represented with great propriety by the venerable Mr. Boman, at

1. Page 78.   2. II, 99–100.

that time verging to the eightieth year of his age. This actor, was the last of the Bettertonian school. By the remains of this man, the spectators might guess at the perfection to which the old masters in acting had arrived. Boman pronounced the sentence upon the several delinquents, in the comedy, with becoming gravity, grace, and dignity.

Robert Wilks died in 1732, and with him the most famous Mosca of the century passed into oblivion. On the occasion of the several pamphlets and lives which his death brought forward, one writer took thoughtful stock of the comedy of humors, which he found especially prevalent in English drama. He perceived the origin of the type in the desire to combat the reigning vices, follies, and impertinences of an epoch, but saw it growing rapidly obsolete.[1] Jonson's plays were to prove him wrong for the forty-five years which followed.

In 1733 there appeared *The Players: A Satire*, possibly by Edward Phillips, which praised the old actors, flayed the new school, and gave instructions for adequate performance of the masterpieces of English comedy:

> In our best Comedies each Part is wrought,
> With some peculiar Air, or turn of Thought;
> Some noted humour, is in each exprest,
> That may distinguish it from all the rest.
> By various Methods to the self-same end,
> See, in *Volpone*, diffrent Humours tend.
> If that which cost the Poet so much Pains,
> Be mangled by the Players want of Brains:
> If those Distinctions which supported *Ben*,
> And to the World preferr'd his artful Pen,
> Be lost; — We lose our Profit and Delight;
> Be it thy Pride to do thy Poet Right:
> 'Tis from his Genius we expect the Treat,
> Not from an Actor's quibling low Conceit.[2]

The year 1733 saw more performances of *Volpone* than any other in its history. In that year and the next there

1. *Memoirs of the Life of Robert Wilks, Esq.*, pp. vii–viii.
2. Sig. C6.

were twelve productions by the two companies, and on
January 2, 1734, it was acted at both houses simultaneously. The reason for the popularity of Jonson's plays at
this time was the revolt of the leading players of Drury
Lane on September 24, 1733. In 1732 Booth sold his share
of the patent to John Highmore, who, after the death of
Wilks, bought his share and that of Cibber. The theatre
was opened, but the comedians almost immediately "found
a happy Assylum" at the Little or New Theatre in the
Haymarket, safe from "the despotic Power of some petu-
lant, capricious, unskilful, indolent, and oppressive Patentees. . . . 'Twas here that upwards of a hundred successive
Nights, as many crouded Audiences loudly spoke in Favour
of our Attempts."[1] The new company was called "The
Company of Comedians of His Majesty's Revels"; the
revolters were headed by the contentious Theophilus
Cibber. The only important actors who remained at
Drury Lane were Bridgewater, Mrs. Clive, and Mrs. Horton. Highmore, thus deserted, enlisted what actors he
could from the strolling companies and the provincial
theatres, but Charles Macklin was his only accession of
promise.

On December 19 the company at the Haymarket began
a notable revival, during which they presented twelve of
Jonson's plays in shortly over a month. The record is
clearly shown in a manuscript diary attributed to Benjamin Griffin,[2] who had played Sir Politick Would-be since
1731. A. Hallam, who had formerly played Bonario, acted
Mosca; Milward, Voltore; Edward Berry, Corvino; Oates,
Bonario; Winstone, Peregrine; since Mrs. Horton was still
at Drury Lane, the flamboyant Charlotte Charke played
Lady Would-be; and Mrs. Butler first appeared as Celia.

Of the new actors, Griffin, who was now fifty-four years
old, attained great fame in low comedy, especially in characters of testy old men. Hired at Drury Lane to supply

1. Theophilus Cibber, *Two Dissertations on the Theatres* [1756], pp. 19–20.
2. British Museum MS. Egerton 2320.

the parts left by Norris, he acted Sir Hugh Evans in *The Merry Wives of Windsor*, and Sir Paul Plyant in *The Double Dealer*. His Tribulation in *The Alchemist* was excelled only by Johnson's Ananias. In 1731 he acted Rabbi Busy at the last appearance of *Bartholomew Fair* in unaltered form. Adam Hallam, who must not be confused with the Thomas Hallam killed in 1735 by Charles Macklin, played Bonario, Mosca, Surly, and Dauphine. William Milward had already played Voltore at Lincoln's Inn Fields, so that the part was not new to him when he joined the rebelling players. He remained with the company after it returned to Drury Lane. Edward Berry, an actor of moderate accomplishment, chiefly noted for his blubbering, played in Jonson for the first time in 1733. He, too, remained with the Drury Lane company, acting Epicure Mammon in 1742, and Garrick chose him to act old Knowell in *Every Man in his Humour*, in 1751, and Captain Otter in *The Silent Woman*, in 1752. Oates — earlier Cutbeard in *The Silent Woman* at Drury Lane, in 1731, and Kastril in *The Alchemist*, in 1732, — was also playing in 1733 the part of Surly.

Charlotte Charke lasted only two years in Jonson's comedies. Of her three rôles, Lady Would-be, Mrs. Otter, and Dol Common, her natural qualifications were perhaps best adapted to the last. Daughter of Colley Cibber, gifted with an impetuous temper, an adventurous spirit, and an ability to reveal herself in writing, she led a varied career as impersonator of male rôles, grocer and oil-woman, puppet-show manager, *valet de chambre* to a gentleman of quality, and, finally, for the support of her child, sausage-maker. Like her father and brother, she was her own press-agent, and her narrative is not outshone by those of Mrs. Pilkington, Mrs. Woffington, or Ann Catley. She shows her knowledge of *Volpone* in a passage of her memoirs.[1]

1. *A Narrative of the Life of Mrs. Charlotte Charke, Youngest Daughter of Colley Cibber, Esq., Written by Herself*, 1755, p. 104.

The revolt of 1733 was the last of importance in the annals of the eighteenth-century stage. On March 12, 1734, the actors returned to Drury Lane under the management of Charles Fleetwood, who had purchased a controlling share in the patent. He was assisted by Theophilus Cibber and Macklin. Fleetwood was a wealthy man, and his power enabled him to manage the theatre until 1745.

An amusing event in the history of *Volpone* during these years was the amateur performance of the play on November 5, 1734, the anniversary of the Gunpowder Plot, by the boys of Bury School, "in the new Theatre there." Fortunately, the occasional prologue and epilogue for this evening have survived. The prologue, *"spoke by* Mr. STEBBING,*"* improvised on the significance of the day, with a wholesome tone of patriotism matched only by its animus against popery:

> With grateful hearts for this auspicious day,
> To heaven does *England* annual praises pay;
> A nation sav'd from such infernal scheme,
> Affords for thanks an everlasting theme:
> Our morning tribute being paid, the night
> To mirth we give and innocent delight.
> Old BEN shall shew ye brought from *Roman* climes
> A set of puny rogues, whose very crimes
> Appear as virtues, when to those compar'd
> Which by the miscreants of this day were dar'd.
> Alas! the papist bred at home ne'er thrives,
> Ne'er to maturity of sin arrives;
> In foreign martyrs, lies *Rome's* greatest boast,
> 'Tis amongst hereticks saints flourish most;
> And that's a miracle *Rome* may defy
> Her most inveterate enemies to deny.
> The sun, no farther than his beams extend,
> Or soils or vegetables can befriend;
> But holy dad no boundaries can confine,
> His warmth invigorates where his rays ne'er shine;
> Most kindly grow his plants of zeal and grace,
> In lands accurs'd, where he ne'er shows his face:

But lands accurs'd by him still thrive the more;
O may his blessing never reach this shore:
But may that providence, whose tender care
So kindly snatch'd us from this fatal snare,
Be ever watchful for our preservation,
Guarding the *British* throne, the church and nation.[1]

The epilogue, "*spoke by* Master Rustal," who, it may be
inferred, acted Volpone, is in a lighter mood, its theme
based particularly on the splendid mountebank scene, in
which Volpone seeks to gain a view of Celia. The topic
was timely. No reader of advertisements in eighteenth-
century periodicals can help wondering at the apparent
credulity of the populace, who were informed of marvelous panaceas in the form of "antiscorbutick ointments,"
lotions, drops, washes, pills, tonics, and powders which
would "correct all the malignity of Pandora's box."
London was full of quacks and empirics who could guar-
antee cures with conviction which would startle modern
delvers into the intimacies of life. The epilogue chose as
its twin victims Sir William Read and Dr. Joshua Ward:

Great minds to strokes of fortune never yield,
But with fresh courage reassume the field;
To night as mountebank I have been drubb'd;
What then? sir *William Read* a knight was dubb'd,
And many drubbings he, no doubt, sustain'd,
Before he that immortal honour gain'd.
I love such public souls, and I'll essay
To benefit mankind as much as they:
Ne'er seem'd the world (since *Adam*) more inclin'd
To favour mountebanks of every kind:
They've learn'd the graduate blockhead to despise;
Ay — 'twas sir *William* open'd first their eyes.
Heav'ns! what a run, about a twel-month past
Crude Mercury had, — the god ne'er mov'd so fast,
Ne'er drove (whatever poets feign) before
Such shoals of spirits to the *Stygian* shore.

---

1. *The Gentleman's Magazine*, IV (1734), 624; *A Collection and Selection of English Prologues and Epilogues*, 1779, III, 125–126.

But now *Ward's* pill unrival'd reigns alone,
Ward's peerless pill, what wonders has it done!
A *Drury* virgin, who convers'd with beaux,
Chanc'd by misfortune to lose half her nose;
She took a single pill, — and I profess,
Nose has been growing from that minute — less.
A noted cuckold, — I conceal his name,
Whose horns were pointed at, where-e'er he came,
Took but a couple in a glass of wine,
And since his forehead is — as smooth as mine.
  An honest tar, being asham'd to beg,
Took half a dozen — for a wooden leg,
And since protests, — (I scorn the truth to smother)
He feels less pain in that than in the other.
What strange prodigious cures are these, O *Ward*!
Thou'lt surely be a knight, perhaps a lord.
Oh how thy glory fires my blood! thy pill
Could not do't more; — but I'll out strip thee still:
Something will I invent, shall youth restore,
And drive death off, tho' rapping at the door;
Then shall *Ward's* pill be never heard of more.[1]

The Sir William Read alluded to had died in 1715, after a picturesque career as an empiric. From a tailor, he became successively a mountebank and an itinerant quack, boasting of cures in many English counties. In 1694 he had settled in the Strand, whence he issued charlatan advertisements which appeared even in *The Tatler*; he guaranteed to remove wens and cataracts and was supposed to have effected so many cures as an oculist, among the sailors of the English fleet, that Queen Anne knighted him in 1705. As late as April 11, 1711, Swift wrote to Stella that Read had "been a mountebank, and is the queen's oculist: he makes admirable punch, and treats you in gold vessels."

Apparently the most famous successor of Read was Dr. Joshua Ward, who professed to cure every human malady

1. *The Gentleman's Magazine*, IV (1734), 624; *The London Magazine*, III (1734), 664; *A Collection and Selection of English Prologues and Epilogues*, IV, 69–70.

with his "drop and pill." Ward returned to England from
France, where he had been staying since 1716, and immediately obtained enormous sales of his pill. He cured the
king of a dislocated thumb, ministered to the poor at royal
expense, and was consulted by even the dying Henry
Fielding. From the close of 1734, however, he was constantly attacked: on November 28, 1734, *The Daily
Courant* declared the pill and drop part of a plot to introduce popery into England, and *The Grub Street Journal*
violently attacked him on the same day. The boys at Bury
anticipated the public attack by three weeks. Even though
the remedies were later discovered to be preparations of
antimony, Ward, like Read, amassed a large fortune. The
relationship between the Gunpowder-Plot prologue and
the Quack-Doctor epilogue is made clear by the account
above. But it is possible to account also for the sources of
the "cases" recounted in the epilogue. On November 1
The Bee [1] published an animated story of the marvelous
cure effected upon a servant girl suffering from a violent
palsy; with this as a beginning, the boys improvised other
and more striking cases. But satire did not injure the sale
of the pills, for the human mind is never more gullible than
when the body is ailing. In 1740 the public was informed
that "the Earl of Waldegrave is now taking Mr. Ward's
Pills," and in 1753 that "the most inflammatory and intrepid fevers fly at the first discharge of Dr. James's pow-
der, and a drop or pill of the celebrated Mr. Ward corrects
all the malignity of Pandora's box." [2] Ten years later
Ward's receipts were printed in full, for the information of
the curious. [3]

In 1735 *Volpone* was performed exclusively at Drury
Lane, for the reason that Quin came over from Covent
Garden during the season of 1734–1735, depriving that

1. No. 90.
2. *All-alive and Merry; or, The London Daily Post,* November 11, 1740; *The World,* June 14, 1753.
3. *The London Chronicle,* February 12–15, 1763.

house of its only actor of the title-rôle. He kept the character until 1741, but for the last performance at Drury
Lane on February 11, 1742, Delane, who had succeeded
Quin as Volpone at Covent Garden, but was now a member of the Drury Lane company, played the part. Quin
went back to Covent Garden, where he played Volpone
again until 1750.

Aside from a command performance before the Prince
and Princess of Wales on May 24, 1738, there is little to
note about the last years of the comedy at Drury Lane.
During the dispute of 1743 between Fleetwood and the
actors, who seceded from him and hoped to obtain a license
for the theatre in the Haymarket, there was, as usual at
such junctures, a vigorous pamphlet war. In one of the
very scarcest pamphlets, *The Dramatic Congress, A Short
State of the Stage under the Present Management* (1743),
many hard remarks are made on the managers of Drury
Lane and Covent Garden, Fleetwood and Rich. The
author, apparently Chetwood the prompter, calls them
"the illustrious Bashas" and purports to have been spying
on them:

You'll observe as you go on, that I have been so long conversant with the Stage, that I have made Use of Drama Names, and
Christen the *Basha Volpone*, and his Colleague *Mosca*.

The managers decided to reduce salaries:

A solemn League and Covenant was entered into between *Volpone* and *Mosca*, to exclude all who had any merit, and only keep
in such who were not of Consequence enough to grumble.[1]

Although *Volpone* had already been dropped from the
repertory of Drury Lane, during the short-lived revolt of
the discontented actors its fame endured and again it furnished nicknames of obloquy.

1. Pages 14-15.

IV

Lincoln's Inn Fields and Covent Garden
1727–1754

The new theatre in Lincoln's Inn Fields had been opened on December 18, 1714, by John Rich, who managed the company uneventfully until December 7, 1732, when he opened the new Covent Garden theatre. He remained in control until he died, aged seventy, in November, 1761. During his management Covent Garden became the home of those pantomimes which debauched the taste of play-goers, Rich himself being the celebrated pantomimist "Lun." But he produced classical plays as well and competed successfully with Drury Lane. In 1725 his revival of *Every Man in his Humour* reached only a third performance; but, not discouraged by his ill success, he revived *Volpone* on November 15, 1727, with a cast already somewhat experienced in Jonson: Volpone, Quin; Mosca, Ryan; Voltore, Boheme; Corbaccio, Hippisley; Bonario, Milward; Would-be, Spiller; Peregrine, Chapman; Lady Would-be, Mrs. Younger; Celia, Mrs. Bullock. On the first night the receipts were £88 9s., and the house issued free orders to the amount of £6 4s. There is no extant review of the play, but increasing receipts indicate eloquently that it was successful.

James Quin after four years at Drury Lane joined the Lincoln's Inn Fields company in 1718. At Drury Lane he had acted Voltore and Winwife in *Bartholomew Fair*; at Lincoln's Inn Fields, Macbeth, Brutus, Sir John Brute, Othello, Falstaff, Pinchwife in *The Country Wife*, old Knowell in the revised *Every Man in his Humour*; and before his death he was famous for Benedick, Thersites in *Troilus and Cressida*, King Lear, Richard III, Henry VIII, the Plain Dealer, the Old Bachelor, Cato, and Tamerlane. He played all "with Universal Applause." [1]

1. "Thomas Betterton" (?William Oldys), *The History of the English Stage, From the Restauration to the Present Time*, 1741, p. 153.

Lacy Ryan, a great friend of Quin, came to Lincoln's Inn Fields in 1718, distinguishing himself as the fine gentleman in comedies with such rôles as Mirabell in *The Way of the World*, Horner in *The Country Wife*, Plume in *The Recruiting Officer*, Jacques, Oroonoko, Hamlet, Edgar, and Iago. Years later, Garrick said that he had learned to play Richard III from Ryan. Ryan had acted Edgworth in *Bartholomew Fair* and Bonario at Drury Lane, as well as young Knowell as Lincoln's Inn Fields in 1725. He continued as Mosca until *Volpone* was dropped at Covent Garden in 1754.

Boheme, too, had been with Rich since 1718. Victor called him a remarkable performer and praised the "natural, musical piercing Tones of his Voice,"[1] which were requisite in the part of Voltore, the pleader in the senate-chamber scenes of *Volpone*. Although his training as a sailor had given him a straddling gait, he acted satisfactorily as the Ghost in *Hamlet*, Lear, Julius Caesar, Shylock, Hotspur, and Banquo, until his tragic death from fever in 1730. Voltore was his sole attempt in Jonson, and he was succeeded probably by Ogden, but for the performances in 1731 the part is not cast in the bills.

John Hippisley, an excellent low comedian, who came to Lincoln's Inn Fields in 1722, played Sir Paul Plyant, the Clown in *The Winter's Tale*, Fondlewife in *The Old Bachelor*, and Scrub in *The Beaux' Stratagem*. In the revival of *Every Man in his Humour* he was obviously miscast as Kitely. In the two productions of *The Alchemist* at Covent Garden in 1740, he played Ananias.

William Milward was a recent accession to the theatre, and Bonario was his first Jonsonian rôle. He succeeded to Ogden's Voltore in 1732 but kept it only a year, assuming it at the Haymarket on December 19, 1733, when the Drury Lane players were there in revolt. He played it until 1741. Among his other rôles were Jaffeir, Oroonoko, and Lusignan in *Zara*.

1. II, 73.

James Spiller, the Brainworm of Rich's revival of *Every Man in his Humour* and one of the original actors of the company, was able to transform himself wholly into the character he represented and was famous for Ben in *Love for Love*, the first murderer in *Macbeth*, and Polonius. Many a jest was fastened upon him.[1]

Thomas Chapman, "a very excellent Comedian," [2] was known for Brazen in *The Recruiting Officer*, Witwou'd in *The Way of the World*, Shallow in *The Merry Wives of Windsor*, and Touchstone. He acted Peregrine and Sir Politick Would-be until 1733, when he inherited Voltore from Milward, who had deserted to the Haymarket. Chapman played Voltore until 1734, but in 1739 he was cast for Cutbeard at Drury Lane, and in 1740 as Abel Drugger for one night only.

Mrs. Younger, already known for Belinda in *The Old Bachelor*, the Country Wife, and Desdemona, had acted Dol Mavis in 1716, as well as Celia in 1717 and Lady Would-be in 1721 at Drury Lane; so that the part was not new to her in 1727. She played it until 1734, when she retired from the stage.

Mrs. Jane Bullock was particularly able in the Restoration type of comedy, in parts such as Lady Fidget in *The Country Wife*, Narcissa in *Love's Last Shift*, Lady Froth in *The Double Dealer*, and Belinda in *The Old Bachelor*. Her best Shaksperean rôle seems to have been Nerissa. Celia, her only rôle in Jonson, she played until 1734, when she was succeeded by Mrs. Horton. Miss Bellamy and four others kept the part until 1754.

For want of reviews in the daily papers at this time, most of the actors have gone down to dusty death unheralded. The main body of criticism comes from later sources, when the old actors began to write reminiscences

1. [George Akerby], *Spiller's Jests; or, The Life and Pleasant Adventures of the late Celebrated Comedian Mr. James Spiller; containing his merry jests, diverting songs, and entertaining tales* [*ca.* 1730].

2. *The General Advertiser*, July 14, 1747.

of the palmy days of Quin, Kitty Clive, Peg Woffington, and the youthful Garrick. For Quin, Ryan, and Hippisley, however, there are appreciations.

Quin played Volpone some forty nights from 1727 to 1750, mostly at Lincoln's Inn Fields and Covent Garden, but he broke the continuity of his performance with Rich's company by seven seasons at Drury Lane, beginning in 1734–1735. While he was acting Volpone at Drury Lane, he was superseded at Covent Garden by Dennis Delane, who curiously enough, when Quin returned to Covent Garden in 1742–1743, went over to Drury Lane and acted Volpone there. Quin became firmly established in this part. An undated and unsigned manuscript, apparently written about 1750, comments on his personal characteristics, his social qualities, and his education.

As to his theatrical character, it has been the fashion of late to depreciate it; but he stands unrivalld in the parts of Fallstaf, the Spanish Fryar, Sir j. Brute, the old batchelor, the Fox and Pinchwife: and had he no merit in Cato, Brutus, Zanga, Coriolanus, Dorax, Ventidius, Pierre, and Caled, no actor at this day is capable of appearing in those characters with any degree of pleasure to those who recollect Quin whose grief was too big for utterance, or in a part that required a suppression of grief. He was manly and great, he grew heavy by age and full living, and had some bad habits wch he contracted in his youth, and were incurable, but his voice was fine and full.[1]

In 1750 Sir John Hill in his treatise, *The Actor*, gives these instructions on the "Manner of Recitation in Comedy":

Nothing can be more evident, than that rhyme and measure always tend to take off greatly from the air of truth, nature and reality, which the dialogue would otherwise have. In consequence of this, the actor's principal care and study ought to be, wherever he is encumber'd with these fetters, to break the one, and, as much as possible, sink and lose the other in the reciting.

1. *Actors and Actresses, Macklin, Quin, Clive*, Harvard Theatre Collection.

Several of our *Shakespear's* and *Ben Johnson's* plays have passages in rhyme and measure, in some parts; and that excellent
composition *Comus* abounds too much in them, in the character
of the God of Revels; yet, to the honour of *Volpone* and *Comus*,
we mean when Mr. *Quin* represents those characters, perhaps it
has not been found out by any body, that has not read as well as
seen those pieces, that there is a line in measure, or a single
rhyme in either of them.[1]

Tate Wilkinson, writing his memoirs of the year 1748,
says:

The rehearsals that year were very regular at Covent-Garden.
The scenes for Volpone, Henry IV. and their stock plays, (for, at
that house, they seldom acted new ones or revived old ones)
were regularly changed — and all was awful silence. — Mr.
Quin was sole monarch, and had a manner most terrible to the
under performers, carpenters, &c.; if he spied me within two
yards of the wings — "Get away, boy!" — and struck his cane
with such violence as made me tremble.[2]

And later he describes Quin's best rôles:

Quin's Harry the Eighth, Sir John Brute, all the Falstaffs,
Old Bachelor, Volpone, . . . were all, with several others, all his
own; nor have those characters already mentioned ever truly
flourished as when inspired by him. But out of his particular
walk he was ever bordering on the ridiculous.[3]

Thomas Davies describes the Corbaccio of Hippisley:

Hippisley pleased every body but the actors of his time, who,
with an envious malignity, would often compare the weakest of
his performances to the best of Colley Cibber and Ben Jonson;
men who, in some parts, were indisputably his superiors. But
no comedian ever excelled him in describing the excesses of avarice and amorous dotage. . . . Corbaccio, in Jonson's Volpone,
is a strong portrait of covetousness, a vice which predominates
in the man when almost all his faculties of body and mind are

1. Pages 188–189.
2. *Memoirs of His Own Life*, York, 1790, I, 33.
3. IV, 80.

extinguished. Corbaccio can neither see nor hear perfectly: Hippisley's look told the audience that he was a deaf man, for his dim eyes seemed to enquire out the words which were spoken to him. In this character it was acknowledged that he excelled his great competitor Jonson.[1]

The four productions at Covent Garden in 1733 called forth a criticism of *Volpone* in *The Universal Spectator*, one of the earliest reviews to appear in the periodicals. After praising the moral power of the theatre, the reviewer commended Jonson's observance of nature and described "Sir Jasper Truby's" visit to *Volpone*:

Sir *Jasper Truby*, who had not seen a Play for many Years, and never above two or three, was engag'd lately to go with us to see a *Comedy*, and we chose that Night on which *Volpone*, or the *Fox*, was acted: We gave the *Knight* timely Notice in the Morning, and he met us punctually at four in the Afternoon at my Chambers, from whence we proceeded to *Covent Garden Theatre*. Our Party consisted of the Knight, *Harry Careless* and my self. When we had plac'd ourselves to the best Advantage in the Middle of the Pit, Sir *Jasper* began to discover some Signs of secret Pleasure he receiv'd in seeing the House fill: the *Lights*, the *Musick*, the Appearance of *Ladies*, and the whole Scene of *Gaiety* put the old Gentleman into an entire good Humour. The Curtain drew up, when I observ'd in the Knight's Countenance, that earnest Attention which every Man of Sense shou'd shew at an Entertainment from which he expects to be agreeably diverted.

Volpone, at the opening of the Play, makes this Harangue to his Gold. . . .

Sir *Jasper* had no sooner heard him, than he whisper'd me softly, a *Villain I warrant him, Hal.* and as *Volpone* open'd his Character more to the Audience, added with a seeming Pleasure, *I told you so; — I knew nothing but a Rogue cou'd prefer the Love of Gold to the Love of Virtue.* At the Lawyer's bringing a Present, in hopes to be *Volpone's* Heir, the Knight by a *Wink* on me, betray'd his Joy at seeing the Gentleman of the long Robe gull'd by Arts more delusive than his own. The Avarice of *Corbaccio*

1. *Memoirs of the Life of David Garrick*, 4th ed., 1784, I, 36–37.

in the succeeding Scene, had, I observ'd, a different Effect on
Sir *Jasper* from the general Part of the Audience. *Corbaccio*
appear'd a Wretch loaded with all the Infirmities of Nature; but
his *Deafness*, which shew'd his Lust of Money the stronger, while
it made every one laugh, Sir *Jasper* did not once put on a Smile.
At the End of the Act he told me, he wonder'd how the Audience
cou'd *laugh* at so miserable a Wretch, who shou'd move their
Detestation rather than their *Pleasure*. On our turning round to
speak to *Harry Careless*, who had placed himself behind us, to
our Surprize we found *Harry* had given us the Slip. . . .

As I was taken up more in observing my Knight than the
Players, I view'd narrowly the Change of his Features, as they
betray'd the Emotions of his Heart. He seem'd very little
affected with *Volpone's* turning Mountebank, and whisper'd me,
he thought it was too long: But in a Scene or two after, he express'd not a little Pleasure in seeing *Corvino*, a Jealous Covetous
Wretch, work'd up by Artifices, and by his own surprizing
Avarice, to make a voluntary Offer of putting his Wife to bed
with *Volpone*.

At the Beginning of the third Act, I overheard the Knight at
Mosca's Soliloquy, muttering to himself — *The cunningest
Rascal I ever saw* — In a following Scene, where *Corvino* urg'd his
Wife to *Volpone's* Bed, she pleading all that a Woman of Honour
cou'd say, and with Tears enforcing her Prayers, I perceiv'd in
Sir *Jasper's* Countenance, a deep Concern, which was heighten'd
when *Volpone* was about to *force* her — But the Moment she was
rescued by *Bonario*, he with a Smile told me that he lik'd the
young Spark, and that he was a very *honest Fellow*, and he hop'd
now the Roguery was detected: When *Mosca* by a new Device
gave the whole a different Turn, Sir *Jasper* seem'd surpriz'd and
wonder'd *where it would all end*.

Our friend *Harry*, whom we left in the *Side Boxes*, was now
got behind the *Scenes*, and had plac'd himself in such a *Posture*,
that the whole Audience had a full View of him. As soon as Sir
Jasper beheld him in that Situation, whispering to one of the
Actresses, he shew'd some Concern, lest in one of his whimsical,
unthinking Fits he shou'd enter farther on the Stage, and entertain the Audience with an *amorous Interlude;* but the Re-en-
trance of the Players put an End to those Fears. Thro' the rest
of the Play, the Knight by Turns was pitying the *falsly accus'd*

Lady, and that *honest young Fellow*, who had defended her Honour; and very often disapproving of the Poet's making *Villany* so *successful*. At the unravelling of the Plot, when the Innocence of the Lady and young Gentleman was clear'd; when *Volpone* and *Mosca* were caught in the *Trap* of their own *Cunning*, and each of the *avaricious Knaves* was order'd to a proper Punishment by a Decree of the Senate, the Knight in the Ecstacy of his Heart, testify'd his *Joy* with such a *Warmth*, as proclaim'd him an *honest Man*, and a *Lover* of *Vertue*. . . . The Crowd a little dispers'd, we conducted the *Knight* safe to his Coach, and left him full of the *Instructive Moral* of the *Play*, and pleas'd with so *severe a Satire* against *Avarice*.[1]

The first important changes in the cast at Covent Garden came on November 15, 1736, when the play had lain dormant a season. Dennis Delane as Volpone and Mrs. Horton as Celia were the very notable accessions. Delane, who was acting for his first season at Covent Garden, was acknowledged to be an imitator of Quin, many of whose rôles he played. His style was somewhat languid, his action never elegant, and the anonymous biographer of Quin assures us that "though the prejudiced, or ill judges might rank Delane in the same class as Quin; the town, whose opinion seldom errs in this respect, by a great majority pronounced our hero still unrivalled." [2] Delane played, during his eighteen years on the stage, Othello, Macbeth, Lear, Antony, Falstaff, Richard III, Hotspur, the Old Bachelor, Jaffeir, and Horatio in *The Fair Penitent*. Volpone was his only character in Jonson.

Mrs. Christiana Horton, whom Davies described as "one of the most beautiful women that ever trod the stage," [3] appeared as early as 1714 at Drury Lane, where she was chosen by Wilks as Mrs. Oldfield's successor. As she grew older, she laced herself so tightly that her figure displayed

1. December 8, 1733. For a partial reprint see *The Gentleman's Magazine*, III (1733), 635.
2. *The Life of Mr. James Quin, Comedian*, 1766, p. 60.
3. *Dramatic Miscellanies*, I, 183.

grotesque under-emphases. Her leading rôles were Estifania in *Rule a Wife and Have a Wife*, Lady Betty Modish, Millamant, Lady Fidget in *The Country Wife*, Lady Brumpton in *The Funeral*, Cleopatra, Desdemona, and Monimia. She had acted Lady Would-be in 1725 at Drury Lane, keeping the part until 1731. In the season 1734–1735 she was engaged at Covent Garden, where she remained until her retirement in 1749–1750, playing Celia from 1736 intermittently until April 21, 1746. She acted Lady Would-be for the last time on January 8, 1750.

Mrs. Clive played Lady Would-be in December, 1743, her only Jonsonian character at Covent Garden, although she had acted Win Littlewit, Dol Common, and Lady Would-be at Drury Lane. She was one of the greatest English comic actresses, especially gifted in strongly marked characters of middle and low life, in chambermaids, country girls, romps, hoydens, dowdies, superannuated beauties, and viragoes. Perhaps she had the perfect temperament for the obnoxious, garrulous English traveler drawn in the wife of Sir Politick.

There is a description of the costumes worn by Volpone and Mosca at this period. In the "great Wardrobe" at Covent Garden in 1744 were "Volpone's bla: plus dress wrapt in a yellow tabby turkish vest Volpone's old blue jacket & breeches d⁰ — Mountebank's dress Mosca's bla: bays dress." [1]

In 1745 George Anne Bellamy, at the age of fourteen, first appeared in her only Jonsonian rôle, Celia, which she played, with some intermission, until 1753. Miss Bellamy was one of those sensational actresses whose lives are more fascinating than their art. As Desdemona she acted well, but *The Dramatic Censor* (1770) found that she "trod close on the heels of Mrs. Cibber, she had, we think, the more amiable countenance of the two, though it was not marked with so much sensibility, her person though small, was very satisfactory, and her expressions of rapture, beyond

1. British Museum Additional MS. 12201.

any thing we have ever heard; she came somewhat nearer comedy, than her great competitor, but never deserved much praise in that stile." [1] Unquestionably her most interesting achievement was the lively apology for her life, published by Bell in 1785.

Critical opinion in 1747 admitted that *Volpone* "still continues to be acted, with the greatest Applause, which, without doubt, it deserves; and yet in this excellent Piece, good Critics are of Opinion, that there are some unnecessary and superfluous Characters." [2] These characters were later eliminated, but there is no evidence that their lines were even cut at this period.

Luke Sparks inherited the rôle of Corvino on December 20, 1748, and five years later he succeeded Quin as Volpone. "Mr. Sparks," wrote Chetwood in 1749, "has, by incessant Attention to the Drama, arrived to be a well-esteemed Person in the Business of the Theatre; and there are many capital Parts in the Compass of his Power; so that he may be accounted a Person in the highest second Class." [3] The Old Bachelor, Maskwell in *The Double Dealer*, and Sir John Brute were his chief rôles in comedy. He was a useful actor at Covent Garden until 1765, but his influence on the acting of Jonson's plays was so small that no contemporary criticism of his Volpone has survived.

The last actor of note to appear in *Volpone* was Edward, or "Ned," Shuter, one of the most brilliant comedians in the annals of the stage, and one of those "characters," like Quin, Pinkethman, Spiller, Josias Miller, and Ben Jonson himself, who gave their names to jest-books. His most famous rôle in Jonson's comedies (and he played *Every Man in his Humour*, *The Alchemist*, *The Silent Woman*, and *Volpone*), was Master Stephen, which he performed during those years when plays received more criticism in news-

1. II, 495–496.
2. *A Compleat List of all the English Dramatic Poets*, appended to Thomas Whincop's *Scanderbeg*, 1747, p. 122.
3. *A General History of the Stage*, pp. 219–220.

papers and poetical satires than formerly; there was much comment on his exceedingly popular performance of the country gull. He played Corbaccio first on November 12, 1753, and twice again before the play was dropped. He resumed the part at a revival in 1771. In a rare periodical, *The Devil* (1786), appeared a parody of *The Deserted Village* describing Shuter:

> Beside Charles-Street, where hackney-coaches meet,
> Where two blue posts adorn fam'd Russell-Street,
> There, in an alehouse, taught to play the fool,
> Good master Shuter first was put to school.
> Nature's adopted son, tho' mean and low,
> Alas, "I knew him well, Horatio."
> Well did the tittering audience love to trace
> The miser's thrift, depicted in his face;
> Well would the busy whisper circle round,
> When, in Corbaccio, at Volpone he frown'd;
> Yet he was kind — but if absurd in aught,
> The love he bore to blackguards was in fault.
> The chimney-sweeper swore how much he knew,
> 'Twas certain he could act, and mimic too;
> Could tip the London cries — nay, it was said,
> He — for his benefit — King Richard play'd.
> In guzzling too, the landlord own'd his skill,
> For, tho' as drunk as muck — he'd guzzle still.
> While Quaker's sermons, given in drawling sound,
> Amazed the prigs, and kiddies rang'd around:
> And still they gap'd, and still the wonder grew,
> That one droll head, could carry all he knew.
>   But past is all his fame, the Rose and Crown,
> Where he so oft got tipsy — is burnt down.[1]

V

Covent Garden, 1771–1773

Although *Volpone* was actually to lie dormant for seventeen seasons, it was not completely forgotten, but seemed to be on the consciences of the managers. Davies wrote in 1783 that "Mr. Garrick had long wished to revive Volpone,

---

1. Page 205.

and to act the principal character. The parts were transcribed and delivered to the actors, but the acting of the
play was superseded by some means not known," [1] a statement substantiated by two notices in the daily press,
occurring at an interval of twelve years. The first, dated
1757, reads:

Ben Johnson's Comedy of *Volpone* or the *Fox*, is to be revived at Drury-Lane, in which Mr. Garrick and Mr. Woodward are to appear (for the first Time) in the Characters of
Volpone and Mosca. [2]

The second, of November 25, 1769, runs:

There is now in Rehearsal at the Theatre Royal in Drury
Lane a Dramatic Piece of Two Acts, called A Trip to Scotland.
The Comedy of Volpone, or the Fox, (not acted there these
thirty Years) will be soon revived at the same Theatre. [3]

Nothing came of the projected revivals, nor can we conjecture why Garrick deserted the comedy. Two of his best
comedians, Woodward and Shuter, were at Covent Garden, and Garrick always realized the difficulties involved
in a revival of Jonson; but, whatever happened, it was at
Covent Garden that the play was presented, in the middle
of a weak season for Jonson at Drury Lane.

A searching analysis of the comedy was written in 1753
by Bishop Hurd in *A Dissertation on the Provinces of the
Drama*, which brought to a focus earlier comments on the
superfluous characters, the double plot, and the farcical
components.

The VOLPONE . . . is a subject so manifestly fitted for the
entertainment of all times, that it stands in need of no vindica-
tion. Yet neither, I am afraid, is this Comedy, in all respects, a
complete model. There are even some Incidents of a farcical
invention; particularly the *Mountebank Scene* and *Sir Politique's*

1. *Dramatic Miscellanies*, II, 100–101.
2. *The London Chronicle*, September 13–15, 1757.
3. *The Public Advertiser*, November 25, 1769.

Tortoise are in the taste of the *old comedy;* and without its rational purpose. Besides, the *humour* of the dialogue is sometimes on the point of becoming inordinate, as may be seen in the pleasantry of *Corbaccio's mistakes through deafness.* . . . [Jonson's] taste for ridicule was strong but indelicate, which made him not over-curious in the choice of his *topics.* And lastly, his *style* in picturing characters, though masterly, was without that elegance of *hand*, which is required to correct and allay the force of so bold a colouring. Thus, the biass of his nature leading him to Plautus rather than Terence for his model, it is not to be wondered that his wit is too frequently caustic; his raillery coarse; and his humour excessive.[1]

When considering the alteration of the comedy as played from 1771 to 1773, it will be well to recall these remarks. In unaltered form the play required two hours and thirty-three minutes for presentation, according to John Brownsmith,[2] the prompter. Two hours and a half was the normal time required for tragedies, most comedies requiring two hours or less. Of Jonson's plays, *Volpone* demanded the longest playing-time, and the managers were becoming conscious that revision was advisable.

On November 26, 1771, *Volpone* was presented at Covent Garden, "Not Acted these Twenty Years," with the following cast, which, with two small changes, remained the same for the ten performances in the next fourteen months: Volpone, William Smith; Mosca, Robert Bensley; Voltore, Thomas Hull; Corbaccio, Edward Shuter; Corvino, Mathew Clarke; Bonario, Richard Wroughton; Would-be, Kniveton, who was succeeded by George III's favorite actor, John Quick, on January 20, 1773; Peregrine, R. Smith; Lady Would-be, Mrs. Gardner; Celia, Miss Miller. Mrs. Bulkley played Celia from January 28, 1772, until the comedy was dropped in 1773.

---

1. [Richard Hurd], *Q. Horatii Flacci Ars Poetica, Epistola ad Pisones*, I, 278–279; *The Works of Richard Hurd, D. D.*, 1811, II, 103. On Sir Politick Would-be see [James Upton], *Remarks on Three Plays*, p. 25, and Peter Whalley, *The Works of Ben. Jonson*, II, 308 n.

2. *The Dramatic Timepiece*, 1767, p. 58.

"Gentleman" Smith had played Kitely at Covent Garden since 1762, a part in which he proved a serious rival of Garrick. Ned Shuter had already acted Corbaccio, Ananias, La Foole, and Master Stephen. Hull had acted Wellbred, young Knowell, and earlier in November, old Knowell. Clarke had appeared as young Knowell; R. Smith, as Matthew; Mrs. Gardner, in 1771, as Dame Kitely; Miss Miller, as Bridget. Bensley, Wroughton, and Kniveton were appearing in Jonson for the first time. Mrs. Mary Bulkley, formerly Miss Wilford, had played Dame Kitely, with some assistance from Mrs. Mattocks, since 1766. The only member of the cast untutored in a major rôle was Bensley as Mosca, which he seems to have performed as satisfactorily as he did Morose in Colman's revival of *The Silent Woman* five years later. At any rate, he was recast as Mosca at the Haymarket in 1783 and at Drury Lane in 1785; so that he was the last actor to play the famous parasite until the twentieth century.

The production was enthusiastically welcomed, and the press noted that the revival "was received with the greatest Applause." [1] The receipts rose as high as £207 10s. and never sank below £117. *The Theatrical Review* for November, 1771, devoted six pages to a consideration of the comedy, and though a large section of the essay is drawn from *The Companion to the Play-House* (1764) and from Colman's *Critical Reflections*, the original remarks give a valuable contemporary critical estimate of Jonson. The review admitted the excellence of Jonson's comic genius and considered *Volpone* paramount:

The Plot is perfectly original; in the Conduct of which, the Author has discovered great Erudition and Correctness. The circumstance of *Volpone's* taking advantage of the depravity of human Nature in others, yet suffering himself to be duped and overreached by the subtility of *Mosca*, (a creature of his own raising) is happily imagined, and executed in a very masterly

1. *The Public Advertiser*, November 27, 1771.

manner. But, with all these perfections, it seems better calcu-
lated to afford pleasure in the Closet, than on the Stage, as there
is an evident deficiency of incident, and interest in the Catastrophe, which renders it incapable of giving that satisfaction in
the Representation, it undoubtedly must afford on a perusal. . . .

As this Comedy is now represented, most of the obsolete Passages and many blameable intrusions upon delicacy of idea, and
expression in the original, are sensibly omitted, the latter being
unsuitable to the professed chastity of the present age; and some
Scenes are transposed, and others omitted as superfluous. . . .

With respect to the Representation of this Play, the principal
Characters . . . are well performed by Messrs. *Smith, Bensley,
Hull, Clarke, Shuter* and *Wroughton*, so well, that they appear to
fill the Author's Ideas very pleasingly and very justly, except,
that Mr. *Hull*, who is generally natural and correct in his playing, rather over-acts his Part in the capacity of the *Advocate*, . . .
in the Senate. With respect to Mr. *Shuter*, in the Character of
Corbachio, we are glad to remark that his Performance throughout, is chaste and attentively correct, without the least taint of
that over-strained luxuriancy of humour, he too frequently displays, and which almost perpetually runs into buffoonery. His
strokes of Bye-play, of endeavouring to hasten the death of *Volpone*, (whom he supposes to be sick, and near his end, on the
Couch) by pressing his stomach with his cane, while *Mosca* is
engaged with *Voltore*, are well imagined, when we consider, that
in this Character, Nature is rather caricatured, which is the general, tho' only fault of this Author, in his Comic Writings.[1]

The enthusiastic reviewer for *The St. James Chronicle*
considered *Volpone* a "Monument of Art," recommending
that the comedy should always be kept upon the stage. He
praised the universality of its theme, observed that Jonson
often overleaped the bounds of nature, and examined the
performance of the actors:

Volpone, is imagined as the bold, wanton, hypocritical luxurious Epicure, by Mr. Smith. Had this Actor (if I may be allowed
to use a Term in Painting) a proper *Keeping*, in the Management

1. *The Theatrical Review*, 1772, I, 226–232.

of his Voice, we should have little to wish for in the Person, Deportment, and Conception of the Character.

The Criticks were greatly disappointed by Mr. Bensly; for he cheated their Expectation, and perhaps never appeared to more Advantage than in the Character of Mosca. Some have wished that Mr. Woodward had been the sly, subtle, shifting, exquisite Parasite, and Mr. Bensly, Corvino.

Mr. Clarke might have had a Character more suited to his Talents, than the quick Transitions and violent Agitations of a Man distracted in the Extremes of Jealousy, and Avarice. — *Corbaccio* was entertaining to a great Degree; when this Comedian (who should from the Appellation of comical Shuter) gives himself the Trouble to study and be right, Pleasure and Applause will always attend him: Let him be wary for his own Sake, as well as the Publick's, whose sober Approbation at the Theatre for well-exhibiting a Character of Shakespear and Jonson, should outweigh in his Opinion all the riotous Clamour and noisy Laughter of Comus and his drunken Court.

Mrs. Gardner, who has her Merit, should know that Hamlet's Advice to the Players is meant to be general; and that the *o'er-doing Termagant*, or *out-heroding Herod*, may be applicable to both Sexes.

Miss Miller is the very Cælia of the Play; her Look, Manner, Voice, Deportment, and Execution, creates every Emotion in the Spectator which that Character should raise! As I suppose the Rest of the Parts are cast to the best Advantage; and as Mr. Baldwin has desired me to mention only General Officers, I hope the Subalterns will excuse me for leaving them so abruptly without calling them over.[1]

VI

THE ALTERATION

Volpone, as has been shown, was frequently censured for its double plot involving the three essentially unnecessary characters of Sir Politick Would-be, his wife, and Peregrine; for inconsistency in the character of Volpone in the fifth act, where he ties a noose for his own neck by allow-

---

1. January 11–14, 1772.

ing Mosca too much freedom in relation to the will; for the
song to Celia, unnaturally introduced at a moment of high
dramatic tension; for the mountebank scene and Would-
be's tortoise, judged too farcical for the best taste; for inordinate humor and frankness in the dialogue; for lack of
incident and interest in the catastrophe. Obviously, some
of these objections are rather philosophical than strictly
dramatic, and an almost complete rewriting would be required to correct all the imputed errors. Revisers usually
take a simpler course, making as little work for themselves
as possible, keeping to the mold of the original as far as
practicable, and altering only for solid theatric reasons.
Jonson, in particular, especially in the comedies of humors
and in highly complicated plots like *The Alchemist*, was
difficult to alter without changing the entire structure. In
writing his version of *Every Man in his Humour*, for instance, in 1751 or earlier, Garrick had sought merely to
reduce the obsolescent qualities of the play as much as he
could. The main design remained the same. And so the
reviver of *Volpone* did not attempt any ambitious alterations, several of the alleged faults listed above being left
unrectified and "unimproved." The critic of *The Theatrical Review* noted that obsolete passages had been omitted,
as well as many speeches intruding upon delicacy of expression, and that scenes were transposed and omitted.

The details of the changes can be treated briefly.[1] They
were of two kinds, designed for reducing the time of presentation and consisting of structural condensations and
omissions of speeches. In the first act there occurs the only
transposition in the play, one which Herr Zweig adopted in
his recent reworking. In the original, Corbaccio precedes
Corvino in paying courtesies to Volpone on his feigned
death-bed; in the alteration, Corvino comes to Volpone

---

1. The text for the alteration is in *Bell's British Theatre*, XIX (1778). References to act and scene of Jonson's original play are made to the edition of William Gifford (1816), followed by Lieutenant-Colonel Cunningham (1875) and
the Mermaid edition (1894).

first. The transposition of the units is simple, but since Corbaccio's scene is longer and stronger than Corvino's, the climax-building of the act was strengthened a trifle.

In Act II the first two scenes of the original were consolidated into one continuous scene, no change of setting being demanded by the nature of the incidents. In the original, after Volpone had played the mountebank scene and had seen the lovely Celia, he unaccountably went home to wax lyrical over her charms. In the altered version, he remains by the mountebank stand, saving a change of setting for a scene only a page and a half long.

In Act III, scenes ii, iii, iv, v, and vi were played continuously with no change of setting. Scenes iii, iv, and v in the original are extraordinarily brief — of paragraph length only — and are intended for the various manipulations of Mosca, who is trying to conceal Bonario in a closet and to attend to Corvino and Celia. The business here could be satisfactorily managed by doors or curtains, without change of scene, and the device of consolidation was highly natural, preserving unity of place and reducing the number of sets required for the act from five to two.

In Act IV the first two scenes were consolidated and played continuously, according to the text, but this arrangement seems impossible, since scene i is a street scene and scene ii is the trial in the Senate House. Unless we quite ridiculously assume that the trial was held in the street, we must suppose that the text fails to indicate the change of scene.

In Act V, by completely omitting scene ii which took place at Sir Politick's house, a change of scenery was made unnecessary, because scenes i and iii both were set in Volpone's house. By omitting scene vii another change was eliminated, inasmuch as scenes vi and viii were both courtroom scenes. Scenes iv and v, representing two parts of the same street, were united, saving a change of setting. All the changes were designed for saving time and maintaining unity of place.

The most important changes came in the treatment given to speeches. In Act I Volpone's opening address to his gold was cut in half, and its Renaissance exuberance of rhetoric was considerably reduced. The by-play of Nano, Castrone, and Androgyno was entirely cut, including the song of "Fools they are the only nation," as was also Volpone's reflection on old age. On the whole, the act was left much as in the original. A few phrases of Mosca's were omitted on grounds of taste; and as Volpone lost his imaginative expansiveness, he became more sordid in his purpose of making fools of the legacy-hunters.

In Act II the opening scene between Sir Politick and Peregrine was cut from four pages to twenty-one lines. The mountebank scene was reduced about two pages, chiefly to avoid smutty allusions and some of the medical technicalities. Entire speeches have gone, but some of the best of the glorious rhetoric remains. The song beginning "Had old Hippocrates or Galen" remained, but the next one was removed. Corvino's anger at Celia's watching by the window was condensed by some thirty-five lines, chiefly for reasons of taste.

In Act III, scene ii, the parts of Nano and Castrone were abbreviated to two single line speeches for Nano. Lady Would-be's toilet scene was condensed, and from her lines during her visit to Volpone were deleted her literary allusions and her characteristically robust comments on Aretine and others. In the seduction scene, the song to "my Celia" was omitted. Volpone's seductive addresses were cut thirty-two lines, and again his poetic and imaginative qualities vanished. He became less like Tamburlaine and more like Horner.

In Act IV the opening scene between Would-be and Peregrine was cut from four pages to twelve lines. In the court-room scene, about twenty lines of Volpone's defense were omitted, and Corvino's description of Celia's moral character was softened from Anglo-Saxon to Latin. Otherwise, the act was left alone.

In Act V, scene i, the parts of Mosca and Volpone were cut, and some objectionable words were replaced by politer synonyms. Scene ii, the tortoise scene, was entirely omitted, eliminating four pages. In scenes iv and v Volpone's taunting of Corbaccio and Corvino was considerably cut. In scene vi, the second court scene, the last twenty-six lines, unimportant conversation among the *avocatori*, vanished. Scene vii was entirely removed. The final scene at court was left intact, except for the deletion of a few sententious remarks. Volpone ended the play with lines given to the first *avocatore* in the original. A few extra lines were added in order to point the moral.

Now, in the light of the revision, one may consider the objections formerly raised against the play. The underplot was so reduced that almost none of it remained except Lady Would-be, who was difficult to eliminate structurally, since she played an important part in the Senate scene by accusing Celia of wantonness and assisting Voltore to build his case against the innocents of the play. The inconsistency in the character of Volpone, like the lack of incident in the catastrophe, was a philosophical objection, and no alteration short of changing the play entirely could have remedied the fault. All the songs were dispensed with except that in the mountebank scene, which Mosca sings to attract Celia to her balcony: the unnatural interruption of Volpone's attack on Celia's virtue vanished. The mountebank scene remained, but it suffered severe contraction. Technically, it served its purpose of a confrontation between Volpone and Celia, but much of the objectionable farce disappeared. Sir Politick's tortoise was completely banished. The revised version was rendered utterly chaste in language: allusions to cuckoldry and incontinence, as well as indecent and offensive phrases were omitted or paraphrased, and the disgusting figures of the dwarf, the eunuch, and the hermaphrodite disappeared in two scenes and were reduced to two lines in the third. Almost all of the eighteenth-century criticisms were answered in this version. Esthetically, the priceless Renaissance spirit was lost to the stage, but through condensation, consolidation, and omission, the play was far better adapted to the demands and possibilities of the later theatre.

Volpone was presented for the last time at Covent Garden on January 20, 1773. Whether a continuation of the revival was planned is uncertain, but difficulties seem to have arisen over the casting of the leading characters. On August 8 William Smith wrote to the manager, Colman:

> In answer to the Business you mention'd I shoud have no objection to *Mosca*, had I not been in possession of the part of Volpone for these 5 years, & rehears'd it twenty times while Woodward was in ye Company, As you have sent it to Mr Ross, I cou'd wish to be out of the Play, & instead of Mosca, employ'd in a longer Part in the Epicœne — which I hear is much improv'd under y^r hand.[1]

Whatever may have been the reason, the play was dropped. At the end of the next season, Colman sold his share of the patent at Covent Garden, and *Epicoene* was produced at Drury Lane in January, 1776. Smith continued acting in *Every Man in his Humour*, but his days as Volpone were over, and the play itself was never again to appear at Covent Garden.

VII

THE LAST REVIVAL, 1783-1785

In 1784 Thomas Davies included in his *Dramatic Miscellanies* a criticism of *Volpone* which repeated previous objections. He censured the language, "which is so pedantic and stuck so full of Latinity, that few, except the learned, can perfectly understand it." He lamented the mountebank scene as "quite farcical."

1. *Posthumous Letters, from Various Celebrated Men; addressed to Francis Colman, and George Colman, the Elder*, 1820, pp. 185-186.

That a man of Volpone's sagacity should venture to appear in public, in the disguise of a mountebank, to be an eye-witness of a lady's beauty, of which he had heard only from report, and after escaping from the apprehended consequences of this exorbitant frolic, which had brought him within the censure of a court of judicature, . . . that he should again assume another shape, . . . make a pretended will; leave all his money, jewels, and effects, pretendedly to so wretched a fellow as a pimp and parasite; and all this with no other view than to mortify, insult, and abuse, those whom he had gulled, while yet the sentence of the court was depending, is a matter as absurd and improbable as any thing acted at the Italian comedy.[1]

The play was clearly beginning to creak in spots, but Colman ventured another revival, with even more re-visions, at the Haymarket on September 12, 1783, "Never Acted Here." It was played seven more times within a year, performances being given even in July, since the Haymarket was a summer theatre taken over from Samuel Foote by Colman in 1777. The cast, except for Bensley as Mosca, was entirely new: Volpone, John Palmer; Voltore, John Bannister; Corbaccio, William Parsons; Corvino, James Aickin; Bonario, R. Palmer; Celia, Mrs. Inchbald. The reviews were enthusiastic:

Ben Johnson's admirable Comedy of the Fox, was last night revived at the Haymarket Theatre, and received with loud and repeated applause. The play is now brought forward with addi-tional alterations to those made by Mr. Colman, when he re-vived it at Covent Garden Theatre; and the alterations are such as manifestly improve the stage effect of the piece very consider-ably. They chiefly consist of the omission of the character of Sir Politick Would-be and Lady Would-be, and consequently of the several scenes in which these characters are employed. It is needless to dilate on the merit of the Comedy, the great art and ingenuity of the plot, the natural and strong play of characteris-tic humor throughout, the power of the ridicule and satire having

1. II, 98–99. The reviewer of this volume for *The Monthly Review*, LXX (1784), 458, thought that Davies treated Jonson "with too little respect and too much severity."

been long since universally felt and admired by every judge of
dramatic excellence. The reviving it in such a stile, does Mr.
Colman infinite honour: — it may be considered as a classical
bonne bouche to the bill of fare he has served up to the town during the past summer. Last night's representation also reflects
very great credit on his Theatre and performers. The characters
were in general well acted, but those of *Corbachio* and *Mosca*,
incomparably, by Parsons and Bensley; nor ought the well-worn
earnestness of *Corvino*, the happy efftonty [*sic*] of *Volpone*, the
comic manner of *Voltore's* pleading, or the innocent zeal of *Celia*,
to escape our particular notice, Aickin, Palmer, Bannister jun.
and Mrs. Inchbald, having every title to an especial expression
of our approbation.[1]

Another impression of the revival has come down in the
biography of John Bannister, where the major actors are
described in detail. Palmer

supported the character of the simulating voluptuary; his declamation, his malignant mirth, his audacious love, and, in the end,
his manly, uncontrollable anger, were all . . . irresistible.

Bensley

was brisk and agile; his eye glared not·with its usual significancy,
but was illumined with archness and satirical pleasantry; and his
voice, unincumbered with his nasal twang, gave out, with sono-
rous vivacity, the sarcastic observations which the other characters provoked.

As Corbaccio, Parsons gave a performance

irresistibly comic. . . . Around this character [he] threw the
charm of his pungent humour, and made it one of the most striking exhibitions the theatre had ever produced. Splenetic impatience, jealous irritability, hasty suspicion, were associated
with stupid misintelligence, idiotic repetition of phrases, and a
blundering assent to propositions which he could not distinctly
hear, or rightly understand.[2]

1. *The Morning Chronicle and London Advertiser*, September 13, 1783.
2. John Adolphus, *Memoirs of John Bannister, Comedian*, 1839, I, 91-97.

James Boaden wrote that "the Volpone of Palmer and the Corbaccio of Parsons, presented a feast to the visitors of Colman's theatre, which has seldom been equalled, and will I believe never be surpassed," [1] and gave a vivid picture of how Parsons acted his rôle. [2] Michael Kelly reports that Parsons himself, whom he considered an exquisite actor, looked regretfully back to the days of Shuter's Corbaccio.

"Ah," said he, "to see Corbacio acted to perfection, you should have seen Shuter; the public are pleased to think that I act that part well, but his acting was as far superior to mine, as Mount Vesuvius is to a rushlight." [3]

In February, 1785, the Drury Lane company revived *Volpone* with the cast which had played at the Haymarket, advertising it as "Not acted these 20 Years." Mrs. Inchbald, who was then connected with the Covent Garden company, was replaced at the second and third performances by Mrs. Ward. Despite some enthusiasm, the comedy was given for the last time for one hundred thirty-six years on April 13, 1785.

Richard Cumberland wrote the last important examen of *Volpone* in the eighteenth century, a masterly essay in *The Observer* (1785). He, too, remarked on the inconsistency in Volpone's character in the fifth act, and the lack of relationship between the two plots. But he could find no other faults. After refusing to compare two such dissimilar dramatists as Shakspere and Jonson, he concluded by confessing that "this drama of *The Fox* is, critically speaking, the nearest to perfection of any one drama, comic or tragic, which the English stage is at this day in possession of." [4]

1. *Memoirs of the Life of John Philip Kemble, Esq.*, 1825, I, 57.

2. I, 62–63.

3. *Reminiscences of Michael Kelly, of the King's Theatre, and Theatre Royal, Drury Lane*, 1826, I, 315.

4. No. CX, IV (1788), 156.

Volpone was described in 1792 as follows:

This comedy is joined by the critics with the *Alchymist* and *Silent Woman*, as the Chef d'Oeuvres of this celebrated poet; and, indeed, it is scarcely possible to conceive a piece more highly finished, both in point of language and character, than this comedy. The plot is perfectly original.[1]

The next year Ludwig Tieck translated the play into German, under the title of *Herr von Fuchs. Ein Lustspiel in drei Aufzügen nach dem Volpone des Ben. Jonson.*[2] His translation kept all the important characters of the original but gave them such romantic names as Louise, Peter, Friedrich, and Birnam. The mountebank scene, the lyrics, and the three household pets of Volpone were omitted. The most striking change was that by which Louise (Celia) became Corvino's ward, not his wife, and was betrothed at the end of the play to Karl (Bonario). This alteration is extremely interesting in the light of subsequent criticism of the play by Coleridge, who, objecting to the fact that "there is no goodness of heart in any of the prominent characters," thought that "Bonario and Celia should have been made in some way or other principals in the plot; . . . a most delightful comedy might be produced, by making Celia the ward or niece of Corvino, instead of his wife, and Bonario her lover." [3] Were reminiscences of Tieck's play welling up from his unconscious memory?

The final word was written by Dibdin at the opening of

1. *A New Theatrical Dictionary*, p. 326.
2. *Ludwig Tieck's Schriften*, Berlin, 1829, XII, 1–154. See Robert Arnold, *Das Deutsche Drama*, München, 1925, p. 495; H. Lüdeke, *Ludwig Tieck und das alte englische Theater*, Frankfurt am Main, 1922, pp. 265–268; "Der Einfluss Ben Jonsons auf Ludwig Tieck," *Studien zur vergleichenden Litteraturgeschichte*, I (1901), 182–227, II (1902), 37–86; Walther Fischer, "Zu Ludwig Tiecks elisabethanischen Studien: Tieck als Ben Jonson-Philologe," *Shakespeare-Jahrbuch*, LXII (1926), 98–131.
3. H. N. Coleridge, *The Literary Remains of Samuel Taylor Coleridge*, II (1836), 276.

the new century. He admired the plot and the characters
of *Volpone*:

Would not one think it, therefore, very extraordinary that this
piece, even supported by admirable acting, has never greatly
succeeded? Nothing, considered superficially, can be so unaccountable; but, when the subject is fairly investigated, nothing
can be more clearly comprehended. Quaint, dry, studied correctness, unsupported by quickness, spirit, and fire, can never
satisfy. The author in this piece conducts us into a uniform and
proportionable building, presents us with an entertainment, and
introduces us to company, but the apartments are cheerless
vaults, the viands are carved marble, and the guests are statues.[1]

The play reposed on the library shelf until the revival
by the Phoenix Society in London, February 1, 1921,[2] the
rewriting by Herr Zweig, and the production by the
Theatre Guild in New York as a "sardonic farce," with as
gifted a cast, perhaps, as it ever had. Zweig's version had
splendid energy and was a notable success, and *Volpone*
may have another three centuries and a quarter ahead.
The glory of its past nothing can diminish.

   1. *A Complete History of the English Stage*, n.d. [1800], III, 294.
   2. For reviews see *The Times*, February 2, 1921; *The London Mercury*, III,
No. 17 (1921), p. 552; *The Times*, June 30, 1923. See Montague Summers,
The Restoration Theatre, 1934, p. 327. The comedy was presented by the Marlowe
Society at Cambridge University, March, 1923, and at the Malvern Festival,
July 30, 1935.

CHAPTER III

The Alchemist

I

1660–1702

OF ALL the comedies of Jonson, *The Alchemist* had the most brilliant stage-history. Written originally to satirize the evil influence of alchemy, as practised by such a man as Dr. John Dee, the play is colored so deeply with technical details of the alchemist's art that one would naturally expect rapid obsolescence when the abuses exposed had ceased to exist. There are, however, many unique features in the stage-history of *The Alchemist*: it was acted oftener than any other Jonsonian play, and consequently there are more facts to record; it held the stage the most steadily, almost exclusively as a Drury Lane piece; there are on years when it ran into a large number of productions at times of revival, as did *Every Man in his Humour* in 1751 and 1762; as it grew older, it elicited more and more critical comment in consequence of superb acting; and always there was a curiously false emphasis in considering the most important acting rôle neither Subtle, the alchemist, nor the wonderfully imaginative Sir Epicure Mammon, but the pusillanimous tobacco-boy, Abel Drugger. The history of *The Alchemist* was virtually the history of the rôle of Abel Drugger, about whom, I believe, more was written up to Garrick's death than about any other comic character except Falstaff. The play itself, considered by Dryden as Jonson's masterpiece,[1] lasted as long

1. Sir Walter Scott and George Saintsbury, *The Works of John Dryden*, X (1885), 418.

as it did, in spite of its rhetorical encumbrances and its
scientific and pseudo-scientific jargon, because of the plot,
which Coleridge thought "perfect," [1] and which is so
firmly wrought in the permutations and combinations of
relationship among the three rogues and the five gulls or
groups of gulls, that tempo and suspense are constantly
increasing. The play as absolute drama, in other words,
is much more exciting and important than the subject it
presents, and the theme is actually less a satire of alchemy
than a repetition of the idea expressed in *Volpone*, the
transmutation of men into fools when they seek to get
rich quickly.

In view of the later history of *The Alchemist*, it was
fitting that the "Several Stroleing Players, Fools, and
Fidlers, And the Mountebancks Zanies" who put on
"Drols and Farces" at Bartholomew Fair, in halls and
taverns, at Charing Cross, Lincoln's Inn Fields, and other
places, should have included among their drolls, as the
only play from Jonson, the Abel Drugger scenes from *The
Alchemist*. In Francis Kirkman's collection of these
favorite scenes from great plays of the past, *The Wits;
or, Sport upon Sport* (1672),[2] there are in all twenty-seven
drolls, two from Shakspere, fourteen from Beaumont and
Fletcher, and only one from Jonson. It is called "The
Imperick," and the argument is given thus: "*Under the
notion of his knowledg in Chymistrie, he cheats a Grocer
and a Precisian.*" The play is composed of Act I, scene iii,
and Act II, scene vi, the Abel Drugger scenes, to which is
added Act II, scene v, a scene with Ananias. Except for
a few transitional sentences, the text appears *verbatim*.

There is no record for the exact date of revival after
the Restoration, but there is extant a broadside *Prologue
to the Reviv'd Alchemist*,[3] undoubtedly published in 1660,

1. W. G. T. Shedd, *The Complete Works of Samuel Taylor Coleridge*, VI, 426.
2. Pages 159–166 (ed. J. J. Elson, Ithaca, 1932, pp. 229–236).
3. *Oxford Bibliographical Society, Proceedings and Papers*, Oxford, 1927, I,
part iv. 281–282. The prologue is here attributed to Davenant, but Mr. C. H.

which suggests that the comedy was revived in November or December by the King's Company.

PROLOGUE

<small>TO THE</small>

REVIV'D
ALCHEMIST.

THE *Alchemist*; Fire, breeding Gold, our *Theme:*
Here must no Melancholie be, nor Flegm.
Young *Ben*, not Old, writ this, when in his Prime,
Solid in Judgment, and in Wit sublime.
   The *Sisters*, who at *Thespian* Springs their Blood
Cool with fresh Streams, All, in a Merry Mood,
Their wat'ry Cups, and Pittances declin'd,
At *Bread-street's Mer-maid* with our *Poët* din'd:
Where, what they Drank, or who plaid most the Rig,
Fame modestly conceals: but He grew big
Of this pris'd Issue; when a *Jovial* Maid,
His Brows besprinkling with *Canarie*, said.
   Pregnant by Us, produce no Mortal Birth;
Thy active Soul, quitting the sordid Earth,
Shall 'mongst Heav'ns glitt'ring *Hieroglyphicks* trade,
And *Pegasus*, our winged Sumpter, jade,
Who from *Parnassus* never brought to *Greece*,
Nor *Romane* Stage, so rare a Master-piece.
This Story, true or false, may well be spar'd;
The *Actors* are in question, not the *Bard:*
How they shall humour their oft-varied Parts,
To get your Money, Company, and Hearts,
Since all Tradition, and like Helps are lost.
   Reading our Bill new pasted on the Post,
Grave Stagers both, one, to the other said,
The ALCHEMIST? What! are the Fellows mad?
Who shall *Doll Common* Act? Their tender Tibs
Have neither Lungs, nor Confidence, nor Ribs.
   Who *Face*, and *Subtle?* Parts, all Air, and Fire:
They, whom the *Authour* did Himself inspire,
Taught, Line by Line, each Tittle, Accent, Word,
Ne're reach'd His Height; all after, more absurd,

Wilkinson, Librarian of Worcester College, doubts his authorship. Surely Davenant would not have composed a prologue for a play apparently in the possession of Killigrew's company.

Shadows of fainter Shadows, wheresoe're
A *Fox* he pencil'd, copied out a *Bear*.
  Encouragement for young Beginners small:
Yet howsoe're we'll venture; have at All.
Bold Ignorance (they say) falls seldome short
In *Camp*, the *Countrey*, *City*, or the *Court*.
  Arm'd with the Influence of your fair Aspects,
Our Selves we'll conquer, and our own Defects.
A thousand Eyes dart raies into our Hearts,
Would make Stones speak, and Stocks play well their Parts:
Some few Malignant Beams we need not fear,
Where shines such Glory in so bright a Sphere.

The first actual performance of *The Alchemist* for which
there is a record after 1660 was on June 22, 1661, when
Pepys saw it at the King's Theatre in Vere Street and
found it "a most incomparable play." [1] On August 14
he saw it again at the same house,[2] and it was acted for at
least a third time during the year on December 16.[3] The
frequency of performance of *Bartholomew Fair* and *The
Alchemist* during 1661, after the establishment of Killigrew's company in Vere Street on November 8, 1660, looks
as though the comedies were enjoying the popularity of
a fresh revival, just as the four or five productions of *The
Silent Woman* in 1660 argue the same.

During 1662 Dr. Edward Browne continued his attendance at "the new new Theatre in Lincolnes Inne fields"
(clearly the Vere Street house) by paying 2*s*. 6*d*. to see the
"Alchymist" produced by the "K. P." (King's Players).[4]
After the Theatre Royal in Bridges Street was opened

1. H. B. Wheatley, *The Diary of Samuel Pepys*, II, 54.
2. II, 76.
3. J. Q. Adams, *The Dramatic Records of Sir Henry Herbert*, p. 117.
4. British Museum MS. Sloane 1900. The play was already furnishing allusions of a sort that became common in the eighteenth century. See *Calendar of
State Papers, Domestic Series, of the Reign of Charles II, 1661–1662*, 1861, p. 540.
For general satirical use see "A Very Heroical Epistle from my Lord All-Pride
to Doll-Common," J. W. Ebsworth, *The Roxburghe Ballads*, Hertford, IV (1883),
575–576; Thomas D'Urfey, *A Fool's Preferment*, 1688, prologue. See also the
Marquis of Lansdowne, *The Petty-Southwell Correspondence, 1676–1687*, 1928,
pp. 121, 267.

in May, 1663, *The Alchemist*, according to John Downes, became one of the "Principal old Stock Plays," and the cast was: Subtle, Wintershall; Face, Mohun; Mammon, Cartwright; Surly, Burt; Tribulation, Bateman; Ananias, Lacy; Dame Pliant, Mrs. Rutter; Dol Common, Mrs. Corey,[1] long to be called familiarly by this rôle.[2] This cast must be slightly altered to be correct for performances before August 3, 1664, for the part of Subtle was played until then by Walter Clun, famous for Iago, Falstaff, Bessus in *A King and No King*, and the Lieutenant in *The Humorous Lieutenant*. Pepys tells the story of Clun's fate. At the theatre on August 4 he heard that "Clun, one of their best actors, was, the last night, going out of towne (after he had acted the Alchymist, wherein was one of his best parts that he acts) to his country-house, set upon and murdered; one of the rogues taken, an Irish fellow. It seems most cruelly butchered and bound. The house will have a great miss of him."[3] A broadside was immediately published, called "An *Egley* Upon The Most Execrable *Murther* of Mr. *Clun*, On of the *Comedeans* of the *Theator Royal*, Who was Rob'd and most inhumanely Kill'd on Tuseday-night being the 2d of *August*, 1664, near *Tatnam-Court*, as he was Riding to his Country-house at *Kentishtown*."[4] The date given by the broadside is apparently incorrect, provided Pepys's account be true, since *Bartholomew Fair* was performed at the theatre on August 2. John Aubrey, the lively collector of biographical anecdotes for Anthony Wood, throws amusing light on Clun, noting that "Ben Johnson had one eie lower than t'other, and bigger, like Clun, the player:

---

1. *Roscius Anglicanus*, pp. 4-5.
2. Pepys, VI, 109, VIII, 188; J. G. Longe, *Martha Lady Giffard Her Life and Correspondence*, 1911, pp. 100-101. See Montague Summers, "Mrs. Corey: Pepys' 'Doll Common,'" *Essays in Petto*, n. d., pp. 113-132.
3. IV, 195.
4. The elegy was reprinted by G. Thorn-Drury, *A Little Ark Containing Sundry Pieces of Seventeenth-Century Verse*, 1921, pp. 30-31, and J. W. Draper, *A Century of Broadside Elegies*, 1928, pp. 100-101.

perhaps he begott Clun," [1] a conjecture which deserves no attention.

After the misfortune of Clun's death, Killigrew's company had so "great miss of him" that *The Alchemist* was seemingly allowed to fall into decline for almost five years. But it was not forgotten. Dryden, while defending himself against the charge of allowing his debauched protagonists a happy conclusion, contrary to the laws of poetic justice, mentioned an occurrence in Ben Jonson:

Ben Jonson himself, after whom I may be proud to err, has given me more than once the example of it. That in "The Alchemist" is notorious, where *Face*, after having contrived and carried on the great cozenage of the play, and continued in it without repentance to the last, is not only forgiven by his master, but enriched, by his consent, with the spoils of those whom he had cheated. And, which is more, his master himself, a grave man, and a widower, is introduced taking his man's counsel, debauching the widow first, in hope to marry her afterward. [2]

In 1668, also, Dryden made his mistake about the origin of *The Alchemist*, when he wrote the occasional prologue for the revival of Tomkis's *Albumazar*, originally published in 1614, four years after the first performances of *The Alchemist*:

To say this Commedy pleas'd long a go,
Is not enough, to make it pass you now:
Yet gentlemen, your Ancestors had witt,
When few men censurd, and fewer writ.
And *Iohnson*, of those few, the best chose this,
And the best modell of his master piece;
Subtle was got by our *Albumazar*,
That *Alchamist* by this Astrologer.
Here he was fashion'd, and I should suppose,
He likes my fashion well, that wears my Cloaths.

---

1. Andrew Clark, *Aubrey's 'Brief Lives,'* II, 14.
2. *Works*, III, 247. That Dryden's example was ill-chosen was proved by Jeremy Collier (*A Short View*, pp. 151–152). *The Alchemist* was not criticized for moral qualities until *The Stage the High Road to Hell*, 1767, p. 15, appeared.

But *Ben* made nobly his, what he did mould,
What was anothere's Lead, became his Gold;
Like an unrighteous Conquerer he raigns,
Yet rules that well, which he unjustly gains.[1]

On April 17, 1669, Pepys went again to see the play:

Hearing that "The Alchymist" was acted, we did go . . . and
it is still a good play, having not been acted for two or three
years before; but I do miss Clun for the Doctor. But more my
eyes will not let me enjoy the pleasure I used to have in a play.[2]

This performance took place before the king, and the
players were given £10,[3] circumstances repeated on November 12, 1674, and October 26, 1675,[4] after which nothing definite is known about the play until on March 27,
1701, Lady Morley saw it at Drury Lane. Langbaine made
no comment about its appearance on the stage in 1691,
and the only evidence of popularity after Pepys comes
from Aphra Behn, in an irate mood, after a "wretched
Fop" had criticized *The Dutch Lover* (produced at Dorset
Garden in February, 1673), as a "woful Play, God damn
him, for it was a woman's." The lady writes:

I'll only say . . . that Plays have no great room for that which
is men's great advantage over women, that is Learning; We all
well know that the Immortal Shakespeare's Plays (who was not
guilty of much more of this than often falls to women's share)
have better pleas'd the World than Johnson's works, though by
the way, 'tis said that Benjamin was no such Rabbi neither, for I

1. *Covent Garden Drolery*, pp. 87–88 (ed. G. Thorn-Drury, 1928, p. 148);
The Works of John Dryden, X, 417; *Miscellany Poems*, 1684, p. 279; Gerard
Langbaine, *An Account of the English Dramatick Poets*, p. 287; Peter Whalley,
The Works of Ben. Jonson, I, xliv; *The Companion to the Play-House*, article
on *Albumazar*; *The Critical Review*, XIX (1765), 140–141; [Philip Neve], *Cursory
Remarks on Some of the Ancient English Poets*, 1789, pp. 42–43; Charles Dibdin,
A Complete History of the English Stage, III, 297; *Notes and Queries*, 3d series
IX (1866), 178, 259, 302, XII (1867), 155, 510; W. C. Hazlitt, *A Select Collection of Old English Plays*, 1875, XI, 294.
2. VIII, 279.
3. Allardyce Nicoll, *Restoration Drama*, p. 306.
4. Page 307.

am inform'd that his Learning was but Grammar high; . . . and I have seen a man the most severe of Johnson's Sect, sit with his Hat remov'd less than a hair's breadth from one sullen posture for almost three hours at *The Alchymist;* who at that excellent Play of *Harry the Fourth* (which yet I hope is far enough from Farce) hath very hardly kept his Doublet whole.[1]

The criticism is not flattering. Langbaine's silence and the fact that there are no records after 1675 may indicate that, for *The Alchemist* at least, Gildon's statement that Jonson's plays had lain dormant twenty years previous to 1695 was correct. Its history after 1700 indicates a broken continuity, as was the case with some of the other major comedies, for there were lapses from 1702 to 1709, and from 1713 to 1721, after which there were only eight seasons before 1776 when the play was not on the stage. The comedy was performed more regularly as it grew older, a fact which forms but one more anomaly in its history.

For the two performances seen by Lady Morley in the spring of 1701, a possible cast can be reconstructed by comparison of the actors known to be playing then at Drury Lane with the known cast of 1709: Subtle, Colley Cibber; Face, George Powell; Dapper, Norris; Drugger, Pinkethman; Surly, John Mills; Kastril, Bullock; Ananias, Johnson; Dol Common, possibly Mrs. Rogers. It is not possible to assign Lovewit, Mammon, Tribulation, and Dame Pliant. For the single revival of *The Alchemist* by Betterton's company on October 9, 1702, at the new theatre in Little Lincoln's Inn Fields, a reconstruction of the cast is impossible. It was the only time that the comedy was ever presented by a company of actors not associated with the fortunes of Drury Lane until the revival, for two nights only, at Covent Garden in 1740.

1. Montague Summers, *The Works of Aphra Behn,* 1915, I, 224.

II

1709-1713

On February 19, 1709, *The Alchemist* was revived at
Drury Lane, "Not Acted these six years," and was played
seven times before the middle of May. If one were to
judge the members of the cast solely from the bill given by
Genest, he might easily fall into the misconception of Mr.
Montague Summers, who writes, "In February, 1709,
there seems to have been a curious revival of 'The Alchemist' at Drury Lane when Dol Common was omitted." [1]
Aside from the obvious fact that there would be very little
to the play if Dol were left out, it is certain that the cast
remained intact. The bills in *The Daily Courant* give the
same actors that have been indicated for 1701, with the
addition of Bickerstaff as Lovewit, Estcourt as Mammon,
and Pack as Tribulation. The only omissions are the two
female rôles. But the newspaper adds, "And all the other
parts to the best Advantage." The women's parts, further-
more, are given in the first acting quarto of the play (1709),
as Dame Pliant, Mrs. Cox, and Dol Common, Mrs.
Saunders.

Two members of the cast were of the lower school of
comic acting, — Richard Estcourt and William Pinkethman. Estcourt, according to Downes, was "*Histrio Natus*;
he has the Honour (Nature enduing him with an easy,
free, unaffected Mode of Elocution) in Comedy always
to Lætificate his Audience, especially Quality, (Witness
Serjeant *Kyte*) He's not Excellent only in that, but a
Superlative Mimick." [2] Like Pinkethman, Theophilus
Cibber, and many other early actors, he improvised his
parts, and one is inclined to accept Cibber's statement
that Estcourt was languid and unaffecting.[3] He played at

---

1. Program notes for the production of *The Alchemist* by the Phoenix Society, London, March 18, 1923.   2. Page 51.
3. *Apology*, 2d ed., p. 97.

Drury Lane only from 1704 until his death in 1712. Captain Otter was his other Jonsonian rôle. Pinkethman, or "Pinky," was "the Flower of *Bartholomew*-Fair, and the Idol of the Rabble. A fellow that over-does every thing, and spoils many a Part with his own stuff," [1] and Downes characterized him as "the darling of *Fortunatus*, he has gain'd more in Theatres and Fairs in Twelve Years, than those that have Tugg'd at the Oar of Acting these 50." [2] He played Abel Drugger for the last time on October 24, 1739, after an absence of sixteen years from the part. Sir Politick Would-be was his one other Jonsonian character. His improvisations were the delight of the galleries, and his practise was used as a horrible example in the satire called *The Players* (1733):

> Quit not your Theme to win the gaping Rout,
> Nor aim at *Pinkys* Leer, with — blood — I'm out.
> An arch dull Rogue, who lets the Business cool,
> To show how nicely he can play the Fool,
> Who with Buffoonery his Dulness clokes,
> Deserves a Cat of nine tails for his Jokes.[3]

The part of Abel Drugger descended from Pinkethman to Theophilus Cibber with Miller as the only intermediary; Cibber merely heightened the absurdities inherited from Pinky.

The performance on May 11, 1709, was reviewed by Steele in *The Tatler*:

This Evening *The Alchymist* was play'd. This Comedy is an Example of *Ben's* extensive Genius and Penetration into the Passions and Follies of Mankind. The Scene in the Fourth Act, where all the cheated People oppose the Man that would open their Eyes, has something in it so inimitably excellent, that it is certainly as great a Masterpiece as has ever appear'd by any Hand. The Author's great Address in showing Coveteousness

1. [Charles Gildon], *A Comparison Between the Two Stages*, p. 199.
2. Page 52.
3. Sig. C7. See *The Spectator*, No. 539.

[*sic*] the Motive of the Actions of the *Puritan*, the *Epicure*, the *Gamester*, and the *Trader;* and that all their Endeavours, how differently soever they seem to tend, center only in that one Point of Gain, shows he had to a great Perfection that Discernment of Spirit, which constitutes a Genius for Comedy.[1]

In September, 1709, the Drury Lane company revolted to the Haymarket on account of Rich's oppressive management, remaining there until November 20, 1710. *The Alchemist* was presented twice, but the cast was necessarily somewhat altered, because of the five players who remained at Drury Lane, — Powell, Norris, Pack, Bickerstaff, and Mrs. Cox. Wilks played Face, and Dogget Dapper; Mills was at the Haymarket and probably continued as Surly; Mrs. Saunders was doubtless Dol Common, but since the casts in the newspapers were abridged, the parts of Tribulation, Lovewit, and Dame Pliant are open to conjecture. None of the actors who played these rôles subsequently was then in the company. Dogget was no doubt well equipped for Dapper. Downes described him as "very Aspectabund, wearing a Farce in his Face . . . the only Comick Original now Extant";[2] and Tony Aston called him "a little, lively, spract Man," who "never deceiv'd his Audience — because, while they gaz'd at him, he was working up the Joke, which broke out suddenly in involuntary Acclamations and Laughter."[3]

Any changes in the casting were but temporary, for when the play was produced at Drury Lane again three times in 1711, the cast was the same as that given in the quarto of 1709. Although no actors are announced for the performances in 1712 and 1713, one may safely assume that there were few changes: the casts for 1709 formed a nucleus of standard actors in Jonson's comedies for many seasons after 1713. After December 22, 1713, *The Alche-*

1. No. 14 (ed. G. A. Aitken, I [1898], 125–126).
2. Page 52.
3. *A Brief Supplement to Colley Cibber, Esq.*, ed. R. W. Lowe, *An Apology for the Life of Mr. Colley Cibber*, II, 309–310.

mist was forgotten for eight years; there was scarcely an allusion until 1718, when John Dennis wrote a short criticism in a letter on Freethinkers:

What my Lord *Rochester* and the Author of *Hudibras* have declar'd in their Verses, our Dramatick Poets have endeavour'd to shew upon the Stage, *viz.* That the Eyes of the Rabble of Mankind are downright Cullies to their Ears, and that they easily believe that they actually See what they are only impudently Told of; . . . has not *Ben*, Learned *Ben*, who is so great a Master of his Art, and consequently of Human life and nature, shewn us the very reverse of this in the Catastrophe of his admirable Alchimist, *viz.* shewn us Persons who what before they had actually seen, are made to believe that they only vainly imagin'd, and for no other Reason but because they are impudently told that they only vainly imagin'd it.[1]

In the same year Gildon analyzed the technique of the opening scene in *The Complete Art of Poetry*:

I shall consider the Division of our Plays into five Acts. . . . The first Act contains the Matter or Argument of the Fable, and the introducing the principal Characters; and this is admirably done by *Ben Johnson*, in his *Alchymist*, where the Audience is let into the Design and Characters, by a Quarrel between *Subtle* and *Face*, who are the chief Managers of the whole Design.[2]

Dennis again alluded to *The Alchemist* in his bitter attack on Sir Richard Steele, in January, 1720, *The Characters and Conduct of Sir John Edgar, Call'd by Himself the Sole Monarch of the Stage in Drury-Lane*:

You, Sir *John Edgar*, have been a Squanderer in Three Elements. . . . When you, and *Burnaby* the Poet, and *Tilly*, the late Warden of the *Fleet*, enter'd into an Indenture Tripartite, as *Face*, and *Subtle*, and *Doll Common* had done before you; but with this Difference, that these last were Cheats, whereas you and your Brethren were Gulls. With an Eagerness, like that of Sir *Epicure Mammon*, were you embark'd in the Search of your

1. *Original Letters, Familiar, Moral, and Critical*, 1721, pp. 39–40. The allusion is to Lovewit's return (*The Alchemist*, V. i).
2. I, 266. Gildon repeated this criticism in *The Laws of Poetry*, p. 205.

Aurum potabile; when you us'd to say to one another, over your Midnight Suppers, *Drink, and be Rich.*[1]

In the second letter, he criticized Steele's *Theatre* and advised him to cultivate the rules, remarking that " The *Fox*, the *Alchymist*, the *Silent Woman* of *Ben Johnson*, are incomparably the best of our Comedies; and they are certainly the most regular of them all," and that " *Ben Johnson* excell'd all in Comedy, who have attempted it after him." [2] *The Fox* and *The Silent Woman* were still to be seen regularly, and it was incredible, no doubt, that the equal merits of *The Alchemist* should be unrecognized. But a national panic as great as the bursting of the South Sea Bubble was necessary to bring it forth from the purlieus of criticism to a living share in the affairs of the day. The Bubble restored the comedy to a vogue which it retained until 1776.

III

1721–1732

Perhaps there was never a period more rife with speculation and desire for the Midas touch than the years following the death of Queen Anne. Continuous warfare had loaded the country with an enormous national debt, for the reduction of which Harley in 1711 had formed the South Sea Company to exploit markets in the new world. It took over government obligations, issuing its own shares in their stead, and looking for profits not only from trade but from a rise in the price of shares. A craze for speculation broke out fiercely; in August, 1720, shares rose 1000 per cent, only to slump in September, carrying other mushroom companies down in the crash, causing a general panic, and beggaring hundreds of families.[3]

1. Page 18. Reprinted in *The Theatre, By Sir Richard Steele*, II, 363. Compare *The Alchemist*, II. i.   2. Pages 29, 31.
3. For the economic details see I. S. Leadam, *The History of England from 'he Accession of Anne to the Death of George II*, 1909, pp. 293–304.

A selection from a contemporary list of the mushroom projects known as "bubbles" will illustrate to how great a degree sound judgment was corrupted. There were projects "for erecting Salt-Pans in *Holy-Island*"; "for furnishing Funerals to any Part of *Great Britain*"; "for erecting . . . Hospitals for Bastard Children"; "for importing Walnut-Tree from *Virginia*"; "for a Wheel of perpetual Motion"; and, even madder, "for carrying on an Undertaking of great Advantage, but no body to know what it is." [1] Obviously, these mad projects gave occasion for countless caricatures and pasquinades, among the wittiest of which was "The BUBBLER'S MEDLEY, or a SKETCH of the Times: Being Europe's Memorial for the Year 1720," [2] which appeared August 10, 1720. After revealing the madness of all classes of society in sinking their gold so wantonly, the ballad reminds them:

> 'Tis said, that *Alchymists* of old
>   Could turn a Brazen Kettle,
> Or Leaden Cistern into Gold,
>   That Noble, Tempting Mettle:
> But if it here may be allow'd
>   To bring in great and small Things,
> Our cunning *South-Sea*, like a God,
>   Turns Nothing into All Things.[3]

Here was a hint broad enough to have warranted a revival of the play, but not until October 25, 1721, was it presented, "Not Acted these Ten Years" (actually only seven years), "By His Royal Highness's Command."

---

1. Abel Boyer, *The Political State of Great-Britain*, XX (1720), 54–57.
2. *Catalogue of Prints and Drawings in the British Museum, Division I, Satires*, II, 415–420. The ballad was printed in Boyer's *Political State*, XX, 177–179; *The Weekly Journal; or, British Gazetteer*, September 3, 1720; *The Second Part of Penkethman's Jests; or, Wit Refin'd*, 1721, pp. 88–89; *The Parliamentary History of England*, VII (1811), 659–660.
3. Compare *The Alchemist*, II. i:
> "*Mammon.* This night I'll change
> All that is metal in my house to gold:
> And, early in the morning, will I send
> To all the plumbers and the pewterers,
> And buy their tin and lead up."

The comedy was played for three nights running, with the following cast: Subtle, Cibber; Face, Mills; Dapper, Norris; Drugger, Pinkethman; Mammon, Harper; Surly, Wilks, Jr.; Tribulation, Griffin; Kastril, Miller; Ananias, Johnson; Dame Pliant, Mrs. Markham; Dol Common, Mrs. Wethereld. The most striking aspect of the revival was the new occasional epilogue, later printed as an engraved broadside,[1] in which a two-headed hydra was slain, the South Sea scandal and its forerunner, the French project known as the Mississippi Company:

An Epilogue spoke to a Play Call'd the Alchymist.

Old *Surly* Ben, *to Night, hath let us know,*
That in this Isle a Plenteous Crop did Grow
Of Knaves *and* Fools, *a Hundred* Years ago:
Chymists Bawds, Gamesters *&* a Numerous Train
Of humble Rogues, Content with moderate Gain,
The Poet *had he liv'd to see this* Age
Had brought Sublimer Villains *on y*[e] *Stage;*
Our Knaves *Sin higher Now then those of* Old,
Kingdoms, *not Private Men, are* Bought *&* Sold,
Witness the South-sea *Project, which hath shown*
How far Phylosophers may be out done
By Modern S——m-n *that have found y*[e] Stone.
Well might it take its Title from the Main,
That Rose *so swift and* Sunk *so soon again;*
Fools *have been always* Bit *by artfull* Lyes,
But here the Cautious *were deceiv'd &* wise,
And Yet, in these Flagitious Monstrous Times,
The Knaves *detected* Triumph *in their* Crimes,
Wallow in Wealth, *have all things at Command,*
And Brave the Vengeance of an Injur'd Land;
Well! *since wee've Learn'd Experience at our Cost,*
Let us preserve the Remnant *not yet* Lost,
Though L-w, *from* France, *be landed on the* Coast,
By Sober Arts Aspire to Guiltless *Fame,*
And Prove that Virtue's *not an Empty Name.*

---

1. *Catalogue of Prints and Drawings in the British Museum, Division I, Satires,* II, 587–588; *The Weekly Journal; or, British Gazetteer,* December 16, 1721; [Richardson Pack], *The Lives of Miltiades and Cimon. With Poems on several Occasions,* 1725, pp. 48–50; *The Gentleman's Magazine,* XCV (1825), part i, 100–102.

When this satire appeared, public resentment had not yet subsided; many of the South-Sea projectors retained their wealth in safety, as a result of the system devised for restoring public credit. The allusion to kingdoms being bought had foundation in the occurrences of the times. One of the few who profited from the Mississippi scheme was Joseph Gage, who offered three millions sterling to Augustus, king of Poland, to resign the crown in his favor, and upon rejection, attempted unsuccessfully to purchase the sovereignty of Sardinia. The allusion to "Law from France" was specially intended for that gentleman's ears, for from the daily papers we learn that "on Wednesday Night their Royal Highnesses the Prince and Princess of Wales were at the Theatre in Drury-Lane, and saw the *Alchymist* acted: There was a splendid Appearance of the Nobility and Gentry; the famous Mr. Law and his Son were there also." [1]

John Law, formerly controller-general of French finance, famous gambler, slayer of Beau Wilson in a duel, and financial projector, had founded a successful private bank in Paris, when he conceived an idea known as the Mississippi scheme for colonizing Louisiana, to pay the French debt. Fabulous profits were expected and speculation raged, as it raged a little later in England; in May, 1720, the value of notes was reduced one-half and a panic followed, during which Law left the country and wandered about Europe, until the English government invited him to visit London, whither he sailed on the Admiral's flagship in October, 1721. On October 22 he was presented to George I, took lodgings in Hanover Square, where he received countless visitors, and attended the theatre. The actor who delivered the epilogue might, if it pleased him, when he mentioned "L-w from France," bow to the man himself. One is tempted to admire the royal irony in ordering this comedy for the entertainment of the famous guest.

1. *The Whitehall Evening Post*, October 26, 1721; *Applebee's Original Weekly Journal*, October 28, 1721.

The new members of the cast were John Harper, playing his first part in Jonson; Wilks, Jr., who had played Winwife in *Bartholomew Fair*, the year before; Benjamin Griffin, new in Jonson; Miller, already experienced as Bartholomew Cokes and La Foole; and the two women, both new in Jonson. Mrs. Markham acted Dame Pliant until 1726; and Mrs. Wethereld, Dol Common until 1732, the longest continuous period for any of the actresses in the part. The actors held their rôles for many years: Norris dropped out in 1723, and Dapper fell to several actors; Wilks, Jr., yielded Surly to William Mills in 1726; Miller played Kastril for two periods, 1721–1726 and 1733–1738, the part falling to Bridgewater and Oates in the interim. The other actors kept their parts for a long period: Colley Cibber played until 1733, being succeeded by young Mills, who then gave up Surly; John Mills kept Face until 1737, when Charles Macklin assumed the rôle; Harper lasted until 1739, and Griffin until 1740, when Taswell inherited Tribulation and played the part until 1759; and Johnson was Ananias until 1740. Of the comedy during this period there is some account by Thomas Davies:

Colley Cibber I have seen act Subtle with great art; the elder Mills at the same time played Face with much shrewd spirit and ready impudence. The two Palmers have successively acted Face with much archness and solid characteristic bronze. Ben Griffin and Ben Jonson were much admired for their just representation of the canting puritanical preacher and his solemn deacon the botcher; there was an affected softness in the former which was finely contrasted by the fanatical fury of the other. — Griffin's features seemed ready to be relaxed into a smile, while the stiff muscles and fierce eye of the other admitted of no suppleness or compliance. There is still to be seen a fine print of them in these characters, from a painting of Vanbleek: they are striking resemblances of both comedians. . . .

I have never seen an adequate representer of Sir Epicure, from Harper down to Love. The first seemed to have been taught by one who had juster conceptions of what was to be done in the part than the player could execute.[1]

Harper, a corpulent and facetious low comedian, said by Tony Aston to have too much of the Bartholomew Fair in his style, played Falstaff, the "female Falstaff" Ursula, the pig-wife, and Captain Otter with his "bulls and bears." Despite the criticism of Davies, he was described by Dibdin[2] as "a kind of a second to Quin in comedy, and played Sir Epicure Mammon and other parts of that description with truth and spirit." Josias Miller, famous for his brogue, played such rôles as Teague in *The Committee*, Ben in *Love for Love*, Sir Joseph Wittol in *The Old Bachelor;* and at least six times he attained the distinction of performing Abel Drugger after Pinky's death and before Theophilus Cibber took the part in 1731.

After 1721 the comedy was unacted until 1723, when it was played three times, once by special desire and once by royal command; then it was again dropped for three seasons. It was revived on October 20, 1726, after which it was presented regularly with no lapse exceeding a year.

An essay in *The Weekly Journal; or, Saturday's Post*, for August 17, 1723, ridiculed the prevailing fashion of writing in ciphers as "Nonsense without Meaning or Design":

I find this Folly ridiculed by *Ben Johnson* in his celebrated Play of the *Alchymist*, where *Abel Drugger* causes his Name to be writ upon his Sign, with the Letter A and a Bell painted, for *Abel*, the Letter D, with a Rug, and a Dog grinning, for *Drugger*. So that we find this is only an old Folly reviv'd.[3]

The author of a *Dissertation on the Art of Selling Bargains* (1728), noted the popularity of *The Alchemist*:

I therefore refer my Reader to the celebrated Comedy called the *Alchymist*, which opens with a high Quarrel between *Face*

1. *Dramatic Miscellanies*, II, 108–109.
2. V, 202.
3. See a letter on sign-post improvement in *The British Magazine*, April, 1750, p. 160.

and *Subtle*, wherein the latter *sells* the other two *Bargains* almost in a Breath. . . . I purposely forbear to quote this choice Passage, that I may the more excite my Reader's Curiosity, to be present at the Representation of the Play, which I doubt not, upon the Hint I have here given, will be frequently called for before the End of the Season; but I must caution him to be in the House as soon as the Curtain rises, otherwise he will be disappointed of his Expectation.[1]

A year later Bolingbroke published a pamphlet advising a conclusion of the war with Spain. Objectors argued that England could have some hopes of being, one time or another, in almost as good condition as before her affairs were thus embroiled:

This puts me in mind of Sir *Epicure Mammon*, in the *Alchymist*; who, when he had spent his *whole Estate* in search of the *Philosopher's Stone*, was comforted after all his *Cost*, though disappointed of his *main End*, with the Hopes of getting a *little something to cure the Itch*.[2]

The only important change in the cast before the comedians deserted their manager for temporary asylum at the Haymarket in September, 1733, was the appearance of Theophilus Cibber for the first time as Abel Drugger on October 7, 1731, a part which he played last on September 25, 1746, thereby furnishing critics an opportunity to compare his portrayal with Garrick's. In October, 1732, a critic made some observations on the state of the stage, remarking on the number of excellent players recently lost at Drury Lane through death and old age, while admitting that the company still had enough good performers to give it the preference to other stages. He praised the elder Cibber especially, and added:

Whoever has seen the Son in the Characters of *Pistol* in the second Part of King HENRY the *fourth*, *Abel Drugger* in the

1. *The Miscellaneous Works of the Late Dr. Arbuthnot*, Glasgow, 1751, II, 166–167.

2. Caleb D'Anvers (Nicholas Amhurst), *The Craftsman*, IV (1731), 249. The allusion is to *The Alchemist*, IV. iii.

Alchymist, and Father *Martin* in the *old Debauchees*, have seen what it is to excel in Characters masterly drawn by the Authors.[1]

Unfortunately, Cibber was not to keep this reputation. Davies describes how Garrick "freed the stage from the false spirit, ridiculous squinting, and vile grimace, which, in Theophilus Cibber, had captivated the public for several years, by introducing a more natural manner of displaying the absurdities of a foolish tobacconist," [2] and in 1755 the querulous and disappointed Cibber was complaining because he thought there was a conspiracy to exclude him from the stage. He published a list of his hundred and twenty parts, including Dapper, Drugger, Cokes, La Foole, and Sir John Daw, and offered to play them at either theatre in alternation with any other actor, without fear of the judicious and candid audience.[3] The more one reads of Cibber, the more pathetic he seems in his egotism, his jealousy, his lack of honor, and his ultimate tragedy.

IV

1733–1743

During the revolt of the Drury Lane actors from High-more in the fall and winter of 1733–1734, *The Alchemist* was chosen five times by the new "company of comedians of His Majesty's Revels," and it was so popular that eleven further performances were given before the beginning of 1736, so that during this period *The Alchemist*, like *Volpone* and *The Silent Woman*, reached its greatest frequency of production. The only notable accession to the cast was Mrs. Charlotte Charke as Dol Common, a rôle for which she was no doubt perfectly trained by her way of life. Until the first appearance of Mrs. Pritchard in the

---

1. *The Comedian; or, Philosophical Enquirer*, 1732, No. VII, p. 39.
2. *Dramatic Miscellanies*, II, 107.
3. *An Epistle from Mr. Theophilus Cibber, to David Garrick, Esq.* [1756], pp. 21–27.

rôle on April 13, 1736, Mrs. Charke was relieved only one evening,— by Mrs. Clive, who, with her talent for romps and hoydens, was doubtless adequate. On March 12, 1734, the comedians returned to Drury Lane, where they presented *The Alchemist* four days later with an unaltered cast, "For the Entertainment of several foreign Ministers." The play was commanded by the queen on September 15, 1735, and *The London Daily Post and General Advertiser* reported that

Last Night her Majesty, their Royal Highnesses the Prince of Wales and the Duke, together with their Highnesses the Princesses Amelia, Caroline, Mary, and Louisa, were present at the Theatre-Royal in Drury-lane, when the Alchemist was perform'd to a crowded Audience with universal Applause.[1]

The play was repeated the following night for those "who could not get Places Yesterday."

In December Aaron Hill rebuked an upstart who had accused him of atheism by calling him

This *Orthodox-Kastryll*, who, like *Ben Johnson's angry Boy*, has learnt the Art of Quarreling to the highest Degree of Perfection, forgetting himself in the Heat of his Fury.[2]

In the same year, also, a plot-outline of *The Alchemist* was included in *The Dramatic Historiographer*, a hand-book containing summaries of the most popular of the Shaksperean, Restoration, and early eighteenth-century plays.[3]

Mrs. Pritchard's début as Dol Common occurred under somewhat unusual circumstances. Mrs. Cibber was to have played for her own benefit in *The Conscious Lovers*, but the inconsiderate birth of a son a few days before forced her to presume on the candor and good nature of the several ladies of quality who had desired her appearance, and *The Alchemist* was substituted. Mrs. Pritchard

1. September 16, 1735.
2. *The Prompter*, No. CXII.
3. Pages 16–20. Reprinted as *A Companion to the Theatre; or, A View of our most celebrated Dramatic Pieces*, 1747 (Dublin, 1751).

was tenacious of the part, holding it intermittently, with aid from Mrs. Macklin, Mrs. Cross, Mrs. James, and Mrs. Lee, until 1768. Davies wrote of her:

Doll Common fell into Mrs. Clive's hands about fifty years ago. How she came afterwards into the possession of Mrs. Pritchard, while her friend was still in the company, I know not. If I remember rightly, the former, by lessening the vulgarity of the prostitute, did not give so just an idea of her as the latter. Mrs. Pritchard, by giving a full scope to her fancy as well as judgement, produced a complete resemblance of the practised and coarse harlot in Madam Doll.[1]

Several changes in the cast were now made. In 1737 Macklin succeeded to Face and William Havard to Surly; in the next year Woodward played Kastril; and in 1739 Richard Yates acted Dapper. Macklin played Face, his first Jonsonian rôle, until 1748, acting in the meantime Cutbeard, Corvino, and Sir John Daw.[2] Havard, a decent and sensible performer, particularly in genteel comedy, appeared in *The Alchemist* until 1746, his other rôles in Jonson being Dauphine, Bonario, and Voltore. Woodward's Bobadill was so much more important than any of his other rôles in Jonson,— La Foole, Ananias, Face, Subtle, and Daw,— that consideration of his acting may be left to the chapter on *Every Man in his Humour*. Yates, later famous as Brainworm and Master Stephen, played Dapper only twice; his experience in Jonson was to include Kastril, Morose, and Otter. He was "seldom beholden to trick for applause," [3] and his most striking peculiarity was a desire to be buried under the center of the stage on which he had so often acted.

In 1740 came two productions of *The Alchemist* at Covent Garden, when Theophilus Cibber was playing for

1. *Dramatic Miscellanies*, II, 110. See *The London Daily Post and General Advertiser*, April 6, 1736.
2. For a satirical print of Macklin's Face see *Catalogue of Prints and Drawings in the British Museum, Division I, Satires*, III (1877), part i, 475–477.
3. *The Dramatic Censor*, II, 493.

his first season there. The comedy, originally announced for June 5, was given with the same cast on December 10 and 31, but it was never acted there again. Cibber went back to Drury Lane, where he was playing Abel Drugger once more by February 12, 1742. The only members of the Covent Garden cast who had subsequent shares in the history of the play were Richard Neale (Tribulation), John Arthur (Lovewit), and Mrs. Cross (Dol Common), who was engaged at Drury Lane soon after. Neale, who acted also Sir Politick Would-be and La Foole, played Kastril until 1745 and Ananias until 1749. Arthur, a specialist in characters of old men, played Lovewit until 1748, when he went back to Covent Garden and acted Sir Politick until *Volpone* was dropped in 1754. Mrs. Cross played Dol last in 1762, varying her parts with Lady Haughty, Dame Pliant, Lady Centaure, and Mrs. Otter.

The last notable change before the début of Garrick as Abel Drugger was that of Edward Berry as Sir Epicure Mammon on February 12, 1742. He was best known in Jonson's comedies for his old Knowell, which he played until two years before his death in 1760. He acted Sir Epicure until 1759. *The Theatrical Review: For the Year 1757* praised him:

This veteran actor, grown grey in the service of the public, listed young under the banners of the theatric muse. He has made one in almost every company that has been raised for upwards of thirty years. . . . As to his exhibition in comedy . . . it is in general masterly, but in nothing more so, than that his performance has more the appearance of reality, looks less like acting, than that of a great many more famous actors. This is what I fancy every spectator must have observed, who has seen Mr. Berry in his favourite characters, such as Sir Jealous Trafick, Sir Epicure Mammon, Jobson, Boniface, Caliban, &c.[1]

On March 21, 1743, for the benefit of Mr. Macklin, David Garrick first acted the rôle of Abel Drugger and

1. Pages 12–13.

thereby created an epoch in the criticism of *The Alchemist.*
Henceforth, the bulk of material written about the play
itself and particularly about his Abel Drugger, which became immediately one of the sensations of theatrical history, was nothing short of amazing, and henceforth, too,
the history of *The Alchemist* became virtually the history
of Abel Drugger.

V

1743–1763

Two months after Garrick's first appearance, *The Gentleman's Magazine* published an essay on "The Character
of an excellent Actor," lauding the new performer:

Of all the Employments in Life I know none so arduous in
every Respect as that of a *Player.* . . . The Statesman, Soldier,
and Man of Letters have their respective Connections *one* with
the *other*, but what in Nature can be more distinct than the Parts
of *King Lear* and *Abel Drugger?* Few Readers who are *charm'd*
with *one* enter at all into the *Humour* of the *other*; how great then
the Merit not only of entering into the *Poet*'s Sentiment thoroughly in *both*, but to out-do *Shakespeare* and *Johnson*, by performing *both* Parts so *naturally*, as that in Truth they are not
perform'd at all; for I have an *Actor* in my Eye whose *greatest
Merit* is that he is *none*; whose Look, whose Voice, whose Action
have nothing of the *Player*, but so much of the *Person* he represents, that he puts the *Playhouse* out of our Heads, and *is* actually to *us* and to *himself*, what *another Actor* would only *seem to
be.* . . . They are separate *Kinds* of *Pleasure* which we take, in
seeing the same Piece on the *Stage*, and *reading* it in our *Closets*.
The *Alchymist* of Ben. *Johnson* moves the *Many* on the *Stage*,
but the *Few* only in *Print*; the *Merit* of the *Play* is, that it *strikes*,
but the *high Reputation* of the *Author* arises from another Motive, that his *Work* is no less pleasing on *Reflection.* . . . There
requires as much Application to *play* one of *Shakespeare*'s Characters well, as to *form* it; and a great deal more to hit *one* of
Johnson's, because the *Poet* follows his own *Genius*, the *Player*
that of *another Man.*[1]

1. XIII (1743), 253–255.

The contrast between Lear and Drugger was to become common, but *The Alchemist* received some questioning from a pamphleteer who was offended by the increased price of tickets, the production of harlequin plays, and the practise of seldom playing pieces with all the good actors in the cast on the same night:

Which would be most likely to gain you a full House To-morrow, the *Fair Penitent*, for Instance, with Mrs. *Cibber*, Mr. *Garrick*, and Mr. *Sheridan*, as the Town thinks they have a Right to see them all three together; this Play alone, I say, or the *Alchymist*, as you have it now perform'd, with one of your *Pantomimes?* Who is there but wou'd crowd to see the one, and who, I had almost said, wou'd even be hired to sit out the other? Here then, Sir, lies a plain and open Method for you to get good Houses and good Credit, to receive at once People's Money and their Thanks.[1]

In 1744 Corbyn Morris wrote a valuable discussion of Jonson's characters, paying particular attention to Abel Drugger, and noting Jonson's skill in drawing despicable characters of whom one easily tires:

Johnson in his Comic Scenes has expos'd and ridicul'd *Folly* and *Vice*. . . . *The Alchymist*, *Volpone* and *Silent Woman* of *Johnson*, are most exquisite Satires. . . .

It may be further remark'd, that *Johnson* by pursuing the most useful Intention of *Comedy*, is in Justice oblig'd to *hunt down* and *demolish* his own Characters. Upon this Plan he must necessarily expose them to your *Hatred*, and of course can never bring out an amiable Person. His *Subtle*, and *Face* are detected at last, and become mean and despicable. Sir *Epicure Mammon* is properly trick'd, and goes off ridiculous and detestable. The *Puritan Elders* suffer for their Lust of Money, and are quite nauseous and abominable. . . .

But in remarking upon the Characters of *Johnson*, it would be unjust to pass *Abel Drugger* without notice; This is a little, mean, sneaking, sordid Citizen, hearkening to a Couple of

1. *Stage Policy detected; or, some select Pieces of Theatrical secret History laid open*, 1744, p. 17.

Sharpers; who promise to make him rich; they can scarcely pre-
vail upon him to resign the least Tittle he possesses, though he is
assur'd, it is in order to get more; and your Diversion arises,
from seeing him *wrung* between *Greediness* to *get* Money, and
Reluctance to *part* with any for that Purpose. . . . However, this
Character upon the whole is *mean* and *despicable*, without any of
that free spirituous jocund Humour abounding in *Shakespear*.
But having been strangely exhibited upon the Theatre, a few
Years ago, with odd Grimaces and extravagant Gestures, it has
been raised into more Attention than it justly deserved; It is
however to be acknowledg'd, that *Abel* has no Hatred, Malice or
Immorality, nor any assuming Arrogance, Pertness or Peevish-
ness; And his eager Desire of getting and saving Money, by
Methods he thinks lawful, are excusable in a Person of his Business; He is therefore not odious or detestable, but harmless and
inoffensive in private Life; and from thence, correspondent with
the Rule already laid down, he is the most capable of any of
Johnson's Characters of being a Favourite on the Theatre.[1]

This critique admits the inconsistency involved in making
Drugger an important rôle in the play and furnishes an
excuse, if one were needed, for his popularity with the
audiences of the day.

Allusions to *The Alchemist* begin to appear once more in
the letter-writers. Horace Walpole, writing to Horace
Mann on February 14, 1746, about Lord Bath's refusal
of the treasury, describes how that gentleman, whose am-
bition and courage could not match his avarice, went to
give his decision to the king, when "Bounce! went all the
project into shivers, like the vessels in Ben Jonson's *Alchemist*, when they are on the brink of the philosopher's
stone." [2]

The Alchemist was described in 1747 as "still frequently
acted with very great Applause," [3] and in the same year

---

1. *An Essay Towards Fixing the True Standards of Wit*, pp. 33–36.
2. Mrs. Paget Toynbee, *The Letters of Horace Walpole*, Oxford, II (1903),
176. This episode was used with considerable sensibility by Mrs. Elizabeth
Montagu: see Matthew Montagu, *The Letters of Mrs. Elizabeth Montagu*, Boston, 1825, III, 189–190. See *The Alchemist*, IV. iii.
3. *A Compleat List of all the English Dramatic Poets*, p. 122.

TICKET FOR *THE ALCHEMIST*

Samuel Foote noted that the play observed the three unities, bonds which did "not hit the Taste and Genius of the free-born luxuriant Inhabitants of this Isle," who would "no more bear a Yoke in Poetry than Religion." [1]

An amusing anecdote is told in Fielding's *Covent-Garden Journal* in 1752:

It happened some Years since, that a low Farce was to be acted for the first Time after *Ben Johnson's Alchymist.* Two Heroes in the Boxes, had come there with an Intent to amuse themselves in damning the Farce. As their Attention to the Play had been taken off by their own more sublime Conversation, together with that of the Ladies who dispense Oranges, they unluckily took the End of the Play for the Beginning of the Farce, and set to hissing with the Voice not of Serpents but of Geese. The House was amazed; nor were they less amazed themselves, not to hear their Musick kindly returned by their Brother-Heroes in the Pit. In short, the Riddle was not solved, 'till one who sat near them, informed them that the Play was not yet over, and of course the Farce not yet begun. This a little discomposed them, but they soon comforted themselves by observing *'twas but a musty Piece of old Johnson's, and so it did not much signify.* [2]

In 1753 Bishop Hurd, studying the local follies exposed in *The Alchemist,* noted the necessity of exaggerating characters for effectiveness on the stage. Exaggeration, he admitted, led to farce, but *The Alchemist,* on the whole, he considered a true comedy:

For as to the *subject* of this Play's being a *local folly,* which seems to bring it directly under the denomination of Farce, it is but just to make a distinction. Had the *end and purpose* of the Play been to expose *Alchymy,* it had been liable to this objection.

1. *The Roman and English Comedy,* p. 20.
2. Ed. G. E. Jensen, New Haven, 1915, I, 289–290. The anecdote is probably true. The farce referred to was *George Dandin,* played only once, on November 25, 1747. See the manuscript account book of Drury Lane, *Tit for Tat,* Harvard Theatre Collection, and Genest, IV, 234.

But this mode of *local folly*, is employed as the *means* only of exposing *another* folly, extensive as our Nature and coeval with it, namely *Avarice*. So that the subject has all the requisites of true *Comedy*. . . . On the whole, the *Alchymist* is a Comedy in just form, but a little *Farcical* in the extension of one of its characters.[1]

The first formal criticism of Garrick in *The Alchemist* may be found in *The London Chronicle*, March 5–8, 1757. After some controversy over the term "Alchymist," the material for which was drawn from Whalley's edition, the reviewer (probably Arthur Murphy) remarked on the obsolescence of alchemy and praised the play:

This Play sets out finely in the Midst of Things: The Plot is admirably conducted; and the fourth Act is, perhaps, one of the finest, for Contrivance, in the English Drama. We may venture, notwithstanding, to assert, that the Alchymist owes its present Reception on the Stage, to the inimitable Performance of Mr. Garrick. It is, indeed, no wonder, that all Degrees of People conspire to applaud the Performer, who has roused all the noblest Emotions of the Soul, when they see him descending to an Imitation of Nature in her meanest Littlenesses of Action. And yet how admirably does he exhibit the minutest Circumstances, with the exactest Precision, without Buffoonry or Grimace: — There is no twisting of Features, no Squinting, but all is as correct as if a real Tobacco Boy were before us. It is really surprizing how he, who has occasionally looked unutterable Things, can present us such a Face of Inanity: The Actor who can amazingly reach the Sublime in a Lear, or Hamlet, and then exhibit the most ridiculous Appearances, must be possessed of such two-fold and opposite Powers, as hardly ever before concentered in one Man, and are not likely to form such a Tragicomic Genius again.

The Alchemist now began to influence political satire, as *Volpone* had done previously. In 1759 the author of *The Pittiad* hid under the pseudonym of "Doll Common," and

1. *The Works of Richard Hurd*, D.D., II, 102.

The London Chronicle printed another satire called *Doll Common. A Fragment.*[1]

In the first period of Garrick's acting in *The Alchemist,*— the twenty years from 1743 until his trip to Italy in 1763 and the temporary inheritance of the part by Thomas Weston,— he played the rôle of Drugger sixty-four times, and it is interesting to observe that at the end of the period he and Mrs. Bennett were the only actors left from the original cast of 1743. Obviously, a continuity of performance so striking left its impression on the outpouring of critics, poets, satirists, and journalists; although many allusions to the rôle are sheerly impressionistic, telling us nothing technically of the actual stage performance, others aid in reconstructing Garrick's mannerisms.

At the outset he was compelled to rid Drugger of the traditions foisted upon the rôle by Theophilus Cibber. There is a favorite story about Abel Drugger in the eighteenth-century jest-books. A young fellow came to seek employment at the playhouse, affirming that his talent lay in comedy; after seeing a specimen of his powers, Quin asked if he had ever played any parts in comedy.

"Yes," said the fellow, "I have played Abel in The Alchymist."

"I am rather of opinion you played Cain," said Quin, "for I am certain you murdered Abel."[2]

So far as the point of the jest goes, the fellow might have been Cibber. Davies suggests that he acquired an extravagant manner from frequently playing Pistol; he mixed so many ridiculous tricks in the part that, although the galleries laughed and applauded, the more judicious spectators were annoyed.[3]

1. February 27–March 1, 1759. The satire was reprinted in *The Universal Magazine*, XXIV (1759), 95–96, and in *The New Foundling Hospital for Wit*, 1786, IV, 29–32.

2. *Ben Johnson's Jests*, p. 15; *Quin's Jests*, 1766, p. 34; H. Bennet (John Pinkerton), *The Treasury of Wit*, 1786, II, 143.

3. *Memoirs of the Life of David Garrick, Esq.*, I, 60–61.

William Cooke said that Garrick was so concerned about the probable jealousy of Cibber, that he held several private rehearsals of the character before Macklin and other friends. Cooke, who could have had the story from Macklin, represents Macklin as saying, "Theophilus, Sir, though laughable in many respects, rather *farcified* this part too much; he was for making *fun for himself*, as well as the audience — a lamentable mistake for an actor! But Garrick's awkward, sober simplicity, at once announced the ignorant, selfish Tobacconist; and he very properly left his audience to *divert themselves* with the very singular absurdities of the character." [1]

The best and most tolerant account, however, was given only four years after Garrick's première, by Samuel Foote, in *The Roman and English Comedy Consider'd and Compar'd*:

Suffer me to confine [the different species of acting comedy] to two, the Comic and the Comical. And, in order to give you a clear Idea of what I mean by the Distinction, cast your Eye on the *Abel Drugger* of G. and the *Abel Drugger* of C. I call the simple, composed, grave Deportment of the former Comic, and the squint-ey'd grinning Grimace of the latter Comical. The first obtains your Applause, by persuading you that he is the real Man. The latter indeed opens your Eyes, and gives you to understand, that he is but personating the Tobacco-Boy: But then to atone for the Loss of the Deception, you are ready to split with Laughter, at the ridiculous Variations of his Muscles. It may indeed be objected, that this Conduct destroys all Distinction of Characters, and may as well become *Sir John Daw*, or *Sir Amorous La Tool* [*sic*], as honest *Nab*. Well, and what then? Don't Folks come to a Play to laugh? And if that End be obtained, what matters it how? [2]

A clue to Cibber's horse-play is given in a "PROLOGUE for Mr. CIBBER, junior, written by Aaron Hill," apparently when Cibber was engaged in the disgraceful action with

---

1. *Memoirs of Charles Macklin, Comedian*, 2d ed., 1806, pp. 109-110.
2. Pages 38-39.

William Sloper over his second wife. Hill pretends that
Theophilus stands silent, twirling his hat "with a half-
suppressed Leer of Irresolution," and striking Drugger's
attitude, with crimped penitential "tweer":

> Not ABEL's three-tir'd *squint* more *queerly* show'd him,
> When the *crack'd urinal* had half-o'erflow'd him.
>
> .   .   .   .
>
> I'm a poor sinful cur — heav'n un-bewhelp me!
> Be-mus'd — be-creditor'd — *be-wiv'd*, God help me!
> Plung'd, in a sea of woes — past all enduring;
> Yet, not one woe, but was — *my own procuring.*[1]

Until 1747 Garrick and Cibber shared the part at Drury
Lane, so that the example chosen by Foote was undoubtedly the most timely one for his illustration. Cibber
played Drugger for the last time on the English stage on
September 25, 1746, but that he continued to give pleasure
with his conception of the tobacconist is witnessed by a
letter from Dublin in 1752.[2]

Praise of Garrick in verse abounds; the earliest poem
mentioning his Drugger was printed in September, 1743,
when Garrick had acted in *The Alchemist* only four times.
It is interesting also as a Miltonic imitation:

> *Roscius, Paris*, of the stage,
> Born to please a learned age,
> Come again to grace the scene
> With the lover's placid mien:
> Quick resume the sword and shield,
> Be the king in *Bosworth* field.
>
> .   .   .   .   .
>
> Now incite our hopes and fears;
> Come and fill our eyes with tears.
> Shift the Scene to scenes of wit;
> Shew the whining, cuckold cit:
> In a face that's not your own,
> Make the foolish lubbard known:

---

1. *The Works of the Late Aaron Hill, Esq.*, 2d ed., 1754, III, 21–22.
2. *A Lick at a Liar; or, Calumny Detected* [1752], p. 21.

Come and shake our sides with joy,
In the droll *Tobacco-Boy*:
Roscius, Paris, of the stage,
Born to please a learned age.[1]

It is singularly fortunate that Garrick was both author and actor and that in his early career he produced several pamphlets as a result of his terror of criticism. In 1744 when he was planning to revive *Macbeth*, he wrote a humorous attack on himself in order to forestall censures. The pamphlet, rich in material on Abel Drugger from the performer himself, tells how he felt in playing the part and throws light on some of his stage business:

When *Abel Drugger* has broke the *Urinal*, he is *mentally absorb'd* with the different Ideas of the *invaluable* Price of the *Urinal*, and the Punishment that may be inflicted in Consequence of a Curiosity, no way appertaining or belonging to the Business he came about. Now, if this, as it certain *is*, the Situation of his Mind, How are the different Members of the Body to be agitated? Why Thus, — His *Eyes* must be revers'd from the Object he is most intimidated with, and by dropping his *Lip* at the some [*sic*] Time *to* the Object, it throws a trembling *Languor* upon every *Muscle*, and by declining the right Part of the Head *towards* the *Urinal*, it casts the most *comic Terror* and *Shame* over all the *upper* Part of the Body, that can be imagin'd; and to make the *lower* Part equally ridiculous, his *Toes* must be *inverted* from the *Heel*, and by *holding* his *Breath*, he will unavoidably give himself a *Tremor* in the *Knees*, and if his *Fingers*, at the same Time, seem *convuls'd*, it finishes the compleatest low Picture of *Grotesque Terror* that can be imagin'd by a *Dutch* Painter. — Let this be compar'd with the *modern Copies*, and then let the Town judge.[2]

Breaking crockery or plaster-of-Paris statuettes on the stage is one of the surest forms of amusing the public,

1. *The Gentleman's Magazine*, XIII, 489. For an early prose appreciation see [James Boaden], *The Private Correspondence of David Garrick*, I (1831), x–xi.
2. *An Essay on Acting: In which will be consider'd The Mimical Behaviour of a Certain fashionable faulty Actor*, pp. 6–8. For adverse criticism of Drugger's urinal see the review of *The Alchemist* as played January 23, 1762, in *The Universal Museum*, January, 1762, p. 46.

but the breaking of Abel Drugger's urinal had a purely accidental origin. Thomas Wilkes tells the following anecdote:

The introducing this incident was first owing entirely to accident. It happened to old Cibber, who was allowed to play this character well. He, while the other personages were employed, rather than stand idle, was fiddling about the table of the Alchymist; and by way of filling up time, took up the urinal, and held it to the light, when it by chance slipping through his fingers, broke to pieces; and he had presence of mind to put on an air of distress happy to the time and the place; it told to admirable purpose. He played the part afterwards as usual; but the audience obliged him to restore the accidental addition; and it has been ever since retained by every other performer. Abel Drugger is certainly the standard of low comedy; and Mr. Garrick's playing it the standard of acting in this species of comedy.[1]

When Garrick acquired the joint patenteeship of Drury Lane with James Lacy in April, 1747, William Whitehead wrote an ode in his honor, in which the news was brought to Parnassus, to the delight of the Nine:

> O thou, where-e'er you fix your praise,
> BRUTE, DRUGGER, FRIBBLE, RANGER, BAYS!
> O join with her in my behalf,
> And teach an audience when to laugh.
> So shall buffoons with shame repair
> To draw in fools at Smithfield fair,
> And real humour charm the age,
> Tho' FALSTAFF shou'd forsake the stage.[2]

But eulogy was not unalloyed. Some people felt that Garrick was already resting on his laurels: in one coffee-house a knot of critics inveighed against him for not acting oftener; at the next a cluster of youths called his honesty into question for playing so much more for himself than

1. *A General View of the Stage*, pp. 257–258. Unfortunately, there is no evidence that Colley Cibber ever played Drugger.
2. *A Collection of Poems In Three Volumes. By Several Hands*, 1748, II, 257; W. Whitehead, *Poems on Several Occasions, with The Roman Father*, 1754, p. 105.

he had for other managers. Other minds, eager to find flaws in a public idol, considered him given up wholly to ease and pleasure, careless of his reputation as an actor, and condemned

your frequent Repetition of Characters of little Consequence, such as *Chamont, Hastings, Lothario,* Capt. *Plume, Abel Drugger,* Sir *John Brute,* &c. and your seldom appearing in those of greater, such as *Hamlet, Richard, Lear, Macbeth,* &c.[1]

Sir John Hill, in 1750, continued the analysis of Drugger by writing that the public should give no applause to an actor representing a fool on the stage, unless it were perfectly certain that he was not a fool in actuality:

If the managers of our theatrical entertainments should chuse to put Mr. *Anderson* or Mr. *Usher* into the part of *Abel Drugger* it is possible that the folly of the part might hang more naturally about them than it does about Mr. *Garrick;* but 'tis not this that an audience expects on such occasions: we may venture to foretel, that neither we nor our children shall ever see that character with so much pleasure as we now see it play'd by Mr. *Garrick,* unless, which is scarce probable, another actor of equal merit should undertake it.[2]

During the same year was published the first of the imitations of *The Dunciad* to concern itself with stage-players, the extremely rare satire, *The Rosciad,* antedating Churchill's more famous *Rosciad* by ten years. England's leading actors are summoned before Melpomene and Thalia, beneath whose thrones are seated Shakspere and Jonson. Quin recites his merits; then Garrick, "the *Cornavian Roscius,*" reviews his rôles,— Richard, Hamlet, Lear, Gloster:

This is my sphere: 'tis pleasure to my soul
To probe the tender parts of *Nature*; tears

1. *D—ry L—ne P—yh—se Broke Open. In a Letter to Mr. G——*, 1748, pp. 20–21.

2. *The Actor,* p. 62. See also pp. 216, 318; *The Actor,* 1755, pp. 147, 279; *The Inspector,* 1753, II, 162.

Nobly to draw, and angelize the mind.
Or, if the sock delights me, *Drugger* there
Exposes folly; and in *Archer* flames
The gay prevailing lover.[1]

The London Daily Advertiser and Literary Gazette on November 21, 1751, published another "Ode addressed to Mr. Garrick," eight days before his first appearance as Kitely in *Every Man in his Humour*:

Now into gayer Scenes descend,
The sportive Rake, or honest Friend:
Sir John we wonder at in thee;
Canst thou put on Absurdity?
     Thou canst: — And Bays is all thy own —
New form'd — new Rapture to the Town;
While Johnson's Humour sways thy Face,
And Drugger charms without Grimace.

The Theatrical Manager: A Dramatic Satire (1751), one of those virulent attacks frequently directed at Garrick by such men as William Shirley and William Kenrick, fretted at the manner in which Garrick directed public taste and imagined a dialogue between Vaticide (Garrick) and Buck (a modern gentleman). Vaticide described how the players had faced empty houses while performing tragedies:

VATICIDE

Mark the Sequel of my Tale: The Day following a Report prevailed, of your humble Servant's appearing in the simple Character of *Ben Johnson's Nab*, which so suited with the idle Humour of the Town, that you would have been surprized at the immediate Dispatches from all Quarters, the Abundance of painted Liveries from People of the first Rank and Quality, and the many ceremonious Epistles from the Ladies, laying themselves under the greatest Obligations for the bare Promise of Admittance; such was their forward Zeal at the Night of Performance, that the House (vulgarly speaking) was stuffed before Five, for fear of being superseded.

1. Lines 356–361.

BUCK

But at so trifling, and so disguising a Character, what could be their Reason?

VATICIDE

A mere Woman's: Because they did.[1]

The public was informed in 1753 that "were it possible to fill the House with *Puritans*, the *Drama's* profess'd Enemies, they would involuntary weep at his *Lear*, and laugh at his *Abel Drugger*," [2] and Mrs. Montagu wrote four seasons later a letter steeped in gentle sensibility:

> We are born to die, and die to be born again, and the fool that laughed, and the other fool that cried, were neither of them true philosophers in my opinion; there is hardly cause for mirth or melancholy in any thing that passes on our stage. He that tops his part like Mr. Garrick, whether it be Abel Drugger the tobacconist, or a great emperor, will leave the world with applause, and at last have a great benefit.[3]

An adverse view was taken in 1758 by a writer who objected to the quantity of attention being paid to the modern Roscius and undertook a candid survey of his merits. In tragedy Garrick was surpassed by others, in middle characters like Ranger, he was excellent, but "in lower comedy, or rather farcical characters, he distinguishes himself more by grimace than humour, such as *Bays*, *Fribble*, *Abel Drugger*, and others." [4] So criticism proceeded, ranging from panegyric to downright abuse. *The London Chronicle* for December 19–21, 1758, lamented his efforts to outdo Woodward as Marplot, objecting that though nature "with the help of chalk and charcoal makes him a *Lear* or an *Abel Drugger*," he had not the physique

---

1. Pages 4–5. *The Monthly Review*, IV (1751), 305, called it a "wretched performance," typical of "the virulence of scriblers."
2. *The Present State of the Stage in Great-Britain and Ireland, and the Theatrical Characters of the Principal Performers . . . Impartially Considered*, p. 21.
3. *Letters*, III, 121.
4. *The Literary and Antigallican Magazine*, January, 1758, p. 20.

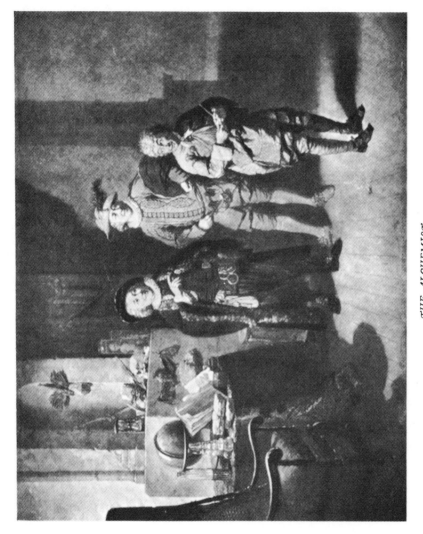

THE ALCHEMIST

BURTON AS SUBTLE, PALMER AS FACE, AND GARRICK AS DRUGGER

for this new part, which he acted compositely, being now Ranger, now Don John, now Abel Drugger, and reminding the critic of the miser who was happy when he picked his own pocket of a guinea and locked it up with joy in his bureau.

In 1759 a pamphleteer was so impressed with the way in which Garrick eclipsed everyone else on the stage at the same time, that he recommended retirement. His account is lively:

I, like a fool, the other night, went to see the *Alchymist:* I saw *Burton* and *Palmer* plain enough, till *Abel Drugger* came on, fiddling with his shop-keeper's apron. He no sooner came on than away went *Subtle*, and captain *Face*: says I, to one near me, is not this monstrous, that *Subtle* and *Face* should go off the stage, at the time when *Nab* wants them. He answered, that he thought it unaccountable, and that he was served so once before the last season; and that if he had recollected himself in that particular, he would not have come to see *Abel Drugger* alone.

'You know the plot, says he, is mixt, and has a variety of persons in the drama, but the devil a one person here, but *Abel Drugger*. — You shall see him fight a parcel of *Shadows*, and beat them off presently: He is excellent in *Skiomachy*. He did so, in a very short time, beating the air, with as much dexterity, as if there had been a dozen people on the stage: Well, said I, to the gentleman near me, I don't like this egotism, for as *Young* the satyrist expresses it,

and I's *the little hero of each tale.*[1]

In *The Alchemist* there is no indication of a boxing-match for Drugger. The business was Garrick's improvisation, as noted in *The Theatrical Review* for February 1, 1763:

If Mr. Garrick has any particular defect as a comedian, 'tis barely this, and from which few actors are exempt; namely, an occasional compliance with the viciated taste of too many of the

1. *Reasons Why David Garrick, Esq., Should not Appear on the Stage, in a Letter to John Rich, Esq.*, pp. 16–17. See *An Enquiry into the real Merit of a certain popular Performer*, 1760, p. 14.

audience, in introducing the outré, for the sake of a laugh, where the author never intended it. The first is that of boxing in Abel Drugger: This character, as drawn by Johnson, is that of a most credulous, timid, pusilanimous wretch; the Broughtonian attitudes, into which Mr. Garrick throws himself, are utterly inconsistent with the part; and consequently the weakness of those who are pleased with, and applaud it, is obviously manifest.[1]

The fault lay wholly with Garrick, who by his own authority, encroached upon the part of Kastril, the "angry boy" (acted "incomparably" by Yates), in the fourth act of the play, where Surly is challenged and driven off the stage. Pugilism was natural to Kastril and in character; it should never have been performed by Abel Drugger.[2] Garrick's reasons for assuming Kastril's scene are obvious: Drugger leaves the stage for the last time immediately after Surly's departure, and Garrick realized the value of a vigorous exit.

Criticism of the first period of Garrick's Drugger ends in a dialogue between the Manager (Garrick) and one of the officers of the theatre, who are discussing the complaints of the public over the increased price of tickets:

Coadj. And then, to talk of the superiority of the actors of those times. What is even Booth, or Wilks, or all of them put together, compared to Roscius, the modern *Roscius*!

Man. O — you compliment, Sir, — pray, good Sir, —

Coadj. Not at all, the world, the impartial world must allow your amazing superiority over all your predecessors and cotemporaries. — Who, besides yourself, could ever gain the amazing height of Comedy and Tragedy? — Who, before you, ever excelled in Lear and Abel Drugger? — Who, before you, ever attempted Fribble and Richard 3. with equal success, with equal applause?

Man. Sir, you are too Kind; — I beg —

Coadj. Not at all. — I appeal to every one in the Green-

1. Page 80.
2. Thomas Davies, *Dramatic Miscellanies*, II, 108. The acting version (*Bell's British Theatre*, XVII [1777], 75) gives the scene to Kastril.

room, if what I have said, is not devoid of all flattery, and nothing but the genuine truth?

Omnes. Nothing but the truth, — nothing else.[1]

On April 9, 1763, the first period ended. In September Garrick set out on the grand tour, and when *The Alchemist* was next presented, on December 17, Abel Drugger was played by Weston, whose simplicity in the part threatened to excel that fine art which in spite of occasionally unfavorable criticism, Garrick must have brought to his playing in order to command such praise. With the exception of Mrs. Bennett, he had outlasted every actor in the original cast. It is necessary to examine by what steps the cast was altered during the two decades. There was little criticism of individuals, for they were mere backgrounds for the tobacconist, who took all the bows to himself.[2]

After Mills gave up acting Subtle in 1749, the part fell to Bridges, who had played it in 1744, as well as Lovewit in 1748; he was succeeded in 1753 by Burton, at the time well-known for Justice Clement. Woodward followed Burton for three years from 1755 to 1758, but Burton reassumed the part in 1758 and acted it for fourteen years without rivalry.

Cross succeeded Macklin as Face in 1748, acting until 1753, when Woodward took the part. Woodward acted as Face for only two years; W. Palmer succeeded and played steadily for fourteen years, after which he acted Dapper until 1774, and J. Palmer played Face until 1768. W. Palmer acted also Master Stephen, Master Matthew, and Truewit.

Henry Vaughan, brother of Mrs. Pritchard, performed as Dapper from 1748 to 1766. His Dapper was mentioned

1. *A Dialogue in the Green-Room upon a Disturbance in the Pit,* 1763, pp. 9–10.

2. There are two unauthentic but amusing anecdotes about Garrick's Drugger. See William Cooke, *Memoirs of Charles Macklin,* pp. 110–111; *The Thespian Magazine,* I (1793), 278; Thomas Davies, *Memoirs of the Life of David Garrick,* I, 61–62.

in *The Rosciad*. Lovewit was played by a succession of
minor actors until Packer took the rôle in 1759 and kept it
until 1776. Berry as Sir Epicure Mammon was followed
in 1759 by Robert Bransby, who had already played four
years as Lovewit, and in 1762 by James Love (whose real
name was Dance), characterized by *The Dramatic Censor*
as "the bloody murderer of blank verse." [1] Bransby assumed the part again in 1774 when Love relinquished it.
Of Love's Sir Epicure, Davies wrote that the outline was
well drawn, but "there was a deficiency of glowing and
warm tints which such a ripe dupe in folly required, and
the character amply afforded. Love's conceptions of the
part were just, but his want of power to execute his meaning rendered his acting imperfect." [2] Sir Epicure required
fewer actors than any other part in the comedy; from the
beginning of the century to 1776 only five performers
played the part, whereas for Tribulation eleven were
needed, and for Dapper and Lovewit twelve each.

Surly was in the hands of Charles Blakes from 1746
until his death in 1763, when Robert Baddeley took the
part and kept it, except for two years, until 1776. His
other Jonsonian rôles were Kastril, and Cutbeard in
Colman's revival of *The Silent Woman* in 1776. Clough
followed Brownsmith as Tribulation in 1759 and acted
until Hartry succeeded him in 1766. Hartry kept the
part until 1774. Phillips, who played Ananias steadily
from 1755 to 1764, had taken the rôle as early as 1744,
but the part was particularly unsteady, and during the
first Garrick period five actors were engaged for it, including Woodward and Shuter.

In the years from 1743 to 1763 there were many performances "By Particular Desire" and two "By Command." No doubt the most far-reaching influence of the
productions was Garrick's innovation on April 14, 1753,
when he showed his interest in the details of accurate his-

1. II, 492.
2. *Dramatic Miscellanies*, II, 109–110.

torical costuming (already displayed two years before at the revival of *Every Man in his Humour*), by advertising the play with "The Characters dress'd in the Habits of the Time." Ten years passed before the managers of Covent Garden adopted Garrick's idea, which was to develop in the nineteenth century into the excessive realism of Sir Henry Irving. Garrick's idea was in itself good, and since this aspect of his managerial genius has scarcely been done justice, it is pleasant to emphasize here the value of researches, which together with Horace Walpole's much-cited bastard-Gothic battlements at Strawberry Hill and William Beckford's artificial ruins at Bath, indicated that new and uneasy desires were stirring the complacency of the mid-century mind with an eagerness for comprehending the past, where, for all they knew, lay the Golden Age.

VI

The Alteration

Garrick's problem in altering *The Alchemist*, a play very long and highly wrought technically, was to reduce the bulk without changing the progress of events, because once the sequence was tampered with, the carefully graded continuity was almost irreparably destroyed and suspense was ruined. The acting version,[1] therefore, consists of a great number of minor cuts, but no characters are wholly eliminated as in *Volpone*, and no scenes are expanded as in *Every Man in his Humour*. It is clearly impossible, without employing a dull tabular scheme, to list each cut, for there were no less than one hundred fifty-four of them, varying from one line to three pages; it is far more important to understand the tendencies followed by the acting-version and the reasons for them.

1. References are made to the scene divisions of the original play in the edition by Gifford (1816), followed by Cunningham (1875) and the Mermaid edition (1894). The acting version is in *Bell's British Theatre*. The acting version of 1770 indicated somewhat fewer omissions and no additions.

The opening scene between Subtle, Face, and Dol, with its abusive language, was reduced about sixty-five lines,— a good change which started the action at once. Farther on, Dapper's part was appreciably condensed; the maker of the stage-version worked consistently, for Dapper was cut again in Act III, scene ii, and almost completely in Act V, scene ii, so that over one hundred thirty lines belonging to, or concerning him, were removed.

More than two hundred fifty lines of Sir Epicure Mammon (II. i; IV. i; IV. iii) were slashed. Mammon is the greatest character in the play, and one may readily conjecture that the portrayer of Abel Drugger did not care to risk having his own rôle dwarfed. But there were other reasons. Mammon, like Volpone, has an exceedingly luxurious imagination, and on the grounds of that delicate taste of which the eighteenth century boasted, whole speeches must fall beneath the scissors of the censor. Mammon's plans for spending his money and his intense interest in the technicalities of the alchemist's art required thorough editing to remove indecencies and obsolete allusions. When these went, the expansive quality of Mammon was destroyed, and to the eighteenth-century spectators the rôle no doubt seemed less important than it deserved. Such revision was parallel to the omission of the mountebank scene in *Volpone:* some of Jonson's most characteristic writing vanished.

The parts of Ananias and Tribulation were greatly shortened, about one hundred fifty lines. Practically the entire scene in which they first appear (III. i) has gone; but as it was concerned both with alchemy and with the tenets of the religious sect to which these preachers belonged, the loss is tolerable. Upon their next appearance (III. ii) their religious discourse was abbreviated almost a hundred lines. Only the fact that they were objects to be gulled remains. The aim here was to minimize the allusions to an obsolete sect.

The last appearance of Drugger (V. iii), which was but

momentary and during which he spoke only one line, was completely omitted, since it would have been a distinct anticlimax after his beating off Surly (IV. iv), a structural change already noted as not indicated in the acting-version and one which received unfavorable criticism throughout the Garrick period. These are the only changes in the conduct of the plot.

Other contractions were made *passim*, however, to reduce casual traits of obsolescence and the highly technical terms of alchemy which could mean little to a latter-day audience. At least fifty lines alluding to the plague, Spanish customs, and the topography of Jacobean London, as well as quibbles, word-plays, and heavy jests disappeared. A hundred lines on the extinct religion of Ananias and Tribulation went, and on alchemy almost two hundred fifty. The burden, but also the impressiveness, of rhetorical jargon was eliminated.

That *The Alchemist* is verbally the most indecent of Jonson's plays is proved by the fact that well over two hundred lines had to go before the comedy was purged, and these are exclusive of the first scene, which is not amenable to actual line counting for this purpose. Mammon's speech in the original is lush; all allusions to Dol Common are inclined to be smutty; Surly, the cynic and doubting Thomas, expresses himself with great frankness; Face has an unclean mind; and Lovewit imagines the worst when he returns to find his house occupied. It is needless to be more specific; let the most carping Puritan edit the original text, deleting all oaths and all dubiously moral references. He will find that the age of Garrick completely anticipated him.

The total number of cuts amounted to well over nine hundred lines; *The Alchemist* was so reduced in bulk that it could easily be performed in two hours and three minutes. The third act was over at 7:27 P.M. and the play at 8:33 P.M.[1] The additions to the comedy were

1. John Brownsmith, *The Dramatic Timepiece*, p. 62.

composed mainly of several single-line speeches for Abel Drugger, which had the effect of increasing his credulity. The alteration was, then, mainly a matter of omissions, which made the play, on the whole, dramatically more compact and more modern, but which destroyed much of the literary greatness of the satire and ruined the greatest character, Sir Epicure Mammon.

When Thomas Weston played the rôle of Drugger for the first time on December 17, 1763, he surprised everyone by his capital performance. It was his first attempt in a comedy by Jonson; his chief characters at Drury Lane, where he had been only since the summer of 1761, were Jeremy in *Love for Love* and Shallow in *The Merry Wives of Windsor;* at the Haymarket he had played the original Jerry Sneak in *The Mayor of Garrat,* written especially for his talents by Samuel Foote. His greatest fame was derived from his portrayal of Abel Drugger in the mutilation of *The Alchemist* known as *The Tobacconist* (1770), which he acted for the last time on September 21, 1775, but his renown began in the two performances during Garrick's absence and the one performance on April 29, 1769, for his own benefit. There are two accounts of Weston's success at his first performance. J. P. Kemble's father-in-law, Mr. Hopkins, the prompter at the theatre, kept a diary of plays which Kemble later transcribed on the playbills now in the Huntington Library. Of this performance Hopkins wrote:

Mr. Yates would not play his Part. — Abel Drugger by Mr. Weston, — who went thro' it much beyond what any one could expect, — and, considering so great a man as Mr. Garrick was his Predecessor, 'twas wonderful. — Upon the whole, I think, he played it very decently. — His Figure is much in his Favour. — He received great applause.

The Public Advertiser, annoyed because the other newspapers were habitually printing incorrect playbills, complained because they had assigned Drugger "to Mr. *King,*

instead of *Weston*, whose first Appearance it was in that
Character, and who justly gained Applause in Performance
of it." [1] King, who had previously played the part once
in 1762, acted Kastril in place of the recalcitrant Yates,
who had held it for eighteen years.

In view of the fact that Weston had played Drugger
only twice, it is curious that his performance was noticed.
But in 1766 when Hugh Kelly wrote his abusive attack
on the Drury Lane actors, he found praise for Weston's
Drugger:

> Born to delight a laughter-loving age,
> And give fresh funds of humour to the stage;
> Mark with what strength of unaffected ease,
> That happy WESTON commonly can please:
> Tho' bold, yet simple; forcible, tho' cool;
> Fine without trick; and finish'd without rule —
> In those still scenes of *scarce existing life*,
> Where SNEAK breathes only to obey a wife;
> Or where poor DRUGGER publicly display'd,
> Hangs out the mere dull animal of trade;
> There WESTON's worth with certainty may rest,
> Nor fear the strictest rigidness of test;
> There a sublime stupidity of face,
> As dead to sense as destitute of grace,
> A fix'd, relaxless vacancy of lines,
> With such true genius generally shines,
> That quite surpriz'd, tho' satisfied we gaze,
> And all is mirth, astonishment, and praise.[2]

In the summer of 1767 Foote's company, of which
Weston was a member, was attacked by George Saville
Carey in a satire called *Momus, A Poem*. Weston fared
thus:

> With face by *Bacchus*, or by *Venus* marr'd,
> For he's with both the mighty powers warr'd;
> In word expressive, and in gesture dry,
> In action simple, with a meaning eye,

---

1. December 21, 1763.
2. *Thespis; or, A Critical Examination into the Merits of all the Principal
Performers belonging to Drury-Lane Theatre*, p. 24.

> See *Weston* gravely force the hearty smile,
> Nor pall with low buffoonery the while:
> Whene'er in *Sneak* or *Drugger* he appears,
> *Garrick* attends with patient eyes and ears,
> And owns his humour natural and true,
> For *Garrick* must give genius her due.[1]

The Town and Country Magazine, a little later, found his province confined to low comedy and his merits very great in Abel Drugger, Scrub, and Dr. Last, in all of which he showed such vacuity of expression and a tone of voice so perfectly concordant, that it was impossible to see him without bursting into roars of laughter.[2] Weston was renowned for going the pace, and the subtitle of his life might well read *Love and a Bottle*. Many anecdotes are related of his exploits.[3] He was always in debt and in such terror of the bailiffs that he would frequently take to his heels and run many streets out of his way whenever he met a man of forbidding countenance.[4] It is possible that his conception of Drugger had less of art than of nature.

VII

1766–1770

Garrick returned to the stage as Abel Drugger on October 31, 1766, with three actors new to the comedy: James William Dodd, as Dapper, which he acted for three years; William Parsons, as Ananias, a rôle which he kept until the end of the Garrick period; and Hartry, making his first appearance on the stage at Drury Lane as Tribulation, which he played until 1774. Fortunately, there is a review of this revival:

This is one of the most excellent Comedies upon the English Stage. The effects it has produced by exposing the folly and imposture of Alchymy, put the Author on a footing with the

---

1. Pages 7–8. As to Garrick's opinion of Weston's Drugger see William Cooke, *Memoirs of Samuel Foote, Esq.*, 1805, I, 131–132.
2. I (1769), 93.   3. See *Garrick's Jests*, n.d., *passim*.
4. *The History of the Theatres of London . . . 1771–1795*, 1796, I, 48.

celebrated Cervantes, who in another kingdom, by his excellent humour and satire, banished the ridiculous passion for Knight Errantry. . . . Perhaps, there was never an Actor who could represent Abel Drugger in so pleasing a light as Mr. Garrick. It has been observed of him in this character, that there is a merit in letting himself down to it, when there would be none in another's performing it naturally, who was not, by nature, at all above it.[1]

The king commanded a performance of *The Alchemist* on November 13, and attended it with the queen and several of the royal family, a theatrical adventure apparently so pleasant that he spent a similar evening on March 7, 1768. At the next production, January 25, 1769, the younger John Palmer first acted Face, and Garrick himself, who had been suffering from a cold, was so well recovered that he could play Drugger. *The Theatrical Register* (1769) included a review of the performance, for notices were becoming more frequent. The newspapers began to make a business of dramatic criticism (begun by *The London Chronicle* in 1757, but soon discontinued), and opened their columns to correspondents eager to express opinions on current entertainments. *The Theatrical Register* judged that

this inimitable comedy is not more universally known, than admired; and is generally allowed to be equal in merit to the *Volpone* and *Silent Woman* of the same author. Considering the age in which it was written, the design was noble, *viz.* to lash the then prevailing passion for Alchymy, and to point out how easy it is for mankind to be imposed on, where some darling folly lends its aid to the imposture. At this period, it seems to owe much of the applause it receives from the admirable performance of Mr. *Garrick* in the part of *Abel Drugger*. [2]

1. *Lloyd's Evening Post*, November 3-5, 1766. For notes on the similarity between *Don Quixote* and *The Alchemist* see Edmund Gayton, *Pleasant Notes upon Don Quixot*, 1654, p. 3; *The Critical Review*, XXVI (1768), 205; the review of *The Alchemist* in *The London Chronicle*, December 10-12, 1771, and in *The Theatrical Review*, December, 1771, pp. 247-248.

2. Part ii, pp. 11-12.

The elder John Palmer's acting of Face, which he played until 1768, won the approval of "Anthony Pasquin, Esq." (John Williams), in *The Children of Thespis* (1785):

> Of PALMER the elder I'll give my opinion,
> No man on the stage holds so wide a dominion;
> Come Tragedy, Comedy, Farce, or what will,
> He still gives a manifest proof of his skill;
> From the BASTARD of SHAKESPEARE, and FACE of old BEN,
> To the dry namby-pamby of CUMBERLAND's pen.
> He's the Muses' great hackney, on which both together
> Oft pace thro' the Commons, in damn'd dirty weather.
> Yet he still claims applause, tho' like Proteus he changes;
> For equal to all, thro' the drama he ranges:
> And bears with much ease its vast weight on his shoulders,
> Till, like Atlas, his powers surprise all beholders,
> So graceful his step, so majestic his nod,
> He looks the descendant from Belvedere's god! [1]

Garrick's Drugger during these four years evoked the usual amount of critical comment. In March, 1765, while he was still absent from the stage, *The Gentleman's Magazine* printed a poem "*To Mr* Garrick *on the report of his leaving the Stage*," begging that, if ever the theatre were so unfortunate as to lose him, he would

> Deign some accomplish'd youths to teach,
> With all thy *nature*, all thy art,
> To mould at will th' obedient heart,
> That wond'ring and transported, we
> May think our *Garrick* still we see.
> And may thy gen'rous labours raise,
> A *Ranger*, *Macbeth*, or a *Bayes*,
> Some stripling *Hamlet*, "to surprize
> "The faculties of ears and eyes,"
> Or on the stage a *Drugger* bring,
> Or *Lear*, "*who's* ev'ry *inch a King*." [2]

---

1. 13th ed., 1792, p. 39. There were two John Palmers. The first played Face (1755–1768). The second was not related to him, but was the brother of Robert Palmer.
2. XXXV, 138. See also p. 478.

In Hugh Kelly's *Thespis* Garrick received the following encomium:

> OTHELLO'S form a BETTERTON might wear,
> And rend the soul with horror and despair;
> BOOTH might with conscious majesty declaim,
> And build on CATO a substantial name;
> In WILDAIR, WILKES most certainly might soar,
> And CIBBER'S fop set millions in a roar;
> But which of these like GARRICK cou'd appear,
> In ROMEO, SHARPE, in DRUGGER, and in LEAR;
> Fill the wide rounds of passion as they fall,
> And shine with equal excellence in all? [1]

The Theatrical Monitor; or, Green-Room Laid Open (1767) did not hold so high an opinion of Garrick: it attributed his rise to the dearth of players on the stage when he first appeared at Goodman's Fields, and lamented that, though his talents were good enough in their way, he was forced to enhance them by artifice and transform himself into such characters as Bayes and Abel Drugger.[2] The fact that Abel Drugger was, in Jonson's text, a pretty worthless figure dramatically was beginning to be acknowledged in the daily press. *The London Chronicle* in 1769 remarked that Drugger, in which Garrick made so distinguished a figure, "is but a wretched character to read; but who can resist its force when animated by his figure and action?" [3] At least one person in London, however, found himself able to resist the charm of Drugger. "Rusticus Theatricus" attended the performance on February 6, 1770, and was so disgusted that he wrote his impressions to *The London Evening Post*:

The character of *Abel Drugger* I look upon, as drawn by the celebrated Ben Johnson, to be that of a credulous, timid, pusilanimous wretch, one who, by the most miserable œconomy, has scraped together a little money, and is so careful in the preservation, and attention to every method of encreasing it, that he becomes an easy dupe to the fraudulent and designing. I must do

1. Page 6.   2. No. II, October 24, 1767.
3. December 31, 1768–January 3, 1769.

Mr. Garrick the justice to say, that the moment he made his appearance on the stage, his whole deportment held him up to be the real character the poet would represent. In his face I could see that stupid stare, and vacancy of thought; and in his manner, all that vulgarism and unfamiliarity, that peculiarly marks low life.

While I was congratulating myself on the pleasure I was receiving, and, at the same time, condemning my former want of taste, I was roused by the sudden alteration of his acting, where he discovers himself duped by the sharpers. Here I thought he would have stood in silent meditation on his folly, or, at most, run about the stage in a state of distraction: but how I was deceived! as if nature and he had instantly shaken hands and parted, he stripped off his cloaths, rubbed his hands, clenched his fists, and threw himself into all the attitudes of a modern Broughtonian bruiser.

I am easily satisfied, that the thirst of applause has induced many an actor to figure away in the *outre*; I have often seen it, and it may do very well from a country performer to a country audience; but for the Roscius of his day, playing before one of the politest audiences in the world, to accommodate his powers to the vicious palate of the rabble, for the sake of raising the momentary roar of vulgar applause, is, in my opinion, not a little derogating from so justly an established character.

The consequences of this don't even end here, for as Mr. Garrick is more copied than nature herself, by most of the present race of players, his vices are equally imitated as his perfections; and I have seen, in this particular instance I have been remarking on, one of the most natural comedians this, or perhaps, any age or nation has produced (I mean Mr. Weston) fall into the same absurdity in the very same part.[1]

But the well-meaning letter did little good. Garrick went on playing *The Alchemist* to prosperous houses which finally brought in box-office receipts of £265, and with Weston as Abel Drugger once mcre, Samuel Foote presented on October 15, 1770, at the Haymarket (as an

---

1. February 10–13, 1770. For the state of journalistic criticism at this period see *The London Magazine*, XLV (1776), 510, and C. H. Gray, *Theatrical Criticism in London to 1775*, New York, 1931, pp. 189–190.

afterpiece to his own play *The Minor*) a wretched farce called *The Tobacconist*, made from a frightfully mutilated *Alchemist*, which was destined to last until 1815, when Edmund Kean was the tobacconist and William Hazlitt the dramatic critic of the evening.

VIII

THE TOBACCONIST

It is almost matter for apology to discuss this monstrous performance, the work of a poetaster, Francis Gentleman, now chiefly remembered for his useful *Dramatic Censor*. Gentleman was an Irishman who emigrated to Bath, where he acted about 1750 at the Theatre Royal, and later to London, where he entered the Haymarket under Foote and stayed three years until his discharge in 1773. He seems to have been peculiarly determined to improve Ben Jonson, for in 1752 he produced a version of *Sejanus*, never acted; in 1770, *The Tobacconist*; in 1773, *The Pantheonites*, which has little to do with *The Alchemist* beyond the fact that the hero Dan Drugger is conceived as being the great-grandson of Abel Drugger; and in 1771, *The Coxcombs*, based on *The Silent Woman*, and, with exceptions to be noted, unpublished.[1] With reference to his mutilations of Jonson, *The Scot's Magazine*, after a summer in which *The Tobacconist* had been frequently acted at the Haymarket, printed a significant "*Epigram on Mr* Francis Gentleman's *late alteration of some of* Ben Johnson's *plays*":

> Mark the commandments, Frank,
>   Go no further —
> Is it not written,
>   *Thou shalt do no murther?*
>   *Ben Johnson's Ghost.*[2]

---

1. For comments on Gentleman see Dibdin, *A Complete History of the Stage*, V, 268; *The Theatres, A Poetical Dissection*, 1771, p. 36, probably by Gentleman himself; G. Parker, *A View of Society and Manners in High and Low Life*, 1781, I, 70–73.   2. XXXIII (1771), 485.

The idea of exploiting Weston's abilities as Drugger apparently occurred to Foote as early as the spring of 1770, for *The London Chronicle* printed in its column of theatrical intelligence:

Mr. Foote has prepared several new pieces for the stage, which are now in rehearsal; . . . *Drugger's Jubilee*, is a burlesque parody upon the Jubilee at both houses; in which Mr. Weston is to personate the modern Roscius. This piece of satire, it is imagined, will have a very fine effect.[1]

The "burlesque parody" was never presented, but on October 15, 1770, bills for *The Minor* announced that there would be "a Farce (taken from the *Alchymist*) call'd the TOBACCONIST, the Part of Abel Drugger Mr. WESTON." The prologue, which appeared immediately in *The London Chronicle*,[2] offered the only excuse for the performance except the advertisement, which confessed that "it was meant to give Mr. WESTON's established merit in the character of *Abel Drugger*, more frequent, familiar, and compact opportunity of shewing itself, than the Old Play [could] possibly afford." The prologue is far superior to the farce:

> BEN JOHNSON'S *name, in ev'ry ear of taste,*
> *Must with respect, and countenance be grac'd;*
> *No pen the lines of nature better drew,*
> *No wit or satire ever higher flew;*
> *An early pillar of the English stage,*
> *His pieces were true pictures of the age;*
> *Time-worn they feel impair — yet still must please.*
> *Nervous and just, though void of modern ease.*
>
> .   .   .   .   .   .
>
> *Search all the world, examine ev'ry part;*
> *You'll find each man an alchymist at heart*
> *In ev'ry clime we find, if truth be told*
> *The universal deity is gold.*
> *Whate'er of merit you perceive this night,*
> *Grant your old bard as his undoubted right*

---

1. June 5–7, 1770.
2. October 18–20, 1770.

My brain has laboured — feebly I confess,
Only to furnish a more modern dress.
My weak endeavours let your candor raise,
They hope indulgence, though they reach not praise.[1]

A brief summary will show how little the farce was inspired
by the original.

The farce opens with a quarrel between Subtle and Face. To
them comes Doll Tricksy, who announces the tobacconist.
Mammon and Headlong (who has a faint resemblance to Kastril) are Doll's admirers. Drugger receives instructions for
building his shop and leaves Subtle preparing for Mammon. In
the second act Mammon describes what he will buy with his
gold. He asks for his Cyprian queen, Doll, who enters, talking
mad jargon toned down from Jonson. But Subtle announces
that the works are blown *in fumo*; Mammon faints, is brought to,
and told to bring more money. Miss Rantipole, a lady of fortune fond of relating her amours, enters, for no particular reason.
Drugger returns to ask about his sign and tells of a young widow
who lives near him; she proves to be Tricksy. When Abels asks
when they are to marry, she sends him to Subtle to ask for a suitable day. Headlong brags to Doll about his boxing; Drugger
returns; Headlong picks a fight, in which, of course, Drugger is
victorious. The prize is Doll. Knowlife returns home with constables; Mammon learns the truth about the impostors. Drugger learns that Doll is Knowlife's chambermaid and comforts
himself with bachelorhood.

Now *The Tobacconist* is clearly wanton patchwork, and,
worse, there is not a single line which would bring a smile
even to a willing reader. The opening scene is vulgar indulgence in affected Billingsgate, the masterly gradations of
plot in *The Alchemist* have yielded to a succession of dull
scenes devoid of suspense, and, worst of all, Garrick's
weakness in making Abel Drugger act out of character in
fighting Surly off the stage has been developed here into a

1. Reprinted in *The London Evening Post*, October 16–18, 1770; *The London
Magazine*, XL (1771), 373; *The Town and Country Magazine*, III (1771), 385;
The Universal Magazine, XLIX (1771), 42. The prologue and a scene were
printed in *The London Chronicle*, July 16–18, 1771.

casual and inorganic climax. *The Alchemist* in "a more modern dress" was a disaster. But what of contemporary opinion?

The first performance in October, 1770, was reviewed in an unprejudiced paper, *The London Evening Post*:

> The *Tobacconist* is . . . a *disfiguration* of Ben Johnson's *Alchymist*. Mr. Gentleman . . . begged hard for mercy before the curtain was drawn up, as he said the players were all imperfect, which no doubt went a great way towards its salvation. To analize this piece particularly, would be soiling the pen of criticism, as it was nothing more than an incoherent mixture of obsolete humour and low buffoonery. What kept down even the resentment of the galleries was, now and then a little seasoning of personality; for on *Drugger's* being told by *Subtle*, "that he was born under a lucky star," he replied, "he hoped it was a *North* star."
>
> The concluding humour of this piece we must confess Mr. Gentleman has a precedent for, that of introducing *two persons boxing on the stage* for the amusement of the audience; as nothing is more common on the Dutch theatre than such gross buffoonery; which is well enough calculated for the gross of their audience, who are composed of the dregs of the people; but for such gross characters to escape the pen of an Englishman, to an English audience, is reprehensible in the highest degree, and its being tolerated can only be accounted for from that great partiality the town has long entertained for Mr. Weston's extraordinary comic abilities.[1]

The reviewer was far more correct than the critic for *The London Chronicle* after the second London performance of the farce the next July:

> Mr. Gentleman . . . seems principally to have designed to preserve the satire and ridicule of the Alchymist, but to lop off the superfluous characters, and to let it appear without its unintelligible, pedantic language, and that quaintness of expression which peculiarly distinguishes the works of Ben Johnson. —

1. October 13–16, 1770.

He has succeeded tolerably well; the modern dress and familiar-
ized diction make the piece infinitely more palatable to the
present frequenters of the Theatre, — those who admire Mr.
Weston are much indebted to Mr. Gentleman, for affording him
an opportunity of still farther exerting his abilities. Abel Drugger is certainly one of the best parts Mr. Weston plays, and the
applause so liberally bestowed on him last night, justifies this
assertion. The two new characters, are Miss Rantipole, a gay,
giddy young Lady of fortune, supported with peculiar spirit by
Mrs. Didier, and Headlong, a bruising, boxing blade, judiciously
played by Mr. Vandermere. The other parts were done justice
to by the several performers, and the whole met with repeated
shouts of approbation. Considered merely as an after-piece, the
Tobacconist has every necessary merit for the Stage, and is
extremely laughable and entertaining.[1]

Various monthly magazines criticized the piece. *The
Town and Country Magazine* [2] paraphrased the foregoing
account. *The London Magazine*, which thought Jonson's
fables "most lamentably uninteresting, his incidents heavy
and unnatural, and his catastrophes wretchedly uninstruc-
tive," insisted that Abel Drugger was what gave *The
Alchemist* its support on the stage and was so pleased with
The Tobacconist that it printed a scene from the farce.[3]
The Monthly Review judged *The Alchemist* itself "heavy
and uninteresting," but dismissed *The Tobacconist* as a
piece "of low vivacity, and that kind of wit which one
may suppose to have been begotten by Punch on the body
of the comic Muse." [4] Despite varying opinions, the farce
flourished, and there were fourteen performances before
the close of 1775. In the winters Weston performed at
Drury Lane; in the summers, at the Haymarket. The fact
that he could have animated this lifeless production is the
strongest argument for his genius, to which there were yet
many tributes before and after his death in 1776. He did
not act in *The Alchemist* after 1769.

1. July 13–16, 1771.   2. III (1771), 356.
3. XL (1771), 362–363.   4. XLV (1771), 152.

In November, 1771, *The Theatres, A Poetical Dissection*, devoted a passage to Weston which seems an excellent summary of his life and character:

> Weston, but wherefore need we speak of him,
> Begot by Momus upon Lady Whim;
> While laughing multitudes declare, with glee,
> His face the essence of true comedy;
> Nor does mechanic manner stiffly spoil
> The pleasure of involuntary smile;
> Scrub, Abel-Drugger, Sneak, and Doctor Last,
> Must stand unrival'd his peculiar cast;
> Tho' in Medea's kettle boil'd anew,
> Garrick would lose by parallel review:
> Then happ'ly plac'd, beyond all public strife,
> Use, Tom, some caution in thy private life;
> So shall not creditors enjoyment damp,
> Nor sordid Managers thy income cramp.[1]

Theatrical Biography (1772) merely confirms one's opinion that Weston found the part of Drugger unusually adapted to his gifts, by ascribing to him a natural simplicity which made him appear to be conducting himself without any art at all. Particularly when the phial broke, he presented a natural mixture of pusillanimity and consternation that made the spectator laugh but also made him pity.[2] He seems, in short, to have combined unconscious comedy with that simple pathos that makes Mr. Charles Chaplin a great comic actor.

In the early fall of 1773, Foote offered another farce by Gentleman, designed to make the most of Weston's comic powers. It was called *The Pantheonites*; the chief characters are Drugger, a tobacconist, and his wife, who, hearing that they have drawn £20,000 in a lottery, affect the manners of people of quality and launch out upon every fashionable extravagance. After two acts they discover that a mistake has been made by the lottery-office, and

---

1. Pages 52–53. *Memoirs of that Celebrated Comedian, and very Singular Genius Thomas Weston*, 1776, gives amusing sidelights on Weston's private life.
2. II, 92. See also *An Essay on Satirical Entertainments*, 1772, p. 8.

that the prize really belongs to Mrs. Drugger's sister.[1] Apparently the farce was an unnecessary addition to the repertory, for the records do not reveal that it was acted more than twice. Of course, its only relation to *The Alchemist* lies in the name of the hero.

A year later, on August 29, 1774, Weston appeared at the Haymarket again in a *jeu d'esprit*, spoken as an interlude during the performance of *The Devil upon Two Sticks*, called *Abel Drugger's Return from the Fête Champêtre at Marybone Gardens*. Although this recitation, spoken by Weston only three times, is apparently not extant, some conjectures may be made about its content. Society went mad during the summer of 1774 over *fêtes champêtres*.[2] Garrick himself, a man of quality and social prominence, entertained his friends on August 19 at his villa at Hampton with lavish hospitality. Parts of the garden and the Temple of Shakspere were illuminated; the house was crowded. Musicians were placed in various parts of the garden, and there were fireworks directed by the famous Signor Torre, who "shewed his Skill likewise in Fireworks adapted for the Water, of which he had not given any Proof in England before." [3]

Ten days later Weston gave his monologue or skit; it was probably a satire of *fêtes champêtres* in general and of Garrick's in particular. He repeated the piece on September 5 and September 6; since it was only a local gag, he probably dropped it then. At any rate, it was probably not very funny, for the author of *The Stage of Aristophanes* (1774) wrote:

> CROWN'D with success in walks of simple nature,
> Why will you *hum us* with your *Fete Champetre*?

---

1. This farce, based on Molière's *Bourgeois Gentilhomme*, was reviewed in *The Critical Review*, XXXVI (1773), 235; *The Town and Country Magazine*, V (1773), 466–467; *The Monthly Review*, XLIX (1773), 232; *The Oxford Magazine*, 1773, pp. 345–346.

2. See *The Letters of Horace Walpole*, IX (1904), 5, 11; *The London Chronicle*, July 19–21, 1774; John Burgoyne, *The Maid of the Oaks*, 1774.

3. *The Public Advertiser*, August 25, 1774.

> Such little arts ill suit your gen'ral fame,
> And leave you open to satiric blame:
> Detest these tricks, — they're low, — don't sit with ease; —
> Nor think the *Novelty* of such schemes can please.
>
> .   .   .   .   .   .
>
> SCRUB, ABEL DRUGGER, and an hundred more,
> Set the two theatres in continual roar.
> Then stoop not, TOMMY, from all nature's rules,
> To paltry shifts to catch the praise of fools.[1]

In September, 1775, Weston resumed playing in *The Tobacconist* for the last two performances of Abel Drugger before his death. The last poetical appreciation of his skill was written in a poem attributed to Hugh Downman, *The Drama* (1775) [2]:

> Without an effort, WESTON gains applause,
> Nature has made him what the poet draws:
> Others, with trick, and stage manœuvre aim,
> To strike the groundlings, and their clap obtain;
> Shew Johnson's Drugger, skill'd in Broughton art,
> And Scrub, instead of fool, a downright smart:
> But he, superior to such paltry aid,
> Ne'er makes a jest but what his author made;
> True humour, free from taint of low grimace,
> Or wild distortion, sits upon his face:
> Tho' laughter shake, unconscious he receives
> The echoing plaudit public favour gives.

He died of chronic alcoholism in January, 1776. An obituary notice in *The Town and Country Magazine* observed:

To mention Mr. Weston as an excellent comedian, would be paying him but a trifling compliment. . . . Untutored, either at school or by a taste for literature, he rushed upon the world as an unlettered mechanic, and evinced himself a real son of Thalia. . . . Scrub and Abel Drugger stampt the seal of his comic merit; and, had we never seen Mr. Garrick in those parts, we should have thought Farquhar and old Ben had Weston in their eye, when they drew those characters. Or rather, if Weston had not

1. Pages 6–7.   2. Pages 15–16.

made his appearance upon the stage till the retreat of Roscius, now so near at hand, we should almost have forgot David to admire Tom.[1]

A biography appeared almost immediately. It is remarkable that none of his critics whitewashed his sins, just as none of them condemned his acting. Whether he was drunk or sober, all agreed that one never saw Thomas Weston, but Sneak, Scrub, Sharp, or Drugger; and so accomplished was he that he never deviated from the conception he had previously formed of a character. Identical performance of a rôle, year after year, is one of the tests of great acting.[2]

IX

1770–1776

In spite of novelties like *The Tobacconist* and *Abel Drugger's Return* and criticisms which admitted more and more frankly that *The Alchemist* was showing distinct traits of obsolescence, the comedy was acted once or twice every year until Garrick's farewell on April 11, 1776. The box-office receipts increased steadily. If ever an ancient comedy left the stage with a brilliant climax, *The Alchemist* did. Ben Jonson was not to mutter in the shades, "Come leave the loathed stage, and the more loathsome age." The Londoners of George III conducted themselves with magnanimity, more perhaps out of deference to their English Roscius, than to a bard much of whose language they could not even understand.

Blue-stockings and politicians now and later found the comedy still rich for embellishing their scribblings. In 1770 a correspondent of *The Public Advertiser* was excited

1. VIII (1776), 15. See also *The London Magazine*, XLV (1776), 149.
2. For an essay on Weston by the delightful critic Thomas Holcroft see *The Theatrical Recorder*, II (1806), 112–124. See also *Memoirs of the Late Thomas Holcroft, Written by Himself, and Continued to the Time of his Death [by William Hazlitt]*, 1816, I, 254.

over a dinner given by the Earl of Chatham; he would "have liked very much to have been present at the Debate, which I dare say was as curious as that between *Subtle* and *Face*, in the first scene of the *Alchymist*, where *Doll Common* acted as Umpire." [1] Mrs. Piozzi, in her anecdotes of Dr. Johnson, recalled the time that Arthur Murphy, who had translated back into English an essay from *The Rambler* printed in French only a month before, came to Johnson to apologize and found him "all covered with soot like a chimney-sweeper, in a little room, with an intolerable heat and strange smell, as if he had been acting Lungs in the Alchymist, making *æther*." [2] And John Lucas, a tobacconist, could find no trade-card more appropriate than a picture of Garrick as Abel Drugger. [3]

The performance of December 3, 1771, received a long review in *The London Chronicle*. After praising Shakspere and Jonson as the two greatest English dramatists, the one for nature and the other for art, the reviewer considered *The Alchemist*:

In this age . . . the *Alchymist* seems to owe much of the applause it receives, from the inimitable performance of our celebrated *English Roscius*, in the character of *Abel Drugger*. Nature is greatly caricatured in this part, but it is the exaggeration of *Drugger's* folly that charms us; for it is to the placing it in a good light that we owe half the beauty of the exhibition. In this particular, Mr. Garrick stands unrivalled, and it is very unlikely we shall ever see this character so well played when this great Actor ceases to perform it. [4]

The Theatrical Review expanded this account with notes on the actors:

1. April 26, 1770.
2. S. C. Roberts, *Anecdotes of the late Samuel Johnson, LL.D., during the last twenty years of his Life. By Hesther Lynch Piozzi*, Cambridge, 1925, pp. 151–152.
3. Freeman O'Donoghue, *Catalogue of Engraved British Portraits in the Department of Prints and Drawings in the British Museum*, II (1910), 285. See also Jacob Larwood and J. C. Hotten, *The History of Signboards*, 1866, pp. 85–86.   4. December 10–12, 1771.

GARRICK AS ABEL DRUGGER
TRADE CARD OF JOHN LUCAS, TOBACCONIST

Mr. Weston has attempted [Abel Drugger] with great success, but not with equal excellence. — *Subtle* is one of the few Characters in which Mr. *Burton* exhibits any tolerable degree of merit. The late Mr. *Palmer* rendered the Part of *Face* very respectable; and the present Mr. *Palmer* is not far behind his predecessor. *Sir Epicure Mammon* is well represented by Mr. *Love*; and the under Parts of *Surly, Ananias, Tribulation,* and *Dapper,* are very well supported by Messrs. *Baddeley, Parsons, Hartry,* and Mr. *W. Palmer.* As to the Female Characters, they are of but little importance to the Piece, and it is well they are not, unless they were better supported in the Representation.[1]

Appreciations of Garrick were now a mere habit, and it was difficult to say anything original about Drugger. Possibly too much had been said already, for that character was commanding almost a monopoly of criticism. Fanny Burney attended the performance of October 14, 1773, and sat in Garrick's box.

Never could I have imagined such a metamorphose as I saw; the extreme meanness, the vulgarity, the low wit, the vacancy of countenance, the appearance of *unlicked nature* in all his motions. In short, never was character so well entered into, yet so opposite to his own. [2]

A poem in *The London Magazine* called "Proteus, Truth and Momus," inscribed to Garrick, remarked on his presenting

> The great delight of Ranger's rake,
> To make the house with laughing shake;
> The vacant looks of Drugger's fool;
> Unrivall'd in great nature's school! [3]

The London Chronicle printed yet another review of *The Alchemist* as performed on November 25, 1775:

1. I, 248–249. Mrs. Johnston played Dame Pliant (1767–1776), and Mrs. Hopkins Dol Common (1769–1776).
2. A. R. Ellis, *The Early Diary of Frances Burney,* 1889, I, 255.
3. XLIV (1775), 484–485.

Mr. Garrick performed the character of Abel Drugger in the Alchymist, on Saturday evening last, for the first time this season, to a very brilliant audience: We fancy this *contrasto* was intended as a compliment to Prince Orloff, who was half the evening however, before he could reconcile it to himself, that the gay and lively Benedick, and Ben Johnson's simple gull Abel, were represented by one and the same man; after the Count was satisfied that the performer was really Mr. Garrick, his features, (which are very expressive) began to relax, and discovered a mixture of pleasure and astonishment, till he came to the boxing scene, when he could not refrain from joining in the extravagant exclamations and bursts of applause that re-echoed through the house.[1]

At the beginning of the new year, Garrick sold his share in the theatre to Sheridan, Linley, and Dr. Ford. Describing the performance of *The Alchemist* on January 18, *The London Chronicle* records that

Mr. Garrick on Thursday night intimated to the audience his having sold his share in Drury-Lane Theatre, by answering in the part of Abel Drugger, on being asked if he had any interest at the Theatre, "I *had* some, I don't know what I *may have*." [2]

Kemble's note on the playbill for the evening indicates that "it had an effect." The last performance occurred on April 11. It was one of Garrick's first farewell appearances, two weeks before the last production of *Every Man in his Humour* and two months before the last of all his performances, Don Felix in *The Wonder*, on June 10. Mrs. Montagu wrote to him asking for a box,[3] and, indeed, everyone who could crowd into the theatre went. *The Oxford Magazine* furnished its readers an excellent account:

Mr. Garrick having publicly declared, that he should never perform the character of *Abel Drugger* in the Alchymist after last night, we were not surprized to find the house full as soon as the doors were open, and the most astonishing overflow we ever remember.

1. November 25–28, 1775.   2. January 18–20, 1776.
3. *The Private Correspondence of David Garrick*, II (1832), 370.

His performance of this character was always an excellent treat to all palates, but last night he seemed determined to give it a *gout* that should not soon be forgotten. — The bottle and boxing scenes, he carried so high that the pladits [*sic*] of the audience repeatedly shook the house. When *Face* asked whether he has any interest with the players? He replied "Yes, I play the fool now and then: — but your worship! — they say I'm old enough to be wiser: — so I intend to leave of [*sic*] now, and grow melancholy and gentlemanlike": — This stroke was universally taken and had a fine effect. However when he had finished his part, a murmur of sorrow run [*sic*] through the house as general as the applause had done during the performance.

As nothing but his singular excellence in *Drugger*, has kept the comedy on the stage for many years past, it bids very fair to lie undisturbed upon the dramatic shelf since *Roscius* has taken his leave of it.[1]

The next day Garrick wrote that he had played Abel Drugger for the last time. "I thought the audience were cracked, and they almost turned my brain."[2] On May 12 Hannah More, who had gone all the way from Bristol for these last performances, wrote to a friend that a few nights before she had seen Garrick in *Hamlet*, and that she should "have thought it . . . as impossible for Milton to have written Hudibras, and Butler Paradise Lost, as for the same man to have played Hamlet and Drugger with such superlative and finished excellence."[3] She sat next to Edmund and Richard Burke, Dr. Warton, and Sheridan, "no vulgar names," as she noted.

When the time came for the retirement, an occasional poet pictured Garrick as summoning the company and giving them notes on acting, not unmixed with satire:

1. April, 1776, p. 118. Hopkins's *Diary* gives the anecdote in substantially the same form. The passage in *The Alchemist* is in IV. iv:

"*Face.* hast thou no credit with the players?
Drugger. Yes, sir; did you never see me play the fool?"

2. Percy Fitzgerald, *The Life of David Garrick*, 1868, II, 391.

3. William Roberts, *Memoirs of the Life and Correspondence of Mrs. Hannah More*, New York, 1836, I, 58-59.

The characters that Roscius *play'd*,
Were now assembled — to a shade.
Poor Benedict, began to stare:
And tho' 'tis odd how he got there
Macbeth, protested he was *glad*,
Roscius, *too oft* had made him mad,
His crimes so painted to the life,
As — Pritchard, us'd to paint his wife:
The pensive Hamlet, smote his breast,
And on poor Yorrick's shoulder press'd:
Even Drugger, seem'd to feel the blow,
Then took a quid, to ease his woe:
Othello, little seem'd to care,
And Jaffier, was not in despair:
Yet royal Lear, sustain'd the stroke,
Tho', Barry — at the *bottom* broke:

.   .   .   .   .   .

Ranger, with nectar almost mellow,
Swore Roscius, was a noble fellow,
Then turning to unfriended Stephen,
Wish'd Ned and Davy both in heaven.[1]

"A Review of the Theatrical Character of the English Roscius" appeared in *The St. James Evening-Post*, hailing Garrick as the great benefactor of the stage, to which he had brought back natural acting and proper use of the human voice, together with a taste for Shakspere and for other almost forgotten authors from England's great literary past.[2] The essay is tinged with the spirit of *Eheu fugaces!* When Garrick died, only three years later, there was a new outburst of prose and poetry. *The Town and Country Magazine* printed an excellent memorial, pronouncing him the greatest phenomenon of the century, who had never, perhaps, had an equal as a universal actor, and never, certainly, a superior:

1. *Garrick's Looking-Glass; or, The Art of Rising on the Stage*, 1776, pp. 59–61. Ned refers to Shuter, the actor of Master Stephen in *Every Man in his Humour*, who died November 18, 1776.
   2. The article was reprinted in *The Gentleman's Magazine*, XLVI (1776), 304.

The adulators of Betterton, Booth, and Wilkes, could only admire them in particular parts, and they were obliged to acknowledge that the latitude of Mr. Garrick's talents, either in the sock or buskin, was never yet rivalled — To view him one night in Lear or Richard, the next in Scrub or Drugger, would almost destroy probability, and make us sceptics to the bills of the day.[1]

On earth nothing new could be said: eulogy could only echo trite phrases which had been bandied about for thirty-five years. So Garrick was admitted to the shades for the last scene, where he was welcomed by Woodward, Quin, Foote, and Weston. The tragedians having greeted him in blank verse, Garrick asked Holland what the shade of Ben Jonson had to say at his arrival.

HOLLAND

Johnson I saw — him poets nickname Ben;
'Though by his godfathers named — assuredly —
Benjamin — and being laureat, titled 'squire —
As managers above are all styled, squires.
Thus then did Johnson say —
"That thou by action excellent — seeming a thing
"Inanimate — a stock — a very stock — did'st to the stage
"Continue a piece, of humour wholly obsolete;
"And to thy Abel Drugger 'tis, he owes
"That now his Alchymist is not forgot —
"For which he thanks thee — not that here,
"Fame, wealth, or glory, ought avail —
"But that it is a tribute due from him to thee."

GARRICK

Well, my dear Holland, this is some comfort however. — He will allow me to be an actor then?

HOLLAND

Oh, that (he says) he neither will, nor dare dispute,
Roscius, the second — not the least — thou still must be,
And by the honourable name of Roscius,
Must to all ages be remember'd.[2]

---

1. XI (1779), vi.
2. *Garrick in the Shades; or, A Peep into Elysium; A Farce: Never Offered to the Managers of the Theatres-Royal*, 1779, pp. 28-29.

As Garrick's funeral procession passed to Westminster Abbey, John O'Keeffe thought of an elegy, which he later printed. Each of the distinguished characters that Garrick had played was fancied as lamenting him. Among them was Abel Drugger.

> For snuff-shop, Abel asked the lucky sign,
>   He bade the stars their awful silence break;
> The glass is shivered, never more to join, —
>   Himself fixed, tongue-tied, never more shall speak!
>
> As Johnson wails his Drugger's hapless fate,
>   Cries Hoadley, — "Ben, you may not weep alone,
> Soon dull oblivion blots me out of date:
>   My darling Ranger's — "Positively gone." [1]

The Alchemist now fell into complete abeyance, and the rôle of Drugger into some contempt.[2] In 1789 Philip Neve, who thought Jonson obsolete, still valued *The Alchemist* alone, considering its fame deservedly established. Although alchemy was not likely to find credence at that late day, Neve thought human avarice strong enough to propagate even this folly and superstition:

As long as it shall exist, the application of the *Alchymist* will remain. Of the characters, Sir *Epicure Mammon* is excellently chosen: a glutton and debauchee, whose judgment is weakened by his passions, and who thereby becomes a fit subject to be the dupe of *Subtle*, and, his helpmate, *Face*.[3]

A New Theatrical Dictionary still judged the play in 1792 "too well known and admired to need any comment on or account of it." [4] The last important critique appeared at the beginning of the new century. Written by Dibdin, it showed acute recognition of many of the points noted in the course of the history of the play:

This comedy . . . must, no doubt, have been greatly successful originally, since we have seen it very much followed and ad-

1. *Recollections of the Life of John O'Keeffe, Written by Himself,* 1826, I, 388. See also pp. 81–82.
2. [John Wolcot], *The Works of Peter Pindar, Esq.,* 1794, I, 33.
3. *Cursory Remarks,* pp. 11–12.   4. Page 6

mired during the time GARRICK ornamented the stage. His incomparable performance, however, of ABEL DRUGGER was a considerable drawback from the proper reputation of the author, and in great measure the cause of the success of the play; at the same time it must be confessed that the best acting can do nothing without good materials, with which the *Alchymist* abounds. . . . *The Alchymist*, however, will probably never again be celebrated; but this is more owing to the subject, which of course grows every day in a greater degree obsolete, than to any deficiency in its dramatic requisites, although the insuperable objection to JONSON in a degree prevails here as well as every where else; for though his comic characters do not actually wear the buskin, yet the sock has such high heels and is made of such stiff materials, that the characters stalk instead of trip, and thus we have quaintness for nature, affectation for grace, and awkwardness for ease.[1]

An additional scene for the play by Joseph Moser, which may have had some point when it was written but which is highly esoteric now, appeared in 1809 in *The European Magazine*.[2] Apparently it was a venture into political satire, but no names are mentioned; an expert in the history of the period might be able to determine its meaning. As a literary effort it will bear little investigation, and it had no effect on the history of the play.

The fame of the old actors continued into the nineteenth century. Leigh Hunt entertained

a very high opinion of Mrs. Pritchard. . . . She seems to have been a really great genius, equally capable of the highest and lowest parts. The fault objected to her was, that her figure was not genteel; and we can imagine this well enough in an actress who could pass from Lady Macbeth to Doll Common.[3]

Coleridge, with his ever-present reconciliation of opposites, hoped for another actor as great as Garrick, who would possess "a knowledge of Man united to an equal knowledge of Men":

1. *A Complete History of the Stage*, III, 295–296.
2. LV, 428–432.   3. *The Town*, 1859, p. 295.

For such a Being possesses the rudiments of every character in himself. . . . He combines in his own person at once the materials and the workman. The precious proofs of this rare excellence in our Greatest Dramatic Poet are in the hands of all men. To exhibit the same excellence in our greatest actor, we can conceive no more lively or impressive way than by presenting him in the two extreme Poles of his Creative and almost Protean Genius — in his Richard the Third and his Abel Drugger.[1]

Less philosophically, but more delightfully, Hazlitt was willing to part with a year's income, could he but see Garrick "act in tragedy and comedy, in the play and the farce, Lear, and Wildair, and Abel Drugger," in spite of the skepticism of his generation, which had its misgivings about this great player, "as if he was probably after all little better than a Bartlemy-fair actor, dressed out to play Macbeth in a scarlet coat and laced cocked-hat. For one, I should like to have seen and heard with my own eyes and ears." [2]

On March 21, 1782, a shortened version of *The Alchemist*, seemingly distinct from *The Tobacconist*, was presented with the following cast: Subtle, Aickin; Face, Palmer; Drugger, Dodd; Lovewit, Packer; Mammon, Griffith; Surly, Wrighten; Kastril, Burton; Dame Pliant, Miss Simson; Dol Common, Mrs. Hopkins.[3] The first performance, noted in *The Morning Chronicle and London Advertiser*, praised Dodd's Drugger.[4] Dodd acted the part

---

1. [Thomas Allsop], *Letters, Conversations, and Recollections of S. T. Coleridge*, 1836, II, 193.

2. "Of Persons One Would Wish to have Seen," *The New Monthly Magazine*, XVI (1826), part i, 32–41; *Literary Remains of the late William Hazlitt*, 1836, II, 347.

3. The names in *The Tobacconist* could easily have been changed back to the original names, but there is an extra character, Surly, not in Gentleman's version. This 1782 version, which was played until 1787, when Genest (VI, 433) noted that it had become "so obsolete that it was hissed by some persons in the gallery," omits three characters in *The Alchemist*, — Dapper, Tribulation, and Ananias. To have been used as an afterpiece, the play must have been cut tremendously.   4. March 22, 1782.

sixteen times, and his performance was recorded in *The
Children of Thespis*:

> Behold sprightly DODD amble light o'er the stage,
> And mimic young fops in despite of his age!
> He poises his cane 'twixt his finger and thumb,
> And trips to the fair, with a jut of the bum.
>
> .   .   .   .
>
> We may swear from his mien, that his humour was cast
> In the light moulds of Fashion, full thirty years past;
> In such acting we look on no effort that new is,
> As he steers in midway between CIBBER and LEWIS;
>
> .   .   .   .
>
> Yet his DRUGGER defies the stern critic's detection,
> And his AGUE CHEEK touches the edge of perfection.[1]

He died in 1796. Michael Kelly described him as an actor
of the old school, particularly fitted for the rôles of fops,
and said that his Abel Drugger, as well as his renown for
telling comic stories, always gave "infinite pleasure." [2]
John Adolphus lamented Dodd's death as depriving the
stage of a particular species of fine gentleman which had
ceased to exist and concluded by observing that, "should
an event so improbable as the revival of 'The Alchemist'
occur, there is no person to compete with him in Abel
Drugger." [3]

The Tobacconist was taken down from the theatrical
shelf again at the Haymarket in the summer of 1784, where
it was presented three times with an actor named Kippling,
new to London, as Drugger. It then remained idle until
July 15, 1800, when Emery played the tobacconist. The
last performances were those by Edmund Kean (1814–
1815). Mrs. Garrick, who saw him act Drugger for the
first time for his own benefit on May 14, 1814, wrote a
note to him: "Dear Sir,— You cannot play *Abel Drugger*,"
to which his reply was equally laconic: "Dear Madam,—

---

1. Pages 53–54.
2. *Reminiscences of Michael Kelly*, II, 101.
3. *Memoirs of John Bannister*, I, 387.

I know it." [1]   The newspaper reviewer for this evening
found much to compliment in his talents for comedy,
praising his awkward gait, foolish terrors, and simplicity,
but observed that the farce had too little business to
please the audiences of his day. He suspected that the
older actors of *The Alchemist* had relied on by-play not
preserved by theatrical tradition.[2] The most favorable
criticism of Kean was written by Hazlitt, who reviewed
the performance of May 25, 1815.[3]

The Tobacconist was spent, and no one had courage
enough to produce *The Alchemist* until it was acted by the
Elizabethan Stage Society at Apothecaries' Hall, Black-
friars, February 24, 1899. The version was advertised as
revised. On April 8, 1916, the Birmingham Repertory
presented the play [4] in an unaltered form, a precedent
adopted by the Phoenix Society on March 18, 1923. The
reviewer found the performance somewhat inferior to that
of *Volpone* but approved in particular the character of Sir
Epicure Mammon, slighted in the eighteenth century:

> Sir Epicure is enough fame for any dramatic poet. Where is
> the dramatist to-day who can create such marvels for us? Where
> is the master of fantastic language that could write such a lip-
> twisting catalogue of extraordinary pleasures as flow from the
> heated brain of that most robust and generous of epicures? [5]

The most recent performances were given at the Malvern
Festival in 1932. One may hope that some enterprising
producer, gambling on the success of the modern *Volpone*,
will dare to restore *The Alchemist* to the professional stage,
where it was acted so brilliantly for one hundred seventy-
five years.

1. J. W. Cole, *The Life and Theatrical Times of Charles Kean, F. S. A.*, 1859,
I, 49.
2. John Genest, *Ana relating to the English Stage, 1815–1818*, Harvard
Theatre Collection. For an unfavorable view of Kean's Drugger see [B. W.
Procter], *The Life of Edmund Kean*, 1835, II, pp. 130–132.
3. *A View of the English Stage*, 1818, pp. 111–112.
4. *The Era Annual*, 1917, p. 114.
5. *The London Mercury*, VIII, No. 44 (1923), 197.

CHAPTER IV

Epicoene; or, The Silent Woman

I

1660–1707

THE only comedy of Jonson's for which there are definite records of performance during that difficult theatrical year 1660 is *The Silent Woman*. Indeed, the performance of the play about June 6, 1660, is apparently the first recorded after the return of the king to England on May 25. The play was acted four times before the end of the year and twice in 1661 before the second Jonsonian comedy, *Bartholomew Fair*, was produced on June 8. Before March 25 (but how much earlier is not known), Rhodes had opened at the Cockpit (the old Phoenix) with Betterton as his chief actor and Kynaston as the portrayer of the leading female rôles.[1] To rival this company, the remnant of the old actors who had survived the Commonwealth formed a company and began to give plays at the Red Bull in St. John's Street. The leading actors were Mohun, Hart, Robert Shatterel, Edward Shatterel, Burt, Cartwright, Clun, and Wintershall,[2] most of whom, as has been noted, were famous in Jonson's plays. The records of Sir Henry Herbert give *The Silent Woman* in a list of dramas acted by the Red Bull actors. The record is undated,[3] and indeed the earliest specific information is the note of Pepys for June 6, 1660, "that the two Dukes do haunt the Park much, and that

1. Allardyce Nicoll, *Restoration Drama*, pp. 269–270.
2. R. W. Lowe, *Thomas Betterton*, 1891, p. 62.
3. J. Q. Adams, *The Dramatic Records of Sir Henry Herbert*, p. 82.

they were at a play, Madam Epicene, the other day." [1]
Where this performance occurred is a puzzle. One would
naturally assume that the old actors were performing at
the Red Bull, for there is no evidence that they used any
other theatre so early in 1660, but it seems somewhat improbable that the dukes would attend a performance in the
large unroofed Clerkenwell public playhouse. Not im-
probably the old actors hired either the Phoenix in Drury
Lane or the house in Gibbons's Tennis Court. They could
not have used Salisbury Court, which was being repaired
between April 5 and June 24. It is barely possible that
the dukes saw the comedy at the Cockpit-in-Court, Monk's
lodging in Whitehall Palace, but the circumstances of the
performance of *The Silent Woman* there on November 19
argue against the theory. It is perhaps wiser to conjecture
that they demeaned themselves sufficiently to visit the Red
Bull, where the Mohun company continued acting during
August.[2] This company was to form the nucleus of the
actors managed by Killigrew, who were to be the sole
possessors of Jonson's comedies. On July 9 and on July
19 the king endorsed the patent to Killigrew,[3] and on
August 21 the patent was issued to him.

On November 8 Killigrew's new company started acting
at Gibbons's Tennis Court in Vere Street, with a company
of the Red Bull actors given above, strengthened by the
addition of Theophilus Bird and Edward Kynaston. Two
days later they played *The Silent Woman*,[4] probably with
the following cast: Morose, Cartwright; Clerimont, Burt;
Truewit, Mohun; Daw, Shatterel; La Foole, Wintershall;
Otter, Lacy; Epicoene, Kynaston.[5] On November 19 these
actors gave in the afternoon, at Gibbons's Tennis Court, a

1. H. B. Wheatley, *The Diary of Samuel Pepys*, I, 160. The dukes were the
duke of York and the duke of Gloucester.
2. See Nicoll, p. 273.
3. Page 270.
4. *The Dramatic Records of Sir Henry Herbert*, p. 116.
5. Based on the list for 1663 in *Roscius Anglicanus*, p. 4.

performance of *The Unfortunate Lovers*,[1] and in the evening another of *The Silent Woman*, at the Cockpit at White-hall, for which there is extant the broadside occasional prologue.[2]

THE
PROLOGUE
TO HIS
MAJESTY

At the first PLAY presented at the Cock-pit in

WHITEHALL,

Being part of that Noble Entertainment which Their MAIESTIES
received *Novemb:* 19. from his Grace the Duke of

ALBEMARLE.

Greatest of Monarchs, welcome to this place
Which Majesty *so oft was wont to grace*
Before our Exile, to divert the Court,
And ballance weighty Cares with harmless sport,
This truth we can to our advantage say,
They that would have no KING, *would have no* Play:
The Laurel *and the* Crown *together went,*
Had the same Foes, *and the same* Banishment:
The Ghosts of their great Ancestors they fear'd,
Who by the art of conjuring Poets rear'd,
Our HARRIES *&* our EDWARDS *long since dead*
Still on the Stage a march of Glory tread:
Those Monuments of Fame (they thought) would stain
And teach the People to despise their Reign:
Nor durst they look into the Muses Well,
Least the cleer Spring their ugliness should tell;
Affrighted with the shadow of their Rage,
They broke the Mirror of the times, the Stage;
The Stage against them still maintain'd the War,
When they debauch'd the Pulpit *and the* Bar.
Though to be Hypocrites, *be our Praise alone,*
'Tis our peculiar boast that we were none.

1. *The Dramatic Records of Sir Henry Herbert*, p. 116.
2. See Leslie Hotson, *The Commonwealth and Restoration Stage*, pp. 208–209; Eleanore Boswell, *The Restoration Court Stage*, Cambridge, Mass., 1932, p. 15. The prologue has been attributed to Sir William Davenant and to Sir John Denham.

What e're they taught, we practis'd what was true,
And something we had learn'd of honor too,
VVhen by Your Danger, and our Duty prest,
VVe acted in the Field, and not in Jest;
Then for the Cause our Tyring-house they sack't,
And silenc't us that they alone might act;
And (to our shame) most dext'rously they do it,
Out-act the Players, and out-ly the Poet;
But all the other Arts appear'd so scarce,
Ours were the Moral Lectures, theirs the Farse:
This spacious Land their Theater became,
And they Grave Counsellors, and Lords in Name;
VVhich these Mechanicks Personate so ill
That ev'n the Oppressed with contempt they fill,
But when the Lyons dreadful skin they took,
They roar'd so loud that the whole Forrest shook;
The noise kept all the Neighborhood in awe,
VVho thought 'twas the true Lyon by his Pawe.
If feigned Vertue could such Wonders do,
VVhat may we not expect from this that's true!
But this Great Theme must serve another Age,
To fill our Story, and adorne our Stage.

The entertainment of November 19, the first play given at court after the Restoration, was mentioned in a letter from Edward Gower to Sir Richard Leveson on November 20:

Yesternight the King, Queen, Princess, &c. supped at the Duke d'Albermarle's, where they had the Silent Woman acted in the Cock-pit, where on Sunday he had a sermon.[1]

Pepys described the king's behavior in an entry for November 20:

This morning I found my Lord in bed late, he having been with the King, Queen, and Princess, at the Cockpit all night, where General Monk treated them; and after supper a play, where the King did put a great affront upon Singleton's musique, he bidding them stop and bade the French musique play, which, my Lord says, do much outdo all ours.[2]

1. *Fifth Report of the Royal Commission on Historical Manuscripts, Part I*, 1876, Appendix, p. 200; J. Q. Adams, *Shakespearean Playhouses*, Cambridge, Mass., 1917, p. 405.   2. I, 268.

The second performance of *The Silent Woman* at Killigrew's theatre, on December 4,[1] Pepys did not see. He has no information about the manner of production until January 7, 1661, when he writes:

Tom and I and my wife to the Theatre, and there saw "The Silent Woman." The first time that ever I did see it, and it is an excellent play. Among other things here, Kinaston, the boy, had the good turn to appear in three shapes: first, as a poor woman in ordinary clothes, to please Morose; then in fine clothes, as a gallant, and in them was clearly the prettiest woman in the whole house, and lastly, as a man; and then likewise did appear the handsomest man in the house.[2]

Kynaston was still playing Epicoene, although on December 8 preceding, occurred probably the first appearance of a woman as a professional actress on the English stage, almost certainly Mrs. Hughes as Desdemona.[3] On January 3 Pepys had seen *The Beggars' Bush*, "the first time that ever I saw women come upon the stage," [4] but some time was required to furnish a supply of actresses. Just how long Kynaston continued as Epicoene it is impossible to say, but surely not later than May 7, 1663, when Downes assigns the rôle to Pepys's friend Mrs. Knepp.[5] At this time began that curious mistake of casting a woman in the title rôle which was corrected only by popular disapproval in 1776, just as the play was to leave the stage. The anomaly of disguising a woman as a woman and then revealing her as a boy should have struck the sensibilities of witty Restoration audiences acquainted with *The Country Wife*. Pepys was pleased with the comedy again on May 25,[6] after which the records are blank until Dr. Edward Browne recorded seeing the play

1. I, 277. 2. I, 297.
3. See Edmond Malone, *Historical Account of the Rise and Progress of the English Stage*, Basel, 1800, p. 138; Hazelton Spencer, *Shakespeare Improved*, p. 39.
4. I, 294.
5. *Roscius Anglicanus*, p. 4.
6. II, 39.

"at the Cock Pit in Drewry Lane" in 1662,[1] where Killigrew's company, as has been pointed out, was performing, probably at the end of the year.

There is an allusion, however, to *The Silent Woman* in a short letter from Elizabeth Bodvile to an unknown correspondent, noting that the king "had giveing my Lord Robarts the privi seall." It reads:

Good night, and pray sleep never the les. I hope y^r good fortune is still to come; and pray bee well to morrow, or I shall bee Mrs. Otter.[2]

There is evidence at this time that Saint-Évremond appreciated *The Silent Woman*, for his editor noted that he was charmed with "La Femme Qui Ne Parle Point."[3]

The play was assigned to Killigrew after April 8, 1663, for the new theatre in Drury Lane;[4] the cast, as given by Downes, remained the same as that noted above, except that Kynaston now played Dauphine; Mrs. Knepp, Epicoene; Mrs. Rutter, Lady Haughty; and Mrs. Corey, famous for Dol Common and Lady Would-be, Mrs. Otter, the termagant wife of the captain of bulls and bears.[5] There are no actual records for the remainder of this season,[6] but on Candlemas, February 2, 1664, *The Silent Woman* was selected by the King's Company for presentation at the Inner Temple,[7] and on June 1 Pepys saw it again at Drury Lane,

but methought not so well done or so good a play as I formerly thought it to be, or else I am now-a-days out of humour. Before the play was done, it fell such a storm of hayle, that we in the

1. British Museum MS. Sloane 1900.
2. E. M. Thompson, *Correspondence of the Family of Hatton, A.D. 1601–1704,* 1878, I, 22. Lord Robartes was appointed to the privy seal on May 18, 1661.
3. *Œuvres,* III, 42.
4. *Roscius Anglicanus,* pp. 3–4.
5. Page 4.
6. For an allusion to Morose in this year see [Katharine Phillips], *Letters from Orinda to Poliarchus,* 1705, p. 170.
7. F. A. Inderwick, *A Calendar of the Inner Temple Records,* III (1901), lxi-lxii.

middle of the pit were fain to rise; and all the house in a disorder, and so my wife and I out and got into a little alehouse, and staid there an hour after the play was done before we could get a coach, which at last we did.[1]

A command performance at court on December 10, 1666, was rewarded by £20. There is some doubt, however, whether the play this night was *The Silent Woman* or *The Scornful Lady*.[2] Pepys, visiting the theatre on April 16, 1667, to see a new play, was surprised to find *The Silent Woman* substituted:

I never was more taken with a play than I am with this "Silent Woman," as old as it is, and as often as I have seen it. There is more wit in it than goes to ten new plays.[3]

In 1665 that extraordinarily frank picaresque tale *The English Rogue* alluded to the comedy. The rogue married but found his wife devirginate. When she was prematurely brought to bed, the rogue was considerably perturbed, despite the protestations of an ingenious midwife, and a domestic war began:

My Wife acted the *Silent Woman* to the life, whilest in a single state; for before we were married all her answers were very short, comprehended within the two Monosyllables of *I*, and *No*; and those two must be forcibly extracted from her; But now her tongue wagg'd in a perpetual motion, and her voice so shrill and loud, that it would be heard distinctly, though a piece of Ordnance were discharged near her at the same time.[4]

It is a somewhat bold transition from this bit of pleasantry to Dryden's keen and serious analysis of *The Silent Woman* in his *Essay of Dramatic Poesy*,[5] published in 1668

---

1. IV, 138–139.   2. Nicoll, p. 305.
3. VI, 259. Pepys alludes to the king's amours in terms of the play (VII, 49).
4. [Francis Kirkman and Richard Head], *The English Rogue Described in the Life of Meriton Latroon* [part i], 1668, p. 200.
5. Sir Walter Scott and George Saintsbury, *The Works of John Dryden*, XV, 348–355.

or possibly in the December preceding. In his character
as Neander, the interlocutor and representer of compro-
mise between the classic and neo-classic points of view,
French and English, Dryden chose this comedy by Ben
Jonson, "the most learned and judicious writer which any
theatre ever had," as "the pattern of a perfect play,"
from which to "make a short examen, according to the
rules which the French observe." In the first place, Dryden examined the manner in which the play observed the
unities. As for time, the amount comprehended was only
three hours and a half, exactly the time required for presentation. The latitude of place was little, the scenes
being all laid in London. The continuity of scenes was
better observed than in any other play except *The Fox*
and *The Alchemist*. The unity of action was observed,
inasmuch as the aim of the play was single, that is, the
settling of Morose's estate on Dauphine. As for the characters, all seemed delightful, and there was a great variety
of humors — Morose, the noise-hater, who is not a forced
character (and here Dryden explained his conception of
humor, which agreed with Jonson's), and at least nine or
ten others, all of which have "several concernments of their
own, yet are all used by the poet, to the conducting of the
main design to perfection. I shall not waste time in com-
mending the writing of this play; but I will give you my
opinion, that there is more wit and acuteness of fancy in
it than in any of Ben Jonson's." Dryden found the conversation of Truewit and his friends more gay and free
than in other plays of Jonson; the plot, elaborate, yet easy;
and the untying of it admirable and "altogether so full of
art, that I must unravel every scene of it to commend it
as I ought. And this excellent contrivance is still the more
to be admired, because 'tis comedy where the persons are
only of common rank, and their business private, not
elevated by passions or high concernments, as in serious
plays." He observed Jonson's habit of describing his
leading characters before they appear on the stage, as he

does Daw, La Foole, Morose, and the collegiate ladies in
Epicoene, and Numps and Cokes in *Bartholomew Fair*. He
praised the rising action and suspense of the play, heightened and varied by the revelation of new characters, and
ended his analysis by venturing the opinion that if *The
Silent Woman* were translated into French prose, the controversy over dramatic excellence would soon be decided
betwixt the two nations.[1]

In 1668 Shadwell, who adored Jonson, made his character
Sir Positive At-all say that he had found two plays that
had a great deal of wit in them, *The Silent Woman* and
The Scornful Lady, which, according to his understanding,
had wit enough in both to make one good play![2] Mrs.
Knepp was still playing the boy's part in *Epicoene*, for
Pepys noted on September 18 that she had "to get her
part against to-morrow, in 'The Silent Woman.'"[3] Except that Hart was still acting in 1673, this information is
the last we have about members of the cast for the rest of
the century, for Pepys ceased writing the next spring,
and other records are wanting. There is scattered information concerning the play, however, before 1700. About
January 12, 1669, it was "allowed of to his Ma[tes] Servants
at y[e] New Theatre,"[4] and in this year the music for the
song beginning "Still to be neat" appeared.[5]

Killigrew's company in 1673 was hard pressed for
money; their theatre in Bridges Street had burned on
January 25, 1672, and from February 26 of that year to

1. Dryden further criticized *The Silent Woman* in *A Defence of an Essay of
Dramatic Poesy* (*Works*, II [1882], 314), and in the preface to *An Evening's Love*
(III [1883], 245–247), where he defended himself against charges of immorality
by citing the successful denouement of Dauphine's intrigues.
2. Montague Summers, *The Complete Works of Thomas Shadwell*, 1927, I, 21.
3. VIII, 101.   4. Nicoll, p. 315.
5. *Select Ayres and Dialogues to Sing to the Theorbo-Lute or Basse-Viol. Composed by Mr. Henry Lawes, late Servant to His Majesty . . . and other Excellent
Masters*, Book II, p. 51. The words only were printed in *Westminster-Drollery*,
1671, part i, pp. 107–108; *Windsor-Drollery*, 1672, No. 189; *The Academy of
Complements*, 1663, p. 205; *Wit's Academy; or, The Muses Delight*, 1677, p. 79;
The Vocal Magazine; or, British Songster's Miscellany, IV (1779), No. 551.

midsummer's day, 1673, they acted at the old Lincoln's Inn Fields theatre, when they were ordered to stop acting for the summer. In the October following, the old Duke's theatre was taken over by Betterton as a nursery for actors. Contemporary documents show the difficulty the King's Company experienced in raising money for a new house,[1] and it was probably in order to raise funds that the actors went down to Oxford to give some of their plays, no doubt for the Act early in July. There are an occasional prologue and epilogue to *The Silent Woman*, written by Dryden, "to the University of Oxford, Spoken by Mr. Hart at the Acting of the Silent Woman,"[2] which show clearly the hardships the company endured also from the competition of French actors, Italian Merry-Andrews, and operatic performances such as that of *Macbeth* at Dorset Garden in 1673.

The new theatre in Drury Lane opened on November 24, 1674, and Killigrew's men acted there until April, 1682. The articles of union were signed on May 4, 1682, but the new company did not start acting until November, the lease of the theatre being dated to run from November 9. The union, which lasted until December 22, 1694, caused many old actors to disappear from the stage, leaving Betterton the acknowledged master.[3] *The Silent Woman* continued to be acted. In 1683 Sir William Soame referred to it in his translation of Boileau's *Art of Poetry*, as he did to *Volpone* and *The Alchemist*:

> You then, that would the Comic Lawrels wear,
> To study Nature be your only care:
> Who e're knows Man, and by a curious art
> Discerns the hidden secrets of the heart;
> He who observes, and naturally can Paint
> The Jealous Fool, the fawning Sycophant,

---

1. Nicoll, p. 289.
2. *Miscellany Poems. By the Most Eminent Hands*, 1684, pp. 263-267; *The Works of John Dryden*, X, 379-384. See also W. D. Christie, *The Poetical Works of John Dryden*, 1902, pp. 420-422; Genest, I, 139; *Roscius Anglicanus*, p. 33.
3. Hotson, pp. 271, 273, 294.

A Sober Wit, an enterprising Ass,
A humorous *Otter*, or a *Hudibras*;
May safely in these noble Lists ingage,
And make 'em Act and Speak upon the Stage:
Strive to be natural in all you Write,
And paint with Colours that may please the Sight.[1]

On January 15, 1685, the United Companies were granted £5 for a performance, "The King and Queene at the Silent Weoman," which occurred just before the death of Charles II in February, and the record notes that "This was before ye late Kinges death." [2] Thereafter no specific data are available for nearly fifteen years until Lady Morley saw the play on December 21, 1700, at the Theatre Royal in Drury Lane. But meanwhile a good deal was written about it.

The merry Tom Brown, in 1690, in his dialogue on Dryden's conversion to Catholicism, made Bayes explain his reasons:

Bays. . . . As the peevish old Huncks, in the *Silent Woman*, hir'd him a House as far from the rattling of Coaches as he could meet with, so I have done the same in relation to a Church; and you might as well wheedle *Ben Johnson's Morose*, if he were alive again, into the *Wits-Coffee-House*, as persuade me now into any of your Churches.[3]

In 1691 Langbaine wrote that "this Play is Accounted by all, One of the best Comedies we have extant; and those who would know more, may be amply satisfied by the perusal of the judicious Examen of this Play made by Mr. *Dryden*." [4] Four years later, John Dennis, whose analysis of *Volpone* has already been examined, continued his research into Jonson's technique in a second letter to

1. Pages 49–50.
2. Nicoll, p. 312. For the possibility that William Mountfort acted Sir John Daw at this performance see A. S. Borgman, *The Life and Death of William Mountfort*, Cambridge, Mass., 1935, pp. 15–16.
3. *A Collection of all the Dialogues Written by Mr. Thomas Brown*, p. 103.
4. *An Account of the English Dramatick Poets*, p. 296.

Congreve, which evoked the famous reply of July 10, 1695, when the dramatist wrote the critic his ideas *Concerning Humour in Comedy.*

The Plots of the Fox, the silent Woman, the Alchimist, are all of them very Artful. But the Intrigues of the Fox, and the Alchimist, seem to me to be more dexterously perplexed, than to be happily disentangled. But the Gordian Knot in the Silent Woman is untyed with so much Felicity, that that alone, may Suffice to show *Ben Johnson* no ordinary Heroe. But, then perhaps, the Silent Woman may want the very Foundation of a good Comedy, which the other two cannot be said to want. For it seems to me, to be without a Moral. Upon which Absurdity, *Ben Johnson* was driven by the Singularity of *Moroses* Character, which is too extravagant for Instruction, and Fit, in my opinion, only for Farce. For this seems to me, to Constitute the most Essential Difference, betwixt Farce and Comedy, that the Follies which are expos'd in Farce are Singular; and those are particular, which are expos'd in Comedy. These last are those, with which some part of an Audience may be suppos'd Infected, and to which all may be suppos'd Obnoxious. But the first are so very odd, that by Reason of their Monstrous Extravagance, they cannot be thought to concern an Audience; and cannot be supposed to instruct them. For the rest of the Characters in these Plays, they are for the most part true, and Most of the Humorous Characters Master-pieces. For *Ben Johnson's* Fools, seem to shew his Wit a great deal more then his Men of Sense. I Admire his Fops, and but barely Esteem his Gentlemen. *Ben* seems to draw Deformity more to the Life than Beauty. He is often so eager to pursue Folly, that he forgets to take Wit along with him. For the Dialogue, it seems to want very often that Spirit, that Grace, and that Noble Railery, which are to be found in more Modern Plays, and which are Virtues that ought to be Inseparable from a finish'd Comedy. But there seems to be one thing more wanting than all the rest, and that is Passion, I mean that fine and that delicate Passion, by which the Soul shows its Politeness, ev'n in the midst of its trouble. Now to touch a Passion is the surest way to Delight. For nothing agitates like it. Agitation is the Health and Joy of the Soul, of which it is so entirely fond, that even then, when we imagine we

seek Repose, we only seek Agitation. . . . I leave you to make
the Aplication to *Johnson* — Whatever I have said my self of
his Comedies, I submit to your better Judgment.[1]

The criticism is excellent, for it touches at the core the
main defects of Jonson's comedies, their lack of universality arising from over-emphasis of the local, the temporary, and the particular, and their intellectual aloofness
from ordinary human emotions.

Congreve answered Dennis's desire for a definition of
humor, by distinguishing it from wit and by showing that
it did not rise from folly, personal defects, external habit
and ridiculous clothing, or affectation, but from a natural
growth, born with us. To illustrate, he chose Morose as a
character of humor, absolving him from charges of un-
naturalness on the grounds that splenetic people actually
do hate noise and clamor, as one may observe daily.

Well; But *Morose* you will say, is so Extravagant, he cannot
bear any Discourse or Conversation, above a Whisper. Why,
It is his excess of this Humour, that makes him become Ridiculous, and qualifies his Character for Comedy. If the Poet had
given him, but a Moderate proportion of that Humour, 'tis odds
but half the Audience, would have sided with the Character,
and have Condemn'd the Author, for Exposing a Humour which
was neither Remarkable nor Ridiculous. Besides, the distance
of the Stage requires the Figure represented, to be something
larger than the Life; and sure a Picture may have Features
larger in Proportion, and yet be very like the Original.[2]

Whether Dennis agreed with Congreve's theory we do not
know, for he never discussed the subject again.

The union ended on December 22, 1694. On April 1,
1695, Rich's company resumed acting at Drury Lane, and
on April 29 Betterton opened at the new theatre in Lincoln's Inn Fields, where he remained for ten years. The
next criticism of *The Silent Woman* came from Jeremy

1. *Letters Upon several Occasions*, pp. 76–79.
2. Pages 87–88. Gildon, in *The Laws of Poetry*, p. 246, agreed with Congreve's defense of Jonson and regarded Morose as a general character.

Collier, who answered Dryden's attempt to defend his *Mock-Astrologer* by urging Jonson's precedent in *Epicoene*,[1] where Dauphine "is crowned in the end with the possession of his uncle's estate, and with the hopes of enjoying all his mistresses":

> This Charge, as I take it, is somewhat too severe. I grant *Dauphin* Professes himself in Love with the Collegiate Ladies at first. But when they invited him to a private Visit, he makes them no Promise; but rather appears tired, and willing to disengage. *Dauphin* therefore is not altogether so naughty as this Author represents him.[2]

The play-reading parson also absolved Jonson from any charge of disrespect for his cloth in this play.[3] The comedy could enter upon a new century clear of the stigma of immorality, for if Collier saw none, there was none to see. Whether it had been acted recently or whether it had fallen into temporary neglect are matters impossible to solve with our present information, but a passage in *Historia Histrionica* (1699) indicates that it was not on the stage then. Lovewit observes that "when the Question has been askt, Why these Players do not revive the *Silent Woman*, and some other of *Johnson's* Plays, (once of highest esteem) they have answer'd, truly, Because there are none now Living who can rightly Humour those Parts."[4] Barely a year later, however, actors were found who could "Humour those Parts." One may guess at the cast seen by Lady Morley on December 21, 1700, although the full list of names was not advertised in *The Daily Courant* until December 31, 1706. The actors in 1700 probably were Morose, Johnson, who acted it subsequently and who was at Drury Lane in 1700; Clerimont, Mills; Truewit, Wilks; Sir John Daw, Cibber; La Foole, Bullock; Cutbeard, Norris; Epicoene, Mrs. Oldfield.

1. Preface to *An Evening's Love*, 1671; *Works*, III, 247.
2. *A Short View*, p. 153.
3. Page 126.
4. R. W. Lowe, *An Apology for the Life of Mr. Colley Cibber*, I, xxiv.

Cibber gives an impression of Wilks about this time. Wilks returned to the Theatre Royal and ousted Powell from many of his stellar rôles. Cibber was given small parts but comforted himself with the thought

that even the coxcombly Follies of a Sir *John Daw*, might as well distinguish the Capacity of an Actor, as all the dry Enterprizes, and busy Conduct of a *Truewit*. Nor could I have any Reason to repine at the Superiority he enjoy'd, when I consider'd at how dear a Rate it was purchased, at the continual Expence of a restless Jealousy, and fretful Impatience — These were the Passions, that, in the height of his Successes, kept him lean to his last Hour, while what I wanted in Rank, or Glory, was amply made up to me, in Ease and Chearfulness. But let not this Observation either lessen his Merit, or lift up my own; since our different Tempers were not, in our Choice, but equally natural, to both of us. To be employ'd on the Stage was the Delight of his Life; to be justly excus'd from it, was the Joy of mine: I lov'd Ease, and he Pre-eminence: In that, he might be more commendable.[1]

Lady Morley saw *The Silent Woman* again on June 5, 1701. In 1702 the comedy was not performed, but George Farquhar used the character of Morose as a typical illustration of a humor in his *Discourse Upon Comedy, In Reference to the English Stage,* pointing out that the English, being a mixed race, must expect a medley of temperaments and humors in excess of other nations, and must find "a *Wildair* in one Corner and a *Morose* in another; nay, the space of an Hour or two shall create such Vicissitudes of Temper in the same Person, that he can hardly be taken for the same Man. . . . We have nothing to do with the Models of *Menander* or *Plautus,* but must consult *Shakespear, Johnson,* . . . and others, who by Methods much different from the Ancients, have supported the English Stage, and made themselves famous to posterity." [2]

1. *Apology,* 2d ed., pp. 211–212.
2. *Love and Business: in a Collection of Occasionary Verse, and Epistolary Prose,* pp. 141–143; Charles Stonehill, *The Complete Works of George Farquhar,* 1930, II, 337–338. Compare *The Works of Mr. Thomas Brown,* 1715, II, 57.

II

1707–1742

Until January 1, 1707, *The Silent Woman* was acted with fair regularity at Drury Lane, twice in 1703 and 1704, and once "At the Desire of several Persons of Quality" in 1706. The usual *divertissements* by the Devonshire Girl, Scaramouch, the du Ruells, and Signora de l'Epine formed part of the bills. The real impetus to productions came, however, during the secession of the Drury Lane actors to Betterton's company at the Haymarket after September, 1706. Before the new union of the Drury Lane and Haymarket companies at Drury Lane under the management of Rich and Brett on January 15, 1708, *The Silent Woman* was performed seven times in scarcely more than a year. For the performance of January 1, 1707, we have the first complete cast. With the exceptions of Betterton as Morose, Booth as Dauphine, and Fairbank as Otter, the actors were those conjectured above for 1700. Betterton acted Morose only three times, his only recorded attempts in Jonsonian comedy, because he was always associated at other periods of his career with a company which did not include Jonson in its repertory. He was succeeded on February 21, 1707, by Benjamin Johnson, who played the rôle as regularly as he played Corbaccio, appearing in it for the last time on February 13, 1742. During this long period he had no rivalry in the part.

Robert Wilks played Truewit until his death in 1732, when he was succeeded by the younger Mills. The anonymous author of *The Laureat* (1740), after furiously attacking Colley Cibber in answer to his animadversions on Wilks in the *Apology*, wrote of Wilks's Truewit:

I have indeed sometimes been surprised. . . to see a Man Master of so exact, so literal, and so strong a Memory. I have known him lay a Wager, and win it, that he wou'd repeat the Part of *Truewitt* in the *Silent Woman*, which consists of thirty

Lengths of Paper, as they call 'em, (that is, one Quarter of a Sheet on both Sides to a Length) without misplacing a single Word, or missing an (*and*) or an (*or*).[1]

Mrs. Oldfield, Mrs. Knight, Mrs. Porter, Mrs. Garnet, and Mrs. Thurmond played Epicoene until 1733, but of these actresses Mrs. Oldfield played most frequently and attained most fame. She appeared for the last time in *The Silent Woman* on January 9, 1722. When she died in 1730, the memoir writers seem to have forgotten her Epicoene, for the only mention of it occurs in a list of her principal parts included in William Egerton's *Faithful Memoirs of the Life, Amours, and Performances of . . . Mrs. Anne Oldfield* (1731).[2]

Of the other actors in *The Silent Woman*, Booth acted Dauphine until replaced by Bridgewater on January 29, 1729; he died in 1733. The elder Mills acted Clerimont last on October 23, 1736, when he must have been much too old for the part. Colley Cibber as Sir John Daw was succeeded by his own son on April 14, 1735. Bullock as La Foole played until January 25, 1716, when Miller assumed the rôle. He acted it until Theophilus Cibber took the part on October 9, 1731, but during the revolt to the Haymarket in 1733, Miller regained his part and kept it until Woodward appeared as La Foole on January 26, 1739. The part of Captain Otter was unstable, requiring four actors before 1733,— Fairbank, who played only one year; Estcourt, who played until 1713; Pack, who performed indeterminately (since the bills do not indicate the part from 1713 to 1720); and Shepard, who acted, with the exception of a few performances when Harper and Marten substituted, until February 13, 1742. Norris was Cutbeard for the last time January 29, 1729; he was followed by Oates.

The most stable parts were, therefore, Morose, Dauphine, Clerimont, Truewit, Daw, and Cutbeard. As for

1. Page 45.   2. Page 207.

the regularity with which *The Silent Woman* held the stage until its first long lapse after 1752, there were only eight years between 1707 and 1752 when it might not be seen, and from the beginning of the century to 1752 there were eighty-seven performances.[1]

The first information about the casting of the collegiate ladies is given in *The Daily Courant* for April 21, 1708. Lady Haughty was acted by Mrs. Saunders; Dol Mavis, by Mrs. Bradshaw. The quarto edition of 1709 indicates Mrs. Powell for Mrs. Otter, and Mrs. Baker for Lady Centaure, but the newspaper bill for January 4, 1709, casts Mrs. Mills as Lady Centaure.

There is little of interest to record in the history of *The Silent Woman* during the year 1709. On May 31 the farceur Pinkethman spoke a popular "Epilogue on an Ass," usually delivered by Jo Haines.[2] The possibility of presenting this epilogue shows the low ebb which theatrical conditions had reached. On June 4, 1709, Drury Lane was silenced by order of the lord chamberlain, and the union of the companies, which had lasted about a year and a half, came to an end. On July 8, as proof of the integrity of Rich's management and of the actors' lack of reason in their revolt against Drury Lane, the patentees of the theatre directed the treasurer to furnish a statement of accounts, showing what salaries were paid. This list records the following payment to Mrs. Oldfield:

And she had for wearing in some plays a suit of boys cloaths on the stage; paid £2 10s. 9d.[3]

---

1. The cast from 1712 to 1730 was noted for its "inimitable Perfection" by W. R. Chetwood, in *Memoirs of the Life and Writings of Ben. Jonson*, p. 72.
2. See *Catalogue of Prints and Drawings in the British Museum, Division I, Satires*, II, 151–152; *The Remains of Mr. Tho. Brown*, 1720, pp. 233–235; *The Second Part of Penkethman's Jests; or, Wit Refin'd*, 1721; Thomas Scott, *The Unhappy Kindness*, 1697, epilogue; *Apollo's Feast; or, Wit's Entertainment*, 1703, pp. 156–157.
3. *The Eccentricities of John Edwin, Comedian. Arranged by Anthony Pasquin* (John Williams) [1791], I, 221. The entry was copied incorrectly by Percy Fitzgerald, in *A New History of the English Stage*, I, 268.

It is barely possible that one of the plays in which Mrs. Oldfield wore boy's clothes was *The Silent Woman*, but the playbills for the period covered by the statement list Mrs. Knight for the rôle.

Pope wrote a letter to Henry Cromwell on August 29, 1709, containing, apparently, his only specific allusion to a play of Jonson's. His acquaintance with Jonson was not very extensive, but he did refrain from using the epitaph "O Rare Bounce" when his faithful dog died, for fear that some people might take it as ridicule of Ben.[1] He wrote Cromwell:

> As for myself, I wou'd not have my Life a very regular Play, let it be a good merry Farce, a G — d's Name, and a Fig for the critical Unities! . . . For the Generality of Men, a true modern Life is like a true modern Play, neither Tragedy, Comedy, nor Farce, nor one, nor all of these: Every Actor is much better known by his having the same Face, than by keeping the same Character: For we change our Minds as often as they can their Parts, and he who was yesterday *Cæsar*, is to day Sir *John Daw*. So that one might with much better Reason ask the same Question of a modern Life, that Mr. *Rich* did of a modern Play; pray do me the Favour, Sir, to inform me; Is this your Tragedy or your Comedy?[2]

The Drury Lane actors revolted to the Haymarket, under Swiney's management, on September 15. Their first performance of *The Silent Woman* was given on January 11, 1710. The abridged cast notes only Morose, Truewit, Daw, La Foole, Otter, and Epicoene, but those parts were played as formerly, with Mrs. Oldfield again the Silent Woman. A later cast for the Haymarket gives Mills for Clerimont and Mrs. Saunders for Lady Haughty. Since Norris remained at Drury Lane, another actor had to be found for Cutbeard. The three performances of the play

---

1. Edmond Malone, *Observations, Anecdotes, and Characters, of Books and Men: By the Rev. Joseph Spence*, 1820, pp. 39–40. On p. 84 Pope is recorded as calling Jonson's works "trash."

2. *Miscellanea. In Two Volumes*, 1727, I, 18–19.

at the Haymarket and the production of *Volpone* on January 9 called forth a passing allusion to Jonson's famous triad of comedies in *The Female Tatler*.[1]   *The Tatler* for February 7 advertised a performance for February 9, "For the Benefit of Mr. Estcourt," who was suffering from gout and stone, and recommended "that admirable play of Ben Jonson's, called, 'The Silent Woman,'" adding that his man and his maid would be present in the first row of the middle gallery.[2]   In 1710, also, Gildon, in his *Life of Mr. Thomas Betterton*, who died April 28, alluded to *The Silent Woman* while giving instructions in voice production and tempo and warning the actors against volubility:

But on the Stage indeed the Case is something different, because there are Parts, and some particular Speeches, where such an extravagant Volubility is beautiful; as in several Places of the Part of *True Wit* in the *Silent Woman*, and some other Parts: . . . there is nothing hurts the Lungs more, than such a Violence and Precipitation of Speech, as allows no Intermission for the regular drawing the Breath, which has cast some into Consumptions, and cost them their Lives.[3]

The company at the Haymarket returned to Drury Lane on November 20, 1710, and eight days later played *The Silent Woman*, with Norris restored to the cast. The comedy, given twice in 1711, once in 1712, and three times in 1713, aroused little comment, but on June 30, 1713, *The Guardian* printed a humorous letter from Oxford, recounting the misfortunes which happened when highwaymen set upon a wagon stocked with theatrical properties, containing

The chains of *Jaffeir* and *Pierre*, the crowns and scepters of the posterity of *Banquo*; the bull, bear, and horse, of captain *Otter*; bones, sculls, pickaxes and a bottle of brandy, and five muskets.

1. No. 82, January 11–13, 1710.
2. No. 130 (ed. G. A. Aitken, III [1899], 91–92).
3. Page 108.

The Silent Woman. Lud. Du Guernier inv. et sculp.

... The robbers ... destroyed the world, the sun and moon, which lay loose in the waggon.[1]

Although the play was performed at least once every year, there was a surprising lack of criticism. There were minor changes in the cast. Jenny Cibber acted Dol Mavis from November 8, 1725, until she was displaced by Mrs. Butler on October 9, 1731, when Theophilus Cibber first appeared as La Foole, Oates as Cutbeard, Mrs. Shireburn as Lady Haughty, and Mrs. Grace as Lady Centaure. Thomas Davies, over fifty years later, described the performers at this period:

> About fifty or sixty years since, great respect was paid to this comedy; for Booth, Wilks, the elder Mills, and Colley Cibber, acted the Dauphin, Truewit, Clerimont, and Sir John Daw. Such an exhibition of comic distress, in old Ben Jonson's Morose, I have hardly ever seen in any other actor. He and Weston are the only comedians I can remember, that, in all the parts they represented, absolutely forgot themselves. I have seen very great players, nay, superior, in some respects, to them, at least in the art of colouring and high finishing, when on the stage laugh at a blunder of a performer or some accidental impropriety of the scene: but these men were so truly absorbed in character, that they never lost sight of it. Jonson stayed on the stage to the last, till within about two years of eighty; but his very dregs were respectable. ... Otter was well acted by Shepherd, and Sir Amorous La Foole with vivacity by Theophilus Cibber.[2]

When the Drury Lane company revolted from John Highmore's management in 1733, few alterations in the cast were necessary. Wilks, who had died the year before, was replaced as Truewit by William Mills; since Bridgewater did not join the revolt, A. Hallam played Dauphine; although Theophilus Cibber led the revolt, he yielded his rôle of La Foole to Miller; Mrs. Grace and Mrs. Wethereld disappeared as Lady Centaure and Mrs. Otter

---

1. No. 95. Otter's bull, bear, and horse are, of course, his drinking glasses. See *The Silent Woman*, III. i.

2. *Dramatic Miscellanies*, II, 105-106.

and were superseded by Miss Mann and Charlotte Charke;
Dol Mavis fell to Miss Robinson, and Epicoene to Mrs.
Butler. Of the new players, the only one who kept his
part steadily was Mills, who acted until the comedy was
dropped at Drury Lane in 1742.

The Silent Woman was given four times while the company was at the Haymarket. Like *The Fox* and *The
Alchemist*, it reached its height of popularity in the next
few years, for from December, 1733, to October, 1736, there
were thirteen performances, after which the play was acted
usually only once a year until 1742, when it was abandoned
at Drury Lane for ten years. On May 22, 1735, the play
was advertised for the "Benefit of Hewitt, Winstone, and
Miss Cole," "with a New Epilogue spoken by Master
Green and Miss Cole." The epilogue shows clearly the
popularity of French comedies, Italian singers, and harlequinades, which were almost driving legitimate drama from
the stage:

> *He.* What shall we say — come Miss, do you begin.
> *She.* I can't, this odious Play has given me the *Spleen*,
>   Must we be teiz'd with *Ben's* old Writings still!
> *He.* How should we please, or ever hope Advance,
>   I'm no *Italian* —
> *She.*   Nor am I from *France*.
>   O Faugh! I hate my self — an *English* Wench! —
>   O dear, dear Ribaldry and *French*.
> *He.* Must *Shakespeare's* Nature, *Johnson's* Humour cease;
>   And to Buffoons and empty Sounds give place?
> *She.* Lard! can your Humour like a Caper charm,
>   Or *Hamlet* like a soft *Piano* warm;
>   What's *Caesar's* Death to a *French* Comic-Scene?
>   Or what is *Cato* to a *Harlequin?*
>
> .   .   .   .   .   .
>
>   But let us still your kind Applauses share,
>   And to deserve the Boon shall be our Care;
>   To rise in *Merit* justly by *Degrees*,
>   And tho' we're *English*, yet we hope to please.[1]

---

1. *The Delights of the Muses: Being a Collection of Poems Never before Published*, 1738, pp. 175-176.

Although "this odious Play" was apparently causing some spleen, it enjoyed considerable patronage from royalty in the next few years. *The London Daily Post and General Advertiser* for December 22, 1735, informs us that "Last Saturday Night his Royal Highness the Prince of Wales was at the Theatre Royal in Drury-Lane," the play that night being *The Silent Woman*. It was given "By Command of their Royal Highnesses the Prince and Princess of Wales" on February 18, 1738, January 26, 1739, and October 23, 1739. Of the last two visits, the daily papers took notice.[1]

A new generation of actors was now appearing. Havard, who played Dauphine at the revival of 1752, first acted the part on November 16, 1737. Harper as Otter, Macklin as Cutbeard, and Mrs. Pritchard as Lady Haughty also appeared in the play for the first time that night. Mrs. Pritchard later acted Epicoene at the Covent Garden revival of 1745, where she continued for three years. In 1752 she resumed the rôle at the unsuccessful revival at Drury Lane. A new character came forward on January 26, 1739, with Woodward as La Foole, a part which he played also at Covent Garden for three years, but exchanged for Sir John Daw at the 1752 revival. After February 13, 1742, *The Silent Woman* suffered the first lapse of more than two seasons since the beginning of the century, for it was not acted again until April 17, 1745, at Covent Garden, under the direction of Rich, and its career on any stage was almost finished. If one may credit the account of Benjamin Victor, who wrote that "The *Morose*, in the *Silent Woman* . . . died" at the death of Ben Jonson in August, 1742, the reason for its disappearance is clear.[2]

1. *The London Daily Post and General Advertiser*, January 26, 1739; October 23, 1739.
2. *The History of the Theatres of London and Dublin*, II, 63.

III

COVENT GARDEN, 1745–1748
DRURY LANE, 1752

The Coxcombs

Concerning the seven performances of *The Silent Woman* at Covent Garden between April 17, 1745, and March 28, 1748, not a scrap of criticism has come down to us. We know nothing but the casts, which remained almost unchanged during the period. There were five actors already familiar with the play: Bridgewater (Morose); Cibber, Jr. (Daw); Woodward (La Foole); Marten (Otter); and Mrs. Pritchard (Epicoene). Of the rest, Hale (Truewit) had acted Peregrine (1733) and Face (1740); James (Cutbeard) had acted Dapper (1740) and Would-be (1742). The rest, — Cashell (Dauphine), Ridout (Clerimont), Mrs. Hale (Lady Haughty), Mrs. Bland (Lady Centaure), Miss Hippisley (Dol Mavis), and Mrs. James (Mrs. Otter),— were new in Jonson.

A writer observed in 1747, "This Play is still acted with great Applause," [1] and its excellence was apparent to such critical minds as admired regularity and carefully graded structure, for the author of *A Dissertation on Comedy* (1750) described *The Silent Woman* as "the correctest Play on the *British* Stage" and "a perfect Standard of dramatic Writing," [2] in that it had a diversity of natural characters, strongly marked and regularly disposed, all conducing to the completion of the main action.

The Silent Woman was revived at Drury Lane on October 26, 1752, "Not Acted these Fifteen Years," "the Characters New Dress'd after the manner of the Time." Garrick, although he did not play a part himself, selected his cast so carefully that there were only three actors inex-

---

1. *A Compleat List of all the English Dramatic Poets*, p. 122.
2. Pages 53–54.

perienced in Jonson: Scrase (Clerimont); Davies (Cut-beard); and Mrs. Price (Dol Mavis). Five were new to this comedy but familiar with other plays of Jonson: Yates as Morose had acted Dapper, Kastril, and Brainworm; William Palmer as Truewit had acted Wellbred; Shuter as La Foole had acted Ananias and Master Stephen; Berry as Otter had acted Corvino, Mammon, and old Knowell; Mrs. Clive as Lady Haughty had acted Win Littlewit, Dol Common, and Lady Would-be. And there was a nucleus of five men and women who had acted formerly in *The Silent Woman:* Havard as Dauphine had played the part earlier (1737), as well as Surly, Bonario, and Volpone; Woodward as Daw had already played La Foole, Kastril, Ananias, and Bobadill; Mrs. Pritchard had previously acted Epicoene (1745), as well as Lady Haughty (1737), Lady Would-be, and Dol Common; Mrs. Bennett had acted Lady Centaure (1736), as well as Lady Haughty (1741); and Mrs. Cross as Mrs. Otter had acted Lady Haughty, Lady Centaure, Dame Pliant, Dol Common, and Cob's wife.

If the comedy could have been successful with any cast, it should have been now. A lively, though unfavorable, review, consisting mainly of a chatty summary of the plot, appeared in "Priscilla Termagant's" (Bonnell Thornton's) *Spring Garden Journal* (1752).[1] The reviewer ridiculed the notion of a silent woman, satirized the collegiate ladies, and analyzed the character of Morose:

The Character of *Morose* is the most extraordinary one that ever appeared upon a Stage; and I am apt to imagine, had a modern Author drawn so unnatural a Part, that the Audience would have shewn very little Complaisance to his Humour. I will take upon me to say, this Character never existed but in Imagination; and I am at a Loss to find out Mr. *Garrick's* Inducement in reviving this Play; for as it is temporary, a very few of the Audience could possibly relish the Wit; and the Scene between the Doctor and Mr. Parson is improper to be repre-

1. No. 1, pp. 12–15.

sented before a polite Audience; and tho' *Every Man in his Humour* met with so general an Approbation, yet it could not insure Success to this Play. I will not pretend to say, Mr. *Garrick* regarded only the filling his House; I would rather impute it, for once, to his Want of Judgment: However, he has given two ingenious young Fellows an Opportunity of shewing themselves to Advantage, I mean Mr. *Shuter* and Mr. *Palmer*, who have each of them more Merit than Encouragement.

A description of the revival was also given by Davies, who had first-hand knowledge of what he wrote:

When it was revived, about thirty years since, under the management of Mr. Garrick, with perseverance it was dragged on for a few nights. The managers acquired neither profit nor reputation by the exhibition of it. Some expressions met with severe marks of the spectators displeasure. The character of Morose, upon whose peevish and perverse humour the plot of the comedy depends, is that of a whimsical recluse, whose disposition can bear no sound but that which he utters himself. If this were the whole of his character, he would still be a good object for comic satire, but the melancholy of Morose degenerates into malice and cruelty. . . .

But, besides the licentiousness of the manners, the quaintness of expression, in the Silent Woman, the frequent allusions to forgotten customs and characters render it impossible to be ever revived with any probability of success. To understand Jonson's comedies perfectly, we should have before us a satirical history of the age in which he lived.[1]

The comedy was acted only five nights between October 26 and November 11, and was then dropped. Echoes of the revival found their way into the pamphlets. In November, 1752, Woodward was disgracefully insulted during his performance by a person in a stage box. In the inevitable controversy which followed, Dr. John Hill took the side of the insulter and attacked Woodward, who replied in a pamphlet called *A Letter from Henry Woodward . . . to Dr. John Hill*. An ironical defense of Woodward, congratu-

---

1. *Dramatic Miscellanies*, II, 101–103.

lating him on his victory as a writer and his ability as an actor, answered his letter. Among other "compliments," it contained the following:

The *Daw* of *Johnson*, view it, examine it! let those who wou'd do Justice to thy Name examine it! how pitiful a Character! Nature, meer, paltry, servile, common, perfect Nature! a Fool, a Coward, a Coxcomb, a Being whom we may pick up at every Coffee-house. What could be expected from a Thing like this upon the Stage? Contempt and not Applause, unless you *Harry* had inspir'd the Scene! Your *Thingum Thangum* to your Sword: Call'd it not forth, that Approbation from the attending Benches which all the Authors cold and pointless Humour in vain so-licited? 'Tis thus thou claim'st our Praises, O inventive Friend? not on the Fund of others Merit, but on the rich Produce of thine own. Vainly shall Men hereafter ask what Talent Nature gave thee for this Purpose. She has done more than all she cou'd have heap'd upon thee, in bestowing, by that she has deny'd. She has taken from thee Modesty.[1]

Palmer's Truewit received appreciation:

Mr. PALMER's first Appearance is very pleasing; his Figure is good one, but he has a Sameness in every thing he does, which makes him sometimes tiresome: He did great Justice to TRUE-WIT in the *Silent Woman*, of which he made much more than the Part seemed capable of; however he has not enough of the *De-gagée* about him, to stand with much Reputation in *Mirable* and *Captain Plume*; there is a Sprightliness in these Characters of which he is not sufficient Master; but the Improvements he has made, since his being first brought forward on the Stage, induce us to believe that Mr. PALMER has not yet reached the Summit of his Abilities.[2]

In 1752 Bonnell Thornton's *Have at You All; or, The Drury-Lane Journal* printed the following notice:

The DISPUTANT SOCIETY for the FEMALE SEX met as usual at the *Silent Woman* in *Broad Saint Giles's*; but Mrs. TERMAGANT

1. *A Letter to Mr. Woodward, on his Triumph over the Inspector. By Sampson Edwards, the Merry Cobler of the Hay-Market* [1752], pp. 8–9.
2. *The Present State of the Stage in Great-Britain and Ireland*, pp. 32–33.

being engaged at Mr. Ryan's Benefit, a Stranger assum'd the Chair, and no Minutes were taken at their Proceedings.[1]

This allusion to an inn named "The Silent Woman" was doubtless purely facetious, but there is ample evidence that many inns actually bore that name,[2] and one author even suggests that Jonson originally derived the title of the play from the name of an inn.   The critics forgot *The Silent Woman*, save for the edition by Whalley (1756), until 1759, when *The Universal Magazine* printed "The Life of Benjamin Jonson, Poet-Laureat," including praise of the perfection of *Epicoene*, "this being generally esteemed the most exact and finished comedy that our nation hath produced," and paraphrasing Dryden's examen.[3] Arthur Murphy in his comedy *The Way to Keep Him* (1761), referred to a person who does not appear in the play, as Sir Amorous La Fool,[4] and three years later Baker noted that *The Silent Woman* "is accounted one of the best Comedies extant, and is always acted with universal Applause."[5] *The Dramatic Timepiece* indicated that the time required to play the comedy was one hour and fifty-nine minutes, and that the play was over at 8:29 P.M.[6]

In 1769 Richard Twiss, the traveler, reported that the play had penetrated to the continent and was acted in Portugal:

A Portuguese translation, in three acts, in prose, was published of Ben Johnson's *Epicœne*: it was acted at Lisbon, though miserably disfigured.[7]

1. Page 237.
2. *Notes and Queries*, 1st series, V (1852), 468, 547, 3d series, IX (1866), 431, 5th series, IV (1875), 88, 136, 252, 337; Fritz Endell, *Old Tavern Signs*, Cambridge, Mass., 1916, pp. 67–69; G. J. Monson-Fitzjohn, *Quaint Signs of Olde Inns*, 1926, pp. 118–119.   3. XXIV, 337–347.
4. II. ii. There is a character named Epicene in Robert Hitchcock's comedy *The Macaroni*, 1773.
5. *The Companion to the Play-House*, I, article on "*Epicœne*."
6. Page 71.
7. *Travels through Portugal and Spain, in 1772 and 1773*, 1775, p. 457. I have not been able to trace a copy.

Desecration was not to end here, for two years later Francis Gentleman, who could not keep his hands off Jonson,
followed his vandalism in *The Tobacconist* with another
mutilation called *The Coxcombs*, a farce made from *The
Silent Woman*, but acted only once, on September 16,
1771, at the Haymarket. *The Public Advertiser* for that
day announced *Love in a Village*, "to which will be added
a Farce (altered from Ben Jonson) by the Author of the
Tobacconist, call'd The Coxcombs. . . . The Prologue
written and spoken by Mr. Gentleman." The same paper
indicated also that *The Coxcombs* was "a Comedy of two
Acts, taken from one of Ben Jonson's most celebrated
Pieces." The principal characters were taken by Vandermere, Fearon, Dancer, Gentleman himself, Didier, and
Mrs. Didier. Hitherto, it has been supposed that the farce
was never printed,[1] but, fortunately or not, the prologue
and an entire scene found favor with the editor of *The
Oxford Magazine*, who printed them in the issue of September, 1771.

PROLOGUE to the COXCOMBS

Our corps disbanded till the next campaign,
When smiling summer takes his chearful reign,
Our able Gen'ral on the wing to France,
Un-officer'd — with tremors we advance:
Tho' all the genuine, jocund pow'r to please,
Is fled with modern ARISTOPHANES
Tho' Bobadil and Drugger now no more
Within these walls create the festive roar,
We venture on a critical review,
Conscious of kind forgiving friends in you.
    The little after-game propos'd this night,
In business, plot, and character, is slight;
Yet, as from Johnson our design we take,
We hope your kind indulgence for his sake.
    Coxcombs our subject — which the muse may deem
For pointed satire an unbounded theme.

---

1. "*The Stage*" *Cyclopædia*, 1909, p. 94; D. E. Baker, Isaac Reed, and
Stephen Jones, *Biographia Dramatica*, 1812, II, 139.

Such characters are found in every sphere,
Thro' all the arts and sciences appear,
Physic, divinity, and quibbling law,
Have each La Foole, and eke a Sir John Daw.
Courts, tho' refined, keep more than equal pace,
And strain their speed in folly's flimsy chase,
The city cramm'd with politics and eating,
Puffs close behind, and hardly bears the beating.
　　Tho' to the males our portraits we confine,
Females in Coxcombry too often shine;
But to their beauty, their resistless charms,
Satire, with much politeness, yields its arms.
　　But hold — don't I, like other authors roam
In search of folly, with too much at home?
'Tis odds against me — let me then retreat,
Lest Truth should censure from her awful seat,
And by this slight excursion of my brains,
Prove I'm a scribbling Coxcomb for my pains. [1]

The scene from the farce was as follows:

Makemirth, Frolic, and Gravely. *Enter to them* Sir Amorous
La Foole.

Sir Amo. Bright shine the morning on you, Charles.
Make. Why not make your compliment as long as the whole day,
　　　　Sir Amorous?
Sir Amo. Well, the whole day, and every day; that's better still.
Make. Friends, give me leave to introduce a matchless Baronet,
　　　　Sir Amorous La Foole, of Simple Hall.
Sir Amo. Yes, of Simple Hall.
Frolic. We are made happy by the Introduction.
Sir Amo. Gentlemen, I kiss your little fingers — you must know,
　　　　friends — for we are all friends now, being so intimately
　　　　acquainted, that I have been at Lord Callepash's to
　　　　borrow his French Cook.
Grave. Borrow a Cook!
Sir Amo. Oh, nothing commoner; I have a negro myself for dressing
　　　　turtle, but the sun-burnt scoundrel powdered my last so
　　　　horribly with Chian, that nothing but the palate of a
　　　　fire-eater could swallow one bit.
Make. What a dreadful disappointment!

---

1. Page 112. Aristophanes was the nickname of Foote, the manager of the
Haymarket summer companies.

Sir Amo. Faith, and so it was, Charles, considering what excellent judges of eating I had; four Aldermen past the chair; three Deputies; two Chaplains; a Major of the Train Bands; ten Common-council men; *and the Ladies of as many as were married.*

Frolic. By your Gusto we may presume some city election is in view.

Sir Amo. No, no, I don't trouble my head with politics.

Grave. No! then you differ much from your name-sakes; for the La Fooles are notorious dabblers that —

Frolic. Nay, Sir Amorous, don't mind cynical Jack, your family is very respectable and ancient.

Sir Amo. Yes, Sir, we are very *antic* — we bear our arms from Adam in Paradise: three fig-leaves pendent and an apple-tree rampant, for the crest.

Make. ⎫
Frolic. ⎭ Ha! ha! ha!

Sir Amo. And as my grandfather, Sir Humphrey, used to say, we are like the Jacobites, scattered all over the earth.

Grave. Jacobites! Israelites you mean.

Sir Amo. Ay, ay, Israelites, they are all the same you know — but, gents, I shall positively expect you to dine with me when I get into my new house on the Terrace Adelphi next week.

Make. Adelphi! a most classical situation.

Sir Amo. True — every one knows I have taste — we shall have steeples, wharfs, timber yards, bridges, barges, and water in abundance there.

Frolic. Objects plenty — but, Sir Amorous, won't your prospect, like a pudding stuck too full of plumbs, be apt to cloy?

Sir Amo. Not at all — I love rich prospects, rich puddings, rich parties, rich purses — rich every thing; besides they tell me for six months together we shan't see further than the ballustrades.

Make. How so?

Sir Amo. Thames fogs won't let us.

Grave. Admirably pleasant and wholesome, to be half the year wrapped round with a wet blanket.[1]

The reference to the new home of Sir Amorous on the Adelphi Terrace must have had the force of every fresh local allusion, for at the time there was much discussion of

1. Page 92.

the project of the brothers Adam, after whom the buildings were named. In July, 1768, the Adelphi buildings were commenced, but court and city were opposed, and the citizens of London were glad to do all in their power to show hostility to the court. It was thought that the Adam brothers had encroached too far upon the Thames; the citizens applied to Parliament for protection, but lost their cause. The Adelphi was on the site of Durham House; Durham yard was occupied by a number of small low-lying houses and coal-sheds, washed by the muddy river. The change effected by the architects was extraordinary. They erected a series of arches, allowed the wharves to remain, "connected the river with the Strand by a spacious archway, and over their extensive vaultings erected a series of well-built streets, [and] a noble terrace toward the river." [1] Gentleman's scene is very flat, and *The Coxcombs* did little to perpetuate the fame of *The Silent Woman*. Nor, in fact, did the revival of the comedy at Drury Lane in January, 1776.

IV

DRURY LANE, 1776

The earliest reference to the projected revival of *The Silent Woman* occurs in a letter dated August 8 (1773), from William Smith, the famous Kitely at Covent Garden, to George Colman, in which Smith refused an offer to play Mosca and expressed a preference for being "employ'd in a longer Part in the Epicœne — which I hear is much improv'd under y^r hand." [2] Colman was at work on an alteration of the comedy to which he had already called Garrick's attention, and on December 20, 1774, Garrick wrote him:

I shall do all I can to produce y^e *Silent Woman* this Season; but it will work us much, if we keep Jephson's tragedy; I shall

1. H. B. Wheatley, *London Past and Present*, 1891, I, 4–5.
2. *Posthumous Letters*, pp. 185–186.

rely upon y^r Attachment to us to excuse our deferring it, if we
find an absolute necessity for it — the Comedy will take thrice
ye trouble & care of a modern one to shew it, as it shall be shewn,
& *ought* to be coming from *you* to *me*.[1]

Garrick always appreciated the difficulty of training a cast
for any of Jonson's plays. How soon he began to select
his actors for *The Silent Woman* is a question, but by
December 12, 1775, his plans were in progress. On that
day he wrote Colman:

I want to talk to you about 'the Silent Woman.' Poor Weston, Moody tells me, will, he thinks, never play again; he wants
to go to Bath: therefore, as we cannot stay his recovery, to whom
shall I give La Fool? We must go to work upon it directly.[2]

On December 16 *The Public Advertiser* printed the first
announcement of the revival, a notice repeated on December 31 and January 9. These bills emphasized the fact
that "the Characters [were to be] dressed in the Habits
of the Times," a custom which had prevailed with Garrick
since the revival of *Every Man in his Humour* in 1751.
The play was produced, "Not Acted these Twenty Years,"
on January 13, 1776, "with a New occasional Prologue
[spoken] by Mr. Palmer":

Happy the soaring bard who boldy wooes,
And wins the favour of, the tragic muse!
He from the grave may call the mighty dead,
In buskins and blank verse the stage to tread;
On Pompeys and old Cæsars rise to fame,
And join the poet's to th' historian's name.
The comick wit, alas! whose eagle eyes
Pierce Nature thro', and mock the time's disguise,
Whose pencil living follies brings to view,
Survives those follies, and his portraits too;
Like star-gazers, deplores his luckless fate,
For last year's Almanacks are out of date.

1. Page 303.
2. R. B. Peake, *Memoirs of the Colman Family*, 1841, I, 390. Weston died
on January 18, 1776.

"The Fox, the Alchemist, the Silent Woman,
"Done by Ben Jonson, are out-done by no man."
Thus sung in rough, but panegyrick, rhimes,
The wits and criticks of our author's times.
But now we bring him forth with dread and doubt,
And fear his *learned socks* are quite worn out.
The subtle Alchemist grows obsolete,
And Drugger's humour scarcely keeps him sweet.
    To-night, if you would feast your eyes and ears,
Go back in fancy near two hundred years;
A play of Ruffs and Farthingales review,
Old English fashions, such as then were new!
Drive not Tom Otter's *Bulls and Bears* away;
Worse *Bulls and Bears* disgrace the present day.
On fair Collegiates let no critick frown!
A Ladies' Club still holds its rank in town.
If modern Cooks, who nightly treat the pit, ⎞
Do not quite cloy and surfeit you with wit, ⎬
From the old kitchen please to pick a bit! ⎠
If once, with hearty stomachs to regale
On old Ben Johnson's fare, tho' somewhat stale,
A meal on Bobadil you deign'd to make,
Take *Epicœne* for his and Kitely's sake![1]

The cast was composed of excellent actors, all but four of whom, Miss Platt (Dol Mavis), Mrs. Millidge (Trusty), Miss Sherry (Lady Haughty), and Mrs. Siddons (Epicoene), had been adequately trained in Jonson's plays. Three of the cast had taken part in the revival of 1752. Palmer (Truewit) had played that rôle previously, as well as Face, Dapper, Stephen, and Matthew. Davies (Clerimont) had played Cutbeard. One wonders if he was not too old for Clerimont in 1776, or at least too much disfigured by disease to play the youthful Ned, for we are told that "O disasterous chance! Hymen, as if inflamed at the

---

1. *Epicœne; or, The Silent Woman. . . . With Alterations,* by George Colman, 1776, sig. A4; *The Gentleman's Magazine,* XLVI (1776), 87–88; *The London Magazine,* XLV (1776), 50; *The Lady's Magazine,* VII (1776), 48–49; *The Universal Magazine,* LVIII (1776), 40; *The Town and Country Magazine,* VIII (1776), 48; *The London Chronicle,* January 20–23, 1776; *The Public Advertiser,* January 22, 1776; George Colman, *Prose on Several Occasions,* 1787, III, 212–213; *The Dramatick Works of George Colman,* 1777, III, 214–215.

indignities offered his rites, bribed Venus to set fire to his *nose*, which the artful baggage did so dexterously, that it is, at present, with the greatest *daily art* he can preserve it from falling into his porter pot." [1] Yates (Otter) had acted Morose in 1752. His other rôles in Jonson have already been noted. Of his acting at this time *Theatrical Biography* noted that he was the oldest actor of any repute then belonging to the theatre, that he had a particular turn for low comedy, the finest understanding of Shakspere's fools, and a genius for dressing his parts with singular propriety. [2]

All the rest of the cast had played in Jonson. Thomas King (La Foole) had acted Bobadill, Wellbred, and Kastril. He was undoubtedly well chosen by Garrick to supply the rôle intended for the inimitable Tom Weston, for *Theatrical Biography* commented on his "pert vivacity, with a sly knowledge of the world, which he possesses both in his face and manner, that are peculiarly his own, and render him an original in these casts of parts." [3] He was notable for Tom in *The Conscious Lovers*, Brass in *The Confederacy*, William in *The Way to Keep Him*, and Lord Ogleby in *The Clandestine Marriage*.

Robert Bensley (Morose) had acted Mosca in 1771. But there were few compliments for his performance on the stage, and *Theatrical Biography* apologized for introducing him as any actor at all; "he has neither *face*, *voice*, nor *manner*, that can any way entitle him to this epithet; there is a horror in the *first*, a sepulchral gravity in the *second*, and a mechanism in the *third*, that must always render him disgusting to those few who are judges of the natural requisites of theatric powers." [4]

Parsons (Daw), a specialist at impersonating old men, had previously acted Ananias. Baddeley (Cutbeard), earlier Surly and Kastril, had been bred a cook, but had

1. *Theatrical Biography*, II, 105.
2. II, 46–47.
3. I, 81. See also *The Dramatic Censor*, II, 493.
4. II, 63.

emerged from the kitchen to play foreign footmen and just such parts as Cutbeard. Of the actresses Mrs. Hopkins (Mrs. Otter) had played Dol Common; and Mrs. Davies (Lady Centaure), Dame Kitely and Bridget.

The receipts for the first night were £192 11s., a reasonably large sum for those times, even when compared with the £265 17s. taken in for Garrick's last performance of *The Alchemist* in April. Of the success of the première there is an opinion, "free of managerial influence," on the playbill for the evening now in the Huntington Library. The note was made by J. P. Kemble from the diary of his father-in-law, Mr. Hopkins, the prompter:

This play is altered by Mr. Colman — received with some applause — but it does not seem to hit the present taste — A little hissing at the End.

Before the reviews can be fully appreciated, some account of Colman's alteration is necessary.

V

THE ALTERATION

Colman's alterations of the text of *The Silent Woman* were of two kinds.[1] First, as in *Volpone* and *The Alchemist*, there was need for condensation in order to reduce some of the expansive Jonsonian verbosity, obsolete allusions, and by-play which might retard lively acting of the farce. In addition, Colman conceived an essential structural change which seemed to improve the climax. Both changes were simple to make, and both had clear advantages. For two acts the play received no alterations sufficiently important to permit of generalization. No character was greatly reduced, like Sir Epicure Mammon, and Colman

1. References to act and scene in Jonson's original play are made to the edition by Gifford (1816), followed by Cunningham (1875) and the Mermaid edition (1894).

made no additions except such as were necessary for co-
herence. First of all, the page's song beginning "Still to
be neat" was sung at the beginning of Act I, instead of
later in the act, and the description of the collegiate ladies
by Clerimont and Truewit was omitted, in conformity with
Colman's practise later in the play, where Lady Haughty,
Dol Mavis, and Lady Centaure were reduced in importance. The reduction here, of more than a page, is the longest single cut in the first two acts, the other cuts consisting
mainly of short omissions of one, two, or three lines only.
The page's description of Morose omitted about ten lines
which referred to an ancient bearwarden. All profanity
and all of the characteristic Jonsonian indelicacies were
expunged.

In Act II, scene i, Truewit's long discourses with the
noise-hating Morose were frequently abbreviated, but as
the force of the scene depended primarily upon Truewit's
garrulity and the agony it caused Morose, it was impossible to reduce his speeches too much. Altogether, the
omissions in his part amounted to well over a page of text
without ruining the effect of the whole. From Act II,
scene ii, were removed some of Sir John Daw's allusions
to classic authors, which could scarcely interest the audience. There were other minor cuts which caused little
change in characterization and none in plot. In Act II,
scene iii, the scene introducing Epicoene to Morose, the
part of Morose was cut about fifty lines, including a description of his hatred of noise, already known to the
audience, and of his ideals for his wife. Act II, scene iv,
remained practically unaltered.

In Act III, scene ii, Colman introduced the sole alteration which demanded labor more exacting than that of an
editor interested in shortening and modernizing an old
comedy. Only here did he deviate from Jonson's structural
plan. At the opening of this scene, the original text showed
Morose happily married (as he supposed) to Epicoene.
After rewarding the parson, however, he was astonished

to hear Epicoene begin to talk. That is, Jonson revealed early in the plot the supreme hoax practised on the surly old man,— indeed, the most terrible misfortune which could happen to him,— a termagant wife. Next Jonson introduced Truewit in voluble conversation with Epicoene and in argument with Morose, who cursed the barber Cutbeard, cause of his woe, in two pages of Jonsonian realism. Then the garrulous collegiate ladies entered, driving Morose into agony with their chattering. The arrival of the musicians and Captain Otter with his bull, bear, horse, and trumpeters, finally drove the desperate husband from the stage.

Now Colman saw clearly that a deferred climax was possible, that the noise created by Truewit, the collegiate ladies, and the musicians would savor less of anticlimax if Epicoene were not permitted to speak until the noise-makers had done their worst. Morose could rid himself of the others, but Epicoene was now his for life, and her chatter would fall upon him like a thunderbolt. The alteration required only a deft transposition of the revelation of Epicoene's volubility (Jonson, III. ii) to a later position in the play. Colman began the act by giving Morose a soliloquy on his happiness in marrying a dumb wife. The minor horrors of Truewit and the collegiates followed, but Epicoene was consistently silent, and Colman was obliged to cut not only her speeches, but the splendid two pages in which Morose cursed Cutbeard, a vivid passage similar to Dr. Slop's excommunication of Obadiah in *Tristram Shandy*. Clerimont and his musicians and Otter nearly drove Morose mad, it is true, but after their departure the act ended with a quiet soliloquy for Morose, composed by Colman, showing him still delighted, after so much uproar, with his charmingly silent bride.

By making sizable deletions of about eight pages, Colman played Act IV continuously without the change of scene indicated in the original. The act had to be adjusted, also, to compensate for the transposition of the climax begun in act three. The altered act began like Jonson's, with Truewit and Clerimont conversing about Morose's recent torture. At this point in Jonson, Dauphine entered and described the activities of the collegiate ladies. All this worldly-wise information about the ways of women Colman judiciously removed. Next came the fun between Otter and his eavesdropping wife, half a page of which disappeared. Morose entered and drove this company away, Jonson's first scene ending here.

Colman was now almost ready to introduce his climax. The collegiates entered with Epicoene, whom they wished to make one of their number. A page of their dialogue vanished. To them came Morose, wildly lamenting the noise-making in his house, only to be scolded, for the first time, by his "dumb" wife. And here Colman introduced the episode from Jonson (III. ii) omitted in his third act. Morose was horrified. The ladies, including Epicoene, departed, leaving him to lament his fate to Dauphine and Truewit. Morose feared that he should go mad. Epicoene returned and talked at length on her husband's approaching mania, but not at such great length as in Jonson, for the discussion on madness, another example of Jonson's learning, was reduced a page, and the entire episode between Trusty and Epicoene concerning a means of putting Morose to sleep was omitted as wordy and obsolete. In both versions Dauphine entered here to announce that Morose had departed to arrange for a divorce. Jonson concluded the act with the fooleries practised by Truewit and Clerimont on La Foole and Daw, but Colman ended his act at once.

The altered fifth act, consisting of two scenes, began with the episode in which Jonson (IV. ii) amused the audience with tricks played on La Foole and Daw, a farcical scene depending on the opening and closing of doors. To make cuts here was difficult. Except for the omission of a few too frank remarks by La Foole and of the admiration for Dauphine's physical charm expressed by the collegiate ladies, together with a few occasional cuts of two or three lines, the episode appeared unchanged.

The second scene of Colman's fifth act (Jonson, V. i) was shortened more than any other scene. The conclusion depended only on the means of securing Morose's divorce, and Colman moved toward this end much more swiftly than Jonson. Indeed, he reduced the text of the original no less than ten pages. The parts of Dol Mavis, Clerimont, La Foole, and Daw were greatly abbreviated. La Foole and Daw in particular were made to wound ladies' reputations more laconically than in Jonson. The assignations between Dauphine and the several members of the collegiates were obliterated, probably as offensive to improved taste and manners. One may recall that Dryden professed to have been somewhat shocked by this scene, although Collier excused it, as he excused almost all of Jonson's offenses against delicate moral sensibility.

The divorce episode was made much more compact. Truewit's instructions to Otter and Cutbeard were written sharply to the point, with little ornamentation. Morose, in keeping with his character, spoke far fewer lines than in the original. But the greatest cut came in the twelve causes for divorce, which were merely mentioned, with little of the learned and perhaps tiresomely casuistical expansion of Jonson. About three pages heavily sprinkled with Latin terminology disappeared, and except as they satirized the procedure in courts of law, there was no loss to theatrical presentation. The removal of Jonsonian erudition at this point was exactly parallel to the cutting of the mountebank scene in *Volpone* and passages describing alchemical processes in *The Alchemist*. Next, Morose's confession of impotence and the admissions of Daw and La Foole concerning their previous relations with the bride were entirely removed, and the divorce was rapidly accomplished by Dauphine, who persuaded Morose to sign the will in his favor and then revealed Epicoene as a boy.

As a whole, then, the alteration was a more compact

comedy, with a more carefully graded climax than Jonson's. But it had lost in its brevity the gusto and occasional portentousness which made the original play a farce in the grand manner.

VI

1776 AND LATER

The comedy was diversely reviewed. *The Public Advertiser*, connected with the theatre because it printed the daily bills, was discreetly favorable, devoting over half of its space to a quotation from Dryden's examen. The original part of the review commended Colman's structural alteration, which had remedied the anticlimax in Jonson, where the lesser tortures had come last:

According to this Idea, the Order of the Circumstances of the Fable was judiciously reversed in the Alteration of Saturday Evening; to effect which it has here and there been necessary to make some few Additions, in which the Stile and Colour of the original Author seemed to be very happily imitated. The Dresses were new and elegant, and the Performance, allowing for a few lapses of a first Representation, very spirited and excellent.[1]

Henry Bate, in *The Morning Post and Daily Advertiser*, contradicted Dryden's praise, judging the fable "trifling, broken, and confused," and the characters unnatural and overcharged. He found Otter "very humerous," but absurd; Dauphine and Clerimont "two poor animals"; and the collegiate ladies "four insignificant females in chalk." Mrs. Otter was, however, "a tolerable likeness of the virago of those times." The horse-play of La Foole, Daw, and Truewit was too farcical and improbable. The classical style of the play he admired. As to Colman's alterations, Bate approved, but wished that more of "the rust of antiquity" had been removed. His most important note, however, concerned the casting of Epicoene:

1. January 15, 1776.

It cannot be an improper intimation, that the character of
Epicoene should be played by a *male*, if the denouement is to be
brought about by any natural means, or produce the least effect
— the coolness with which the audience received the discovery,
is a proof of the propriety of this remark.

Upon the whole we cannot esteem it a striking comedy, even
with the assistances it has now received, the fine manner in
which it is certainly got up, and the great expence which the
managers have been at in habiting the whole *dramatis personae*,
in splendid and characteristic old English dresses.

As to the performers they exerted every nerve; Mr. King did
more than possibly could have been expected in *La Fool*: Mr.
Parsons was very great in *Daw*; Mr. Bensley's *Morose* was capital; now and then he forgot the surly old man, and sunk into
the superannuated driveller: It must be considered as a great
undertaking for a young man, and no doubt his apprehensions
on the first night, prevented a. regular display of his powers: —
We conceive Mr. King should have played it. Mr. Yates's *Otter*,
and Mr. Baddeley's *Cutbeard* were all we could expect. — Mr.
Palmer was admirable in the long unprofitable part of *True-wit*,
and discovered great spirit and comic vivacity through every
scene: *Cleremont* and *Dauphine*, altho' trifling parts, were well
performed by Mess. Brereton, and Davis. The ladies in general
played well. Mrs. Siddons acquired great applause in the spirited part of *Epicoene*; and Mrs. Hopkins was not behind hand
in Mrs. Otter. — Upon the whole the play had great justice done
it in representation by the performers as well as the managers.[1]

The Westminster Magazine copied most of Bate's review, but disagreed with him about the cast:

All the Actors, except Mr. King and Mr. Parsons, performed
but indifferently. Bensley is the worst Old Man we ever saw.
He presents the countenance of a sickly old Woman, and the
uniform goggle of his eyes, by which he means to express in-
firmity and distress, is the look of a man in anguish from the
colic. Mr. Palmer, Mr. Brereton, and Mr. Davis, have a bloated

---

1. January 15, 1776. See C. H. Gray, *Theatrical Criticism in London*, pp.
232-233. *The London Chronicle*, January 13-16, 1776, printed a composite review, taken from *The Public Advertiser* and *The Morning Post*.

vulgarity about them, which should ever deter the Manager from assigning them the parts of cavaliers or men of fashion. Baddeley, as usual, over-did his part; and Mr. Yates, as usual, was not very perfect in his.[1]

The London Magazine lamented Jonson's preoccupation with the rules and praised Shakspere for displaying how far genius is superior to art in the portrayal of human nature.

To describe the human heart, as actuated from within, or affected from without, and strip it of its various coverings; to analyse and mark the human mind in its innumerable operations; to connect those with the manners, habits, humours, and prevailing follies of the times, are the true qualifications of a dramatic writer. Ben Jonson was certainly possessed of those talents, but he as certainly sacrificed too much to the opinion of others, and the prevailing taste of the age in which he wrote. On the other hand, he too frequently indulged his genius, and gave way to the impressions he received at an early period of his life; . . . his juvenile habits led his attention to objects not always the best selected, or worthy of his pen. Ben was besides a pedant, as well as a scholar, and like his cotemporary *Cervantes*, was tinctured with the very folly which was the fixed object of his most pointed ridicule.

These, we take it, were some of the chief reasons, that Jonson's plays do not bear the high reputation they did for almost a century after they were written; and will remain, we may venture to predict, an insurmountable bar to their ever recovering their former reputation, except where indeed they happen to be uncommonly *well-supported* in the representation; which, truth compels us to say, was not the case on Saturday evening.[2]

The Silent Woman was repeated on Monday, January 15, and *The Public Advertiser* for the next morning observed that it was "received with very great Applause." The receipts were £200 13*s*. 6*d*. The third night, January 17, it was played to a house of £146 8*s*., and the next morning *The Public Advertiser* announced:

1. January, 1776, p. 30.   2. XLV (1776), 48-49.

As many Admirers of Ben Jonson have expressed a Desire to see the Silent Woman performed as the Author originally intended it, Mr. Le Mash will perform the Part of Epicoene on Monday next.

When the comedy was presented on Tuesday, January 23, Epicoene was played by Philip Lamash, a protégé of Garrick's, who had acted Dapper in 1774. J. P. Kemble noted on the playbill for the evening:

By this Time it was discovered that Epicœne should be acted by a man, and Mr. Lamash performed it.

What, aside from Bate's review, gave Colman and Garrick the idea for the substitution? It is possible that Mrs. Siddons gave a weak performance,[1] but it is equally likely that the restoration of a boy as Epicoene was determined by a letter from Dr. Hoadly to Garrick on January 14. Hoadly suggested that King act Morose and urged that by no means should Epicoene be played by a woman.

A young *smooth-face* certainly, if you have *one* in the company; the force is entirely lost by its being acted by a woman. *Sex* is so strong in every body's mind, especially of your more vulgar hearers, that it is impossible to be separated.

He suggested cutting most of Truewit's exploits, but advised keeping Otter, and was consumed with admiration for the Congrevian quality of the dialogue,— its wit, naturalness, and ease.[2]

The receipts for January 23 were only £134 6s. *The Public Advertiser* for January 24 remarked:

1. James Boaden, in his *Memoirs of Mrs. Siddons*, 1827, I, 37, thought she played one of the collegiate ladies; for the first discussion of her apparent failure as Epicoene see Percy Fitzgerald, *The Kembles; An Account of the Kemble Family* [1871], I, 54–55.
2. [James Boaden], *The Private Correspondence of David Garrick*, II, 123–124. On the female Epicoene see William Gifford, *The Works of Ben Jonson*, 1816, III, 336–337.

The Performance of this character [Epicoene] by an Actor rather than an Actress, according to the original Intention of the Author, was received with particular Marks of Approbation, and the Comedy will be repeated (for the 5th Time) on Saturday.

But on Saturday Colman's *Jealous Wife* was given, and again *The Silent Woman* was banished from the stage.[1]

After the play was withdrawn, Colman brought out his altered version, explaining that he had always believed it the duty of a director to atone for the mummery served up daily by bringing forward the productions of the most esteemed writers. The alterations of the present comedy had been generally approved, and he had no intention of vindicating the established reputation of Jonson against critics who found his plays unnatural and lacking in ingenuity. The alteration was reviewed by *The Monthly Review* in April, which commended Colman's attempt to keep an ancient writer before the public, but judged *The Silent Woman* in every respect inferior to *Volpone*. As for the revision, the reviewer praised Colman for purging the dialogue of grossness and pedantry, for correcting the anticlimax, and for artfully interweaving his new matter with the original, and concluded with the hope that "for the credit of the present age, we could . . . see both Volpone and Epicœne restored to the theatre."[2]

The play was done, but the business aspects of the venture still remained unsettled. Garrick, who had a reputation in certain circles for niggardliness, had not yet paid Colman for his share in the revival. On May 25 Colman wrote him and jogged his memory.[3] With his usual policy, Garrick fought off the application, told Colman that he had thought the alteration a gift, and wondered why Colman had delayed writing until this distressing period of farewell performances.[4] Colman replied that he had not

1. For an allusion in verse to its passing see *The London Magazine*, XLV (1776), 52. 2. LIV (1776), 312-313.
3. *Memoirs of the Colman Family*, I, 401-402.
4. I, 402.

intended making a present of his version, and that he regretted the failure of the play, which, for the honor of the managers, ought to hold the stage.[1]

It is perhaps unimportant to know whether Garrick accepted the alteration as a gift or whether Colman's name was finally entered among the creditors of Drury Lane. The play was soon forgotten by the public. In 1777 Thomas Davies attempted an analysis of the progress of humor in society, noting that in Elizabethan times the ideal of every fashionable young fellow was to pass for a man of humor. Shakspere and Jonson held up mirrors to the manners of the times, but Jonson's portraits had confined themselves to dry and disagreeable absurdities, and Morose was a "disagreeable picture of a man who secludes himself from the world to enjoy his own perversities":

Let any man read Morose's soliloquy, in the second act of the Silent Woman, where he enjoys the ruin of his nephew, and then tell me if the writing does not smell most rankly of the lamp. Shakespeare, like the sun shining upon a landscape, brightens and beautifies every object. Jonson degrades human nature, Shakespeare exalts it.[2]

Critical opinion of Jonson had become captious in the century after Dryden.

On April 26, 1784, the intrepid managers of Covent Garden, untaught by the ill fortune of the play eight years earlier, ventured on another revival, using Colman's version. The first and only performance was for the benefit of John Edwin. The cast was Morose, Aickin; Dauphine, Whitfield; Clerimont, Davies; Truewit, Wroughton; Daw, Quick; La Foole, Edwin; Otter, Booth; Cutbeard, Wewitzer; Epicoene, Mrs. Bates; Lady Haughty, Mrs. Wilson; Lady Centaure, Miss Platt; Dol Mavis, Miss Stuart; Mrs.

---

1. I, 403.
2. *A Genuine Narrative of the Life and Theatrical Transactions of Mr. John Henderson, commonly called the Bath Roscius*, p. 50.

Otter, Mrs. Webb; Frederick (with a Song), Brett; Mute, Stevens.[1]

The production was reviewed in *The Morning Chronicle and London Advertiser* for the next morning:

What with the strength of one of our strongest old comedies . . . and . . . the attraction of his own benefit, Edwin . . . contrived to draw together, as well filled a house, as has been seen this season. All the parts of Ben Johnson's comedy were well played; Edwin, Quick, and Mrs. Bates, were excellent — Wroughton, Whitfield, Mrs. Webb, were very sufficient; together, making these scenes, almost every one of which abounds with point, go off with good impression.

After this single performance the play was ignored for one hundred forty years.

In 1792 *The Silent Woman* was "accounted one of the best comedies extant, and is always acted with universal applause,"[2] but eight years later Dibdin could write that "nothing can prove that it has that sterling attraction which begets for a dramatic production universal satisfaction; not even that judicious and sensible alteration of it by COLMAN, which was brought out, yet not with very warm success, in 1776, at Drury Lane."[3]

Ludwig Tieck translated the comedy in 1800 as *Epicoene oder Das stille Frauenzimmer*,[4] a version which followed the original very closely, without the alterations and romantic adjustments noted in his translation of *Volpone*.

When Coleridge was making his *Notes and Lectures upon Shakespeare*, he called *The Silent Woman* "the most entertaining of old Ben's comedies," and thought a successful revival possible if an actor for Morose could be found. He considered the comedy frankly a farce, and his analysis of the singularity of Morose's character agreed fundamentally not with Congreve but with Dennis, in that the defect

1. *The Public Advertiser*, April 26, 1784.
2. *A New Theatrical Dictionary*, p. 77.
3. *A Complete History of the Stage*, III, 294–295.
4. *Schriften*, XII, 155–354.

of Morose grows not from his character, but the character rises from the accident. Jonson's characters

are, either a man with a huge wen, having a circulation of its own, and which we might conceive amputated, and the patient thereby losing all his character; or they are mere wens themselves instead of men, — wens personified, or with eyes, nose, and mouth cut out, mandrake fashion.[1]

The first modern revival of *The Silent Woman* occurred on February 7, 1895, when the students of the American Academy of Dramatic Art, trained by Mr. Franklin Sargent, played an adaptation by Abby Sage Richardson. This production was so successful that the comedy was given as completely in the Jacobean style as possible on March 20, 1895, in the Sanders theatre at Harvard College.[2] On May 8, 1905, the comedy was revived, apparently in its original form, by the Mermaid Repertory, under the direction of Philip Carr at the Great Queen Street theatre, with Cyril Cattley as Epicoene.[3] The most recent performance was given on November 16 and November 18, 1924, by the Phoenix Society at the Regent theatre, with Cedric Hardwicke as Morose and Godfrey Winn as Epicoene.[4]

In 1895 the critic for *The Boston Herald* thought *The Silent Woman* the most modern of Jonson's comedies, but thirty years later, opinion of the play had changed. The reviewer for the production by the Phoenix Society, bored with the horseplay and "ragging," regarded Morose as a tragic figure, tormented by a corps of eupeptics in a full-

1. W. G. T. Shedd, *The Complete Works of Samuel Taylor Coleridge*, IV, 192.
2. See *The Boston Herald*, March 17, 21, 1895, for sketches of the stage and the actors. For a full critical account see G. P. Baker, "The Revival of Ben Jonson's Epicoene; or, The Silent Woman, March 20, 1895," *The Harvard Graduates' Magazine*, III (1894–1895), 493–501.
3. The reviewer for *The Times*, May 12, 1905, considered Morose a neuropath, not a comic figure.
4. Program notes by Mr. Allan Wade. For a French version, *La Femme Silencieuse*, see *The New York Herald-Tribune*, December 20, 1925.

blooded age, and consigned the play to the "museum of dramatic antiquities," [1] from which, alas, it is not likely to emerge.

1. *The Times*, November 19, 1924. Stefan Zweig has renewed his interest in Jonson in *Die Schweigsame Frau, Komische Oper in Drei Aufzügen frei nach Ben Jonson von Stefan Zweig, Musik von Richard Strauss*, Berlin, 1935. The première was at the State Opera House, Dresden, June 24, 1935. For accounts see *The Times*, July 6, 1935; *Boston Evening Transcript*, July 13, August 3, 1935. Zweig's libretto is a very free version of *Epicoene*.

CHAPTER V

Bartholomew Fair

I

1660–1702

NONE of Jonson's comedies had a more brilliant stage-record during the Restoration than his magnificent *Bartholomew Fair*, a play comprehending a multitude of characters with such deft pattern of plot that the reader is never bewildered or compelled to refer constantly to the *dramatis personae*, as he is apt to do when reading *Every Man in his Humour* or *Every Man out of his Humour*. Indeed, to the true lover of Jonson, this picture of the Jacobean public on holiday must remain the greatest achievement of the comedy of humors. But just so far as it is the greatest, it has had to pay most dearly the price of ardent worship at the shrine of that myopic muse, local color — early and complete obsolescence. As Ward observed, "the amount of odd 'learning'— for so it must be called — crowded into the play is astonishing; it is a perfect dictionary of slang, and of slang of all sorts. . . . *Bartholomew Fair* is of its kind without a rival." [1] The comedy was weighted so heavily with the brand of realism which after a century requires notes and glossaries that it sank to intermittent performance in 1722 and to neglect in 1731, after which it was not revived for exactly one hundred ninety years.

Bartholomew Fair was, according to the records, the second of Jonson's plays to be revived after the Restora-

1. A. W. Ward, *A History of English Dramatic Literature to the Death of Queen Anne*, 1875, I, 573. Also see Henry Morley, *Memoirs of Bartholomew Fair*, 1859, pp. 145–181.

tion by the king's players. It was not acted until June 8, 1661, a year after the first production of *The Silent Woman*. The companies were well settled, and the play was given in the house at Vere Street, for Pepys wrote:

Then to the Cook's with Mr. Shepley and Mr. Creed, and dined together, and then I went to the Theatre and there saw Bartholomew Faire, the first time it was acted now-a-days. It is a most admirable play and well acted, but too much prophane and abusive.[1]

The first two productions of the play omitted the puppet-show in the last act. The puppets were not restored until September 7, a performance coinciding in time with the fair itself, which was not restricted to August 23, 24, and 25 until 1708 (and even then the restriction was not enforced). Pepys saw the play:

So I having appointed the young ladies at the Wardrobe to go with them to a play to-day, I left him [Wm. Joyce] and my brother Tom who came along with him to dine, and my wife and I took them to the Theatre, where we seated ourselves close by the King, and Duke of York, and Madame Palmer, which was great content; and, indeed, I can never enough admire her beauty. And here was "Bartholomew Fayre," with the puppet-show, acted to-day, which had not been these forty years (it being so satyricall against Puritanism, they durst not till now, which is strange they should already dare to do it, and the King do countenance it), but I do never a whit like it the better for the puppets, but rather the worse. Thence home with the ladies, it being by reason of our staying a great while for the King's coming, and the length of the play, near nine o'clock before it was done.[2]

Like *The Silent Woman* in 1660, *Bartholomew Fair* was presented so frequently in 1661 that even if we did not have Pepys's word for the freshness of the revival, the records would argue for it. There were two more produc-

1. H. B. Wheatley, *The Diary of Samuel Pepys*, II, 47.
2. II, 92–93.

tions before the end of the year, on November 12 and
December 18. Pepys attended the first:

> My wife and I to "Bartholomew Fayre," with puppets which
> I had seen once before, and the play without puppets often, but
> though I love the play as much as ever I did, yet I do not like the
> puppets at all, but think it to be a lessening to it.[1]

The record for December 18 is given by Sir Henry Herbert.[2]

In the last decades of the seventeenth and in the early
years of the eighteenth century many tracts and pamphlets
about the fair appeared. They may have carried some
allusion to the famous comedy which, rather than *Every
Man in his Humour*, had stripped "the ragged follies of
the time, Naked as at their birth," but, being of the most
ephemeral nature, few have survived. There are records
enough, however, to argue for the popularity of the comedy
before 1700.

Dr. Edward Browne paid 1*s.* 6*d.* in 1662 to see "*Bartholomew faire*" at "the new new Theatre in Lincolnes
Inne fields,"[3] an alternative designation, as has been
noted, for the theatre occupied by Killigrew's company.
On April 8, 1663, the play was assigned to the king's men
for representation at the Theatre Royal in Bridges Street,
opened on May 7. It was one of the plays which were
"Acted but now and then; yet being well Perform'd, were
very Satisfactory to the Town."[4] For these plays which
were performed somewhat infrequently, Downes unfortunately does not give the casts. He notes only that "Mr.
Wintersel, was good in Tragedy, as well as in Comedy, especially in Cokes in *Bartholomew Fair*; that the Famous
Comedian *Nokes* came in that part far short of him."[5] It
seems likely that Wintershall, one of the king's actors, pre-
ceded James Nokes in this part, for Nokes was connected

1. II, 127.
2. J. Q. Adams, *The Dramatic Records of Sir Henry Herbert*, p. 117.
3. British Museum MS. Sloane 1900.
4. John Downes, *Roscius Anglicanus*, p. 9.   5. Page 17.

with the company at Lincoln's Inn Fields and presented such "a plain and palpable Simplicity of Nature, which was so utterly his own, that he was often as unaccountably diverting in his common Speech, as on the Stage."[1] His performances in *Bartholomew Fair* seem to belong to the era of the union of the companies, during which we know that the play was acted. Wintershall died in July, 1679. He played Subtle and La Foole, the latter rôle furnishing excellent practise for that of Cokes, the foolish "Esquire of Harrow" who is determined to purchase everything he sees at the fair.

Pepys saw the play again on August 2, 1664:

> To the King's play-house, and there saw "Bartholomew Fayre," which do still please me; and is, as it is acted, the best comedy in the world, I believe.[2]

From June 5, 1665, to about November 20, 1666, the theatres were closed on account of the plague, and the next performance of the play, on April 27, 1667, was given by royal command, the actors receiving £10 for the afternoon.[3] In August of this year Dryden's *Sir Martin Mar-All* was produced at Lincoln's Inn Fields, and one of the characters, Warner, alludes to Cokes:

> Why, sir, are you stark mad? have you no grain of sense left? He's gone! Now is he as earnest in the quarrel as Cokes among the puppets; 'tis to no purpose, whatever I do for him.[4]

Despite Pepys's dislike of the puppet-show, the scene in the last act where Rabbi Busy is vanquished by the puppet Dionysius made more impression on audience and critic in the Restoration than anything else in the play except possibly the pig-woman Ursula.

1. Colley Cibber, *Apology*, 2d ed., p. 118.
2. IV, 193.
3. Allardyce Nicoll, *Restoration Drama*, p. 305.
4. V. i. The allusion is to *Bartholomew Fair*, V. iii. For passing allusion to Cokes see also Anon., *The Woman turn'd Bully*, 1675, IV. iii.

Pepys saw the comedy again, during the time of the fair, on September 4, 1668:

Up . . . and at noon my wife, and Deb., and Mercer, and W. Hewer and I to the Fair, and there, at the old house, did eat a pig, and was pretty merry, but saw no sights, my wife having a mind to see the play "Bartholomew-Fayre," with puppets. Which we did, and it is an excellent play; the more I see it, the more I love the wit of it; only the business of abusing the Puritans begins to grow stale, and of no use, they being the people that, at last, will be found the wisest. And here Knepp come to us, and sat with us.[1]

Dryden gave his opinion of the play in *A Defence of an Essay of Dramatic Poesy* (1668), praising Jonson's art as a selective realist:

In "Bartholomew Fair," or the lowest kind of comedy, that degree of heightening is used, which is proper to set off that subject: It is true the author was not there to go out of prose, as he does in his higher arguments of comedy, "The Fox" and "Alchemist"; yet he does so raise his matter in that prose, as to render it delightful; which he could never have performed, had he only said or done those very things, that are daily spoken or practised in the fair: for then the fair itself would be as full of pleasure to an ingenious person as the play, which we manifestly see it is not. But he hath made an excellent lazar of it; the copy is of price, though the original be vile.[2]

The comedy was beginning to furnish literary allusions. A reference to that "sow of enormity," Ursula, occurred in *The English Rogue*. The Rogue, being hard up, was taken into keeping by an oldish woman with pig eyes, but, tiring of the city, he decided to bid her farewell and go to the country:

She retrived my intentions, clasping me in her arms; I should rather have chosen the imbraces of a she-Bear, as thinking her

1. VIII, 91-92.
2. Sir Walter Scott and George Saintsbury, *The Works of John Dryden*, II, 296.

breath far sweeter; and truly I have often wondred at my recovery in so impure and unwholsom air. Being on Horse-back
she so bathed her Cheeks with tears (wanting no moisture, derived from an everlasting spring of humours distilling from her
head) that you would have sworn she was the representation of
the Pig-woman in *Ben's Bartholomew*-fair.[1]

About January 12, 1669, *Bartholomew Fair* was "allowed of to his Ma^tes Servants at ye New Theatre,"[2] and
on February 22 the Theatre Royal company performed it
by command at the Cockpit at Whitehall and received
£20.[3] Pepys made his way thither and wrote the last entry
for this comedy in his diary:

And in the evening I do carry them [his wife and two girls] to
White Hall, and there did without much trouble get into the
playhouse, there in a good place among the Ladies of Honour,
and myself also sat in the pit; and there by and by come the
King and Queen, and they begun "Bartholomew Fayre." But
I like no play here so well as at the common playhouse; besides
that, my eyes being very ill since last Sunday and this day
se'nnight, with the light of the candles, I was in mighty pain to
defend myself now from the light of the candles.[4]

About April, 1670, Charles Sackville, Earl of Dorset,
wrote an epilogue to Matthew Medbourne's *Tartuffe*
(1670). Since the comedy concerned a Puritan, the poet
naturally remembered Rabbi Busy:

Many have been the vain Attempts of Wit,
Against the still-prevailing Hypocrite.
Once (and but once) a Poet got the day,
And vanquish'd *Busy* in a Puppet-Play.
But *Busy* rallying, Arm'd with Zeal and Rage,
Possest the Pulpit and pull'd down the Stage.

---

1. [Francis Kirkman and Richard Head], *The English Rogue Described in the
Life of Meriton Latroon* [part i], 1668, pp. 228-229.
2. Nicoll, p. 315.   3. Page 306.
4. VIII, 221. For a delightful burlesque of *Bartholomew Fair* see *A Garland
for the New Exchange*, 1669, no. xiv (1845, pp. 44-51).

To laugh at English Knaves is dangerous then,
Whilst English Fools will think 'em honest Men.
But sure no zealous Rabby will deny us
Free leave with this our Monsieur *Ananias*.[1]

There is evidence that the play was being acted at this period on the Irish stage, for on December 27, 1670, Robert Bowyer wrote to Robert Southwell from Dublin:

Yesterday there being very many people at the playhouse the lofts fell down, three or four killed dead in the house, whereof a maid of Mr. Savage's was one. My Lord Lieutenant was hurt a little, one of his son's much hurt, the Countess of Clanbrasill ill hurt, very many wounded, some of which it is said cannot live. The play that was acted was Bartholomew Fair, in which it seems there is a passage that reflects upon a profession of holiness, and it is said when they were entering upon that part the scaffold fell.[2]

In the same month Shadwell, the most loyal disciple of Ben Jonson in the Restoration, came to the defense of his master in the preface to *The Humorists* (1671), replying to those critics who accused Jonson of dullness:

The most Excellent *Johnson* put Wit into the Mouths of the meanest of his People, and, which is infinitely Difficult, made it proper for 'em. And I once heard a Person of the greatest Wit and Judgment of the Age say, That *Bartholomew-Fair* (which consists most of low Persons) is one of the wittiest Plays in the World.[3]

Bartholomew Fair was performed once more before royalty on November 30, 1674, the actors receiving £10.[4] The number of performances commanded by Charles II supports the popular tradition that the comedy was one of his

1. Page 66. The epilogue was reprinted in *A Collection of Poems Written upon several Occasions By several Persons*, 1673, pp. 59–61, and *A Collection of Poems*, 1702, pp. 289–291. See *Bartholomew Fair*, V. iii.
2. *Historical Manuscripts Commission. Report on the Manuscripts of the Earl of Egmont*, Dublin, II (1909), 24.
3. Montague Summers, *The Complete Works of Thomas Shadwell*, I, 188–189.
4. Nicoll, p. 307.

favorite plays.[1] It was also a favorite with Saint-Évremond, who noted the English love for plays dealing with an exhibition of public follies, such as *Bartholomew Fair* and *Epsom Wells*,[2] a practise possible for a nation which cared little for the unities.

That the ancient customs of the fair, as described by Jonson, were propagated during the Restoration, one may assume from a notice for August in a contemporary almanac:

> In this month is a Fair kept at *West-Smithfield*, which the men of the world call *Bartholomew-Fair*, whither resort many Wenches with painted faces and black patches. Those Wenches (Friends) though they are not Whores of *Babylon*, yet they are Whores; who when they meet with their Cullies, for pig and Pork give them the outlandish disease into the bargain; therefore Friends, as you dread the charge of a Chirurgeons, or Apothecaries Bill, keep from this lac'd Mutton; yea, rather let the Man of Authority carry them to the Hemp-office, and let their backs suffer for the crimes of their other parts.[3]

The race of Ezekiel Edgworth, Nightingale, Captain Whit, Ursula, and Alice still stalked the earth, making it odious with their disrepute.

The two patent companies, united on May 4, 1682, began acting on November 15. In Downes's list of the plays revived by the "mixt Company," the only play of Jonson's is *Bartholomew Fair*.[4] Although there are no specific records of performance from 1674 to 1682, one may reasonably suppose that it was acted often enough to warrant in-

1. John Nichols, *The Progresses, Processions, and Magnificent Festivities, of King James the First*, 1828, III, 28.

2. *Œuvres*, III, 241–242; *Mixt Essays upon Tragedies, Comedies, &c.*, 1685, p. 17; *The Remains of Mr. Thomas Brown*, p. 329. See Langbaine, *An Account of the English Dramatick Poets*, p. 446.

3. *A Yea and Nay Almanack For the people call'd by the men of the World Quakers*, 1679; see also *Poor Robin's Almanack* for the same month; *Wit and Drollery, Jovial Poems*, 1682, pp. 227, 304; "A Description of Bartholomew Fair," H. E. Rollins, *The Pepys Ballads*, Cambridge, Mass., III (1930), 77–81.

4. *Roscius Anglicanus*, p. 40.

clusion in the repertory. Among frequent allusions to the characters in the play,[1] the most interesting occur in a letter from Sir Robert Southwell, written on August 26, 1685, to his son Ned, who was in London with his tutor during the time of the fair. The letter points out the inclusiveness of Jonson's panoramic view and recalls Leatherhead, Edgworth, Nightingale, Trouble-all, Joan Trash, Alice, and Ursula. Sir Robert advised Ned to read the play before visiting the fair,

for then . . . you wou'd note, if things and humours were the same to-day, as they were fifty years ago, and take pattern of the observations which a man of sence may raise out of matters that seem even ridiculous . . . and you wou'd note into how many various shapes humane nature throws itself, in order to buy cheap, and sell dear. . . . The main importance of this fair is . . . a sort of Bacchanalia, to gratifie the multitude in their wandring and irregular thoughts. . . . When you see the toy-shops, and the strange variety of things, much more impertinent than hobby-horses or gloves of gingerbread, you must know there are customers for all these matters. . . . 'Tis out of this credulous croud that the ballad singers attrackt an assembly, who listen and admire, while their confederate pickpockets are diving and fishing for their prey. . . . There is one corner of this Elizium field devoted to the eating of pig, and the surfeits that attend it. . . . There are various corners of lewdness and impurity.[2]

That lover of city life, Thomas D'Urfey, who, like Thomas Brown and Edward Ward, delighted to write of the sights and sounds of London streets and the adventures which one might experience without traveling far from the Strand, published in 1690 a burlesque poem, *Collin's Walk through London and Westminster*, an entertaining forerunner of Gay's *Trivia*. Wednesday's walk took Collin to the playhouse, which D'Urfey described with virulent satire. And there the following surprising drama took place:

1. *The Observator*, February 28, 1682; John Crowne, *City Politiques*, 1683, sig. A2; *Poor Robin's Almanack*, 1684, "Observations on August"; *The Pleasures of Matrimony*, 1688, p. 19.
2. Morley, pp. 288–290.

    To this rare place where Wit is taught,
The Major now had *Collin* brought;
The House was Peopled with all sorts,
The Cities product and the Courts,
An Ancient Comick Piece they knew,
Intitled the Fair of *Bartholomew*,
Collin first thought as he came in,
It had a Conventicle bin,
And that mistaking of the day,
The Major brought him there to pray;
He saw each Box with Beauty crown'd,
And Pictures deck the Structure round;
Ben, Shakespear, and the learned Rout,
With Noses some, and some without.
Loud Musick sounding through his Ears,
That were more sanctified than theirs,
Made him a great while doubting stand,
Till seeing Brother *Zeal o' th Land*,
Give to his Canting Sister Greeting,
Confirmed him this must be a Meeting;
With Eyes turn'd up and shake of Head,
He now repeated all was said;
Admir'd the Habit of the Prig,
And wink'd at stealing of the Pig,
As wisely knowing all those Slips,
Natural to their Apocalips;
And that the Brethren may Steal,
As well as Lie, to shew their Zeal;
He had not long been in this Rapture,
Which pleas'd him more than any Chapter;
But by the Nature of the Play,
His Mood was turn'd another way;
For finding that a little after,
Meerly to urge the Peoples Laughter,
The Rabbi with loud Shouts and Mocks,
Was for Slight reason set ith' Stocks;
In *Breast* a suddain Anger glow'd,
And instantly revenge he vow'd,
As thinking this a base affront,
To the whole Tribe of those that Cant;
This Maggot working in his Pate,
He starts from off the Bench he sate;
And getting near half choak'd with Rage,
Thus spoke to those upon the Stage.

What Carnal Motion of the Beast?
What *Dæmon* Sirs has you possessest? [*sic*]
Or what curst Law is there that Grants,
This Licence to affront the Saints,
That labour in their strict Vocation,
And sweat to teach Regeneration?
Is now th' eleventh Tryal come,
In Persecution taught at *Rome*;
That thus you dare disturb their Zeals,
And tye unerring Truth by th' Heels?
If so, we have no more to do,
Both He and I will suffer too;
If not, it never shall be said,
An Elder to the Stocks was led,
For all the Rabble to deride,
Whilst I wear Bilboe by my side.

The Actors when he first begun,
By th' Noyse were stopt from going on;
Nor was the Audience less amaz'd,
Who all on *Collins* out-side gaz'd;
Who now possess't with zealous Rage,
Was getting up upon the Stage,
With Sword in Hand resolv'd on War,
With those who stock'd the Presbiter,
For sake of Brotherhood to ease him,
And from his Wooden Shame release him;
When Blew Coat Bully that stood by,
And heard his Chattring Lunacy,
Wondring to see a Country Lout,
In *Cassock* Vile to make that Rout,
His Noddle reaching with Battoon,
Gave him a thump that brought him down:
And now the Hubbub was so great,
That each one rose from off his Seat;
All Laughing at his Garb and Look,
Whom now they for a Madman took;
Till *Collin* who resolv'd to show,
He was a Wiser Man then so;
Nor *Begger* as they might suppose,
By the Humility of's Clothes;
Oth' suddain stopping the Discourse,
Out of his Pocket pull'd his Purse,
With twenty pieces in't of Gold,

His proper Right to have and hold;
Yet this ceas'd not the loud uproar,
But rather made the Laughter more;
And tho the Major fretting try'd,
To take him off to tother side;
And to inform him did his best,
That what he saw was but a Jest;
Yet he with late ill usage heated,
Would forward, and had bin worse treated
Had not a Female Wastcoateer,
Came up, and whispering in his Ear,
The ill match'd Combatant drawn off,
Leaving the Crowd to showt and laugh.[1]

Collin's implicit tribute to the excellence of the playing at this performance makes one wish more than ever that the cast were known. What with a visitation of God on the playhouse by way of dislodged balconies, and with acting mistaken for dire reality, *Bartholomew Fair* was having a lively career.

Langbaine noted in 1691: "This Play has frequently appear'd on the Stage, since the Restauration, with great applause."[2] In this year, too, there was an early discussion concerning the restriction of the fair itself, which was worrying the officials by its lawlessness and disorder.[3] Whether the comedy continued to be acted until the end of the union in 1695, there is no means of telling. But in 1695 Congreve analyzed the low type-characters in the play:

The Character of *Cob* in *Every Man in his Humour*, and most of the under Characters in *Bartholomew-Fair*, discover only a Singularity of Manners, appropriated to the several Educations and Professions of the Persons represented. They are not Humours but Habits contracted by Custom. Under this Head may be ranged all Country-Clowns, Sailers, Tradesmen, Jockeys,

---

1. Pages 148–153. For pictures of Jonson and Shakspere used as decoration in the theatre see *The Censor*, April 9, 1717.
2. Pages 287–288.
3. R. J. Kerr and I. C. Duncan, *The Portledge Papers*, 1928, p. 118.

Gamesters and such like, who make use of *Cants* or peculiar *Dialects* in their several Arts and Vocations.[1]

He gave a receipt for the composition of such characters.

In spite of its satire of professing Puritans and the fun made at the expense of Rabbi Busy's appetite and sanctimony, the comedy passed lightly through the controversy with Collier, who seems to have had sense enough to realize that Jonson, himself a great moralist and a great Puritan, was rather railing against the abuses of the new sect than pillorying their virtues. So he merely remarked that Vanbrugh, in *The Relapse*, had borrowed the spirit of some of his insolent profaneness "from *Ben Johnson's Bartholemew Fair*; only the Profaneness is mightily improved, and the Abuse thrown off the *Meeting-House*, upon the *Church*." [2]

The character of the fair was changing, and the abuses of good manners and good morals to be observed there were within a few years to lead to a restriction of its liberties to three days instead of fourteen, although the restriction was not enforced. Tom Brown noted the changing aspects of the fair,— the growth of theatrical entertainments, drolls, farces, and operas. On August 30, 1699, he wrote from "the Gun Musick-Booth in Smithfield" a thoughtful letter to George Moult:

I cou'd say a thousand things more in behalf of the *Vacation*, but I shall content myself at present with observing, that it produces *Bartholomew*-Fair; and when I have said that, I think it needs no *farther* Panegyrick. . . . Fourscore Years ago, and better, it afforded *Matter* enough for one of our best *Comedians* to compose a Play upon it: But *Smithfield* is another sort of a Place now to what it was in the Times of *Honest Ben*; who, were he to rise out of his Grave, wou'd hardly believe it to be the same numerical spot of Ground where Justice *Overdo* made so busie a Figure, where the *Crop-ear'd Parson* demolish'd a *Ginger-*

1. *Letters Upon several Occasions*, p. 89.
2. *A Short View*, p. 109. See *The Stage-Beaux toss'd in a Blanket; or, Hypocrisie Alamode*, 1704, p. 34.

bread Stall, where *Nightingale*, of harmonious memory, sung *Ballads*, and *fat Ursula* sold *Pig* and *bottled Ale*.

As I have observ'd to you, this noble *Fair* is quite another thing than what it was in the last Age; it not only deals in the humble Stories of *Crispin* and *Crispianus*, *Whittington's* Cat, *Bateman's* Ghost, with the merry Conceits of the little Pickleherring; but it produces *Opera's* of its own Growth, and is become a formidable Rival to both the Theatres.[1]

Bartholomew Fair, like the rest of Jonson's plays, does not appear in the lists of plays seen by Lady Morley before 1700, and it was probably acted infrequently from the close of the union until the first performance listed in *The Daily Courant* for June 3, 1702. Although the fair was giving the legitimate stage some competition, there was one virtue not discerned by Brown. The farces and drolls were developing a school of comic actors, like Johnson, Pinkethman, and Jo Haines, where the managers of the theatres found many of their best players. After the production of short plays at the fair succeeded the earlier puppet-shows, no group of individuals was better qualified to make money from the eager public than the trained actors themselves. They set up their theatrical booths, and there was complete interaction between the regular and occasional stages in the early eighteenth century; the actors in *Bartholomew Fair* could play with gusto and understanding, in spite of changed times, because they had seen the fair itself in all its moods.

The music for Nightingale's ballad beginning "My masters, and friends, and good people, draw near," "To the tune of Paggington's pound, sir," [2] was printed by Tom D'Urfey in *Wit and Mirth; or, Pills to Purge Melancholy* (1700).[3] The tune, although very old, was certainly not originally composed for these words.[4] It seems to have

1. *The Works of Mr. Thomas Brown*, I, 212 (see also p. 217).
2. III. i.
3. Part ii, pp. 1–2. The words were reprinted in *Wit and Drollery, Joviall Poems*, 1661, p. 97 (1682, pp. 169–171).
4. The words were unquestionably written for the play by Jonson. See C.

been virtually a folk-song, and during the seventeenth and eighteenth centuries innumerable sets of words were written to the music.[1]

II

1702 AND LATER

On August 18, 1702, just before the time of the fair, Drury Lane offered "that celebrated Comedy call'd *Bartholomew Fair*; Written by the Famous *Ben. Johnson*." The play was given but once and was not revived again until March 25, 1704. Indeed, it does not seem to have been very popular on the stage until 1707, when the Drury Lane actors were playing at the Haymarket. It was acted, however, three times in 1704, once during the season of the fair, but the bills were cluttered with those entertainments of singing and grotesque dancing which were stifling the vitality of the theatres. After January 8, 1705, the comedy was not presented for two and a half years. There is no hint about the cast at the beginning of the century, but as with the other plays an approximate list of some of the actors may be inferred. Cokes was doubtless played by Bullock, Littlewit by Norris, Quarlous by Mills, and Waspe by Johnson. Other assignments are beyond conjecture, for Booth, Pack, and Husband, who later acted Edgworth, Rabbi Busy, and Winwife, were at this time connected with the Lincoln's Inn Fields theatre. About the women characters it is, as always, dangerous to guess.

The first complete cast is that for the production of August 12, 1707, at the Haymarket. The comedians were those already noted, with the addition of Keen as Overdo, Fairbank as Nightingale, Cross as Ursula, Mrs. Porter as

---

R. Baskervill, "Some Parallels to *Bartholomew Fair*," *Modern Philology*, VI (1908–1909), 117–118.

1. See Sir John Hawkins, *A General History of the Science and Practice of Music*, 1776, IV, 381; William Chappell, *Popular Music of the Olden Time*, I [1855], 123; *The Roxburghe Ballads*, I (1871), 370, III (1880), 395, 471, 491–495.

Mrs. Welborn, and Mrs. Powell as Dame Purecraft. The other prominent characters, Leatherhead, Trouble-all, Joan Trash, and Alice, were not indicated. The comedy was performed four times during the revolt.

John Mills played Quarlous as faithfully as his other rôles in Jonson: Powell relieved him for one night only. Mills had a thorough Bartholomew Fair training, for early in the century he acted Captain Lovewell in a droll, *The Siege of Barcelona*, and later with Miller and Oates he managed a theatrical booth.[1] Josias Miller succeeded Bullock as Cokes in 1715, when Bullock joined the Lincoln's Inn Fields company, making another actor who knew both the fair and the play. His rôles as La Foole and Drugger formed excellent complements to that of the foolish squire. Bullock, also well known as La Foole and Kastril, was probably large enough in person to have played Ursula. He, too, was proprietor of a booth at Smithfield, along with Pinkethman and Mills,[2] and had acted Captain Blunderbuss in *The Siege of Barcelona*, and Ezekiel in *Jephthah's Rash Vow* (1704), at Pinkethman's booth.

Pack, trained for his later rôle of Tribulation by his short career as Rabbi Busy, the "superlunatical hypocrite," which he played with some competition from Colley Cibber and Bickerstaff, was to have experience at Bartholomew Fair at Pinky's booth in 1717 as Tim in *Twice Married and a Maid Still*. Bickerstaff, who also played Winwife apparently only once, enlivened his career by playing Corporal Scare Devil in *The Siege of Barcelona*. Keen, who had previously acted Volpone, played Justice Overdo, so far as the bills tell us, until succeeded on June 28, 1715, by Shepard, who played the part until 1722. Booth as Edgworth was followed by Lacy Ryan in 1715 and by Tom Walker in 1718. Walker was another hero of the fair; his talents were discovered by Booth, who witnessed his performance of the part of Paris in *The Siege of Troy*, at Mrs.

1. See *Memoirs of the Society of Grub-Street*, II, 123.
2. See *Bartholomew-Fair: An Heroi-Comical Poem*, 1717, pp. 6–7.

Mynn's booth. Walker, a famous drinker, kept sober long enough to write two ballad operas expressly for Bartholomew Fair.[1]

Ben Johnson held the rôle of Waspe as tenaciously as his Ananias, Morose, and Corbaccio: no one else played it. He, too, had been associated with the fair in 1694, the year he joined the theatre. There was a booth at the fair called "Ben Jonson's booth," named not for the actor but for the dramatist.[2] Norris, "Jubilee Dicky," acted Littlewit with only one night's absence, during the revolt from Drury Lane in 1709, when he remained faithful to the old house. He acted Squib in *The Siege of Barcelona*. His friend Pinkethman, "the flower of Bartholomew Fair," never acted in the comedy.[3]

For the comedian Cross, who acted Ursula, there is little information. One may safely remark that he was probably a "tun of man," though his rôles as Face and Surly would not require a fat man. He played also Roger in *Aesop*, Charino in *Love Makes a Man*, and Sir Henry Atall in *The Double Gallant*. He acted Ursula until 1720, with slight aid from Leigh. Nightingale had to be acted by a man with a good voice for the ballad of the cutpurse. Fairbank was succeeded by Bowman, an excellent singer, often billed to sing between the acts, and he, in turn, by Burkhead.

Of the actresses there is little to note beyond the fact that Mrs. Porter, Mrs. Powell, Mrs. Saunders (Win Littlewit), Mrs. Baker (Dame Purecraft), Mrs. Bradshaw (Grace Welborn), Mrs. Mills (Grace Welborn), and Mrs. Moor (Dame Overdo), all had other rôles in Jonson's comedies. Mrs. Cox (Dame Overdo) played only this part in Jonson, but she retained it from 1708 to 1720. Mrs. Powell played for thirteen years and Mrs. Willis for eight, but the rest of the actresses had fitful careers in the play. Only Mrs.

1. See *Notes and Queries*, 2d series, VII (1859), 410.
2. See Errol Sherson, *London's Lost Theatres of the Nineteenth Century*, 1925, p. 329.
3. See John Dennis, *Original Letters, Familiar, Moral, and Critical*, p. 113.

Bartholomew Fair. Lud. Du Guernier inv. et Sculp.

Willis seems to have acted at the fair — as the Dame of Honor in *The Siege of Barcelona*. Grace Welborn was her only Jonsonian rôle.

The parts requiring the fewest changes of actors were Littlewit, Dame Purecraft, Quarlous, Waspe, and Ursula. There were at least eight actors at this period who performed also at theatrical booths in Smithfield, so that the stage presentation of *Bartholomew Fair* should have possessed a great degree of verisimilitude.

In 1708, after the new union of the Drury Lane and Haymarket comedians under Rich and Brett, the comedy was presented three times during the summer. Then it was dropped until June 1, 1710. From that year until the first long lapse in 1722, *Bartholomew Fair* was played every season except 1714 and 1721. Meanwhile the fair was changing in character, and the authorities were seeking to quell it. Scenes of gross indecency were common,[1] and the morality of an age which was rapidly being improved by Addison, Steele, and the dramatists of sensibility, was set against the idle disorder of the rabble. Actual restriction was deferred until 1735, but feeling was aroused against organized crime observable to any visitor. As the fair changed from what it had been in the days of Ben Jonson, the comedy became more and more antiquated. It was destined to die early, but it died hard. After performances on an average of only one a year from 1710 to 1718, it was played ten times from 1718 to 1722, was then dropped for nine years (the bills said seven), and was acted only once more in its original form, on October 30, 1731.

From 1710 to 1720 little critical notice was taken of the play. On April 25, 1711, *The Spectator* described a company of strolling players, so poor that Lord Foppington had no better means to show himself a fop than by wearing stockings of different colors. Only one part was dressed with propriety:

1. *Reasons for the Punctual Limiting of Bartholomew-Fair in West Smithfield*, 1708. See *The Observator*, June 26–30, 1708.

That was Justice *Clodpate*: This was so well done that it offended Mr. Justice *Overdo*, who, in the midst of our whole Audience, was (like *Quixote* in the Puppet-Show) so highly provok'd, that he told them, If they would move Compassion, it should be in their own Persons, and not in the Characters of distressed Princes and Potentates.[1]

On June 28, 1715, Quin acted Winwife, his first part in Jonson. He continued playing in *Bartholomew Fair* until the summer of 1717, when he appeared at Pinky's booth at the fair as Vincent in *Twice Married and a Maid Still*. On August 13, 1716, Lady Mary Wortley Montagu wrote from Nimwegen to an early friend, Sarah Chiswell, describing her visit to a French church, where she "stared very much at their manner of service."

The parson claps on a broad-brimmed hat in the first place, which gave him entirely the air of *what d'ye call him*, in Bartholomew Fair, which he kept up by extraordinary antic gestures, and talking much such stuff as the other preached to the puppets.[2]

After December 21, 1722, when *Bartholomew Fair* was performed by royal command, the play was neglected and aroused no critical notice. Unfortunately, the playbills have been cut out of the newspapers for several months in 1731, so that for the cast at the revival on October 30, one is compelled to rely on the incomplete list given by Genest. The revival was not noted by Latreille, and no other files of newspapers have been available. Of the actors, only two were old in the play,— Johnson and Shepard. Theophilus Cibber (Cokes) and Griffin (Busy) probably had no experience at the actual fair until 1733, when reduced profits at the theatre, resulting from the popularity of foreign operas, caused an unusual number of the players to draw treasure there. Cibber had acted Dapper, and in 1731 was playing La Foole, a rôle which seems always to have been

1. No. 48.
2. W. Moy Thomas, *The Letters and Works of Lady Mary Wortley Montagu*, 1898, I, 106. For another allusion to Rabbi Busy, on May 14, 1718, see *The Entertainer*, No. XXVIII.

given to the actor of Cokes. Mrs. Clive, or as she was known then, Miss Raftor, with her "inexpressible comicalness," [1] made her first appearance in Jonson as Win Littlewit. John Harper (Ursula), who acted Falstaff at Drury Lane, was beautifully cast for that rogue's fat female counterpart, for he was "happy in his Corpulence," and was said by Tony Aston to have had "too much of the Bartholomew-Fair," [2] surely no handicap for Ursula! He was a fat, round-faced man, with a jolly laugh that qualified him for his position as the Falstaff of his time. He acted Rustego in *The Siege of Bethulia*, a droll presented at the fair.

By 1731 the glory of Bartholomew Fair was gone. James Ralph, writing on public diversions in *The Taste of the Town*, lamented the disappearance of the expansive old days:

My Old Friend *Bartholomew's* Wings are close clipp'd; his Liberties retrench'd, and Priviledges invaded. How alter'd!— how sunk from his former Golden State!—Those merry, drunken, whoring Days!—when immortal *Ben* thought it no mean Subject for his comick *Muse*. . . . It happens at that dead Time of Year, when Business and Diversions in *London* sink under the Weight of a long Vacation, when Trade lies dead, and Pleasure languishes; whilst there they raise their drooping autumnal Heads, and revive to charm us with new budding Delights, as in the Spring.[3]

In 1735 the Court of Aldermen and the strong mayor Sir John Barnard forbade acting, limited the fair rigorously to three days, and permitted the erection of stalls for merchandise only. At last Bartholomew's wings were indeed close-clipped.[4]

1. *The Works, in Verse and Prose, of William Shenstone, Esq.*, III (1769), 52.
2. *A Brief Supplement to Colley Cibber, Esq., His Lives*, ed. R. W. Lowe, *An Apology for the Life of Mr. Colley Cibber*, II, 300.
3. Page 230.
4. Puppet-plays continued, and the regulations were subsequently unenforced. Tate Wilkinson saw the puppets at the fair about 1744. See *Memoirs of His Own Life*, I, 19.

An altered version of *Bartholomew Fair* was acted at Lincoln's Inn Fields on August 25, 1735, with a fairly obscure cast. The only players who became well known later were Mullart, Aston, Miss Brett, Miss Mann, and Mrs. Charke. Several characters were unquestionably new: Ananias, Valentine, Rover, Silence, Florella, Lovewit, Nut Woman, and Pickle Herring. Apparently, of the original characters, only Cokes, Overdo and his lady, Waspe, the toyman, and the gingerbread-woman remained. The alteration must have been but a sad mutilation, for it was played only once. Mullart, who acted Holofernes in *The Siege of Bethulia* in 1732, was the one new actor who had had experience before the throngs at Smithfield.

The final restriction of the fair came in 1762, when the Court of Common Council recommended that plays should be interdicted. At the legal close of the fair, the mayor, Sir Samuel Fludyer, sent constables to prevent its unlawful continuance. This legal action brought the fair into the public eye and produced at least one poetical broadside, written by George Alexander Stevens, part of which deserves quotation as a memento of what had passed:

> There was drolls, Hornpipe dancing, and shewing of Postures,
> With frying black Puddings, and op'ning of Oysters;
> With salt Boxes, Solos, and Gallery folks squawling;
> The Tap-house guests roaring, and mouth pieces bawling.
> Pimps, Pawn-brokers, Strolers, fat Landladies, Sailors,
> Bawds, Bailies, Jilts, Jockies, Thieves, Tumblers, and Taylors.
>
> Here's Punch's whole play of the Gun-powder plot Sir,
> Wild Beasts all alive, and pease Porridge, all hot Sir;
> Fine Sausages fried, and the Black on the Wire,
> The whole Court of France, and nice Pig at the Fire.[1]

Bartholomew Fair has apparently been acted only once since 1731, when the Phoenix Society revived it in London on June 28, 1921. But Garrick seems to have been interested in reviving it, for Dr. John Brown, the author of two

1. Original broadside, Harvard Theatre Collection; *The Universal Magazine* XXXI (1762), 96.

tragedies, *Athelstan* and *Barbarossa,* an impracticable person with tendencies towards madness,— he cut his throat in 1766,— wrote several letters to the manager about a version of the play which he was making. On August 10, 1765,[1] he informed Garrick:

As to the comedy [*Bartholomew Fair*], my good friend, I must brush up your memory a little. It was your own proposal (in your garden at Hampton,) that I should try my hand at it. Its comic merit, in point of *character*, is universally allowed to be of the first degree. In point of *plan*, it goes on well upon the whole, till the third or fourth act, and then falls into nonsense and absurdity. This, I really think, I have removed; retaining, at the same time, every the least scrap of what is thinly scattered through the bad parts of it, such as might be worth preserving. This is all I pretend to: and as to the excellence of the other parts, it is generally allowed to be supreme. The Pig-woman certainly cannot be removed without spoiling the whole; for on *her* depend all the fine comic scenes between Busy, John Littlewit, and Justice Overdo; as well as some of Coke's and Wasp. In short, she is the *great connecting circumstance* that *binds* the *whole together.* If the scene of her scolding be thought rather too coarse, it may easily be softened. But as to all these matters, I can only give my reasons: you are to judge of them. Upon the whole, therefore, you will oblige me much if you can bring on either of these pieces this season. If you declare this impossible, I cannot for the present say any thing farther on this matter.[2]

It is said that Garrick, shortly after his marriage in June, 1749, had taken Mrs. Garrick to the booth at the fair kept by Yates and Shuter. He could have carried away only an impression of roughness, for he was so rudely pushed about by the crowds that he was compelled to call upon Palmer, his bill-sticker, for aid. Palmer, who took money at the entrance of the booth, although a very strong man, could

1. The letters were badly edited by James Boaden, in *The Private Correspondence of David Garrick,* 1831. Boaden dated the first two letters 1762 and the last two 1765, but it is clear that three years could not have passed between them. From an allusion to Dr. Johnson's *Preface to Shakespeare,* 1765, I am persuaded to date them all 1765.   2. I, 146.

lend little assistance, alleging that few people at the fair knew Garrick off the stage.[1] Perhaps the play seemed as likely to succeed as *Every Man in His Humour*, or perhaps the suppression of the fair made a revival of the comedy seem desirable.

Garrick's attitude is open to conjecture, inasmuch as his correspondence with Brown has disappeared. A week after the first letter, Brown sent another, informing Garrick that he had forwarded the version:

> I pique myself more on rectifying this plan, than on any plan I ever struck out in my life. It is amazing to think how any writer could do so well, and so ill, at the same time, as Ben Jonson did in this comedy. However, so far as I am a judge, there are admirable materials left, enough to make out a first-rate comedy after the trash is thrown out. But I will not anticipate. As to the little connecting scenes which I have added, I have made them as short as possible, because I know that my comic composition is nothing. As soon as you have well considered it, let me have your thoughts. I can furnish you with some songs that will be proper for the purpose: that which is inserted is the finest that ever Purcel composed; and if Miss Wright can *act it* as well as she can *sing it* (for both will be necessary), that very song will draw an audience. You will see that I have struck out four of the *dramatis personæ*. . . . But I am like honest Justice Overdo, when he was set in the stocks, and defy Dame Fortune to hurt my mind, come what will.[2]

It is not certain that Garrick ever received Brown's packets. On September 4 Brown wrote a letter of inquiry,[3] and on October 27, from Newcastle, he sent his last letter on the matter:

> As to "Bartholomew Fair," my sentiment, in a word, is this: the comedy was, in its essentials, *excellent*, and that it wanted nothing but a *plan*. This I have attempted to give it; and I wait for your decision in this point.[4]

1. William Hone, *The Every-Day Book*, 1826, I, 1244.
2. *The Private Correspondence of David Garrick*, I, 147–148.
3. I, 198–199.   4. I, 205.

What became of the alteration is not known. But it had no effect on the history of the play.

Bartholomew Fair, rapidly becoming a museum-piece, was described in 1792 as having "an infinite deal of humour in it, and is, perhaps, the greatest assemblage of characters that ever was brought together within the compass of one single piece." [1] In our own day the Phoenix Society does not seem to have made a great success with its revival. Mr. W. J. Turner found the production "a triumph for the producer and the actors" and "very amusing entertainment," but it seems that he completely misunderstood Jonson's attitude towards Puritanism when he remarked that Ben Jonson "did not concern himself with the Puritan principle at all." [2] Even Jeremy Collier understood that Jonson did almost nothing else. The less literary critic for *The Times* dismissed as a question of taste the enthusiastic account written by Mr. Montague Summers, who considered it "a supreme effort of Jonson's titanic genius, a masterpiece where the richest humour and most brilliant realism combine with immortal satire." [3] He confessed to being exceedingly bored at the personified eccentricities, never human beings, who pursued their irrational ways.

The fun of the fair is always noisy and sometimes nauseous, and the "richest humour" of . . . the pig-woman is too rich for our stomach. We were very glad, exceeding glad, very exceeding glad, when the play was over. We speak of it, of course, as an entertainment. As a "document" *Bartholomew Fair* is full of interest — but that is another matter. [4]

Rugged old *Bartholomew Fair* must submit to the weakness of the modern stomach, which no longer craves hot roast pig, but prefers orange juice and toast Melba.

1. *A New Theatrical Dictionary*, p. 19.
2. *The London Mercury*, IV, No. 22 (1921), 422.
3. Program notes for the production.
4. June 28, 1921.

CHAPTER VI

Every Man in His Humour

I

RESTORATION AND EARLY EIGHTEENTH CENTURY

ALTHOUGH *The Fox, The Alchemist,* and *The Silent Woman* held the stage as regular repertory plays from the Restoration until Garrick's retirement in 1776,— with intervals of relapse, it is true, as long as twenty-five years,— the illustrious stage-history of *Every Man in his Humour,* with a total of over one hundred fifty performances, was confined to the last quarter-century of Garrick's management. From 1751, indeed, not a year found the play in abeyance, and its average of six performances in a season of some hundred fifty playing nights, with about fifty plays in the repertory of each theatre, is an extraordinary record of popularity. That this comedy of Jonson's which, if we except *Bartholomew Fair,* most thoroughly portrays Elizabethan manners, should have achieved its record one hundred fifty years after composition and should have competed not only with Shakspere's comedies and the always popular plays of Congreve, Farquhar, Cibber, Steele, and Mrs. Centlivre, but with the new plays of Colman, Foote, Goldsmith, and Sheridan, is little less than a miracle. But its popularity is unquestionable, for no play, except possibly *The Alchemist,* excited more criticism in newspapers, theatrical pamphlets, satires, and memoirs. Frequently selected for actors' benefits, it made many a reputation at both Drury Lane and Covent Garden, and was the only Jonsonian comedy, except the disfigurement of *The Alchemist, The Tobacconist,* to last into the nineteenth-century theatre of Edmund Kean.

Records of *Every Man in his Humour* in the Restoration are scarce. When Killigrew was assigned the Theatre Royal in Drury Lane on May 7, 1663, the play was allotted to his company, not as one of the "Principal Old Stock Plays," but as one of those which were "Acted but now and then; yet being well Perform'd, were very Satisfactory to the Town." [1] Pepys never saw the play, at least during the years covered by his *Diary*, but on February 9, 1667, he wrote:

At noon home to dinner, and then to my office again, where also busy, very busy late, and then went home and read a piece of a play, "Every Man in his Humour," wherein is the greatest propriety of speech that ever I read in my life: and so to bed.[2]

About January 12, 1669, the play was "allowed of to his Ma^tes Servants at ye New Theatre," [3] and it is likely that it was performed about that time, but certainly before June 16, 1673, when the occasional epilogue by Charles Sackville, Earl of Dorset, appeared in print:

EPILOGUE
To every Man in his humour

Intreaty shall not serve nor violence,
To make me speak in such a Playes defence.
A Play where Wit and Humour do agree
To break all practis'd Laws of *Comedy*:
The Scene (what more absurd) in *England* lies,
No Gods descend, nor dancing Devils rise;
No captive Prince from nameless Country brought
No battel, nay, there's not a duel fought.
And something yet more sharply might be said,
But I consider the poor Author's dead;
Let that be his excuse. . . . Now for our own,
Why . . . Faith, in my opinion, we need none.
The parts were fitted well; but some will say,
Pox on 'em Rogues what made 'em chuse this Play?

---

1. John Downes, *Roscius Anglicanus*, p. 9.
2. H. B. Wheatley, *The Diary of Samuel Pepys*, VI, 158.
3. Allardyce Nicoll, *Restoration Drama*, p. 315.

I do not doubt but you will credit me,
It was not choice, but meer necessity;
To all our writing friends, in Town, we sent,
But not a Wit durst venture out in *Lent*;
Have patience but till *Easter*-Term, and then
You shall have Jigg and Hobby-horse agen,
Here's Mr. *Matthew*, our domestique Wit,
Does promise one of the ten Plays h'as writ;
But since great bribes weigh nothing with the just
Know, we have merits, and in them we trust;
When any Fasts, or Holy-days, defer
The publick labours of the *Theatre*,
We ride not forth although the day be fair,
On ambling Tit to take the Suburb-air,
But with our Authors meet, and spend that time
To make up quarrels between sence and rhyme.
Wednesdays and *Fridays* constantly we sate
Till after many a long and free debate,
For divers weighty reasons 'twas thought fit
Unruly sence shu'd still to rhyme submit.
This the most wholesom Law we ever made.
So strictly in this *Epilogue* obey'd,
Sure no man here will ever dare to break.

       [*Enter* Johnson's *Ghost*.
Hold, and give way, for I my self will speak,
Can you encourage so much insolence,
And add new faults still to the great offence
Your Ancestors so rashly did commit
Against the mighty Powers of Art and Wit?
When they condemn'd those noble works of mine
Sejanus, and my best lov'd *Cataline*:
Repent, or on your guilty head shall fall
The curse of many a rhyming Pastoral:
The three bold *Beauchamps* shall revive again,
And with the *London* Prentice conquer *Spain*
All the dull follies of the former age
Shall rise and find applause upon this *Stage*.
But if you pay the great arrears of praise
So long since due to my much injur'd Plays,
From all past crimes I first will set you free,
And then inspire some one to write like me.[1]

---

 1. *A Collection of Poems Written upon several Occasions By several Persons*, 1673, pp. 29–32; *A Collection of Poems By Several Hands*, 1693, pp. 117–120.

Dorset is, of course, only ironically damning Jonson's play; he is really satirizing the low tastes of the audience.

From February 26, 1672, to midsummer's day, 1673, because of the burning of the theatre in Bridges Street on January 25, 1672, the King's Company played at the Lincoln's Inn Fields theatre recently deserted by Davenant, and it is possible that the performance was given there, although one is tempted to date it rather nearer 1669 than 1673. "Mr. Matthew" was the eminent Matthew Medbourne. There is no trace of ten plays written by him, but he did translate, according to Langbaine,[1] Molière's *Tartuffe*, printed in June, 1670,[2] for which Dorset had also supplied the epilogue, spoken by Medbourne himself. Now Medbourne was famous as an actor at the Duke's theatre, but the printed *Tartuffe* stated that it had been "Lately Acted at the Theatre Royal" (the customary name for the King's Company's theatre), a fact which enables us to explain the dilemma of Thomas Davies,[3] who was convinced that *Every Man in his Humour* must have been revived at both theatres, because Dorset had referred to Medbourne as the "domestique Wit" at the King's theatre. In short, Medbourne had probably been connected with Killigrew's company about 1668 and was doubtless still there when Jonson's comedy was revived between January, 1669, and June, 1673. Dorset's real opinion of Jonson appears to lie in the words spoken by Jonson's ghost, and the device of allowing staunch Ben to answer those smart detractors who preferred the *deus ex machina*, the foreign scene, and the activities of Belphegor, was quite in the spirit of an author who could write of his own work, "By God! 'tis good, and if you like 't, you may!"

1. *An Account of the English Dramatick Poets*, pp. 366–367.
2. Edward Arber, *The Term Catalogues*, I, 50.
3. *Dramatic Miscellanies*, II, 62–63. He thought the play was not revived until 1675 by the Duke's Company at Dorset Garden, and he assigned a conjectural cast from the Duke's actors. Of the actors he chose, only Betterton acted in a Jonsonian comedy, and he only three times at the Haymarket in 1707, according to extant evidence, as Morose.

It is true that Dryden held an unfavorable opinion of the diction of *Every Man in his Humour*, directly opposite to that of Pepys noted above. Regarding Jonson's occasional meanness of expression, he wrote:

Nay, he was not free from the lowest and most grovelling kind of wit, which we call clenches, of which "Every Man in his Humour" is infinitely full; and, which is worse, the wittiest persons in the drama speak them. . . . Gentlemen will now be entertained with the follies of each other; and, though they allow Cobb and Tib to speak properly, yet they are not much pleased with their tankard, or with their rags.[1]

If this allusion was influenced by the performance of the play, light is thrown on the date of production, which would be before February, 1671.

In 1691 Langbaine remarked only that "This Play has been reviv'd since the Civil Wars, and was receiv'd with general Applause," [2] a statement which confirms the opinion that *Every Man in his Humour* was not indifferently received by the Restoration audience. But it did not hold the stage, and the revival, which seems to have been an isolated one, was not duplicated until 1725.

Concerning the revival in 1725 at Lincoln's Inn Fields under the management of John Rich, there is, as usual at this time, a scarcity of critical material. Newspapers did not review plays, no one has left reminiscences of the performance, and there are no extant facts beyond the bills in *The Daily Post* and the box-office receipts culled from the ledgers in the British Museum. So little was known about the revival even in the eighteenth century that Davies remarked: "I was informed, many years since, that Every Man in his humour was revived at the theatre in Lincoln's-inn-fields about the year 1720: how the parts were distributed I could not learn." [3] The bills announced the play as

1. Sir Walter Scott and George Saintsbury, *The Works of John Dryden*, IV (1883), 237–243.
2. Page 290.   3. II, 64.

"Never acted Before. Revis'd with Alterations from Ben Johnson," and the cast was: old Knowell, Quin; young Knowell, Ryan; Brainworm, Spiller; Stephen, William Bullock; Downright, Hulet; Wellbred, Walker; Kitely, Hippisley; Bobadill, Hall; Clement, Christopher Bullock; Marwit, Egleton; Clara, Mrs. Moffett; Lucinda, Mrs. Butcher.[1] The comedy was acted on January 11, 12, and 13. The receipts the first night were £51 18s.[2]

The altered play, no printed copy of which seems to have been made, omitted seven characters from the original,— Matthew, Cash, Cob, Formal, Wellbred's servant, Bridget, and Tib,— but contained three new ones,— Marwit, Clara, and Lucinda. Genest conjectured that "either Hippisley was totally out of his element, or the part of Kitely was spoilt so as to make it suit the talents of the actor."[3] *Biographia Dramatica* observed, "strange to say, the part of Kitely was allotted to the buffoon Hippisley; Bobadil by Hall, the original Lockit. . . . In such hands, it will be no wonder that it ended in three representations only."[4] John Hippisley, who had acted in no other Jonson play, had succeeded to all of Pinkethman's characters; he was an excellent low comedian, and his performance was much heightened by a distortion of his face occasioned by an accidental burn in his youth. No doubt with his "joke-abounding physiognomy,"[5] he was seriously miscast as the sober Kitely.

William Bullock had played La Foole, Cokes, and Kastril before 1710, but as young Master Stephen, the country gull, he must — before the wonderful days of plastic surgery — have presented an incredible figure, for he was no less than sixty-eight years old, of a large frame suitable for playing the host in *The Merry Wives of Windsor*, and

1. *The Daily Post*, January 12, 1725.
2. British Museum Additional MSS 32249–32252.
3. III, 166. See *The Thespian Dictionary*, 2d ed., 1805, Quin.
4. II, 204.
5. *The Works, in Verse and Prose, of William Shenstone, Esq.*, III, 52.

Sir Tunbelly Clumsey in *The Relapse*! Quin had already
played Winwife and Voltore; Lacy Ryan, Edgworth and
Bonario; Thomas Walker, who had already played Edgworth, and was in three years to act the original Mac-
heath, was so seldom sober that he devoured sandwiches
backstage to allay the fumes of alcohol; James Spiller,
famous for his portrayals of old men, must have been ill
cast as the lively Brainworm. The younger Bullock had
played Edgworth. None of the women had played Jonson
previously.

The receipts for the third day, "Benefit of Capt. Phillips," reached £100 15s. 6d., after a second night's house
worth only £28, and the play was abandoned, not to appear
again for twenty-six years. The venture should have
proved to the managers that Jonson's comedies required
only the minor alterations which they were to receive at
the hands of Garrick and Colman.

II

DRURY LANE, 1751–1762

When Garrick revived *Every Man in his Humour* at
Drury Lane in November, 1751, he had already appeared
in the chief classical rôles on which his fame is based: Hamlet, Richard III, Romeo, Macbeth, Lear, Pierre, Jaffeir,
Lord Foppington, Bayes, Benedick, and Abel Drugger.
Even if he had not been interested from the scholar's point
of view in reviving great Elizabethan plays, his own success for seven years as the Tobacco Boy and the popularity
of *The Fox* at Covent Garden would have warranted
trial of another play by Jonson. Most of his rôles in plays
which had been repertory pieces in the early years of the
century he had inherited from predecessors and reclaimed
in the interests of greater naturalism, as he had rescued
Drugger from the grimaces of Theophilus Cibber. But it
was indeed a sporting venture to revive a play which had
not been a success for over a century, especially one which

was almost irremediably stamped with an epoch; a play
with burly wit, robust humor, practically no plot, no love
story; a play cast for thirteen men and only three women,
all of whom must be perfectly selected in order to bring
forth emphases and differentiations in characters which
even after much study leave a confused impression.

With so many difficulties facing him, it is not strange
that Garrick prepared for this revival as for no other. A
year before the first performance, *The General Advertiser*
announced that the play was about to be revived.[1] Again
in October, 1751, *The London Daily Advertiser and Literary
Gazette* noted that *Every Man in his Humour* had "some
time been in Rehearsal, and will be very shortly performed,"[2] and we have Garrick's own account of the labor
necessary to produce it with the perfection which he desired. In March, 1759, a command performance having
been ordered at a time when only seven of the original
sixteen actors remained, he wrote to Robert D'Arcy,
fourth Earl of Holderness, that he was not prepared and
feared the performance would disgrace the company:

> The Language & Characters of Ben Jonson (and particularly
> of the Comedy in question) are much more difficult than those
> of any other Writer, & I was three years before I durst venture
> to trust the Comedians with their Characters, when it was first
> reviv'd.[3]

The revival on November 29, 1751, had beyond doubt
been highly anticipated, and its success as a social event
was guaranteed by the expected presence of the king, for
The London Daily Advertiser informed the public:

> We hear that his Majesty intends to go to the Theatre-Royal
> in Drury-Lane this Evening, to see the Comedy of *Every Man
> in his Humour*, wrote by Ben Johnson in 1598, acted the same
> Year by the then Lord Chamberlain's Servants, and dedicated

---

1. December 17, 1750.   2. October 5, 1751.
3. George Pierce Baker, *Some Unpublished Correspondence of David Garrick*,
Boston, 1907, pp. 79–80. The command performance was given on March 31.

to the great Mr. Camden; and was revived since the Revolution with great Applause, having a new Epilogue spoken by Ben Johnson's Ghost, written by the late Earl of Dorset.[1]

For some reason, the king deferred his attendance until the second performance on December 1.[2]

The General Advertiser, which furnished the theatrical bills at this time, announced the cast and advertised that "the Characters will be dress'd in the old English Manner," a fact that is highly important, because it has been declared even recently [3] that no effort towards historical accuracy in costuming period plays was made until the revival of *Every Man in his Humour* at Covent Garden in October, 1762.

The play had a new occasional prologue, not by Garrick, as some have supposed,[4] but by William Whitehead.

PROLOGUE

At the Revival of *Every Man in his Humour*
Spoken by Mr. Garrick

Criticks! your Favour is our Author's Right —
The well-known Scenes, we shall present to-night,
Are no weak Efforts of a modern Pen,
But the strong Touches of immortal *Ben*;
A rough old Bard, whose honest Pride disdain'd
Applause itself unless by Merit gain'd —
And wou'd to-night your loudest Praise disclaim, ⎫
Shou'd his great Shade perceive the doubtful Fame, ⎬
Not to his Labours granted, but his Name. ⎭

1. November 29, 1751.
2. *The General Advertiser*, December 3, 1751.
3. See D. T. Mackintosh, "New Dress'd in the Habits of the Times," *The Times Literary Supplement*, August 25, 1927, where Colman the elder is considered the innovator of this custom. *The Silent Woman* in 1752 and *The Alchemist* in 1753 were historically costumed. See an article "On Dramatic Costume," *The Gentleman's Magazine*, XCV, part i (1825), 4.
4. *A Collection and Selection of English Prologues and Epilogues*, III, 215–216; *Every Man in his Humour*, 1780, p. 2; H. H. Carter, *Every Man in his Humor*, New Haven, 1921, p. xxi. There is a fragment of a variant version of the prologue in Garrick's handwriting in the Harvard Theatre Collection. The prologue was reprinted in *The London Magazine*, XX (1751), 568; W. Whitehead, *Poems on Several Occasions*, 1754, pp. 139–140.

Boldly he wrote, and boldly told the Age,
"He dar'd not prostitute the useful Stage,
"Or purchase their Delight at such a Rate,
"As, for it, he himself must justly hate:
"But rather begg'd they wou'd be pleas'd to see
"From him, such Plays, as other Plays shou'd be:
"Wou'd learn from him, to scorn a motley Scene,
"And leave their Monsters, to be pleas'd with Men."
Thus spoke the Bard — And tho' the Times are chang'd,
Since his free Muse, for Fools the City rang'd;
And Satire had not then appear'd in State,
To lash the finer Follies of the Great;
Yet let not Prejudice infect your Mind,
Nor slight the Gold, because not quite refin'd;
With no false Niceness this Performance view,
Nor damn for *Low*, whate'er is just and true:
Sure to those Scenes some Honour shou'd be paid,
Which *Cambden* patroniz'd, and *Shakespear* play'd.
Nature was Nature then, and still survives;
The Garb may alter, but the Substance lives.
Lives in this Play — where each may find complete,
His pictur'd Self — Then favour the Deceit —
Kindly forget the hundred Years between;
Become *old Britons*, and admire *old Ben*.

The cast was as follows: old Knowell, Edward Berry, who had played Corvino (1733) and Mammon (1742); young Knowell, David Ross; Brainworm, Richard Yates, who had played Dapper (1739) and Kastril (1745); Master Stephen, Edward Shuter, who had played Ananias (1750); Downright, Richard Winstone, who had played Peregrine (1733); Wellbred, William Palmer; Kitely, Garrick, who had played Drugger since 1743; Cash, Charles Blakes, who had played Surly (1746); Bobadill, Henry Woodward, who had played La Foole (1739), Kastril (1739), and Ananias (1749); Master Matthew, Henry Vaughan, who had played Dapper (1748); Cob, Thomas Mozeen; Justice Clement, Taswell, who had played Tribulation (1740); Formal, Costollo; Dame Kitely, Mrs. Ward; Bridget, Miss Minors; Cob's wife, Mrs. Cross, who had played Lady Haughty (1735), Dame Pliant (1735), Dol

Common (1740), and Lady Centaure (1742). Ten of the players had previously acted a variety of characters from Jonson's comedies; it was a tutored and sophisticated cast, the oldest actors of which connected the mid-century theatre with the traditions of the earlier stage. That the first night was an extraordinary success is not surprising, although there is a report that there was "some hissing . . . from the rash, minor Critics."[1]

After the second night the papers announced that "His Majesty . . . was greatly pleas'd with the old reviv'd Comedy of Every Man in his Humour; written by Ben Johnson."[2] He had been attended by the Right Hon. the Marquis of Hartington and several other nobles.[3] The play took the fancy of the town by storm. There were nine performances before the end of the year, and sixteen before the end of the season in May, a notable tribute to Garrick's skill in altering the text and in training his actors. In January, 1752, *The Gentleman's Magazine* printed a critique of the play, "The public having been lately entertained with *Every Man in his Humour*, a revived play of *Ben Johnson's*," noting that in Jonson there are few passages that want correction and that his editor should concern himself with pointing out references to the customs of that age and to Jonson's classical borrowings.[4] The article made no comments on the acting at Drury Lane.

Of the critical pamphlets, the earliest to appear takes an unfavorable view of the revival. The Inspector meets Ben Jonson among the shades. Offended by Ben's patronizing attitude, he remarks:

Why damn me, old *Ben*, for all that Puff upon your Monument, if I see any Reason why you should take such Airs upon you. You may thank the Ignorance of the Times, Sir, for your Success; but your *every Man in his Humor*, would not do with us; besides, one of the best Scenes in it is visibly pilfer'd from the

1. Benjamin Victor, *The History of the Theatres of London*, II, 127.
2. *The General Advertiser*, December 3, 1751.
3. *The London Daily Advertiser*, December 3, 1751.   4. XXII, 3-4.

Suspicious Husband; and but for *Woodward*, your Bobbadil would never pass. Why, Sir, you never had the Genius of my learned and worthy Friend *Sam. Foote*; I'll pawn my Reputation, Posterity will think you never had; for there is infinitely more genuine Wit, more of the true *Vis Comica* in his *Taste*, than in your *Alchymist*.[1]

The fame of the comedy continued, spread, and found its way even into a novel, *The Cry: A New Dramatic Fable* (1754), by Sarah Fielding and Jane Collier:

The *Cry* . . . began to accuse [Portia] of a total want of humour, in not being pleased with such entertaining characters, as are drawn by *Ben Johnson*. Then some were sounding the praises of *Bobadel*, others of the jealous *Kitely*, and all joined in admiration of the diverting figure of master *Stephen*, when he saw his broken toledo.

Portia. Very justly, O ye *Cry*, have you pointed out the humour of three very entertaining comic characters, which have lately gained such merited applause; nor is there any one amongst you, who can admire the beauties of some of *Ben Johnson's* writings more than I do. For, besides the foregoing ones, which by the force of inimitable action have made such an impression on your memories, there is *Morose, Macilente*, lady *Woud-be*, and many other strong pictures of nature, in his comedies.[2]

Much of the play's success must be attributed to the fashion in which Garrick had eliminated the obsolete features of the play and given it greater concentration. Before the comments of the critics can be appreciated, it is necessary to study the alteration.

1. *The Inspector in the Shades*, 1752, pp. 14–15.
2. I, 165–166. Sarah Fielding alluded to Bobadill and Stephen in *The History of the Countess of Dellwyn*, 1759, I, 140, 237. See also *The Adventures of Jack Wander* [1766], p. 156. Allusions appeared also in prologues and epilogues: see Arthur Murphy, *The Upholsterer*, 1758, sig. A3; *The Court of Thespis*, 1769, p. 123; *The Universal Magazine*, XXII (1758), 209; *A Collection and Selection of English Prologues and Epilogues*, IV, 138. For allusions to Bobadill and Downright in political satire see [Hugh Dalrymple], *Rodondo; or, The State Jugglers*, 1763; *A Collection of Scarce, Curious and Valuable Pieces, Both in Verse and Prose*, Edinburgh, 1773, pp. 2, 16; *Notes and Queries*, 1st series, IX (1854), 589.

III

THE ALTERATION

Garrick's method of altering old plays was caustically described by his rival Theophilus Cibber, who hinted that Garrick gave the original to his cat to play with. "What Puss claw'd off, the Actor left out." [1] Whatever wantonness the manager practised on Shakspere's plays, there can be no doubt that he approached *Every Man in his Humour* with the utmost respect and altered only enough to make it intelligible and attractive. He perceived that the main outlines of this complex comedy of humors could scarcely be changed without making a new play, and contented himself, therefore, with removing traits of obsolescence, indecencies in expression no longer tolerable, obscure allusions, and puns. He made as few structural changes as possible. *Volpone*, *The Alchemist*, and *The Silent Woman*, which still held the stage, all had dramatic interest arising from plots or characters based on some fundamental human quality. *Every Man in his Humour*, however, depended on its force as a realistic picture of an epoch, resembling a Dutch painting, with a large group of characters representing different passions or "humors," which moved here and there with slight centrifugal control. Garrick saw that the danger of diffuseness could be averted by emphasizing the most promising emotional possibility of the comedy,— Kitely's jealousy. The development of the rôle of Kitely necessitated, in the fourth act, some structural alterations, which gave Garrick a far better opportunity for displaying his abilities continuously on the stage. Inasmuch as he rearranged rather than rewrote the original episodes by Jonson, the alteration retained the spirit of the original and presented a really improved stage-

1. *Two Dissertations on the Theatres*, pp. 34–35.

piece. Without the change, the play would probably have failed, for even with revision the comedy appeared strange to the audience.[1] Garrick explained his reasons for taking liberties with Jonson's play in the advertisement of his alteration:[2] "the Distance of 150 Years from the Time of Writing it, [has] occasioned some of the Humour to be too obsolete, and dangerous to be Ventur'd in the Representation at present."

Inasmuch as there have been two minute comparisons of the alteration with the original,[3] only a recapitulation need be made here. The cast of characters remained the same, but Garrick throughout the play reduced the part of Cob, a low-comedy figure no longer familiar to the inhabitants of London. Other characters were incidentally reduced as he ridded the comedy of obsoleteness and verbosity. On the other hand, the rôles of Kitely and Dame Kitely were somewhat expanded. Structurally, some changes were advisable as the result of improved technical resources in the eighteenth-century theatre: the use of scenery made necessary a coalescence of several scenes, improving the continuity of action.

Garrick left Act I practically unaltered. The scene divisions remained the same as in Jonson. The revision omitted short allusions to Hogsden, Pickthatch, Master John Trundle, and Drake's old ship at Deptford on grounds of their obscurity. In scene iii Cob's account of his lineage was cut a page. In scene iv the conversation of Bobadill

1. Thomas Davies, *Dramatic Miscellanies*, II, 66–67.

2. *Every Man in his Humour. A Comedy. Written by Ben Jonson. With Alterations and Additions. As it is Perform'd at the Theatre-Royal in Drury-Lane*, 1752.

3. Franz Krämer, *Das Verhältnis von David Garrick's "Every Man in his Humour" zu dem gleichnamigen Lustspiel Ben Jonson's*, Halle, 1903; Heinrich Maass, *Ben Jonson's Lustspiel "Every Man in his Humour" und die gleichnamige Bearbeitung durch David Garrick*, Rostock, 1903. Krämer ignored the acting versions of 1752, 1754, and 1759, thinking the edition of 1768 the first printed copy of Garrick's alteration. Compare H. H. Carter, pp. xxi–xxii. References to act and scene of Jonson's original play are to the edition of Gifford (1816), followed by Cunningham (1875) and the Mermaid edition (1894).

and Matthew on *The Spanish Tragedy* was cut, together with a half-page of Bobadill's boasting about his prowess in fencing. Woodward's acting could doubtless have justified inclusion of the passage.

Act II, scene i, was unaltered, except for the omission of four short passages of one sentence each, including an ancient proverb, a reference to antiquated forms of clothing, and an allusion to Gargantua by Downright, removed for reasons of taste. The passage of Cob across the stage was eliminated. Garrick played continuously scenes ii and iii of the original, thereby saving a change of scenery. In scene ii two lines for Brainworm were cut,— one a pun, the other a reference to motley. In the original scene iii, the elder Knowell lost sixteen lines on the education of the youth of his day, and Brainworm lost a line alluding to the musters at Mile-end.

The scene divisions of Act III remained unchanged. Scene i appeared unaltered from Jonson, but for the omission of an allusion to Symmachus, twelve lines on sonnet writing by young Knowell, Stephen, and Matthew, and the lines of Wellbred and Brainworm on the porters of Thames Street. Scene ii was liberally reduced. Kitely's conversation with Cash on cuckoldry was shortened by ten lines, but the important cut was the removal of Cob, a reduction of two pages of low wit. The rest of the scene was slashed here and there, some of the cuts amounting to a half-page. They included young Knowell's reference to the Seven Wise Masters and to the beggars on the outskirts of the city, Wellbred's proverb on crafty knaves, Bobadill's eulogy of tobacco and Cob's aspersions on the weed. The total of cuts amounted to about four pages. In scene iii Cob lost three lines of soliloquy on his "vinegar and mustard revenge" and on Tib's kindness to Bobadill. This scene was the most reduced of all, for with deletion of the episode between Cob, Clement, Knowell, and Formal, where Cob sought redress for the beating he had received from Bobadill, three pages of text vanished.

Garrick paid most attention to building the climax in Act IV by strengthening the rôle of Kitely. Scene i lost about two pages. The cuts included an old proverb, one of Stephen's curious oaths, a play on words in Latin, and Matthew's lines on *Hero and Leander*. The labor spent on this scene was justified; much of the heaviness and obsoleteness was removed. Scene ii was entirely omitted; Garrick saved a page and a half and a change of scenery. Scene iii of Jonson, which Garrick played as scene ii, was indicated for the Windmill Tavern, but Garrick placed it on Moorfields, for it could be played as naturally out-of-doors as in the tavern. The change was part of a clever structural device by which the original scenes iii, iv, and v of Jonson were played continuously at Moorfields; two changes of scenery were saved. Garrick cut nothing in scene iii, and only one line in scene iv. In scene v, however, he reduced Bobadill's reminiscences of his fencing by a half-page, a passage which in any case would have given Woodward little opportunity. Garrick added a line for Bobadill at the end of the scene, to heighten his attempted explanation of his cowardice: "I was planet-struck certainly."

Jonson's scene vi, presented as Garrick's scene iii, received more structural alteration than any other scene in any revision of Jonson's comedies. The nearest approach to the method employed here was Colman's alteration of *Epicoene* (III. ii; IV. i). Garrick simply manipulated the episodes of the scene, rearranging them so as to give Kitely a continuous appearance on the stage, and expanding some of them so as to heighten Kitely's suspicion of his wife's fidelity. A short summary will display his method. Jonson's scene fell into the following episodes:

(a) Kitely rebukes Wellbred for disturbing the peace of his house; Wellbred answers that no harm is done. Dame Kitely asks what harm could possibly be done, anyway, and (b) Wellbred replies that her husband might have been poisoned. Kitely, who has just drunk, immediately imagines that he is ill, and

Wellbred remarks that jealousy has poisoned him. (c) Brain-worm enters in Formal's clothes and tells Kitely that Clement wishes to see him. Exit Kitely to seek Cob and Cash as guards during his absence. (d) Wellbred recognizes Brainworm and asks where he found Formal's clothes. Brainworm explains that he has made Formal drunk and taken his clothes. Wellbred sends him back to his master. (e) Kitely reenters with Cash. Reveal-ing great jealousy and suspicion, he bids Cash guard his honor and watch every visitor's actions. Cash promises to be faithful, and Kitely goes out, calling for Cob. (f) Dame Kitely wonders why her husband is always calling for Cob. Wellbred excites her suspicion by telling her that Cob's wife is a bawd and that Kitely resorts there. Dame Kitely orders Cash to accompany her thither. (g) Bridget and Wellbred are left alone. Wellbred in-forms her of young Knowell's admiration of her beauty and asks if she will see him. (h) Kitely returns, lamenting because he was called on a false errand. (g) Finding his wife gone, he suspects a plot. Bridget tells him that his wife has gone with Cash, and Kitely believes that Cash is deceiving him. When Wellbred tells him that Dame Kitely has gone to Cob's house, Kitely supposes that she is cuckolding him and departs for Cob's house, followed by Wellbred and Bridget.

Garrick's scene was arranged as follows:

(a) Since Dame Kitely has appeared to admire young Knowell, Kitely's jealousy is terrific. He thinks his wife and her lover are laughing because they have deceived him, and sends Cash to spy. Cash reports that Wellbred and the ladies have been laughing at the strange clothing of Formal. (b) Brainworm en-ters, clad as Formal, and asks Kitely to call on Clement. Kitely bids Cash be on his guard and makes him swear fidelity. Cash tells Kitely that his suspicions are unreasonable and bids him treat Dame Kitely as formerly. (c) Wellbred enters and asks Kitely why he muses so much; Kitley rebukes him for upsetting the peace of his house. Wellbred assures him that there has been no harm done, and Dame Kitely asks what harm could possibly be done, anyway. (d) Kitely is momentarily pleased with her, but tells her that she ought to stay at home more. If she must go out, he will go too, to stifle the tongue of slander and prevent his being "pointed at, as one disturbed with jealousy."

She asks him if he has ever been thus pointed at, and he indulges in a long and agitated denial. Then he departs seeking Cob. (e) Wellbred analyzes Kitely's trouble as jealousy, and Dame Kitely cannot deny it. She asks why her husband is always calling for Cob. Wellbred tells her that Cob's wife is a bawd and that Kitely haunts their house. Dame Kitely calls Cash and bids him accompany her to Cob's house. Wellbred laughs at the sport he has made. (f) To him comes Brainworm, still dressed as Formal. Wellbred asks how he came by the apparel, and Brainworm tells how he has made Formal drunk and stripped him. Wellbred sends Brainworm back to his master. (g) Bridget inquires what Wellbred means by all this trickery. Wellbred tells her that young Knowell is mad about her. (h) To them comes Kitely, inquiring for his wife. Finding that she has gone to Cob's house, he believes her unfaithful and himself the most miserable of men, betrayed by his wife, pointed at by his neighbors, and despised by himself. He decides to avenge and then hang himself. Bridget and Wellbred are left on the stage. Wellbred assures her that all will end well.

Jonson's episode (a) has become Garrick's (c). Garrick omitted Jonson's (b); his own (b) expanded Jonson's (c). Jonson's (d) was the same as Garrick's (f). Jonson's (e) was greatly expanded in Garrick's (a), and Jonson's (f) was slightly expanded in Garrick's (e). Episode (g) was the same in both. Jonson's (h) was slightly expanded in Garrick's (h), and Garrick's (d) was entirely new. From the point of view of Kitely as the leading rôle, the advantages of Garrick's version are apparent. Kitely was allowed to play continuously four episodes, Garrick's (a), (b), (c), (d), instead of three, Jonson's (a), (b), (c). Thus Garrick was given a big scene instead of several episodes interrupted by departures from the stage. Jonson had allowed no confrontation between Kitely and his wife in which the former specifically displayed his jealousy. The revelation of the consuming jealousy of Kitely to Dame Kitely, as added by Garrick in his (d), formed one of the most dramatic moments of the play. Arthur Murphy described Garrick's acting at this point:

To disguise his suspicions, he assumed an air of gaiety, but under that mask the corrosions of jealousy were seen in every feature. Such was the expression of that various face, that the mixed emotions of his heart were strongly marked by his looks and the tone of his voice.[1]

This scene was the climax of the play. Although Jonson continued his fourth act for three more scenes, Garrick ended his immediately.

Garrick, by beginning his fifth act with the seventh scene of Jonson's fourth act, gave an opportunity to the scene-shifters to arrange the setting for the Stocks-Market. Jonson had indicated a street for this scene. The alteration omitted some lines on Venice, on fencing, and on Elizabethan clothing. Garrick's scene ii (Jonson, IV. viii) received larger cuts. Cob's appearance was entirely omitted, and Garrick added a few lines for Kitely at his entrance, showing his agitation when he finds his wife at Cob's house. Kitely challenges Knowell and threatens to bring the entire company before Justice Clement. The alteration expanded this episode as the climax of the scene. Garrick played scene iii (Jonson, IV. ix) with the same set used for scene i, instead of in a street, as Jonson intended. There were no important cuts. Jonson's Act V, scene i, was greatly abridged to form Garrick's Act V, scene iv, the cuts amounting to two and a half pages. The part of Clement was greatly reduced. Garrick added a few lines for him, when he advises the jealous husband to retire and think coolly about the tricks that have been played on him. Kitely takes the advice, and the play ends practically as in the original, with a happy reunion between Kitely and his wife.

Arthur Murphy noted Garrick's acting at the beginning of the last scene, when Dame Kitely informs Clement that Cob's house is a place of ill fame and that she went thither to seek her husband:

1. *The Life of David Garrick*, 1801, I, 205–206. Murphy adds an interesting analysis of the characters in the comedy.

"*Did you find him there?*" says the *Justice*. In that instant *Kitely* interposes, saying, in a sharp eager tone, "*I found her there.*" He who remembers how Garrick uttered those words, slapping his hand on the table, as if he made an important discovery, must acknowledge, trifling as it may now be thought, that it was a genuine stroke of nature.[1]

IV

THE ACTORS

The uniform excellence of Garrick's production of *Every Man in his Humour* was noted by critics throughout the century. "It was excellently acted. Those who remember the original performers do not expect to see a play ever so completely filled again in every character."[2] "A comedy so completely acted was hardly ever seen on the English stage."[3] "Every part in that production of old Ben's was so well acted, it was hard to point out how any one in that very difficult composition could be amended."[4] Even Garrick's contemporaries, however, considered the revival a *tour de force*, alteration or no, and as early as 1764 *The Companion to the Play-House* observed that although the comedy had been a stock play since 1751, it owed its success to Garrick's masterly casting and would probably never again appear to the same advantage.[5]

The masterpieces of acting were created by Garrick as Kitely, Woodward as Bobadill, and Shuter as Master Stephen. Brainworm, Clement, Cash, and Wellbred were mentioned now and then, but the other rôles were changing performers so rapidly that the actors, and especially the actresses, did not become established in their parts. From 1751 to 1776 only two actors at the major theatres played

1. I, 207–208.
2. *The Gentleman's Magazine*, XLIX (1779), 339.
3. Arthur Murphy, I, 208.
4. Tate Wilkinson, *Memoirs of His Own Life*, IV, 167.
5. Article on *Every Man in his Humour*.

Kitely,— Garrick at Drury Lane, and Smith at Covent Garden; only three played Bobadill,— Woodward at both theatres, and Yates and King at Drury Lane; four played Downright and Formal; five, Brainworm and Tib; six, Stephen and old Knowell; seven, Cash and Cob; eight, young Knowell and Matthew; nine, Wellbred and Bridget; ten, Justice Clement; eleven, Dame Kitely. Obviously, one cannot expect much critical comment on the female performers, and obviously, too, one will find most of it on Garrick and Woodward, who played continuously for twenty-five years.

The fullest account of the ensemble is given by Thomas Davies, whose knowledge of the play was intimate:

Kitely, the jealous husband, which requires great art in the performer, he took upon himself; to Woodward he assigned Bobadil, which has been thought, by many good judges, to have been his masterpiece in low comedy. Brainworm was played with all the archness and pleasantry that could be assumed by Yates: Wellbred and Young Knowell by Ross and Palmer. Shuter entered most naturally into the follies of a young, ignorant, fellow, who thinks smoking tobacco fashionably, and swearing a strange kind of oath, the highest proofs of humour and taste. Winstone, who was tolerated in other parts, in Downright was highly applauded. Old Knowell became the age and person of Berry. Mrs. Ward, a pretty woman, and an actress of considerable talents, acted dame Kitely. Miss Minors, since Mrs. Walker, was the Mrs. Bridget. I must not forget master Matthew, the town gull, which was given, with much propriety, to Harry Vaughan, a brother of Mrs. Pritchard, a man formed by nature for small parts of low humour and busy impertinence.[1]

The character of Kitely, as has been pointed out, was emphasized in the alteration in the interest of expanding the one genuine emotion in a collection of follies and humors. Naturally, the manager chose for his own talents this desirable rôle in a museum of freaks and originals; with

1. *Dramatic Miscellanies*, II, 65-66.

Bayes, Ranger, Don Felix, Benedick, and Abel Drugger it built his fame as a comedian and invited both censure and praise. Even Theophilus Cibber, no friend of Garrick, who described Garrick's "studied Tricks, his Over-fondness for extravagant Attitudes, frequent affected Starts, convulsive Twitchings, Jerkings of the Body, sprawling of the Fingers, . . . his forc'd Conceits," admitted that his performance of Kitely was "so excellent a Piece of Nature, — so truely comic, — it makes Amends for all the Farce with which that indelicate Piece of low Humour abounds." [1] Cibber's view was supported in the next year by *The Theatrical Examiner* (1757), which stupidly considered *Every Man in his Humour* "a coarse bad play," but confessed that Garrick had "greatly supported it by very masterly acting: — but even here, he will not divest himself of stage-trick and clap-traps, — yet must allow him all due praise; — a great actor he must be thought by all, yet not without great faults." [2]

Much of the criticism of actors in the eighteenth century is either plain panegyric or downright abuse, with little pointing of specific beauties. Since acting is the most evanescent of the arts, the most difficult to preserve for future generations, it is valuable to find an interpretative criticism based on definite passages. In 1759 Thomas Wilkes analyzed *Every Man in his Humour*, the main design of which was "to cure a wrong-headed husband of a ridiculous, ill-grounded jealousy." In appreciation of Garrick he wrote:

How beautifully does he paint the jealousy of common life in Kitely. . . . The anxiety and fears here natural to the part, and the aukward endeavour at disguising the ruling passion, are capital, both in the poet and the player, particularly where the husband unawares drops it that he has been,

1. *Two Dissertations on the Theatres*, pp. 46, 47, 56.
2. Page 34.

	pointed out as one
	Disturbed with jealousy.
Dame Kitely.	*Why were you ever jealous?*
Kite.	*What? — ha! never! never! ha, ha, ha! She*
	stabs me home! Jealous of thee! No, do
	not believe it — Speak low, my love.

Garrick's laugh here is, as his wife afterwards expresses it, "Seemingly without mirth, constrained, and affected to the utmost." His supposed detection of old Knowell, in an intrigue with his wife, at Cob's house, is a scene which would make an exceeding good picture. In a few words here, before the justice, and, indeed, through the whole part, he shews a deep knowledge of the human heart; and it is equal to any acting that ever was seen.[1]

After the revival of the play at Covent Garden on October 25, 1762, it was produced only twice at Drury Lane before 1767 (in 1763 and 1766), after which for seven years a spectator might have seen it at both theatres. Woodward had gone over to Covent Garden in 1757; Shuter, Costollo, and Mrs. Ward were to be found acting at Covent Garden at the time of the revival; from 1763 to 1765 Garrick was traveling; consequently, the history of the play at Drury Lane was meager from October 4, 1762, to October 9, 1767. There was, however, occasional criticism, for the years of consecutive playing had established Kitely as one of Garrick's masterpieces. *The Theatrical Review* (1763) declared that comedy was his peculiar forte and praised him for the judgment, infinite vivacity, invention, and every other quality which composed that genuine *vis comica* of his Bayes, for his sprightly and humorous Benedick, his jealous Kitely, and the debauched Chalkstone.[2] Eulogy was at its most extravagant in the article on Garrick in *The Companion to the Play-House*, which insisted that time itself appeared to stand still or advance, as Garrick willed, and that anybody who had seen his Lear,

---

1. *A General View of the Stage*, pp. 258–259. The passage quoted was entirely of Garrick's composition.   2. Page 79.

Hamlet, Romeo, Drugger, Kitely, and Brute would admit
that nature had "bestowed on him such Powers of Expression in the Muscles of his Face, as no Performer ever yet
possess'd."

On May 22, 1766, the play was acted at Drury Lane for
the first time in three years, "with an Occasional Prologue" which does not appear to have been printed. The
proceeds were to go "towards raising a FUND for the Relief of those, who, from their Infirmities, shall be obliged to
retire from the Stage." [1] There were five new actors, and
Dunstall was borrowed for the evening from Covent Garden to play Brainworm. The comedy was cordially received and called forth immediately in *The Public Advertiser* a little poetical appreciation:

ON SEEING MR. GARRICK IN THE CHARACTER OF KITELY

> If ev'ry Talent, ev'ry Power to please,
> Sense join'd with Spirit, Dignity with Ease;
> If Elocution of the noblest Kind,
> Such as at once inflames and melts the Mind;
> Looks, strongly piercing as the Bird of Jove,
> Address, insinuating, soft as Love;
> Politeness, such as Art can ne'er bestow,
> And from the well-turn'd Mind alone must flow;
> Action by no mechanic Rules restrain'd;
> Passion, that strikes the Soul, because unfeign'd;
> If these can form a Character compleat,
> All these in GARRICK, you are sure to meet.
>
> CLIO [2]

If Garrick was great as Kitely, Henry Woodward was
equally renowned as the braggart Bobadill. Although his
powers as an actor were confined almost exclusively to
comedy, harlequinades, and pantomimes, he was master of
his art as Marplot, Lord Foppington, Touchstone, Scrub,
Parolles, Captain Flash, and Petruchio, and was famous
as the author of two popular afterpieces, *Harlequin a Sorcerer* and *Queen Mab*. Unquestionably his most renowned

---

1. *The Public Advertiser*, May 22, 1766.
2. May 28, 1766; *The Jester's Magazine*, June, 1766, p. 278.

rôle was Bobadill, which he played at Drury Lane from November, 1751, until March 31, 1759, when he was succeeded by Richard Yates, and at Covent Garden from the revival on October 25, 1762, until January 21, 1774, after which the play appeared only at Drury Lane until Garrick's farewell. Woodward acted in more performances of *Every Man in his Humour* than any other actor in the period, with a total of one hundred thirty-one nights in comparison with Garrick's ninety; he chose the comedy seven times for his benefit, and it is not strange that Bobadill and Woodward became almost synonymous in the poetical squibs and reviews. Bobadill is a character far inferior to Falstaff, because he is a theory and not an individual, but he is one of the most memorable humors in the comedy, and in the scenes of his cowardice on Moorfields there is considerable physical action which could be effectively interpreted by a clever pantomimist. How Woodward was allowed his own interpretation of the part during the rehearsals is narrated by Thomas Davies in an anecdote which reveals Garrick's methods of direction:

During the greatest part of the rehearsals of Every Man in his Humour, Woodward seemed very attentive to Garrick's ideas of Bobadil. But, in his absence one morning, he indulged himself in an exhibition of his own intended manner of representation. While the actors were laughing and applauding Woodward, Garrick entered the playhouse, and, unperceived, attended to the transaction of the scene. After waiting sometime, he stept on the stage, and cried, "Bravo, Harry! bravo! upon my soul, bravo! — Why, now this is —— no, no, I can't say this is quite my idea of the thing — Yours is, after all — to be sure, rather — ha!" — Woodward perceiving the manager a little embarrassed, with much seeming modesty, said, "Sir, I will act the part, if you desire it, exactly according to your notion of it." — "No, no! by no means, Harry. D—n it, you have actually clenched the matter. — But why, my dear Harry, would you not communicate before." [1]

1. *Dramatic Miscellanies*, II, 69. See Tate Wilkinson, IV, 167.

HENRY WOODWARD AS BOBADILL

Woodward was insulted in November, 1752, by a man
in a stage box,[1] and a controversy followed with the usual
train of pamphlets. Dr. John Hill sided with the insulter
and attacked Woodward, but Hill was honored in turn
with a mock defense, which contained vivid praise of
Woodward in his comic rôles:

> Pox o' your comical Pate! — You have made me laugh many
> a Time and oft, when I have been among the Gods, as you call us
> there in the upper-Gallery; - - - with your fine Gentleman in
> *Lethe* - - - and your *Captain Bobadil*, . . . and your *Scrub*; - - -
> between you and I, Master *H* - - - would have given any Thing
> he could have made so good an Actor. But why insult him for his
> want of Parts.[2]

In 1753 the "vast Success" of *Every Man in his Humour*
was largely attributed to Woodward, who was deservedly
"a Favourite of the Town," and his Bobadill was praised as
"certainly very great acting; 'tis what the *French* call *Jeu
de Fin*; and for which we have no *English* Word sufficiently
expressive." [3]

The Theatrical Review (1757) made a significant note on
Woodward's physical qualifications as a comedian. It
considered him a Proteus, who had played all species of
characters with great applause:

> This success has ever appeared to me remarkable, by a very
> peculiar oddity; to wit, that this excellent comedian has always
> met with a more general approbation from the public in those
> parts, for which nature, one would imagine from his exterior
> powers, least designed him. His figure is perfectly genteel, his
> voice smart, agreeable, and pliant, and both seem to point out
> the parts of a genteeler cast, as those which he is likeliest to look,
> and consequently to perform; and yet, as I said, I have ever
> observed, that it is not in those he succeeds best; and he never
> pleases his audience more, than when he is obliged to distort

1. See above, pp. 198-199.
2. *A Letter to Henry Woodward, Comedian, Occasion'd by his Letter to the
Inspector, By Simon Partridge, the Facetious Cobler of Pall Mall*, p. 5.
3. *The Present State of the Stage in Great-Britain*, p. 23.

that genteel figure, into the aukward deportment of a Scrub, or the like; or to swell his voice out of its natural tenour, into the hectoring accents of a Bobadil.[1]

Thomas Wilkes noted that "Bobadil, by which he has acquired a vast increase of reputation, is a part of his own creation, and a proof of his genius." His best acting came at the point where he trampled on Master Stephen's sword, with "This is a toledo! pish!"[2]

Woodward found, to be sure, only grudging praise in the caustically brilliant lines of Churchill's *Rosciad* (1761):

> W—dw—rd, endow'd with various pow'rs of face,
> Great master in the science of Grimace,
> From Ireland ventures, fav'rite of the Town,
> Lur'd by the pleasing prospect of Renown.
> His wit and humour in Distortion lye,
> And all his merit enters at the eye.
> We laugh, we clap, — but, on Reflexion's birth,
> We wonder at ourselves, and curse our mirth.
> His walk of parts he fatally misplac'd,
> And Inclination fondly took for Taste.
> Hence hath the Town so often seen display'd,
> Beau in Burlesque, high-life in Masquerade.
> Merit he had, some merit in his way,
> But seldom found out in what part it lay.
> In BOBADIL, indeed, such praise he bore,
> Such worthy praise, that KITELY scarce had more.[3]

Woodward played Bobadill at Drury Lane for the last time on May 31, 1758. His desertion of Garrick's company in the winter of 1758–1759 was a serious blow, since he was the entire support of all the comedies in which Garrick did not play, such as *The Busy Body*, *The Man of Mode*, and *The Relapse*, and an actor of the first importance in many where he played second lead to Garrick. He was responsible for all the pantomimes in the afterpieces. The success of his Bobadill he carried over to the feebler com-

1. Page 6. Compare *The Theatrical Examiner*, 1757, p. 41; William Hawkins, *Miscellanies in Prose and Verse*, 1775, pp. 42–43.
2. Pages 263–264.   3. Page 11.

pany at Covent Garden, and three years later (1762) *Every Man in his Humour* was revived there. Seventy-four performances followed in the next twelve years, in all of which Woodward played his rôle with no competition.

The third famous player was Ned Shuter as Master Stephen, the country gull, which he acted at Drury Lane for only three years, until March 19, 1754, when Vernon succeeded him. Yates assumed the rôle on December 6, 1755, and kept it until O'Brien displaced him on March 31, 1759. The important period of Shuter's activity in *Every Man in his Humour* coincides exactly with that of Woodward at Covent Garden; for twelve years he played Stephen with no rivalry; not a performance did he miss. Although criticism seems to have been inexhaustible in sounding the praises of Bobadill, it was not so voluminous about Stephen, but its enthusiasm is incontestable. Ned Shuter was the kind of character who, like Ben Jonson himself, found his way into the jest-books. A follower of George Whitefield, he was said sometimes to have attended five meeting-houses of a Sunday. What with religion and drink, he was befuddled when he died in November, 1776. Garrick called him the greatest comic genius he had ever known, and his performance was admitted to rest entirely upon genuine humor, without grimace or buffoonery. In particular, he had great control of his facial muscles. His forte was old men; he was the original old Hardcastle and Sir Anthony Absolute, and his leading rôles were Scrub, Trapolin, Clincher, and Falstaff. Although he had begun with little success at Drury Lane, Garrick recognized his talent. Believing that Shuter needed only proper direction, he planned the revival of *Every Man in his Humour*, it is said, so that Shuter might have the part of Stephen. Shuter carried off equal honors with Garrick and Woodward.[1] Wilkes thought Shuter's comic performance nearer

---

1. *Theatrical Biography*, II, 42. For an amusing anecdote illustrating Shuter's gifts as an impersonator see *The Macaroni, Scavoir Vivre, and Theatrical Magazine*, March, 1773, p. 270, and *The Encyclopedia of Wit* [1804], p. 467.

to nature than that of any comedian on the stage and praised particularly the "setness and risible turn of his features," his "fine vacancy of look," and "an inexpressible and inimitable simplicity in Master Stephen, which is finely contrasted by the blustering air of Bobadil." [1]

Richard Yates, the original Brainworm of the revival, inherited the rôles of Stephen on December 6, 1775, and of Bobadill on March 31, 1759, when O'Brien, carefully schooled by Garrick himself, succeeded to Stephen. Yates, in 1753, was considered to have "a great deal of Merit in his Way; *Brainworm*, in *Every Man in his Humour*, . . . he fills with Humour and Propriety," [2] and in 1759 Wilkes credited him with an eminent distinction of humor, propriety, and a close adherence to nature. "His Brainworm was no less a masterpiece than Woodward's Bobadil; nay, if we consider the various powers it required to support differently the serving-man, the disbanded soldier, the justice's clerk, and the varlet of the city or bailiff, and how he excelled in each, in all, we shall perhaps rank him next to Kitely." [3] On his performance of Stephen there are no memorable comments, but it was probably as excellent as his Malvolio.

William O'Brien, whom Benjamin Victor praised for his easy and elegant deportment in genteel comedy, was satirized by Churchill in *The Rosciad*:

> SHADOWS behind of F[oo]TE and W[oo]D [war] D came;
> W[il]K[in]S[o]N this, OB[r]I[e]N was that name.
>
> .   .   .   .
>
> With not a single comic pow'r endued,
> The first a mere mere mimic's mimic stood.
> The last, by NATURE form'd to please, who shews,
> In JOHNSON's STEPHEN which way Genius grows;
> Self quite put off, affects, with too much art,
> To put on WOODWARD in each mangled part;

---

1. Pages 300–301.
2. *The Present State of the Stage in Great-Britain*, p. 32.
3. Page 272.

Adopts his shrug, his wink, his stare; nay more,
His voice, and croaks; for WOODWARD croak'd before.
Thus the dull copyer simple grace neglects,
And rests his imitation in defects.[1]

At the revival of May 22, 1766, the rôle of Stephen
fell to James William Dodd, who acted it until 1788. He
was good in genteel fops and coxcombs, but his voice was
weak, and the large theatres were almost fatal to his art.
He was the "paragon representative of all *fatuity*; from
the Town-gull, or Master Stephen, . . . with Master
Slender, Roderigo, and Sir Andrew Ague-cheek by Shakspeare, through all the comic varieties." [2] The only other
actor who merits consideration, although Bransby was
praised for Downright and Taswell for Clement, is Charles
Holland, who succeeded Ross and Usher as young Knowell
on March 31, 1759. But he considered this part unworthy
of his talents, which were indeed promising in a man of
twenty-eight, and was chafed to the extent of writing
Garrick from Liverpool on June 18, 1762, to ask for a
relief.[3] Garrick was not moved, and on October 4 Holland
played the part again, although for his last bow. In 1766
he was replaced by the vain coxcomb Lee, and in 1769
he died of smallpox.

The first long newspaper review of *Every Man in his
Humour*, based on the performance of March 31, 1757,
appeared in two instalments in *The London Chronicle*.[4]
The first section begins:

This Evening was performed, to one of the most numerous
and polite Audiences that have been seen this Season (for the
Benefit of Mr. Beard) Ben Jonson's Comedy, called, *Every Man
in his Humour*. If we consider that this Piece was exhibited in
the Year 1598, being near 160 Years ago, it must be allowed that

1. Page 12. See *The Churchiliad*, 1761, p. 30.
2. James Boaden, *The Life of Mrs. Jordan*, 1831, I, 306.
3. [James Boaden], *The Private Correspondence of David Garrick*, I, 142.
4. March 31–April 2, April 2–5, 1757. The reviewer was probably Arthur
Murphy.

it is a Proof of an uncommon Genius to entertain us at this Time of Day with Ideas and Manners totally obliterated. It shews that the Painter's Pencil must have been faithful to Nature, otherwise we should hardly please ourselves, at present, with Portraits whose Originals are no more; for, excepting the Picture of Jealousy in the Drawing of Kitely, there is not one Personage in the whole Groupe known to our modern Critics. Besides, the Business lies so much in what we call middle Life, or perhaps low Life, and in Parts of the Town disgustful to People of Fashion, . . . that nothing but the strong Colouring of old Ben could support the Piece.

The reviewer discussed the original Italianate version of the comedy and explained that Jonson's use of the word "humour" did not correspond to the modern acceptation, which expected "Men deeply tinged with Habits and Oddities discolouring their whole Conduct." Of this kind of humor, he thought Kitely alone representative. Bobadill's oddities were not strong enough for him to be considered a humorist, although he had some ridiculous affectations.

We should therefore be inclined to think that Ben Johnson took Advantage of a Phrase in Vogue, and intended merely an Exhibition of Manners or Humours in the loose Sense of the Word . . . and not a Picture of People under the Operation of one strong Foible, not vainly assumed out of Levity, or imitative Folly, but rooted in the Mind, and engrossing all their Thoughts. Kitely indeed is a Character of this latter Class, and his Spirits and Powers all run one Way, which may be said to be a Humour.

The second part of the review is an excellent example of detailed analytic and interpretative criticism, rarely found as early as the fifties. The reviewer commended the organization of the plot, the unity in variety of the characters, a sprightly tumult which fell by degrees into order, all forwarding the main action and all brought together by probable and natural means. "Perhaps no Writer had greater Art in the Conduct of his Plots than Johnson," who prepares us in advance for the reception of each character,— old Knowell, Bobadill, Downright, and Wellbred. "We are thus let into a Knowledge of all the *Dramatis Personæ*, except Kitely, whose Jealousy being of a secret Nature, that Matter could only come from himself. And how finely is this developed!"

Thus very artificially all Parties are brought together; the Denouement is skilfully made out; Kitely is convinced of his Error, and the jolly Temper of the old Justice prevails on them to conclude the Evening in Chearfulness and Good humour. . . . We could with Pleasure review separately the Characters of Kitely and Bobadil, the two conspicuous Figures in this Piece; but this perhaps is unnecessary, as they are both so well performed by Mr. Garrick and Mr. Woodward. The latter, in our Opinion, never conceived a Character better than that of Bobadil, who is the best Braggadocio on the Stage; his Assurance has a Mixture of Modesty, and is heightened by it; While he pretends to be a consummate Master of every Branch of military Knowledge as well as Courage, he protests he has only some small Rudiments of the Science, 'as to know his Distance or so.' — When he is sure his Friends will prevent Mischief, he begs them to let his Enemy come on with 'I won't kill him,' and when at last he takes a Beating, 'he is planet-struck, fascinated, &c.' — All this Mr. Woodward performs with such a Reserve and Gravity, and such a judicious Jeu de Theatre, that he is justly a Favourite with the Audience all through the Piece. . . . [In] Mr. Garrick's Performance . . . every Thing has Manners, every Thing has real Life, and whatever his Author may have done, he does not any where exceed the natural Workings of Jealousy. But this Disquisition must be adjourned till he performs this Part again, when we shall trace Mr. Woodward and Mr. Garrick through all their various Shapes in this justly admired Comedy.

The sequel never followed, unfortunately, for *The London Chronicle* ceased reviewing plays. But the criticisms have already indicated the fortunes of the play at Drury Lane and of the actors who played it for the pleasure of the town sixty-one times, including fourteen times "by Desire," and four command performances in ten seasons. Its history at Covent Garden was almost equally brilliant.

V

COVENT GARDEN, 1762–1774

On October 25, 1762, the company at Covent Garden under the management of John Beard presented a revival of *Every Man in his Humour*, "Never Acted there before," "The characters new dress'd in the Habits of the Times," with a nucleus of four players from Garrick's cast of 1751, — Shuter, Woodward, Costollo, and Mrs. Ward,— all playing their original rôles. Woodward's Bobadill was already an acknowledged classic, and the history of the comedy for the next twelve years of continuous playing was virtually the history of his remarkable portrayal of the braggart captain. Mrs. Ward and Costollo had not played in this comedy for a decade, nor Shuter since 1753. The play reached sixteen performances the first season, with a royal command night, four nights "by particular desire," and three benefits. The rest of the cast was: old Knowell, Sparks; young Knowell, Dyer; Brainworm, Dunstall; Downright, Walker; Wellbred, Mattocks; Kitely, Smith; Cash, Perry; Matthew, Hayes; Cob, Buck; Clement, Marten; Bridget, Miss Miller; and Cob's wife, Mrs. Pitt.[1]

Luke Sparks had acted Corvino (1748) and Volpone (1753); Marten, Otter (1745); and Mrs. Pitt, Dame Pliant (1748). Covent Garden theatre at this time had no actor so preëminent as Garrick; it was the particular resort of musical entertainment such as *The Maid of the Mill* and *Love in a Village*, but the managers endeavored to produce their plays adequately. The theatres were becoming sensitive to such matters of technical perfection as costuming,

---

1. *The Public Advertiser*, October 25, 1762.

although Garrick had been conscious of the problem for ten years. Critics were beginning to see the absurdity of clothing Macbeth in a tie-wig and eighteenth-century court costume and Lady Macbeth in a voluminous confection of pleats, tucks, pipings, and ruffles designed more fittingly for the Assembly Rooms at Bath or the Pantiles of Tunbridge Wells than the blasted heaths of Forres. The reform was going on at both houses. The new dresses were praised in *The Public Advertiser*, which hoped that in the future all of the old English plays would be as appropriately costumed.[1] The same issue of the paper praised the revival:

We went for the sake of Mr. Woodward's Bobadil, and we were not disappointed of the Pleasure, which we used to receive from him in that Character. Yet we returned with equal Admiration of the Performance of Mr. Shuter, who was very, very Master Stephen. We scarce remember to have seen a more chaste and accurate Piece of Acting.

There was a dissenting voice, however, when the reviewer for *The London Chronicle* noted his opinion of the production on October 22, 1766:

Great praise is due to Mr. Garrick for reviving this play some years since. . . . The parts were most judiciously cast, and as well supported in the performance. I am sorry to observe, that though several of the principal parts are now performed by those very actors who then play'd in it, yet the whole does not produce that agreeable effect which it did at the time of its revival: not that I mean to undervalue the performance of it at this theatre, as many of the characters are well supported; tho' I cannot help observing, that Mr. Woodward seems to have departed from his originality in Bobadil.[2]

A striking aspect of the Covent Garden revival is the stability of the casts as compared with those at Drury Lane, where Garrick was the only one to act his part for twenty-five years. Of course, the play was presented for

1. November 5, 1762.   2. October 23–25, 1766.

only twelve years at Covent Garden, but the changes were fewer than for the same number of years at Drury Lane. For instance, five actors did not miss a night,— Woodward, Shuter, Smith, Dunstall, and Mrs. Pitt; only two actors shared Downright, Cash, and Bridget; three, old Knowell, young Knowell, Matthew, and Formal; four, Wellbred; five, Cob and Dame Kitely; and six, Clement. The rôles for women were much more stable, it is clear, but no criticism was wasted on them. Memoirs, reviews, and satires, as formerly, saw but three memorable performances,— those of Woodward, Shuter, and William Smith. Woodward received prodigious attention.

On March 15, 1763, he played Bobadill for his own benefit "with a New occasional Prologue by Mr. Woodward," the literary merits of which may be determined by reading:

'*Tis strange* (excuse my gravity) '*tis passing strange*
How much this giddy world is given to change!
The days, the seasons change, and men and women,
All change their minds — and all that can their linen.
Let the grave moralist, with curious eye
Observe the busy throng that vend and buy —
Change, Sir, I must have *change* — is all the cry.
The World, a meer *Change-alley* we may call;
Stars, stocks, and tides, and actors, rise and fall —
Thus I, who late with worse than tragic face,
With shrug repentant, and with sad grimace,
Most humbly sued you'd take the wand'rer in,
Am tempted now to more than comic grin;
Am forc'd to give these deep reflections birth,
And shew my wisdom to disguise my mirth. —
Truth is, the strange delight your smiles impart, ⎫
Has often rais'd too high my conscious heart;   ⎬
Inspir'd my airs, and sometimes — spoil'd my part.⎭
  Hence has a *Giant-Bard* — you all know who,
In lines most sage, and as 'tis said, most true,
Remark'd on *Woodward's tricks, his starts, and whims.*
His twisted features, and his tortur'd limbs,
His wink impertinent, his saucy stare,
His grin ridiculous, his careless air,

His more than Idiot *vacancy of face*,
His monkey arts, and mountebank grimace,
That furrow'd cheeks with *untaught laughter fill*,
And make sad Critics *smile against their will*.
Alas, poor wisdom! doom'd to vile disgrace,
While antic laughter sits upon her face!
While grins detested, and usurping mirth,
That make her *hate herself*, and curse her birth —
I'm sorry — but these pangs she must endure,
Unless *you* force me to apply the cure;
If *you* indeed should threat to *lay the switch on*,
I straight shall own myself a *grave physician*;
To cure all lamentable mirth profess,
All grief phantastical, and droll distress. —
   This when we need — to-night I cannot fear
Th' extorted simper, or the ready sneer,
When all around such partial smiles I see,
And each kind aspect seems to beam on me. —
Oh! should your favour haply be misplac'd, ⎫
Let it, like my imputed errors, last; ⎬
And *inclination kindly take for taste*; ⎭
So shall I still indulge a grateful heart,
And feel unchecked the pleasure you impart.
   Yet under *Bobadil's* grave masque tonight,
I'll hide the antic bauble from your sight,
In calm composure smoak my *Trinidado*,
And taste, for all my faults, the *bastinado*.[1]

Not to mention grammar, the poetry is execrable. Woodward could not reach the heights of polysyllabic rhyme attained by the poets of *The Anti-Jacobin*, Reverend Richard Barham, Lord Byron, and W. S. Gilbert. But the prologue as valuable self-criticism scarcely deserved the long and dreadfully literal example of carping, verbal, and negative criticism which appeared in *The Theatrical Review* on April 1. Woodward must indeed have realized

1. The prologue was given great publicity: it was printed in *The Public Advertiser*, March 16, 1763; *The London Chronicle*, March 15–17, 1763; *The London Magazine*, XXXII (1763), 160; *The Universal Magazine*, XXXII (1763), 158; *The Royal Magazine*, VIII (1763), 157–158; *The Theatrical Review*, April 1, 1763, pp. 138–139; *The Spouter's Companion; or, Theatrical Remembrancer* [177?], pp. 23–24. The Giant-Bard was Charles Churchill.

the significance of the date when he read a labored and scornful *jeu d'esprit* which tore his "celebrated poetical take-in" to pieces metaphor by metaphor and reduced it to complete absurdity, as a single paragraph will show:

In the next two lines we have some most extraordinary pieces of intelligence — "The days, the seasons change" — wonderful! nay what is stranger, "men and women change." — Change what? — Why, their minds" — good lack! — good lack! — Bless us Sir Sampson! But what is still more strange than all, we are told, that all, who *can*, change their linen" — What a most delicate Idea has Harry here raised, of some men and women *not* changing their linen! [1]

On February 12, 1767, Hugh Kelly's *Thespis; or, A Critical Examination into the Merits of all the Principal Performers belonging to Covent-Garden Theatre* was published. It judged Woodward a stage veteran who had been long acclaimed by the crowd. But Kelly wondered if any sensible judge could defend his bad taste and vacuity of mind:

Endu'd with talents singular as these,
Who can expect but what his fools must please;

.   .   .   .

When paltry trick and ignorant grimace
Assume the mask of judgment and of grace;

.   .   .   .

When praise from martyr'd nature must be wrought,
And fame built only on the base of fault?
Hence with delight his BOBADILL we meet,
Hence find PETRUCHIO a delicious treat,
And join in MARPLOT's mirth-exciting cause
With all the warmth of passionate applause. [2]

His other rôles, according to Kelly, merely disgusted the competent beholder.

When Woodward played four nights at York in April, 1771, Tate Wilkinson wrote of the lukewarm audience

1. Page 140.
2. Book II, pp. 21-22.

there as compared with the usual enthusiastic London audiences to which Woodward was accustomed. The actor was so chagrined that Wilkinson was obliged to go among his friends, begging them to give more generous applause. They took the hint, and when Woodward acted Bobadill the next night, he was "so surprised and elated, that he sat up till past two, after all his fatigue (aged 57) in the highest spirits." [1] *The Public Ledger* for June 24, 1771, honored Woodward by printing a eulogistic article, and the next year more praise followed in a poetical review of his abilities, *The Theatres. A Poetical Dissection*: [2]

> Come, chearful HAL, whom time, with gentle hand,
> Hath kindly strok'd, conclude the comic band;
> Lively, descriptive, graceful WOODWARD, come,
> With merit that may strike e'en malice dumb;
> CHURCHILL --- the best absurdities advance, —
> When he beheld thee, view'd with eyes askaunce;
> Else, had he judg'd impartially thy cause,
> He must have honour'd thee with warm applause:
> For sure, in Fops, and parts of *outré* kind,
> All thy competitors fall far behind:
> All must acknowledge thy superior glee,
> In the gay cast of laughing Comedy.

The poet did not like Woodward's performance of Ironsides in Cumberland's *The Brothers*:

> And we acknowledge, with reluctant will,
> Thro' all his scenes we trace thy BOBADIL:
>
> .   .   .   .   .   .
>
> Yet, we behold with pleasure, and admire,
> Thy sportful countenance, thy youthful fire.

The London Evening Post paid its tribute to the Covent Garden cast of *Every Man in his Humour*:

> In Woodward's gesture, speech, and face,
> Rare Ben's own Bobadil we trace:
> In Shuter's vacant eye we ken
> The simple gull, hight Master Stephen.

---

1. IV, 24.   2. Pages 74–75.

Smith strongly marks the jealous Kitely,
Whose mind diseas'd, affects the sprightly;
Whilst Bulkley's modest, winning graces,
Discord repels, and peace replaces.[1]

An epigram on Bobadill and Stephen appeared in 1774:

Mr. Love

In JEMMY LOVE, let Drury-Lane
A living FALSTAFF boast;
He's dead at t'other house 'tis plain,
For SHUTER plays his Ghost.

The Answer, J. CUNNINGHAM.

We can't admit of FALSTAFF's Ghost,
Yet still we're more than even;
While you your living FALSTAFF boast,
We've BOBADIL and STEPHEN.[2]

Woodward acted Bobadill for the last time on January 21, 1774. He had but three more years to live, and until his death his critics had for the most part nothing but praise as they recalled the quarter-century during which he had amused them. Perhaps there was nothing novel to be said, but henceforth dramatic critics copied each other shamelessly, and there are curious echoes of earlier writings. The last pathetic words on Woodward's acting jeer unkindly at age, that withers beyond the power of cosmetics or stage-illusion, when life has fallen into the yellow leaf. For that reason, they seem doubly heartless. *The Drama, A Poem* (1775) gave Woodward ample reasons for making his last bow:

That part, an actor in the bloom of life
Plays with success, he takes to him for wife,
Simpers and ogles with a wither'd face,
And trips the beau with antiquated grace.
Tho' WOODWARD once might boast of sprightly ease,
And ev'ry frolic wantonness to please,

---

1. December 7–9, 1773.
2. *Miscellaneous Pieces in Verse; with Cursory Theatrical Remarks*, p. 25.

Why must he gambol after youth is fled,
And winter scatters hoar upon his head?
Still there's a cast his talents to employ,
Razor or Bobadil can never cloy.[1]

He died on April 17, 1777. Thus Woodward and Garrick, the two veterans, left the stage almost simultaneously, and the greatest actors in the play were gone forever. Woodward "was always perfect in his parts, and never deviated from the spirit of his Author." [2] No actor could hope for a more handsome epitaph. As late as 1794 the following poetical appreciation appeared:

On Mr. Woodward.

KNIGHT of the wooden sword, whose tricks and capers
Prov'd a *catholicon* for spleen and vapors,
Peace to thy manes — *thy* blithe *Mercutio*
Our spirits cheer'd, and banished all our woe.
At *Bobadill's* fierce strut, or fiercer stare, ⎫
At *Tuchstone's* quipps, *at Fopplington's* grand air, ⎬
Say who the well-earn'd plaudit could forbear? ⎭
So great thy comic pow'rs that ev'ry part
Display'd "a grace beyond the reach of art." [3]

William Smith, known as "Gentleman" Smith, was about thirty-two years old when he assumed the rôle of Kitely. Excellently educated at Cambridge, he moved in the highest circles of society and was famous for the elegance of his manners. In comedy he was the fine gentleman *par excellence*; he was perfectly cast as Charles Surface. It is said that he made it an indispensable article of agreement with the manager that his face was never to be blackened, and that he was never to be lowered through a stage-door. Churchill described him as "Smith the genteel, the airy, and the smart." As Kitely he did not encourage the mass of prose and poetic allusion which kept Garrick's Kitely and Woodward's Bobadill always before the public; this is a curious fact, for in the rôle he was deemed equal,

1. Pages 11–12.
2. *The History of the Theatres of London, 1771–1795,* I, 53.
3. *The Thespian Magazine,* September, 1794, p. 347.

if not superior, to Garrick himself. But not until 1767,
after five years of continuous playing, did he stimulate
verse criticism:

> SMITH, to preheminence in tragic fame,
> In the most rigid eye has lawful claim,
> Yet in the comic cast, he fails to please,
> By wanting action, sprithliness and ease;
> Let not his action to the eye appear,
> His elocution captivates the ear:
> Whene'er the poet has with spirit writ,
> And laid a train of fascinating wit,
> By attitude he never gives it fire,
> In lifeless eloquence his words expire:
> Frantic and mad with jealousy and rage,
> In desp'rate mood when Kitely quits the stage,
> Why can with SMITH's good sense that *noke* prevail,
> His arm t'envelope in his garments tail.[1]

He played Kitely at Drury Lane from January 2, 1778,
until May 23, 1788, for sixteen performances, after which
the comedy disappeared from the stage until the revival
at Covent Garden on May 15, 1798, with Holman as
Kitely, Munden as Clement, and Fawcett as Bobadill.

Ned Shuter continued to please the town with Master
Stephen, but again, no one in the cast excited applause
and hissing to so great a degree as Woodward. The best
account of Shuter's acting at this time appeared in *The
Rational Rosciad*: [2]

> SHUTER, the muse a perfect master deems,
> Who is in every part the thing he seems;
> His tones so various and so just, surprize,
> His vast command of features charms our eyes;
> His strict propriety in all he plays,
> Critics themselves, into applause, betrays;
> What beauties he exhibits to the sight,
> When master STEPHEN is in fearful plight;
> When aged PHILPOT, impotently lewd,
> With posture quaint and features strangely screw'd,
> In full detection strikes the ravish'd eye,
> And lifts our souls in raptures to the sky.

---

1. *The Rational Rosciad*, pp. 27–28.   2. Page 30.

John Walker, who made his first appearance on the
Covent Garden stage as Downright, kept the part until
September 17, 1767, when he was succeeded by Gardner.
Hugh Kelly approved his performance:

> Where plain hot DOWNRIGHT, with too fierce a rage,
> Arraigns the harmless follies of the age;
> Admits no plea whatever for the times,
> But foams at trifling levities as crimes:
>
> .   .   .   .   .   .
>
> There, finely warm, and accurately clear,
> No harsh remark need WALKER ever fear;
> Nor dread the bard's most scrutinizing plan
> While candour guides him with a ray of man.[1]

The Covent Garden performance began shortly after
five o'clock and was over at 8:57 P.M. The average length
of each act was half an hour.[2] On November 12, 1771,
The Public Ledger reviewed the play:

This excellent Comedy, is one of the *Chef d'Oeuvres* of this
great Writer, who was one of the most considerable dramatic
Poets of the last Age. The Plot is perfectly original, and the
Piece is very highly finished, both in point of Language and
Character; yet there is an unimpassioned coldness in the Language, and a labour'd stiffness in the general Conduct, that
renders the whole uninteresting, notwithstanding the Author
has exerted great Correctness, and displayed considerable
Erudition. And, for this reason, it is highly probable, it will
afford more pleasure to the real Critic in the Closet, than in the
Theatre, where it receives advantages from dramatic Execution,
which proves, that it is easier to write to the judgment, than to
the feelings of the heart. . . . This Play is in a reputable State of
Action here, notwithstanding that some of the under Characters
are very indifferently performed; but those of *Kitely*, *Bobadil*,
and *Master Stephen*, as represented by Messrs. *Smith*, *Woodward*, and *Shuter*, cannot fail giving critical Satisfaction. The
infinite humour displayed by the two last, must unbend the
most rigid brow.

1. *Thespis*, Book II, sig. H1.
2. John Brownsmith, *The Dramatic Timepiece*, p. 59.

This opinion was reënforced by the review of the performance of February 13, 1773, in *The General Evening Post*:[1]

When the heap of theatrical rubbish is thus reviewed, which passes under the title of Every Man in his Humour, it may not be unnecessary to ask how a play can be frequently exhibited with applause, which is so egregious a compound of absurdity? To this we answer, that nobody goes to see the *play*, but the *performers*. Garrick's Kitely is so exquisite a piece of acting, that it would croud fifty theatres: Woodward, at the other house, is to the last degree masterly as Bobadil, and Shuter inimitable as Stephen. Let us not, therefore, compliment the *poet* at the expence of the *player*, nor suppose, when we run to the representation of Ben Johnson's pieces, that it is the *composition* with which we are captivated; his works are as heavy on the stage, as they are tiresome in the closet, and will fall into oblivion the instant they cease to be capitally executed.

Concerning the box-office receipts for the comedy at Covent Garden from October 22, 1766, to January 21, 1774, it does not seem possible to draw any valuable conclusions. Too many variables determine the income of a theatre. The receipts rose as high as £255 16s. 6d. and sank as low one evening as £26 18s. 6d., an unusual fact, for they never fell before or later to less than £101 7s. The average for eight years was £162 a night, a very respectable sum even when compared to the average of £258 a night at Drury Lane for the two years from 1774 to 1776, when *Every Man in his Humour* might be seen only at that theatre.

VI

Drury Lane, 1767–1776

From October 9, 1767, to the final appearance of Garrick as Kitely on April 25, 1776, *Every Man in His Humour* was played nineteen times, or about twice a year, whereas

1. February 13–16, 1773.

during the same period it was played about four times a
year at Covent Garden. It may not seem curious, therefore, that Woodward's Bobadill during these years at-
tracted more critics than Garrick's Kitely. But the play
as given at Drury Lane was still famous. The cast on the
opening night had five new actors, — Aickin as young
Knowell, who was to play the part for the entire period;
Baddeley as Brainworm, who was to miss only one performance, when Moody substituted; Mrs. Baddeley as
Dame Kitely, who after playing for three years was to be
superseded by Miss Younge and Mrs. Greville; Miss
Simson as Bridget, for one night only, to be followed by
six other actresses in the rôle; and Wingfield as Matthew,
which he played for two years. The bills stated that
Thomas King was playing Bobadill for the first time, but
this information was erroneous, since he had appeared in
that part on April 1, 1761, for his own benefit. From 1767,
however, he acted Bobadill until Garrick's retirement. He
had received training in the part of Wellbred in 1763,
which he played but once, and as Kastril in 1762; he was
to play La Foole in Colman's revival of *Epicoene* in 1776.
King's powers, confined to comedy, were displayed in
such parts as Tom in *The Conscious Lovers*, Brass in *The
Confederacy*, William in *The Way to Keep Him*, and
Lord Ogleby in *The Clandestine Marriage*. *The Town
and Country Magazine* observed that he had "stept out
of his usual walk, and given us great satisfaction in the
truly comic part of Captain Bobadil; and probably if
we had never seen Woodward in the same character,
we should have imagined it could not have been better
performed." [1]

Robert Baddeley's Brainworm,— a part which he acted
until May 23, 1788, when the play was dropped at Drury
Lane, twenty-five years after his première,— inspired a
squib:

1. II (1770), 593.

With crab-apple phiz, and a brow that's disdainful,
See BADDELY smile with fatigue that is painful;
From his dissonant voice, and the form of each feature,
You'd swear him the favorite child of Ill-nature;

. . . .

He snarls through his parts, be they easy or hard,
Like a mastiff that's chain'd to bay thieves from a yard.
Tho' none the misanthrope can copy so well,
As an actor, he's slovenly — Candor must tell;

. . . .

His enacting coarse BRAINWORM's a noble exertion,
And POLONIUS and TRINCULO feed our diversion.[1]

James William Dodd, "the theatrical cockatoo, spirited
and pleasing in the coxcomb-stile," [2] shared the rôle of
Stephen with William Palmer and Thomas Weston, and
continued in it until May 23, 1788. In the character of
genteel fops Dodd was without rival, and his powers as a
stage beau were praised in *Theatrical Portraits* (*ca.* 1785):

None on the stage so well as he can shew
The various traces of that thing, *the beau*,

. . . . . .

Superior rank should be to Dodd assign'd,
Were he to foppish parts alone confin'd,
And yet his pow'rs, not limited to these,
In simple characters can often please;
No better Master Stephen have we found,
Since poor old Shuter spread the laugh around.[3]

The part of Cob was played from January 5, 1763, to
April 25, 1776, by John Moody, famous for the excellence
of his Irish characters, such as Captain O'Cutter in *The
Jealous Wife*. His Sir Lucius O'Trigger was said to be
without humor, and we have no criticism of his Cob, but
it was no doubt satisfactory.

The performance of January 27, 1769, was reviewed in
The Theatrical Register, which considered the comedy equal

---

1. "Anthony Pasquin, Esq." (John Williams), *The Children of Thespis*, pp.
73-74.
2. *The Dramatic Censor*, II, 492.   3. Pages 31-32.

to any of Jonson's other works. The characters and the language were lauded for imagination and correctness, but most of the credit for its success was due to Garrick's "own inimitable performance in the part of *Kitely*," [1] praise echoed fulsomely by Mrs. Elizabeth Montagu in a letter to Garrick. She feared for poor Shakspere: "if Mr. Garrick often acts Kitely, Ben Jonson will eclipse his fame. . . . Kitely will never sink into oblivion. Fie upon Mr. Garrick! he alone can raise a rival to Shakspeare." [2] Louis, Prince of Hessen-Darmstadt, also wrote a remarkable letter of adulation to the great portrayer of Kitely:

I have read *Every Man in his Humour*, *Rule a Wife and have a Wife*, and the *Suspicious Husband*, these Plays are so handsome and spiritfull, that uppon the Theater the Plays cannt are agreable from itself, when but the ilustrious Garrik Plays itself and we poor Strangers when he hear him alors, nous serons dans la plus grande satisfaction d'avoir vu la plus belle chose de l'Angleterre. [3]

On November 12, 1771, *The Public Ledger* published a review of the performance of November 8, as a companion-piece to the review of the production at Covent Garden on November 7. The critic boasted independence of managerial influence, a condition none too common:

Mr. *Garrick's* original excellence in the Part of *Kitely* is universally known, and generally admired. Abstracted from this particular, we think the Performance here is, on the whole, more respectable than at the other House, the under Parts being well supported. We have acknowledged the great Merit of Messrs. *Woodward* and *Shuter*, in the Parts of *Bobadil* and *Master Stephen*, notwithstanding which, we think, these Characters are represented with an equal degree of Merit by Messrs. *King* and *Weston*, though the latter appeared this Evening for the first Time in the Character of *Master Stephen*; and in one respect, they are highly praise-worthy, viz. that of playing from their

1. Part ii, p. 12.
2. *The Private Correspondence of David Garrick*, I, 385–386.
3. II, 636.

own Ideas and Feelings, without discovering one single trace of endeavoring to imitate the above-mentioned Performers, who may be considered as the Originals, having played the Characters ever since the revival of the Play.[1]

In October, 1773, Garrick was still playing Kitely "in the full vigor of his limbs and judgment," [2] and on October 6 he had acted the part "By Command of their Majesties," but he played it only six more times. On December 18, 1775, the first time he had acted Kitely that season, he was a good deal disconcerted during the performance, when in his scene with Thomas Cash (William Brereton) "just as he is going to trust Thomas with the secret, the House was very silent, and Mr. Garrick was speaking, a Fellow in the Gallery bawls out — 'Speak out.' " [3] His last appearance, and the last time the play was performed at either house for two years, was on April 25, 1776. He had already bidden farewell as Lusignan and Abel Drugger, and May and June were given to that series of brilliant final performances to which the society of all England rushed. The occasional poets in particular found these adieux painful and exhausted their superlatives. It was incredible that the little man should never be seen on the stage any more. *The London Chronicle* printed some "VERSES *occasion'd by Mr.* GARRICK'S *quitting the* STAGE," bursting with allusions to Niobe, the Loves and Graces, Melpomene, the Cherub Charity, sweet Benevolence, modest Worth, Drama's Genius, and Fate. "The dreaded hour is come! the curtain falls!" And there are hearts filled with pain, and deep woe, and smiles quench'd in tears, and sad lamenting voices, and an incomparable *ubi sunt*:

> Oh, where is Richard? Where is now old Lear?
> Where is young Hamlet? — We have lost Macbeth:

---

1. The criticism was reprinted in *The London Chronicle*, November 12-14, 1771, and *The Theatrical Review*, 1772, I, 171.

2. *The Westminster Magazine*, I (1773), 580.

3. *Hopkins's Diary*, transcribed by J. P. Kemble on the playbill for December 18 in the Huntington Library.

They all have suffered now a *real* death.
Where the gay Ranger? Where is Kitely gone?
Where's Abel, Felix, Benedict, Don John?
With flowers strew their graves, for they are dead;
Th' informing soul of all, alas! is fled.

Eheu! Eheu! And the stricken poet, "the meanest of the Muses train," hopes that his god may live

Long, very long, in thy retirement blest,
With the dear lovely partner of thy breast.[1]

But Garrick had only a little more than two and a half years to live. When he died, on January 20, 1779, *The London Chronicle* furnished yet another elegy, in which the author invoked the kindly aid of Milton, Shakspere, Otway, Rowe, Dryden, Beaumont and Fletcher, and "learned Ben" in building a monument of fame.

What *Hamlet* was, in Garrick's shape we saw,
And *Kitely's* acting gave the *Jealous* law.
With modern *Chalkstone* could we fail to laugh,
Nor with old *Drugger* with one pipe to quaff?

.　　.　　.　　.　　.　　.　　.

GARRICK shall live while mem'ry fills the brain
With ought she feels of *pleasure* or of *pain*.
In fine — so vast, so various were his powers,
HIS the immortal gain — the ceaseless loss is OURS![2]

Horace Walpole considered his death "not a public loss, for he had quitted the stage," [3] and to him the pomp of the funeral was "perfectly ridiculous," although he did not intend to detract from Garrick's merit as an actor. In his way Garrick was never equaled in both tragedy and comedy, but Walpole did not consider the ability to act the writings of some one else an astonishing talent. "I suppose that in Garrick I thought I saw more of his art;

1. June 11-13, 1776. Reprinted in *The Gentleman's Magazine*, XLVI (1776), 328.
2. January 23-26, 1779; *The Town and Country Magazine*, XI (1779), 47-48.
3. Mrs. Paget Toynbee, *The Letters of Horace Walpole*, X (1904), 367.

yet his Lear, Richard, Hotspur, . . . Kitely, and Ranger, were as capital and perfect as action could be. In declamation, I confess, he never charmed me; nor could he be a gentleman." [1]

Even the clergy rose to do Garrick honor, and the Reverend W. Tasker saw his "ELEGY *on the Death of Mr. GARRICK*" printed on March 9 in *The London Chronicle*. How inept that it should be in the burlesque tail-rhyme stanza of *Sir Thopas!*

> Where is aspiring Richard fled?
> In Roscius' grave, Macbeth lies dead;
>   And Hamlet is no more!
>
> Ye sons of mirth and gallantry,
> No more your sprightly Ranger see!
>   Or Benedict admire;
> Lost with the archness of his eye,
> Drugger and Leon breathless lie,
>   And Kitely shall expire.

And in an anonymous "Monody on the Death of Mr. Garrick," the poet praised the actor for bringing to view "In Shakespeare, beauties that scarce Shakespeare knew":

> In Kitely's sufferings gave us more than mirth,
> Or rais'd to fame poor Drugger's humble birth;
> Taught every Muse a shorter, surer art,
> To strike, or shine, to melt, or please the heart.[2]

For ten years yet *Every Man in his Humour* might have been seen once, sometimes twice a year at Drury Lane. In 1798 it was revived for a few seasons, and Edmund Kean played Kitely in 1816, with a far better reviewer in the audience than Garrick had found,— William Hazlitt, who thought that the play "acts much better than it reads." To him Bobadill as played by Harley was the only striking character; the rest was droll, and Kitely's pathos "as dry as the remainder biscuit after a voyage."

1. X, 370.
2. *The New Foundling Hospital for Wit*, II, 200.

Munden's Brainworm and Oxberry's Stephen were praise-
worthy, but the play was like a revival of the dead.[1] In
1825, in a jest-book, we are given the character of a humorous man as one who is "for a new reading of Ben Jonson's
old play of '*Every Man in his Humour.*' "[2] The play had
retreated to the library again and was acknowledged at last
to be a genuine antique. There it was to remain undisturbed except for the few performances by Charles Dickens
with his company of brilliant amateurs in 1845, the production at the Gaiety theatre, Manchester, in November,
1909, and non-professional performances by college dramatic clubs. But it is doubtful if any Elizabethan comedy
had a more remarkable stage-record for twenty-five years,
a century and a half after composition, than *Every Man
in his Humour* under the genius of David Garrick.

1. *Criticisms and Dramatic Essays of the English Stage*, 2d ed., 1854, pp. 232–
234. See [B. W. Procter], *The Life of Edmund Kean*, II, 161.
    2. "John Bull, Esq.," *The Laughing Philosopher*, p. 540.

CHAPTER VII

Every Man out of his Humour

A S A stage-play *Every Man Out of his Humour* may be said to have perished with the age which produced it. To the modern reader it is an extraordinarily difficult, not to say dull, play. It abounds in classical learning, and the theory of humors creeps along on all fours: Jonson was so far influenced by his theory, which he took pains to define in the Induction, that he prefixed descriptive characters of the *dramatis personae* in the fashion of character-writers like Earle, Hall, and Overbury. A long literary colloquy precedes the action, which is slow throughout. The cast of characters is extremely long for a comedy which displays little of the brilliant concrete realism of *Bartholomew Fair,* and one may doubt if a later age could interest itself in the obsolete affectations of Sogliardo, Puntarvolo, and Fastidious Brisk. It would be cause for wonder if *Every Man out of his Humour* had succeeded on the Restoration stage. There was one revival, it is true, in July, 1675, but probably only a short one. Of more modern revivals there is no evidence.

The play was not one of the principal old stock plays of Killigrew's company after they became established in Bridges Street in May, 1663, but as Downes says, it was among those pieces which were "Acted but now and then; yet being well Perform'd, were very Satisfactory to the Town."[1] About January 12, 1669, it was "allowed of to his Ma^tes Servants at ye New Theatre,"[2] but it was probably not acted until 1675. Dryden made passing reference to the characters Fungoso and Fastidious Brisk

1. *Roscius Anglicanus,* pp. 8–9.
2. Allardyce Nicoll, *Restoration Drama,* p. 315.

in 1673,[1] and in 1691 Langbaine wrote: "This Play was reviv'd at the Theatre-Royal, in the Year 1675, at which time a new Prologue, and Epilogue were spoken by *Jo. Heyns*, which were writ by Mr. *Duffet*. . . . This is accounted an excellent Old Comedy." [2]

Of this isolated revival there is nothing left except the two scraps of doleful verse by Thomas Duffett.[3] It is difficult to understand how even the renowned humor of Jo Haines could have amused an audience with such utter trash.

Prologue to Ev'ry Man out of his Humor, *Spoken by Mr*. Hayns,
July, 1675

So fast from Plays approv'd and Actors known,
To drolling, stroling Royal Troop you run,
That *Hayns* despairing is Religious grown.
So Crack enjoy'd, the queazy Gallants slight,
And she, though still her beauty's in its height,
In rage turns Nun and goes to Heav'n in spight.
O Novelty, who can thy pow'r oppose!
Polony Bear or strange Grimace out-goes
Our finest language and our greatest shows.
   As thick-scul'd Zealots, who from Churches fly,
Think doleful nonsense good that makes them cry;
Y'are pleas'd and laugh because — you know not why.
There ign'rant crouds round travel'd Gallants sit,
As am'rous youths round Vizards in our Pit,
And by their motions judg the Farces Wit.
   If thy but grin, a jest is understood,
All laugh outright and cry — I'gad that's good;
When will our damn'd dull silly rogues do so?
Y'are very complaisant, I fain would know
Where lies the wit and pow'r of (*il ohe*).
   The modish Nymphs now ev'ry heart will win,
With the surprising ways of *Harlequin*.
O the fine motion and the jaunty mene,
While you Gallants —

---

1. Sir Walter Scott and George Saintsbury, *The Works of John Dryden*, IV. 376.   2. *An Account of the English Dramatick Poets*, pp. 290–291.

3. *New Poems, Songs, Prologues and Epilogues*, 1676, pp. 72–76; *New Songs, and Poems, A-la-mode both at Court, and Theatres, Now Extant. Never before Printed. By P. W. Gent.*, 1677, pp. 72–76.

Who for dear Missie ne'r can do to much,
Make Courtships *alamode de Scarramouch.*
Ha —— ha ——
I could have taught you this, but let that pass,
Y'have heard I've wit, now you shall know I've grace,
I will reform —
But what Religion's best in this, lewd Town,
My friends I'm yet like most of you, of none.
If I commence, I fear it will not do,
Religion has its *Scarramouchys* too,
Whose hum's and ha's get all the praise and pence,
For noise has still the upper hand of sense.
Well since 'tis so —
I'll keep my Station till your humors come,
Though like the longing woman, now you rome,
And leave all dainties for the Butchers thumb.
    You and vile husbands equally proceed
Like rambling Bees, you quit your balm to feed
On ev'ry gaudy flow'r and painted weed.
When Winter comes you will again grow wise,
And visit home the wife that you despise,
With empty purses and with laden thighs.

Epilogue to Ev'ry Man out of his Humor

How crossly and how kindly things do go!
Though Forreign troop does very pow'rful grow,
Kind Justice beats down our domestick foe.
Th' inchanted Castle's once more overthrown,
That nursery where all the youth in Town,
Such deeds of Valour and of Love have shown.
Britains Low Countreys, where at mighty rates,
The younger Brothers urg'd their needy Fates,
And th' Elder got diseases for Estates.
    See how the scatter'd Cracks in parties fly,
How like a nest of Wasps disturb'd they ply,
And fiercely fix on any Fop that's nigh.
I warn you, though your presence theirs will bring,
Be not too eager for the pretty thing.
The bag of Hony's sweet, but 'ware the sting.
Play round the light, but from the heat retire;
For if y'are joyn'd between hot Love and Ire
Like *Samsons* Foxes you'l set all on fire.
Reform your selves, Reformers of the Stage,
Blame not my Zeal, who can suppress their rage?

When Love and Wrath spare neither Sex nor Age.
For our Play we say nothing. —
The merit of it will your plaudits gain,
Or else new Wit would strive to prop in vain,
What *Johnsons* sacred mem'ry can't sustain.

There is a later Restoration allusion to the play,[1] but no criticism appeared until Hurd wrote his *Dissertation on the Provinces of the Drama* (1753). His view represented, no doubt, normal critical opinion of the comedy in the middle of the eighteenth century:

If the reader would see the extravagance of building dramatic manners on abstract ideas, in its full light, he needs only turn to B. Jonson's *Every man out of his humour*; which under the name of a *play of character* is in fact, an unnatural, and, as the painters call it, *hard* delineation of a group of *simply existing passions*, wholly chimerical, and unlike to any thing we observe in the commerce of real life. Yet this comedy has always had its admirers.[2]

In June, 1759, *The Universal Magazine* reprinted Hurd's criticism and expanded it:

To this censure it hath been observed, on the part of Jonson, 'That the characters are indeed very strongly marked, yet some of them have been thought to glance at particular persons of the author's acquaintance . . . so that, far from being thought, at that time, to build his characters upon abstract ideas he was really accused of representing particular persons then existing; and that even those characters which appear to be most exaggerated are said to have had their archetypes in nature and life.' But this solution does not go to the bottom; nay indeed, rather eludes than dissolves the force of the objection; which does not mean to assert the exaggeration of the leading or predominant quality above nature or the life, in any of the characters; but that every other quality, as it really exists in nature, is dropped, of which nature affords no specimen.[3]

1. *Familiar Letters: Written by the Right Honourable John, late Earl of Rochester*, 1697, p. 229.
2. *The Works of Richard Hurd, D.D.*, II, 53. This passage was reprinted in *The Town and Country Magazine*, VII (1775), 292.   3. XXIV, 338.

The Companion to the Play-House commented on the obsolete dramatic device of the *Grex* as employed in *Every Man out of his Humour*, praised the characters as "perfect Originals, all painted in the strongest Colours and apparent Likenesses of several well known Existents in real Life," and thought that "with very little Alteration more than an Omission of the Grex, this Play might be render'd extremely fit for the present Stage." [1]

The last criticism of the comedy in the eighteenth century was written by Thomas Davies, who also thought that the play might be successfully revived:

This piece has, in my opinion, a great share of comic pleasantry, and, with some judicious alterations, would now afford rational amusement. Some of the characters, it is true, are obsolete through age; others, such as the Envious Man and the Parasite, are of all times and all nations. Macilente and Carlo Buffone will last till doomsday: they are admirably well drawn. The objection of Dr. Hurd . . . is ill-founded. Some of these parts are to be seen now in some shape or other; fashionable shadows of foppery and custom vary with times and circumstances. Who does not see every day a Sogliardo and Fungoso, differently modified, in our metropolis at this instant? In a rude unpolished age, when the people were just emancipated from barbarism by the renovation of literature and the light of reformation, a groupe of new and absurd characters must naturally spring up which would furnish ample materials of ridicule to the comic writers; and who can deny that Jonson has, in this play, laid hold of many growing follies of the times in which he lived? [2]

This defense of the comedy was noble, but modern criticism would choose the judgment of Dr. Hurd. With all the alteration in the world, *Every Man out of his Humour* would still be a dismal failure on the modern stage. Its entire past is against it.

1. Article on *Every Man out of his Humour*.
2. *Dramatic Miscellanies*, II, 74–75.

CHAPTER VIII

Catiline

THE tragedies of Jonson have suffered from criticism much more than his comedies. They have been censured for their learning, their rhetoric, their classical allusions and borrowings, and their coldness. Essayists have customarily dismissed *Sejanus*, with its foot-noted references to Latin literature, as the prototype of the modern doctoral dissertation, a judgment no doubt as damning as one could conceive. So far as the relative merits of *Catiline* and *Sejanus* are concerned, the choice has apparently been between two unnecessary evils. Swinburne and Ward preferred *Catiline*; the most recent editors of Jonson are inclined to favor *Sejanus*. Closet dramas though they be, the "impartial critick" who goes to the trouble of actually reading them finds them surprisingly good. Despite long speeches which would exhaust the lungs of all but the most stalwart actors, despite local color plastered on the canvas from a palette enriched with the rhetorical "colors" of Sallust, Cicero, and Livy, Jonson displayed a keen knowledge of human passions, of purpose and counter-purpose, and particularly of the psychology of women, which made his materials for tragedy almost original.[1] Whatever may be said against them as acting plays, as closet dramas *Catiline* and *Sejanus* are works artistically far superior to most of the closet dramas of the romantic poets. The terse virility of the language alone is a proof of strength unsupported by wanton emotionalism. To praise any play as poetry is, in the minds of most modern critics, to admit its failure as drama; dramatically, these two tragedies, doomed almost as soon as

1. See John Palmer, *Ben Jonson*, New York, 1934, pp. 124–144.

written, were to play the important but less spectacular rôle of "influences." [1] There is slight documentary evidence that *Sejanus* was played after the Restoration.[2] *Catiline*, on the other hand, seems to have received a cordial reception at least until 1691.

Downes in his list of plays acted at the Theatre Royal after April 8, 1663, included *Catiline* as one of those which were "Acted but now and then; yet being well Perform'd, were very Satisfactory to the Town." [3] But it was certainly not revived until December, 1668. Exactly five years before the revival, Pepys read *Catiline* and found it "a very excellent piece." [4] The actors planned the production long before the actual opening, for on December 7, 1667, Pepys learned that

Catelin is likely to be soon acted, which I am glad to hear, but it is at the King's House. But the King's House is at present and hath for some days been silenced upon some difference [between] Hart and Moone.[5]

Four days later, Harris, the actor, told Pepys that the play was to be performed at once at the King's House, in spite of the fact that everyone agreed that there were not enough good actors to fill the long list of characters:

And Burt acts Cicero, which they all conclude he will not be able to do well. The King gives them £500 for robes, there being, as they say, to be sixteen scarlett robes.[6]

1. See W. D. Briggs, "The Influence of Jonson's Tragedy in the Seventeenth Century," *Anglia*, XXXV (1911-1912), 277-337.

2. *Roscius Anglicanus*, p. 8. *Sejanus* had some influence on the continent during the Restoration: see A. W. Ward, *English Dramatic Literature*, 1899, II, 339; Johannes Bolte, "Ben Jonsons Sejanus am Heidelberger Hofe," *Shakespeare-Jahrbuch*, XXIV (1889), 72-88. The name "Sejanus," like "Volpone," was used frequently in political satire for a favorite for over a century after 1660. In 1751 Francis Gentleman published an alteration of *Sejanus*, acted at Bath, which formed the basis for a second alteration, *The Favourite*, 1769. For criticism of Jonson's *Sejanus* see *The True Briton*, January 10, 1724; *Old Common-Sense; or, The Englishman's Journal*, January 27, 1739; *The Universal Magazine*, XXIV (1759), 342.   3. Pages 8-9.

4. H. B. Wheatley, *The Diary of Samuel Pepys*, IV, 289.

5. VII, 216.   6. VII, 221.

But on January 11 Pepys learned from his friend Mrs. Knepp that

"Catelin," which she thinks, for want of the clothes which the King promised them, will not be acted for a good while.[1]

While the play was on the verge of production, Dryden undertook criticism of it in *An Essay of Dramatic Poesy.* Lisideius, representing the French point of view, objected to the mingling of comedy and tragedy:

Even Ben Jonson himself, in "Sejanus" and "Catiline," has given us this olio of a play, this unnatural mixture of comedy and tragedy, which to me sounds just as ridiculously as the history of David with the merry humours of Golias. In "Sejanus" you may take notice of the scene betwixt Livia and the physician, which is a pleasant satire upon the artificial helps of beauty: in "Catiline" you may see the parliament of women; the little envies of them to one another; and all that passes betwixt Curio and Fulvia: scenes admirable in their kind, but of an ill mingle with the rest.[2]

The revival came on December 18, 1668, and the performance was before royalty, the actors receiving £10 from the king.[3] The tragedy was repeated the next night:

At noon . . . my wife and I by hackney to the King's playhouse, and there, the pit being full, sat in a box above, and saw "Catiline's Conspiracy," yesterday being the first day: a play of much good sense and words to read, but that do appear the worst upon the stage, I mean, the least diverting, that ever I saw any, though most fine in clothes; and a fine scene of the Senate, and of a fight, that ever I saw in my life. But the play is only to be read, and therefore home, with no pleasure at all, but only in sitting next to Betty Hall, that did belong to this house, and was Sir Philip Howard's mistress; a mighty pretty wench.[4]

1. VII, 260.
2. Sir Walter Scott and George Saintsbury, *The Works of John Dryden*, XV, 321. For a modern opinion of Dryden's criticism see C. H. Herford and Percy Simpson, *Ben Jonson*, II (1925), 126–127.
3. Allardyce Nicoll, p. 306.
4. Pepys, VIII, 171–172.

John Evelyn was also present. His record is laconic:

I went to see yᵉ old play of "Cataline" acted, having ben now forgotten almost 40 yeares.[1]

The cast was: Catiline, Hart; Cethegus, Mohun; Cicero, Burt; Sempronia, Mrs. Corey; the rest,— Beeston, Kynaston, Reeves, Wintershall, Cartwright, Gradwell, and Bell,— are unassigned.[2] The tragedy was introduced and concluded by Nell Gwyn, who spoke the occasional prologue and epilogue, her only recorded appearance in Jonson.

Prologue

To be merrily spoke by Mrs. *Nell*.

A Woman's Prologue! This is vent'rous News;
But we a *Poet* wanting, Crav'd a *Muse*.
Why should our Brains lie Fallow, as if they
Without His fire, were meer *Prometehan* [*sic*] Clay?
In Natur's Plain-Song we may bear our Parts.
Although we want choice Descant from the Arts,
Amongst *Musicians*; so the *Philomel*
May in Wild-Notes, though not in Rules excell.
And when i' th weaker Vessel Wit doth lye;
Though into Froth it will work out, and flye.
But, Gentlemen, You know our formal way,
Although we're sure 'tis false, yet we must say,
Nay Pish, Nay Fye, in truth it is not good,
When we the while, think it is not understood:
Hither repair all you that are for *Ben*;
Let th' House hold full, we're sure to carry 't then,
Slight not this Femal Summons; *Phoebus-rayes*,
To crown his *Poets*, turn'd our Sex to *Bayes*.
And Ladies sure you'l vote for us entire,
(This Plot doth prompt the Prologue to conspire)
Such inoffensive Combination can
But show, who best deserves true worth in Man.
And You, with Your great Author taking Part;
May chance be thought, like him to know the Art,

---

1. William Bray and H. B. Wheatley, *Diary of John Evelyn*, II, 233.
2. *Catiline his Conspiracy. A Tragœdie, As it is now Acted by His Majestie's Servants at the Theatre Royal*, 1669. Mrs. Corey's name was not included in "The Persons of the Play." All rôles were unassigned.

Vouchsafe then, as you look, to speak us fair,
Let the Gallants dislike it, if they dare:
They will so forfeit the repute of Judges,
You may turn *Am'zons*, and make them Drudges.
Man's claim to Rule is, in his Reason bred;
This Masculine sex of Brain may make you Head.
'Tis real Skill, in the Right place to praise;
But more, to have the Wit, not to Write Playes.[1]

Epilogue
By the Same.

No *Dance*, No *Song*, No *Farce?* His lofty Pen,
How e're we like it doubtless Wrote to Men.
Height may be his, as it was *Babel's* fall;
These *Bricklayers* turn'd to Linguists, ruin'd all.
I'de ne're spoke this, had I not heard by many,
He lik'd one silent Woman, above any:
And against us had such strange prejudice;
For our Applause, he scorn'd to Write amiss.
For all this, he did us like Wonders, prize;
Not for our Sex, but when he found us Wise.
A *Poet* runs the Gantlet, and his slips,
Are bare expos'd to regiments of Whips:
Among those, he to *Poetick* Champions Writ;
As We to gain the Infancy of Wit.
Which if they prove the greatest number, then
The House hath cause to thank *Nell*, more than *Ben*.
Our *Author* might prefer your praise, perhaps,
Wee'd rather have your Money, than your Claps.

There were several new actors in this tragedy, who so
far as is known never appeared again in Jonson's plays.
It is interesting to observe that Mohun, one of the greatest
tragedians of the King's Company, did not play Catiline,
but "raged" as Cethegus, another conspicuous member
of the conspiracy with fewer lines. The long speeches of
Cicero, who after the first act half effaces Catiline, required
no less than "Stentorian lungs," as Davies observed.[2]
Burt must have been an actor of great endurance to have

1. The 1674 quarto of *Catiline* indicates that the prologue was "Merrily
spoke by Mrs. *Nell*, in an *Amazonian* Habit."
2. *Dramatic Miscellanies*, II, 90.

declaimed sections of verse as long as one hundred seventy continuous lines.

Of the actors of unassigned rôles there is little to note. George Beeston, an unimportant actor, probably did not join the Theatre Royal company until 1666. Reeves and Richard Bell "were Bred up from Boys under the Master Actors." [1] Poor Bell was "blown up" when the Theatre Royal burned on January 25, 1672, the fire beginning "under the stairs where Orange Moll keeps her fruit." [2] Thomas Gradwell joined the Theatre Royal about November 4, 1662. Few of his parts are known.

The robes which the king seems to have furnished were unquestionably in the style of costume *à la Romaine* which came early to the Restoration stage. The actors probably wore the conventional cuirass and helmet, but the toga was not used so early.[3]

Catiline, although an unsuccessful play in the judgment of Pepys, was to prolong its life on the Restoration stage by a *succés de scandale*, the details of which are now beyond discovery. The tragedy was acted on January 2, 1669, the king paying £20,[4] and about January 12 it was "allowed of to his Ma^tes Servants at ye New Theatre." [5] It was presented again, by royal command, on January 13, the actors receiving £10.[6] The scandal centers round these royal performances. On January 15 Pepys wrote:

Up, and by coach to Sir W. Coventry, where with him a good while in his chamber, talking of one thing or another; among others, he told me of the great factions at Court at this day, even to the sober engaging of great persons, and differences, and making the King cheap and ridiculous. It is about my Lady Harvy's being offended at Doll Common's acting of Sempronia, to imitate her; for which she got my Lord Chamberlain, her kinsman,

---

1. *Roscius Anglicanus*, p. 2.
2. *Second Report of the Royal Commission on Historical Manuscripts*, 1874, Appendix, p. 22.
3. G. C. D. Odell, *Shakespeare from Betterton to Irving*, New York, 1920, I, 207–208. 4. Nicoll, p. 306.
5. Page 315. 6. Page 306.

to imprison Doll: when my Lady Castlemayne made the King to release her, and to order her to act it again, worse than ever, the other day, where the King himself was: and since it was acted again, and my Lady Harvy provided people to hiss her and fling oranges at her: but it seems the heat is come to a great height, and real troubles at Court about it.[1]

Pepys's account is supported by a contemporary letter which throws a little light on the quarrel between Lady Castlemaine and Lady Harvey. Lady Sunderland (Dorothy Sidney) wrote to Martha, Lady Giffard, the sister of Sir William Temple, the following note, undated:

Your sister will now bee satisfied her intelligence was true, concerning my Lady Harvie, for I suppose she knowes that she has not bine at Court since the King's seeing that she tooke to herself represented affter she had made so publicke a complaint of it and now she expects some favourable expressions from his Ma.[tie] to encourage her coming again . . . but the King being a very civill person, and she having a mind to be sattisfied the busynesses will probablye be don. Tis a dangerous thinge I finde for Ladyes to brage of power in State affaires and I am confident it has caused that to be don that would not have bine to any other gentlewoman. Her brother is extremely concerned in her disgrace wh. has bine nowe a greate while to satisfy those who did not wishe her in favour. I believe nobody is unwillinge she should showe herselfe in the Drawing-roome, the Queene has taken no notice of this businesse except very privately.[2]

If Lady Harvey was to be satirized for interfering in state affairs (and Saint-Évremond's editor described her as having "un génie propre à entrer dans les affaires d'Etat les plus délicates"),[3] no better play could have been selected than *Catiline*, and no better character than Sempronia, "the queen — a little *passée* — of an intellectual Bohemia"[4] similar to the Restoration court of Charles.

1. VIII, 187–188. Doll Common was, of course, Mrs. Corey.
2. J. G. Longe, *Martha Lady Giffard, Her Life and Correspondence*, pp. 98–99.
3. *Œuvres*, I, 197.
4. Herford and Simpson, II, 127. For an allusion in 1680 to Hortensia Mancini as "*Sempronia in Catiline's Conspiracy*," see J. W. Ebsworth, *The Roxburghe Ballads*, IV (1883), 663. Also see Thomas D'Urfey, *The Banditti*, 1686, sig. A2.

It seems reasonably certain that *Catiline* was acted with some frequency from the time of the revival, for allusions to it were common.   There is a pleasant tradition concerning the manner in which the inimitable Jo Haines rendered the part of a senator one evening after a small quarrel with Hart:

Jo, being vex'd at the slight Mr. *Hart* had put on him, found out this method of being reveng'd on him: He gets out a Scaramouch dress, a large full Ruff, makes himself Whiskers, from Ear to Ear, puts on his head, a long Merry Andrews Cap, a short Pipe in his mouth, a little three Leg'd stool in his hand, and in this manner, follows Mr. *Hart* on the Stage, sets himself down behind him, and begins to smoke his Pipe, to Laugh, and Point at him.

Which Comical Figure, put all the House in an uproar, some Laughing, some Clapping, and some Hollowing. Now Mr. *Hart*, as those that knew him can aver, was a Man of that Exactness and Grandeur on the Stage, that let what wou'd happen, he'd never discompose himself, or mind any thing but what he then Represented, and had a Scene fall'n behind him, he wou'd not at that time look back, to have seen what was the matter, which *Jo*. knowing, remain'd still Smoking, the Audience continued Laughing, Mr. *Hart* Acting, and Wondering at this unusual occasion of their Mirth, sometimes thinking it some disturbance in the House; again, that it might be something amiss in his dress; at last, turning himself towards the Scenes, he discover'd *Jo*. in the aforesaid Posture, whereupon he immediately goes off the Stage, Swearing he wou'd never set foot on it again, unless *Jo*. was immediately turn'd out of Doors; which was no sooner spoke, but put in Practice. So our Grave Senator, was presently dismis'd the Senate, and turn'd out of the House in *Querpo*.[1]

On March 8, 1675, *Catiline* was acted before Charles for the last recorded time, the players receiving the usual £10.[2]

---

1. *The Life of the Late Famous Comedian, Jo. Hayns*, 1701, p. 24; Edmond Malone, *Historical Account of the English Stage*, pp. 355–356. There is difficulty as to which scene in *Catiline* the anecdote indicates, since IV. iii, the Senate scene, is Cicero's scene, composed of his speech against Catiline (Hart).
2. Nicoll, p. 307.

The records reveal no further performances during the Restoration, but that they continued there is no reason to doubt, since Langbaine wrote in 1691 that "This Play is still in Vogue on the Stage, and always presented with success," [1] and since the tragedy was frequently criticized.

In 1677 Saint-Évremond held a high opinion of Jonson's tragedies,[2] and in 1678, when the precisian Thomas Rymer made his terrible attack on the tragedies of the last age, he wrote of *Catiline* that

though the contrivance and œconomy is faulty enough, yet we there find (besides what is borrow'd from others) more of Poetry and of good thought, more of Nature and of Tragedy than peradventure can be scrap't together from all those other *Plays*. Nor can I be displeas'd with honest *Ben*, when he rather chooses to borrow a *Melon* of his Neighbour, than to treat us with a *Pumpion* of his own growth.[3]

In *A Short View of Tragedy* (1693), he continued his analysis by racily objecting to Jonson's presentation of Sylla's ghost, and to the continuous presence of the chorus, "which is not to be drawn through a Key-hole, to be lugg'd about, or juggl'd with an *hocus pocus* hither and thither." In distinction from other critics, who left Jonson's structure alone, Rymer found that he had abused the unity of place.

One would not talk of rules, or what is regular with *Shakespear*, or any followers, in the Gang of the *Strouling* Fraternity; but it is lamentable that *Ben. Johnson*, his Stone and his Tymber, however otherwise of value, must lye a miserable heap of ruins, for want of Architecture, or some Son of *Vitruvius*, to joyn them together.[4]

About the mixture of comedy and tragedy, Rymer agreed completely with Dryden. "It was bad enough in him . . .

1. *An Account of the English Dramatick Poets*, p. 288.
2. *Œuvres*, I, 150, III, 223. For praise of *Catiline* see the broadside *The Character of Wits Squint-Ey'd Maid, Pasquil-Makers*, 1681.
3. *The Tragedies of the Last Age*, p. 143.
4. Page 161.

to interlard so much fiddle-faddle, Comedy, and *Apocry-phal* matters in the History." Rymer's neo-classic excitement always coined amusing turns of speech, but it invalidated many of his critical judgments. Even to the most literal-minded critic, *Catiline* must remain one of the "correctest" tragedies ever written. Compared, for instance, with *Cato*, where the requirement for unity of place brought even love-making into the Senate House, the faults of ghost and chorus in *Catiline* seem petty.

Almost the only information concerning the staging of the play, aside from the comments of Pepys, comes from an old newspaper, *The New Heraclitus Ridens; or, An Old Dialogue between Jest and Earnest Revived*, for May 24, 1689:

> *Earn.* Why, to tell you true, I have seen, - - - I can't tell you well what my self. 'Twas the World turn'd *in and out*. The grand Scene of Prodigies in *Catiline* or *Mackbeth*: Thunder and Lightning: Bloody Axes and Razors: a whole Troop of pale Heads flew glaring by me: One of 'em I think was *crown'd*; but I'm sure there were several *Coronets* among them. After all, when I was terribly frighten'd, comes a hand out o' the Clouds, and sets all right agen.[1]

When Collin took his walk through London in 1690, he not only broke up a performance of *Bartholomew Fair*, but learned from the Major, his guide, some facts about *Catiline*. Collin had been beaten for arguing about the naked figures on St. Dunstan's clock. The Major comforted him by pointing out that a solid beating is the best cause of wise dispute:

> The Soul and Spirits being more
> Alarm'd than they were before,
> Nay, fear of beeting may in some
> Produce the same, as once at *Rome*,
> For as, when *Cataline* a League
> Had made the Senators to fegue,

---

1. See *Catiline*, III. v, IV. i. Most of the allusion seems to be to *Macbeth*.

And strumpet had told *Marcus Tully*,
The close intentions of that Bully,
He not so much the cause revenging
O' th' State, as t'hinder his own swinging,
Made the best speech to quell that strife,
(Tis said) that e're he made in's Life,
Since when, 'tis found upon Record,
In th' Tragedy, writ word for word:
So thou since frighted by the Rabble,
Hast spoke like him most admirable.[1]

About 1690 Verbruggen acted in *Catiline*. Colley Cibber's critic, the author of *The Laureat* (1740), wondered that Cibber "hardly ever mentions Mr. *Verbruggen*, who was in many Characters an excellent Actor, as we remember him in *Cassius*, *Oroonoko*, *Ventidius*, *Chamont*, *Pierre*, *Cethegus*, as well as in several Parts in Comedy, as the *Rover*, &c. He was an Original, and had a Roughness in his Manner, and a negligent agreeable Wildness in his Action and his Mein [*sic*], which became him well." [2] Jack Verbruggen was described by Aston as "wild and untaught," "that rough Diamond," who "shone more bright than all the artful, polish'd Brillants that ever sparkled on our Stage." [3] His person was tall and well built, the only defect consisting in his being "a little In-kneed, which gave him a shambling Gate." His wildness should have been an asset to his Cethegus.

The decade from 1690 to 1700 produced no significant criticisms of the tragedy, but in 1700 Samuel Cobb praised *Catiline* in his poem *Of Poetry*:

> The Coyn must sure for *currant Sterling* pass,
> Stamp'd with old *Chaucer's Venerable Face*.
> But *Johnson* found it of a gross *Alloy*,
> Melted it down, and flung the Dross away

---

1. *Collin's Walk*, pp. 84-85. See *Catiline*, III. ii.
2. Page 58.
3. *A Brief Supplement to Colley Cibber, Esq., His Lives*, ed. R. W. Lowe, *An Apology for the Life of Mr. Colley Cibber*, II, 311.

He dug pure Silver from a *Roman Mine*,
And prest his Sacred Image on the Coyn.
We all rejoyc'd to see the pillag'd Oar,
Our Tongue inrich'd, which was so poor before.
Fear not, Learn'd Poet, our impartial blame,
Such Thefts as these add Lustre to thy Name.
Whether thy labour'd Comedies betray ⎫
The Sweat of *Terence*, in thy Glorious Way, ⎬
Or *Catliine* [*sic*] plots better in thy Play. ⎭
Whether his Crimes more excellently shine, ⎫
Whether we hear the Consul's Voice Divine, ⎬
And doubt which merits most, *Rome's Cicero*, or Thine. ⎭
All yield, consenting to sustain the Yoke,
And learn the Language which the Victor spoke.
So *Macedon's Imperial Hero* threw
His wings abroad, and conquer'd as he flew.
Great *Johnson's* Deeds stand Parallel with His,
Were *Noble Thefts, Successful Pyracies*.[1]

Apparently the first criticism after Rymer which stated directly that Jonson possessed no genius for tragedy came from the pen of John Dennis, in a letter of February 8, 1711, "On the Writings and Genius of Shakespear." Rymer criticized Jonson's technique, but Dennis hit at the soul of *Catiline* and *Sejanus*. He observed that although Jonson's "incomparable Talent" had produced "Comedies, by which he has born away the Prize of Comedy both from Ancients and Moderns," he had "chosen two Subjects, which . . . were utterly incapable of exciting either Compassion or Terror for the principal Characters, which yet are the chief Passions that a Tragick Poet ought to endeavour to excite." [2] Dennis's attack on Jonson's coldness and objectivity was the foundation of subsequent criticism, which has found little to admire in the two Roman plays.[3]

1. *Poems on Several Occasions*, 1707, pp. 189–190.
2. *Original Letters, Familiar, Moral, and Critical*, p. 402.
3. The poetic beauties of *Catiline* were the only selections from Jonson included in Edward Bysshe's *Art of English Poetry*, 4th ed., 1710, pp. 219, 288. See also *Thesaurus Dramaticus*, 1724, I, 187, II, 53, 80, 81, 215, 282, 298; *The Beauties of the English Stage*, 1737, I, 9, 188.

Steele, it is true, praised the portrayal of Fulvia:

The Scene between *Fulvia* and *Curius*, in the second Act of *Johnson's Catiline*, is an excellent Picture of the Power of a Lady over her Gallant. The Wench plays with his Affections; and as a Man of all Places in the World wishes to make a good Figure with his Mistress, upon her upbraiding him with Want of Spirit, he alludes to Enterprizes which he cannot reveal but with the Hazard of his Life. When he is worked thus far, with a little Flattery of her Opinion of his Gallantry, and Desire to know more of it out of her overflowing Fondness to him, he brags to her till his Life is in her Disposal.[1]

After Steele the play rested in limbo. Since it had not been acted at all in the new century, it sank to the dull honors of a library piece. In 1747 it was included as the only play of Jonson in the collection of French translations known as *Le Théâtre Anglois*. The author of the preface, although he admired the methodical outline of Jonson's tragedy, the conduct of the intrigue, and the sustained style, compared Ben with Shakspere and concluded that nature was superior to art, that one applauded Jonson, but that one admired Shakspere.[2] Such comparisons between the two great dramatists increased during the latter half of the eighteenth century, and as Shakspere was performed more and more with the rising tide of romanticism, Jonson's reputation declined. In 1753 Bishop Hurd wrote to the detriment of the tragic values of *Catiline*, remarking that in using well-known subjects for poetical themes, authors should not follow the "trite, obvious round of the original work," nor be translators instead of imitators, nor adopt any particular incident which decency and the nature of the work would reject. *Catiline*, or "the Catilinarian war of Salust, put into poetical dialogue" transgressed in all three respects, and Hurd objected especially to the long, direct translations in the speeches:

1. *The Spectator*, No. 510.
2. V, vii–ix.

Nothing can be more flat and disgusting, than this calm impertinent pleading; especially in the very heat and winding up of the plot. But the poet was misled by the beauty it appeared to have in the original composition, without attending to the peculiar laws of the drama, and the *indecorum* it must needs have in so very different a work.[1]

This condemnation of Jonson for his classical borrowings was propagated by Edward Young, in his *Conjectures on Original Composition* (1759). In the midst of his adulation of Shakspere, he included a neatly figured objurgation, clearly based on Hurd:

> *Johnson*, in the serious drama, is as much an imitator, as *Shakespeare* is an original. He was very learned, as *Sampson* was very strong, to his own hurt: Blind to the nature of tragedy, he pulled down all antiquity on his head, and buried himself under it; we see nothing of *Johnson*, nor indeed, of his admired (but also murdered) antients; for what shone in the historian is a cloud on the poet; and *Cataline* might have been a good play, if *Salust* had never writ.[2]

Despite a veritable avalanche of hostile opinion, *The Companion to the Play-House* judged *Catiline* to be endowed with great merit, but "too declamatory for the present dramatic Taste."[3] There was slight chance of revival, and after James Beattie's attack on the play in 1769, when he accused Jonson of want of taste in his rigid attachment to historical truth and want of invention in confining himself so strictly to the letter of the story,[4] criticism of *Catiline* waned.

Apparently, all possible fault had been found with the tragedy. It was an unnatural mixture of comedy and

---

1. *Q. Horatii Flacci Ars Poetica, Epistola ad Pisones*, I, 85. Compare *The Universal Magazine*, XXIV (1759), 342.

2. Page 80. Compare [Mrs. Elizabeth Montagu], *An Essay on the Writings and Genius of Shakespear*, 1769, pp. 151–152; *The Universal Magazine*, XXIV (1759), 341–342.

3. Article on *Catiline*.

4. *Essays on Poetry and Music*, 1778, pp. 527–528.

tragedy, the least diverting of any ever seen on the stage; the contrivance and economy were faulty, the ghost and chorus utterly incorrect according to the rules for the unities; Jonson had no notion of tragedy, although he knew the rules; and so, without genius to abet him, by wholesale copying from the ancients, he had concocted a dull piece of rhetoric, incapable of exciting pity or terror and displaying in a wealth of extraneous material no evidence of a selective imagination. In plan and technique the play was characterized by nothing more than by its indecorum. It was cold, turgid, extravagant, undramatic. Curiously enough, no critic found specific fault with the poetry.

To fly in the face of all the adverse criticism of *Catiline* is, perhaps, hazardous. But one may safely suggest that the eighteenth-century mind was distinctly unphilosophical in attempting to compare and evaluate geniuses as widely different as Jonson and Shakspere, proving Shakspere's virtues by Jonson's faults. One might as well describe an aquarelle in terms of a lithograph. Coleridge perceived the difficulty:

A fondness for judging one work by comparison with others, perhaps altogether of a different class, argues a vulgar taste. Yet it is chiefly on this principle that the Catiline has been rated so low. Take it and Sejanus, as compositions of a particular kind, namely, as a mode of relating great historical events in the liveliest and most interesting manner, and I can not help wishing that we had whole volumes of such plays. We might as rationally expect the excitement of the Vicar of Wakefield from Goldsmith's History of England, as that of Lear, Othello, &c. from the Sejanus or Catiline.[1]

Many of the faults found formerly in *Catiline* no longer seem so grave as they did to earlier critics. Abuses of the unities have not bothered us much since Dr. Johnson's *Preface to Shakespeare*, and through a long series of closet dramas we have become accustomed to a type of dramatic

1. W. G. T. Shedd, *The Complete Works of Samuel Taylor Coleridge*, IV, 193.

literature which is none the less excellent as poetry because it fails as drama. *Catiline* could not now be acted. But as a reading play, its scenes are by no means so impossible as Dibdin suggested, when he wrote that "to read them a first time is an effort, a second a task, and a third impossible." [1] If one can accept Coleridge's *apologia* for historical plays, there is no longer any ground for criticizing Jonson's method. And if the tragedy does at moments appear emotionally cold, the reader may enjoy the comfort of realizing that, like a spring, it is also very pure.

1. *A Complete History of the Stage*, III, 99.

APPENDIX

APPENDIX

A CHRONOLOGY OF THE PERFORMANCES
OF BEN JONSON'S PLAYS 1660–1776

THE chronological table of performances of Jonson's plays has been mainly compiled from the following sources: newspaper files in the Burney Collection in the British Museum; playbills in the Huntington Library and the Harvard Theatre Collection; the diaries of Pepys and Evelyn; Allardyce Nicoll, *A History of Restoration Drama*; Leslie Hotson, *The Commonwealth and Restoration Stage*; British Museum Additional MSS. 32249–32252, *Performances at London Theatres, 1702–1746, bequeathed by Frederick Latreille*; British Museum MS. Sloane 1900, *Dr. Edward Browne's Memorandum Book*; British Museum MSS. Egerton 2269–2278, *Accounts of Covent Garden Theatre, 1735–1767*; British Museum MS. Egerton 2320, *Diary of Plays, Lincoln's Inn Fields, 1715– 1721; Drury Lane, 1721–1738; Haymarket, 1733–1734, attributed to Benjamin Griffin*. The table contains almost three hundred and seventy-five performances not listed by Genest.

The following abbreviations have been used: DL, Drury Lane; CG, Covent Garden; Hay, Haymarket; LIF, Lincoln's Inn Fields; DG, Dorset Garden.

1660	n.d.	Epicoene	Red Bull
	about June 6	Epicoene	Probably at the Red Bull
	November 10	Epicoene	Gibbons's Tennis Court
	November 19	Epicoene	Cockpit-in-Court
	December 4	Epicoene	Gibbons's Tennis Court
1661	January 7	Epicoene	Gibbons's Tennis Court
	May 25	Epicoene	Gibbons's Tennis Court
	June 8	Bartholomew Fair	Gibbons's Tennis Court
	June 22	Alchemist	Gibbons's Tennis Court
	June 27	Bartholomew Fair	Gibbons's Tennis Court
	August 14	Alchemist	Gibbons's Tennis Court
	September 7	Bartholomew Fair	Gibbons's Tennis Court
	November 12	Bartholomew Fair	Gibbons's Tennis Court
	December 16	Alchemist	Gibbons's Tennis Court
	December 18	Bartholomew Fair	Gibbons's Tennis Court

1662	n.d.	Bartholomew Fair	Gibbons's Tennis Court
	n.d.	Epicoene	Cockpit in Drury Lane
	n.d.	Volpone	Gibbons's Tennis Court
	n.d.	Alchemist	Gibbons's Tennis Court
	October 16	Volpone	Cockpit-in-Court
1663	January 1	Volpone	Oxford
	January 6	Volpone	Oxford
1664	February 2	Epicoene	King's Company at the Inner Temple
	June 1	Epicoene	Theatre Royal in Bridges St.
	August 2	Bartholomew Fair	Theatre Royal in Bridges St.
	August 3	Alchemist	Theatre Royal in Bridges St.
1665	January 14	Volpone	Theatre Royal in Bridges St.
1666	December 10	Epicoene	King's Company at Court
1667	April 16	Epicoene	Theatre Royal in Bridges St.
	April 27	Bartholomew Fair	Theatre Royal in Bridges St.
	August 28	Volpone	King's Company at Court
1668	September 4	Bartholomew Fair	Theatre Royal in Bridges St.
	September 19	Epicoene	Theatre Royal in Bridges St.
	December 18	Catiline	Theatre Royal in Bridges St.
	December 19	Catiline	Theatre Royal in Bridges St.
1669	January 2	Catiline	Theatre Royal in Bridges St.
	January 13	Catiline	Theatre Royal in Bridges St.
	February 22	Bartholomew Fair	Cockpit-in-Court
	April 17	Alchemist	Theatre Royal in Bridges St.
1670	December 26	Bartholomew Fair	Dublin
1674	November 12	Alchemist	Cockpit-in-Court
	November 30	Bartholomew Fair	Theatre Royal in DL
1675	March 8	Catiline	Theatre Royal in DL
	n.d.	Every Man out of his Humour	Theatre Royal in DL
	October 26	Alchemist	Theatre Royal in DL
1676	January 17	Volpone	Theatre Royal in DL
1685	January 15	Epicoene	United Companies at DG and DL

1691 Plays noted by Langbaine as still being acted at the theatres:
Bartholomew Fair, Catiline, Epicoene, Volpone, Every Man
in his Humour.

1700	May 2	Volpone	DL
	December 21	Epicoene	DL
	December 27	Volpone	DL
1701	March 18	Volpone	DL
	March 27	Alchemist	DL
	April 1	Alchemist	DL

1701	June 5	Epicoene	DL
1702	June 3	Bartholomew Fair	DL
	August 18	Bartholomew Fair	DL
	October 9	Alchemist	LIF
1703	May 21	Volpone	DL
	May 25	Volpone	DL
	June 12	Volpone	DL
	October 11	Epicoene	DL
	November 3	Volpone	DL
	November 24	Volpone	DL
	December 13	Epicoene	DL
1704	February 14	Epicoene	DL
	February 23	Volpone	DL
	March 25	Bartholomew Fair	DL
	April 8	Bartholomew Fair	DL
	June 17	Volpone	DL
	September 28	Bartholomew Fair	DL
	October 23	Epicoene	DL
	November 29	Volpone	DL
1705	January 8	Bartholomew Fair	DL
	June 5	Volpone	DL
	November 8	Volpone	DL
1706	February 2	Epicoene	DL
	December 3	Volpone	Hay
1707	January 1	Epicoene	Hay
	January 2	Epicoene	Hay
	January 7	Epicoene	Hay
	February 21	Epicoene	Hay
	August 12	Bartholomew Fair	Hay
	August 14	Bartholomew Fair	Hay
	August 22	Bartholomew Fair	Hay
	October 22	Bartholomew Fair	Hay
	October 28	Epicoene	Hay
	November 13	Epicoene	Hay
1708	January 7	Epicoene	Hay
	April 21	Epicoene	DL
	April 27	Volpone	DL
	July 15	Bartholomew Fair	DL
	August 26	Bartholomew Fair	DL
	August 31	Bartholomew Fair	DL
1709	January 4	Epicoene	DL
	February 19	Alchemist	DL
	February 21	Alchemist	DL
	February 22	Alchemist	DL

1709	February 26	Volpone	DL
	February 28	Alchemist	DL
	March 1	Epicoene	DL
	March 26	Alchemist	DL
	April 4	Alchemist	DL
	May 11	Alchemist	DL
	May 27	Volpone	DL
	May 31	Epicoene	DL
1710	January 9	Volpone	Hay
	January 11	Epicoene	Hay
	January 14	Alchemist	Hay
	January 23	Alchemist	Hay
	February 9	Epicoene	Hay
	June 1	Bartholomew Fair	Hay
	June 9	Epicoene	Hay
	November 25	Volpone	DL
	November 28	Epicoene	DL
1711	February 10	Alchemist	DL
	March 5	Epicoene	DL
	March 8	Bartholomew Fair	DL
	April 6	Alchemist	DL
	August 24	Bartholomew Fair	DL
	November 1	Epicoene	DL
	December 8	Alchemist	DL
1712	February 19	Alchemist	DL
	April 1	Epicoene	DL
	April 29	Volpone	DL
	August 26	Bartholomew Fair	DL
	November 17	Volpone	DL
1713	January 14	Bartholomew Fair	DL
	March 3	Epicoene	DL
	November 2	Epicoene	DL
	November 24	Volpone	DL
	December 1	Bartholomew Fair	DL
	December 14	Epicoene	DL
	December 21	Alchemist	DL
	December 22	Alchemist	DL
1714	May 12	Volpone	DL
	October 27	Epicoene	DL
1715	March 3	Epicoene	DL
	March 19	Volpone	DL
	June 28	Bartholomew Fair	DL
	November 3	Epicoene	DL
1716	January 25	Epicoene	DL

1716	January 26	Volpone	DL
	December 4	Epicoene	DL
	December 10	Bartholomew Fair	DL
1717	January 31	Volpone	DL
	May 15	Volpone	DL
	May 25	Epicoene	DL
	July 16	Bartholomew Fair	DL
1718	January 20	Epicoene	DL
	March 24	Bartholomew Fair	DL
	June 27	Bartholomew Fair	DL
	October 16	Volpone	Hampton Court
	October 17	Volpone	DL
	November 18	Epicoene	DL
	November 26	Bartholomew Fair	DL
1719	April 28	Bartholomew Fair	DL
	August 4	Bartholomew Fair	DL
	November 3	Epicoene	DL
1720	January 13	Bartholomew Fair	DL
	March 19	Volpone	DL
	March 22	Volpone	DL
	June 10	Bartholomew Fair	DL
	September 15	Epicoene	DL
	October 31	Bartholomew Fair	DL
	November 12	Volpone	DL
	November 16	Epicoene	DL
1721	January 31	Volpone	DL
	February 28	Epicoene	DL
	October 25	Alchemist	DL
	October 26	Alchemist	DL
	October 27	Alchemist	DL
	November 22	Alchemist	DL
	December 22	Volpone	DL
1722	January 9	Epicoene	DL
	May 23	Epicoene	DL
	July 10	Bartholomew Fair	DL
	October 10	Volpone	DL
	October 24	Epicoene	DL
	December 21	Bartholomew Fair	DL
1723	February 14	Epicoene	DL
	March 23	Volpone	DL
	October 10	Alchemist	DL
	November 6	Epicoene	DL
	November 21	Volpone	DL
	December 4	Alchemist	DL

1723	December 13	Alchemist	DL
1724	February 10	Epicoene	DL
	May 15	Volpone	DL
	October 28	Epicoene	DL
	December 31	Epicoene	DL
1725	January 11	Every Man in his Humour	LIF
	January 12	Every Man in his Humour	LIF
	January 13	Every Man in his Humour	LIF
	April 6	Epicoene	DL
	April 15	Volpone	DL
	November 8	Epicoene	DL
1726	January 5	Volpone	DL
	October 15	Volpone	DL
	October 20	Alchemist	DL
	October 25	Epicoene	DL
	November 17	Alchemist	DL
1727	January 10	Alchemist	DL
	January 12	Volpone	DL
	November 15	Volpone	LIF
	November 16	Volpone	LIF
	November 23	Volpone	LIF
1728	March 9	Alchemist	DL
	May 29	Volpone	LIF
	October 21	Volpone	LIF
	October 26	Alchemist	DL
1729	January 29	Epicoene	DL
	January 31	Volpone	DL
	February 3	Alchemist	DL
	March 27	Volpone	LIF
	October 17	Volpone	LIF
	December 3	Alchemist	DL
1730	June 1	Volpone	LIF
	September 24	Volpone	DL
	December 31	Epicoene	DL
1731	January 4	Volpone	LIF
	January 8	Alchemist	DL
	October 5	Volpone	DL
	October 7	Alchemist	DL
	October 9	Epicoene	DL
	October 30	Bartholomew Fair	DL
	December 11	Volpone	LIF
1732	February 5	Volpone	LIF
	March 7	Alchemist	DL
	March 9	Epicoene	DL

1732	November 9	Alchemist	DL
	November 11	Volpone	LIF
1733	January 11	Volpone	CG
	January 19	Alchemist	DL
	February 3	Volpone	CG
	April 19	Volpone	CG
	November 3	Volpone	CG
	November 24	Volpone	CG
	December 19	Volpone	CG
	December 20	Alchemist	Hay
	December 22	Epicoene	Hay
	December 27	Volpone	Hay
	December 28	Alchemist	Hay
	December 29	Epicoene	Hay
	December 31	Alchemist	Hay
1734	January 1	Epicoene	Hay
	January 2	Volpone	Hay
	January 2	Volpone	CG
	January 4	Alchemist	Hay
	January 5	Epicoene	Hay
	January 25	Alchemist	Hay
	February 26	Volpone	CG
	March 16	Alchemist	DL
	March 21	Epicoene	DL
	April 6	Alchemist	DL
	April 15	Epicoene	DL
	April 24	Volpone	CG
	April 27	Alchemist	DL
	September 19	Alchemist	DL
	November 5	Volpone	Bury School
	December 3	Alchemist	DL
1735	February 1	Alchemist	DL
	March 13	Volpone	DL
	April 14	Epicoene	DL
	April 26	Alchemist	DL
	May 7	Volpone	DL
	May 22	Epicoene	DL
	August 25	Bartholomew Fair	LIF
	September 15	Alchemist	DL
	September 16	Alchemist	DL
	November 17	Volpone	DL
	November 18	Alchemist	DL
	November 20	Epicoene	DL
	December 18	Volpone	DL

1735	December 19	Alchemist	DL
	December 20	Epicoene	DL
1736	March 29	Epicoene	DL
	April 13	Alchemist	DL
	May 8	Volpone	DL
	May 28	Epicoene	DL
	October 21	Volpone	DL
	October 22	Alchemist	DL
	October 23	Epicoene	DL
	November 15	Volpone	CG
	November 17	Volpone	CG
	December 30	Volpone	CG
1737	March 19	Volpone	CG
	April 19	Volpone	CG
	October 10	Volpone	CG
	November 14	Volpone	DL
	November 15	Alchemist	DL
	November 16	Epicoene	DL
1738	February 18	Epicoene	DL
	February 20	Volpone	DL
	February 21	Alchemist	DL
	May 24	Volpone	DL
	May 27	Alchemist	DL
	October 23	Volpone	CG
	November 16	Volpone	CG
1739	January 26	Epicoene	DL
	March 20	Alchemist	DL
	March 26	Alchemist	DL
	October 22	Volpone	DL
	October 23	Epicoene	DL
	October 24	Alchemist	DL
	December 21	Volpone	CG
1740	October 9	Volpone	DL
	October 10	Alchemist	DL
	October 11	Epicoene	DL
	December 10	Alchemist	CG
	December 31	Alchemist	CG
1741	April 13	Volpone	DL
	May 12	Epicoene	DL
1742	February 11	Volpone	DL
	February 12	Alchemist	DL
	February 13	Epicoene	DL
	February 17	Alchemist	DL
	October 15	Volpone	CG

1743	February 4	Volpone	CG
	March 21	Alchemist	DL
	April 8	Alchemist	DL
	April 21	Alchemist	DL
	May 7	Alchemist	DL
	November 24	Volpone	CG
	December 16	Alchemist	DL
	December 17	Volpone	CG
1744	January 2	Alchemist	DL
	January 17	Volpone	CG
	January 28	Alchemist	DL
	February 4	Alchemist	DL
	April 9	Alchemist	DL
	November 6	Alchemist	DL
	December 22	Alchemist	DL
1745	January 10	Alchemist	DL
	February 8	Alchemist	DL
	February 11	Volpone	CG
	April 17	Epicoene	CG
	April 17	Alchemist	DL
	September 28	Alchemist	DL
	November 21	Alchemist	DL
	November 23	Epicoene	CG
	December 3	Epicoene	CG
	December 28	Epicoene	CG
1746	February 18	Epicoene	CG
	February 22	Alchemist	DL
	March 8	Epicoene	CG
	March 31	Alchemist	DL
	April 21	Volpone	CG
	September 25	Alchemist	DL
1747	October 21	Alchemist	DL
	November 12	Alchemist	DL
	November 25	Alchemist	DL
1748	March 24	Alchemist	DL
	March 28	Epicoene	CG
	April 18	Volpone	CG
	April 29	Alchemist	DL
	November 7	Alchemist	DL
	December 20	Volpone	CG
	December 23	Volpone	CG
1749	April 12	Alchemist	DL
	October 14	Alchemist	DL
	November 14	Alchemist	DL

1749	November 18	Volpone	CG
	December 2	Alchemist	DL
1750	January 8	Volpone	CG
	April 18	Alchemist	DL
	November 14	Alchemist	DL
	November 30	Alchemist	DL
	December 13	Alchemist	DL
1751	January 9	Alchemist	DL
	January 25	Alchemist	DL
	May 2	Alchemist	DL
	November 29	Every Man in his Humour	DL
	December 2	Every Man in his Humour	DL
	December 4	Every Man in his Humour	DL
	December 6	Every Man in his Humour	DL
	December 9	Every Man in his Humour	DL
	December 11	Every Man in his Humour	DL
	December 13	Every Man in his Humour	DL
	December 19	Every Man in his Humour	DL
	December 21	Every Man in his Humour	DL
1752	January 10	Every Man in his Humour	DL
	January 16	Every Man in his Humour	DL
	January 25	Every Man in his Humour	DL
	January 31	Every Man in his Humour	DL
	March 10	Every Man in his Humour	DL
	April 4	Every Man in his Humour	DL
	May 8	Every Man in his Humour	DL
	October 26	Epicoene	DL
	October 27	Epicoene	DL
	October 31	Epicoene	DL
	November 1	Epicoene	DL
	November 11	Epicoene	DL
	November 30	Every Man in his Humour	DL
	December 1	Every Man in his Humour	DL
	December 23	Every Man in his Humour	DL
1753	January 15	Every Man in his Humour	DL
	January 29	Every Man in his Humour	DL
	March 1	Every Man in his Humour	DL
	March 20	Alchemist	DL
	March 31	Every Man in his Humour	DL
	April 14	Alchemist	DL
	April 27	Every Man in his Humour	DL
	April 30	Alchemist	DL
	May 3	Every Man in his Humour	DL
	November 12	Volpone	CG

1753	December 15	Volpone	CG
1754	March 19	Every Man in his Humour	DL
	April 4	Every Man in his Humour	DL
	May 24	Every Man in his Humour	DL
	October 17	Volpone	CG
	October 30	Every Man in his Humour	DL
	December 3	Every Man in his Humour	DL
	December 12	Every Man in his Humour	DL
1755	January 31	Every Man in his Humour	DL
	March 17	Every Man in his Humour	DL
	April 3	Every Man in his Humour	DL
	May 7	Every Man in his Humour	DL
	December 6	Every Man in his Humour	DL
	December 11	Alchemist	DL
	December 12	Alchemist	DL
	December 17	Every Man in his Humour	DL
	December 20	Alchemist	DL
	December 30	Alchemist	DL
1756	January 17	Alchemist	DL
	February 5	Alchemist	DL
	February 17	Every Man in his Humour	DL
	February 19	Alchemist	DL
	April 5	Every Man in his Humour	DL
	April 21	Alchemist	DL
	December 10	Every Man in his Humour	DL
1757	January 12	Every Man in his Humour	DL
	February 21	Every Man in his Humour	DL
	March 7	Alchemist	DL
	March 31	Every Man in his Humour	DL
	April 19	Alchemist	DL
	April 27	Every Man in his Humour	DL
	October 19	Every Man in his Humour	DL
1758	January 27	Alchemist	DL
	February 9	Every Man in his Humour	DL
	February 18	Alchemist	DL
	April 11	Every Man in his Humour	DL
	May 31	Every Man in his Humour	DL
	November 9	Alchemist	DL
	November 22	Alchemist	DL
1759	January 2	Alchemist	DL
	March 15	Alchemist	DL
	March 31	Every Man in his Humour	DL
	October 9	Alchemist	DL
	November 6	Alchemist	DL

1759	November 13	Every Man in his Humour	DL
	December 22	Every Man in his Humour	DL
1760	January 1	Alchemist	DL
	January 12	Every Man in his Humour	DL
	January 21	Alchemist	DL
	March 4	Every Man in his Humour	DL
	April 17	Alchemist	DL
	October 15	Alchemist	DL
	October 24	Every Man in his Humour	DL
	December 18	Alchemist	DL
	December 31	Every Man in his Humour	DL
1761	April 1	Every Man in his Humour	DL
	April 14	Alchemist	DL
	April 15	Every Man in his Humour	DL
	October 16	Alchemist	DL
	October 20	Every Man in his Humour	DL
	October 22	Every Man in his Humour	DL
	November 27	Alchemist	DL
	December 18	Every Man in his Humour	DL
1762	January 23	Alchemist	DL
	March 9	Alchemist	DL
	April 20	Alchemist	DL
	October 4	Every Man in his Humour	DL
	October 25	Every Man in his Humour	CG
	October 26	Every Man in his Humour	CG
	October 28	Every Man in his Humour	CG
	November 2	Every Man in his Humour	CG
	November 4	Every Man in his Humour	CG
	November 10	Every Man in his Humour	CG
	November 13	Every Man in his Humour	CG
	November 18	Alchemist	DL
	November 19	Every Man in his Humour	CG
	November 27	Every Man in his Humour	CG
	December 2	Alchemist	DL
	December 3	Every Man in his Humour	CG
	December 15	Alchemist	DL
	December 16	Alchemist	DL
1763	January 5	Every Man in his Humour	DL
	January 12	Every Man in his Humour	CG
	January 26	Every Man in his Humour	CG
	February 11	Every Man in his Humour	CG
	March 15	Every Man in his Humour	CG
	April 9	Alchemist	DL
	April 13	Every Man in his Humour	CG
	May 6	Every Man in his Humour	CG

1763	October 10	Every Man in his Humour	CG
	November 23	Every Man in his Humour	CG
	December 17	Alchemist	DL
	December 22	Every Man in his Humour	CG
1764	January 2	Alchemist	DL
	January 5	Every Man in his Humour	CG
	February 16	Every Man in his Humour	CG
	March 26	Every Man in his Humour	CG
	April 14	Every Man in his Humour	CG
	May 22	Every Man in his Humour	CG
	September 1	Every Man in his Humour	Hay
	November 1	Every Man in his Humour	CG
	November 21	Every Man in his Humour	CG
1765	January 5	Every Man in his Humour	CG
	January 24	Every Man in his Humour	CG
	March 12	Every Man in his Humour	CG
	April 12	Every Man in his Humour	CG
	May 6	Every Man in his Humour	CG
	October 8	Every Man in his Humour	CG
	November 16	Every Man in his Humour	CG
	December 18	Every Man in his Humour	CG
1766	February 4	Every Man in his Humour	CG
	March 18	Every Man in his Humour	CG
	April 9	Every Man in his Humour	CG
	April 30	Every Man in his Humour	CG
	May 22	Every Man in his Humour	DL
	October 22	Every Man in his Humour	CG
	October 31	Alchemist	DL
	November 13	Alchemist	DL
	November 15	Every Man in his Humour	CG
	December 8	Every Man in his Humour	CG
1767	January 5	Every Man in his Humour	CG
	February 12	Every Man in his Humour	CG
	March 10	Every Man in his Humour	CG
	April 22	Every Man in his Humour	CG
	May 5	Every Man in his Humour	CG
	May 14	Every Man in his Humour	CG
	September 17	Every Man in his Humour	CG
	October 9	Every Man in his Humour	DL
	October 20	Alchemist	DL
	November 7	Every Man in his Humour	DL
	November 24	Every Man in his Humour	CG
1768	January 7	Every Man in his Humour	DL
	January 26	Every Man in his Humour	CG
	February 18	Every Man in his Humour	CG

1768	February 25	Alchemist	DL
	March 7	Alchemist	DL
	April 16	Every Man in his Humour	CG
	April 21	Every Man in his Humour	DL
	September 21	Every Man in his Humour	CG
	November 1	Every Man in his Humour	CG
	December 9	Every Man in his Humour	CG
1769	January 9	Every Man in his Humour	CG
	January 25	Alchemist	DL
	January 27	Every Man in his Humour	DL
	February 9	Every Man in his Humour	DL
	February 25	Every Man in his Humour	CG
	April 29	Alchemist	DL
	April 29	Every Man in his Humour	CG
	May 10	Every Man in his Humour	CG
	May 24	Every Man in his Humour	CG
	September 27	Every Man in his Humour	CG
	November 22	Alchemist	DL
	November 22	Every Man in his Humour	CG
	November 29	Every Man in his Humour	DL
1770	January 20	Every Man in his Humour	CG
	February 6	Alchemist	DL
	May 24	Every Man in his Humour	DL
	October 15	Tobacconist	Hay
	November 16	Every Man in his Humour	DL
	December 6	Alchemist	DL
1771	May 17	Every Man in his Humour	Hay
	July 15	Tobacconist	Hay
	July 22	Tobacconist	Hay
	August 12	Tobacconist	Hay
	September 4	Tobacconist	Hay
	September 10	Tobacconist	Hay
	September 16	The Coxcombs	Hay
	September 20	Tobacconist	Hay
	November 7	Every Man in his Humour	CG
	November 8	Every Man in his Humour	DL
	November 14	Every Man in his Humour	CG
	November 26	Volpone	CG
	November 27	Volpone	CG
	November 29	Volpone	CG
	December 2	Volpone	CG
	December 3	Alchemist	DL
	December 18	Every Man in his Humour	CG
	December 31	Volpone	CG
1772	January 6	Volpone	CG

1772	January 8	Every Man in his Humour	CG
	January 28	Volpone	CG
	February 18	Volpone	CG
	February 20	Every Man in his Humour	CG
	March 19	Every Man in his Humour	CG
	April 21	Tobacconist	DL
	October 14	Every Man in his Humour	CG
	October 29	Every Man in his Humour	DL
	November 20	Alchemist	DL
	December 15	Every Man in his Humour	CG
1773	January 7	Volpone	CG
	January 20	Volpone	CG
	February 13	Alchemist	DL
	February 13	Every Man in his Humour	CG
	April 17	Tobacconist	DL
	May 18	Every Man in his Humour	CG
	August 4	Tobacconist	Hay
	August 23	Tobacconist	Hay
	August 31	Tobacconist	Hay
	October 2	Every Man in his Humour	DL
	October 6	Every Man in his Humour	DL
	October 14	Alchemist	DL
	November 23	Every Man in his Humour	CG
1774	January 21	Every Man in his Humour	CG
	August 29	Abel Drugger's Return	Hay
	September 5	Abel Drugger's Return	Hay
	September 6	Abel Drugger's Return	Hay
	October 20	Every Man in his Humour	DL
	October 24	Alchemist	DL
	December 6	Alchemist	DL
	December 29	Every Man in his Humour	DL
1775	September 19	Tobacconist	Hay
	September 21	Tobacconist	Hay
	October 5	Every Man in his Humour	DL
	November 25	Alchemist	DL
	December 18	Every Man in his Humour	DL
1776	January 13	Epicoene	DL
	January 15	Epicoene	DL
	January 17	Epicoene	DL
	January 18	Alchemist	DL
	January 23	Epicoene	DL
	February 9	Every Man in his Humour	DL
	April 11	Alchemist	DL
	April 25	Every Man in his Humour	DL

EDITIONS OF BEN JONSON'S PLAYS, 1660-1777

(Place of publication London, unless otherwise noted)

Catiline, His Conspiracy. A Tragœdie, As it is now Acted by His Majesties Servants at the Theatre Royal. The Author B. J., 1669.

Catiline His Conspiracy. A Tragœdie. As it is now Acted by His Majestie's Servants; at the Threatre [sic] Royal. The Author B. J., 1674.

The Works of Ben Jonson, Which were formerly Printed in Two Volumes, are now Reprinted in One. To which is added A Comedy, Called The New Inn. With Additions never before Published, 1692.

Volpone, or The Fox. A Comedy. As it is now Acted at the Theatre-Royal, by Her Majesty's Servants. Written by Ben. Johnson, 1709.

The Alchemist: A Comedy. As it is now Acted at the Theatre-Royal, . by Her Majesty's Servants. Written by Ben Johnson, 1709.

Epicoene, or, The Silent Woman. A Comedy. As it is now Acted at the Theatre-Royal, by Her Majesty's Servants. Written by Ben. Johnson, 1709.

Four Select Plays. Viz. The Silent Woman. Volpone, or the Fox. Cataline's Conspiracy. The Alchemist. By Ben. Johnson [ca. 1712].

Volpone: or, The Fox. A Comedy. Written by Ben Johnson. Printed for T. Johnson. In the Year 1714.

The Works of Ben. Johnson. In Six Volumes. Adorn'd with Cuts, 1716.

Volpone; or, The Fox [A Collection of the Best English Plays. Printed for T. Johnson, 1721, vol. IV].

Ben. Johnson's Plays in Two Volumes. Containing Volpone; or, the Fox. Catiline his Conspiracy. Bartholomew Fair. Sejanus his Fall. Epicœne: or, the Silent Woman. Every Man in his Humour. Every Man out of his Humour. The Alchemist, Dublin, 1729.

The Three Celebrated Plays Of that Excellent Poet Ben Johnson. Viz. The Fox, a Comedy. The Alchymist, a Comedy. The Silent Woman, a Comedy. To which is added, A compleat Catalogue of all the Plays that were ever printed in the English Language, to the Year 1732, 1732.

Volpone: or, The Fox. A Comedy. . . . The Author B. J., 1736 (This is the edition of 1732 with a new title-page).

Volpone: or, The Fox. A Comedy. . . . The Author Ben. Johnson. The Alchemist. A Comedy. . . . The Author Ben. Johnson. Epicœne: or, The Silent Woman. A Comedy. . . . The Author Ben Johnson. Bartholomew Fair. A Comedy. . . . The Author Ben. Johnson. Catiline His Conspiracy. A Tragedy. . . . The Author Ben. Johnson, 1739.

O Rare Ben Johnson! Or, The Favourite and Celebrated Comedies Of that Excellent Poet Ben Johnson. Viz. The Fox, The Alchymist, The Silent Woman; and Bartholomew Fair. The Whole Newly Corrected from the Errors of former Impressions [ca. 1740].

Every Man in his Humour. A Comedy. Written by Ben Jonson. With Alterations and Additions. As it is Perform'd at the Theatre-Royal in Drury-Lane, 1752.

Three Plays of Ben Johnson. I. Volpone the Fox. II. The Alchemist. III. Epicoene, or the silent woman, Glasgow, 1752.

Every Man in his Humour. . . . With Alterations and Additions by D. Garrick. As it is performed at the Theatre-Royal in Drury Lane, 1754.

Every Man in his Humour. . . . With Alterations and Additions by D. Garrick. As it is perform'd at the Theatre-Royal in Drury Lane, 1755.

The Works of Ben. Jonson. In Seven Volumes. Collated with All the former Editions, and Corrected; with Notes Critical and Explanatory. By Peter Whalley, 1756.

Every Man in his Humour. A Comedy. Written by Ben Jonson. With Alterations and Additions, By D. Garrick. As it is Perform'd at the Theatre-Royal, in Drury-Lane, 1759.

The Alchemist. With alterations. As performed at the Theatres, 1763.

Ben Jonson's Plays. Viz. I. Volpone: or, The Fox. II. The Alchemist. III. Epicoene: or, The Silent Woman, Glasgow, 1766.

Every Man in his Humour. A Comedy. By Ben Johnson. With Alterations and Additions. By D. Garrick. To which is prefixed, The Life of the Author, Edinburgh, 1768.

Every Man in his Humour. A Comedy. Altered from Ben. Johnson [The Dramatic Works of David Garrick Esq., n. p., 1768, II, 259-347].

Every Man in his Humour. A Comedy. By Ben Johnson. With Alter-
ations and Additions, by D. Garrick. To which is prefixed, The
Life of the Author [The Theatre; or, Select Works of the British
Dramatic Poets, Edinburgh, 1768, vol. II].

Epicoene: or, The Silent Woman. A Comedy, By Ben Johnson [The
Theatre; or, Select Works of the British Dramatic Poets, Edinburgh, 1768, vol. XII].

Every Man in his Humour. A Comedy. Written by Ben Johnson.
With Alterations and Additions, By D. Garrick. As it is performed
at the Theatre Royal in Drury-Lane, 1769.

The Alchemist. A Comedy, Written by Ben. Jonson. With Alterations, As performed at the Theatres, 1770.

Every Man in his Humour. A Comedy. By Ben Johnson. With
Alterations and Additions. By D. Garrick. To Which is Prefixed, The Life of the Author, Edinburgh, 1774.

Epicœne; or, The Silent Woman. A Comedy, Written by Ben Jonson.
As it is Acted at the Theatre Royal in Drury-Lane. With Alterations, By George Colman, 1776.

Volpone: or, The Fox. A Comedy, As altered from Ben Jonson, and
Performed at the Theatre-Royal in Covent-Garden [Bell's British
Theatre, 1776, vol. XIX].

The Alchymist. A Comedy. As altered from Ben Jonson. Distin-
guishing also the Variations of the Theatre, As Performed at the
Theatre-Royal in Drury-Lane [Bell's British Theatre, 1776, vol.
XVII].

Every Man in his Humour. A Comedy, Written by Ben Jonson.
With Alterations and Additions, By D. Garrick. As performed
at the Theatre-Royal in Drury-Lane. A New Edition [Bell's
British Theatre, 1776, vol. II].

Every Man in his Humour. A Comedy. Written by Ben Johnson.
With Alterations and Additions by D. Garrick. Marked with the
Variations in the Manager's Book, at the Theatre-Royal in Drury-
Lane [The New English Theatre, 1776, vol. V].

Epicœne; or, The Silent Woman. A Comedy, Written by Ben Jonson.
With Alterations [The Dramatick Works of George Colman, 1777,
III, 211–324].

INDEX

INDEX